PORSCHE 911
PERFORMANCE HANDBOOK

Second Edition

Bruce Anderson

MBI Publishing Company

Printed in USA

This second edition published in 1996 by MBI Publishing Company, PO Box 1, 729 Prospect Avenue, Osceola, WI 54020-0001 USA

The information in this book is true and complete to the best of our knowledge. All recommendations are made without any guarantee on the part of the author or Publisher, who also disclaim any liability incurred in connection with the use of this data or specific details.

We recognize that some words, model names and designations, for example, mentioned herein are the property of the trademark holder. We use them for identification purposes only. This is not an official publication.

MBI Publishing Company books are also available at discounts in bulk quantity for industrial or sales-promotional use. For details write to Special Sales Manager at Motorbooks International Wholesalers & Distributors, 729 Prospect Avenue, PO Box 1, Osceola, WI 54020-0001 USA.

Library of Congress Cataloging-in-Publication Data
Anderson, Bruce.
    Porsche 911 performance handbook/ Bruce Anderson.—2nd ed.
        p. cm.
    Includes index.
    ISBN 0-7603-0033-X (pbk.: alk. paper)
    1. Porsche 911 automobile—Performance—Handbooks, manuals, etc. I. Title.
TL215.P75A63   1996
629.222'2—dc20   96-43706

On the front cover: This line-up of fantastic 911s is being wrenched on at Connecticut's Automobile Associates of Canton, Inc. Co-owners Jim Newton and Jim Kelly tackle all levels of Porsche work. *Rick Whitley*

On the back cover: top: The ultimate 911? The factory's 1996 mid-engine GT1 racer pushes the 911 performance envelope. **center:** Cutaway showing wheel and brake details from the 1993 911 3.6-liter Turbo. **bottom:** Super-charging of Knoxville's blower fitted to a 3.2-liter Carrera.

Printed in the United States of America

Table of Contents

Acknowledgments

I owe a great deal of thanks to all of the people who have helped with my Porsche education. My Porsche education started with my first Porsche, a 356 Super, which I bought new in 1961 and continues today with my constant contact with the car and people who own and work on them. Many thanks to all of the individuals who have helped with my education over the years and contributed to this book directly by providing information for the book or sharing in the experiences that have been the basis for much of the book. I would like to give everyone who helped credit, but I am sure that I will miss someone. My apologies to anyone that I may have missed or whose request for anonymity will not allow me to mention them.

Bob Akin, Clark Anderson, Stephanie Anderson, my wife who puts up with all of this, Manfred Bantle, Jürgen Barth, Cecil and Carol Beach, Hartmut Behrens, Paul Bingham, Glen Blakely, Gerhard Blendstrup, Howard Blitz, Gary Bohrman, Alexander Bornscheuer, Helmuth Bott, Kevin Buckler, *Car and Driver*, Bob Carlson, Stephania Cohen, Miles Collier, John Daniels, Philippe de Lespinay, Steve Doudy, Dan Fleck, Heinz Dorsch, Lillian Fuess, Chuck Gaa, Bob Garretson, Fred Garretson, Gemballa Automobilinterieur Gmbh, Wolfhelm Gorissen, Begonia Gosh, Chas. R. Green, Robert Grigsby, Harry Hall, Jon Hammill, Roger Hamlin, Fred Hampton, Tom Hanna, Paul Hensler, Tony Heyer, Terry Hunt, Ursula Jopp, Dave Klym, Scott Krag, Kremer Brothers Porsche Racing, Olaf Lang, Eugene Lemke, Bill. F. Martin, Hans Mezger, Dale Miller, Dwight Mitchell, James Newton, Joe Padermderm, Rick Parker, Klaus Parr, Richard Parr, Porsche Aktiengesellschaft, Porsche Cars North America, Inc., Leo F. Rapp, Greg Raven, Klaus Reichert, Richard Riley, Ted Robinson, Alois Ruf, Ruf Automobile Gmbh, Paul Schenk, Lori Schutz, Peter Schutz, Doug Speer, Scott Spence, Rolf Sprenger, Alwin Springer, Robert Strange, Auto Design Strosek, Achim Stroth, Hans Struffert, Dave Truax, Unocal, Tom Urbaniak, Gary Walton, Jim Weber, Pete Weber, Jerry Woods, Tim Wusz, and Ekehard Zimmermann

Preface

I bought my first Porsche in 1961 and have owned one or more Porsches ever since. I ran a Porsche repair business for the better part of 10 years in the late 1970s and early 1980s. Before getting into the Porsche repair business full time I had worked for Hewlett Packard as a technical writer and publications manager for 17 years. I have been a member of the Porsche Club of America for over 32 years and the national technical chairman since 1981, I have been the technical editor for *Excellence* magazine since 1987, and I write about Porsches for other magazines both in the United States and abroad. I have written for the French magazines *Flat 6* and *Talon Pointe*; the British magazines *Porsche Post* and *911 & Porsche World*; *Christophorus*, the Porsche factory magazine; *Porsche Panorama* the Porsche Club of America's magazine; and Japan's *The 911 & Porsche Magazine*.

I have been working on Porsches since 1962 and Porsche 911s since 1966. In the winter of 1966–67, some friends and I bought a half dozen engines that were badly damaged, but not totally lost, in a shipwreck in the Azores. These engines had started out in cars, but when the ship they were being transported in was hit by another ship, the 911s broke loose in the flooded hold. Please note that I said "engines," my first 911 experience was just with the engines. I didn't actually work on one of the cars until about a year later when we installed one of our refurbished engines into a 912 making it into a 911. By the time we had resurrected all of our engines we had learned quite a bit about the 911 engines and cars.

My Porsche education continued with rebuilding and hot-rodding 911 engines, and working on a race team that won the prestigious Porsche Cup, Porsche Team Cup, IMSA GTR, GT, GTO, and GTU championships and the World endurance championship. My education continues today as I help others learn about these great cars through my technical articles and books, by offering instruction through Porsche training courses that we started in 1986, and by giving technical presentation lectures on Porsche and the 911 engine.

As technical editor of *Excellence* magazine, I have an ongoing technical question-and-answer column as well as feature articles in *Excellence* and the other magazines listed above. I have written articles on all aspects of interest to Porsche enthusiasts from technical articles, to coverage of events such as the Porsche Parade, Speedsterfest, La Carrera Panamericana, Daytona, and Le Mans.

I saw the original *Porsche 911 Performance Handbook* as an opportunity to write down all of the things that I knew about 911s so that I would have a place to look them up the next time I needed that same information. Before that book, my Porsche knowledge was documented on scraps of paper and notes. With this second edition I have expanded all sections of the original to include the latest 911s and information I have learned since the first edition. I hope you find most of what you want to know about the Porsche 911 is in the *Porsche 911 Performance Handbook, 2nd Edition.*

—*Bruce Anderson*

Chapter 1

Porsche 911 Performance History

The Porsche 911, like the 356 before it, has always been a performance car. Enthusiasts had heard rumors before the 911 was introduced that the replacement for the beloved 356 would not be a performance car or sports car at all, but instead it would be a four-passenger grand touring car. Fortunately that turned out to be not true and the "new car" was in fact a more efficient, comfortable, and sporting two plus two.

In the postwar years, the British tried to convince the world in general, and the United States in particular, that sports cars needed side curtains, a top that didn't work, and an ox-cart ride to actually be considered "true" sports cars. By the time the 911 came along sports car fans had already been spoiled by the 356 and knew that a sporting car did not have to be a hard-riding uncomfortable car.

Porsche built the Speedster for its customers who needed to be reassured that they had indeed bought a "real" sports car. But the Porsche Speedster didn't even do that right. The top actually worked pretty well and the ride was great. Of course the side curtains leaked,

but did you ever hear of a car that used side curtains that didn't leak?

I first heard about the coming of the 911 from a friend and fellow 356 owner in the early 1960s. He had just returned from a European business trip, where he toured the Porsche factory. On the tour he had seen Porsche's "new car," which turned out to be the not-yet-introduced 911. He came back concerned that Porsche was ruining our car and that it was going to make it too costly for any of us to afford. At the time he and I had plain-Jane, pushrod, 356 Porsches that sold for $4,000 to $5,500. The high-performance and high-priced Porsche of the era was a 2.0 Carrera which was available for about $7,500 in the United States.

Porsche helped finance the 901's development by asking its 100 best dealers to put up what in effect was a deposit on one of the new cars. The deposit was DM 8,000, which back in 1962 was $2,000.

911 Debut

The 911 was introduced at the Frankfurt International Auto Show in

September 1963. Actual production started in September 1964. The new 911 cost DM 22,900 ($5,800) in Germany and $6,500 in the United States. The reason the 901 was renamed 911 was that the French automaker Peugeot had registered the use of three-digit numbers where the center digit was a zero. Porsche was ready for production at the time of this decision, which explains why so many of its parts numbers and designations for the 911 use the 901 prefix.

Competition with the new 911 started as early as 1965 when Porsche prepared a 911 for competition in the Monte Carlo Rally. It placed seventh in that first attempt. The 911 then went on to win most of the major European rallies, including three victories at the famed Monte Carlo Rally and a win in the tour of Corsica. The special race preparation of these very early cars was limited to minor suspension modifications, a more powerful version of the 901 six-cylinder engine, and a wide selection of different gear ratios. As the 901 or 911 has matured there have been several special versions of the 911 built for touring car races and grand touring (GT) racing and rallying. These 911 derivatives have, at one time or another, won most of the world's major races and rallies. Competition is an integral part of the Porsche 911 performance history.

At the 1965 Frankfurt Motor Show Porsche introduced its new, unconventional open car, a cabriolet-like car. Porsche called this new model the Targa to honor its many successes at the Sicilian Targa Florio race. This cabriolet was marked by its 6-inch wide stainless-steel-covered roll bar—it couldn't help but be noticed. Some people called it "the Porsche with a handle" and others called it "the safety cabriolet." Porsche said it was its car with four personalities: (1) "Targa Spyder," a fully open car with the roof off and the rear window folded flat; (2) "Targa Bel Air," like a sunroof, with the top off and the rear window in place for draft-free sunshine; (3) "Targa Voyage," with the soft cabriolet top in place and the rear window folded flat;

The rear of the preproduction 901 prototype. Note the twin tailpipes and the 356-derived rear Porsche script and steering wheel. Porsche AG

and finally (4) "Targa Hardtop," with the roof attached and the rear window zipped in place. The Targa made Porsche the first manufacturer to put a roll bar on a production car, an idea that several other manufacturers would follow. It was more than a year before the Targa was finally added to the Porsche line-up in the 1967 model year.

1967

When the 911 was first introduced it was available only in coupe form and with only one engine configuration, the 130-DIN-hp engine. The coupe body had been designed by Ferdinand Alexander "Butzi" Porsche who had also designed the body for the 904 and who went on to establish his own company, Porsche Design. It was no surprise that with the 1967 model introduction Porsche added a new higher performance model, the 160-DIN-hp 911S. The price for the new 911S was $6,990, while the price of the normal 911 was lowered $500 dollars to $6,000.

In addition to the increased power, the 911S also introduced the Fuchs forged-aluminum wheels which added character to the appearance of the 911 for the next 20-odd years before they were replaced. The originals were 4.5x15 inches and had all-silver spokes. The Fuchs wheels were standard on the 911S and a $375 option for the 911 and 912. When these wheels were first introduced they were not considered attractive. In fact, a friend once remarked that they looked like they belonged on a circus bandwagon! Looks aside, the wheels were lighter, stronger, and provided better brake cooling than the steel disc wheels.

The 1967 911S also marked the addition of a rear antisway bar which improved the 911's already superb handling. In addition to the wheels, different side trim and bumper trim with a larger squared-off rubber insert marked the visual differences between the 911S and the standard 911 and 912 models. The 911S also had an all-leatherette dashboard, the leatherette replacing the wooden inserts of the earlier standard 911, and a new leather-covered steering wheel. For 1967 an aluminum dash insert was used for the standard 911 and the 912.

At the end of 1967, Porsche built a small run of 23 911 models for racing and designated them as the 911R. The 911Rs were extensively modified 911s with fiberglass bodywork, plexiglass windows, and a 210-hp Carrera 6-type engine. These Spartan 911Rs weighed only 1,830 pounds, and although really not very much was done with the

The 1966 model introduction for the United States was held in San Francisco by Porsche Car Pacific on July 23, 1965. Porsche Car Pacific

911Rs, they showed the way for future 911 racing cars. One 911R was fitted with the type 916 engine for the Targa Florio in 1969. The Type 916 four-camshaft version of the 901 engine produced 230 hp, 20 more than the Carrera Six engine. The only notable accomplishments for the 911R were establishing a series of 14 international and 5 world records at the Monza track in 1967 and winning the 1969 84-hour Marathon de la Route.

1968

For 1968 Porsche added a cheaper version of the 911, the 911T, which for 1968 would only be sold in the European market. For the European, or the rest of the world (R.o.W.), market then there were three different 911 models:

the 911T, the 911L, the 911S, and the four-cylinder 912. The 911L was the successor to the 911 Normal for the R.o.W.

While Porsche was expanding the product line for the rest of the world it was actually reducing the models available to the U.S. market. Only the 911 and the 912 were available in the United States for the year. Admittedly there were two models of the 911. In addition to the plain 911, there was now a 911L, the L standing for "luxury." The 911L had most of the appointments of the 911S save one—the important one—the engine; the 911L had the same engine as the standard 911. The reason for this was stricter U.S. emissions laws.

New for the 1968 models was the dual-circuit brake system for the world market; it included a warning light for the U.S. market. The 1968 models had wider 5 1/2-inch wheels replacing the original 4 1/2-inch wheels for all models. The wiper blades now parked on the left side instead of the right side as they had done previously. The move took them out of the driver's line of sight so that they would not interfere with driving.

An interesting addition for the 1968 model year was the semiautomatic Sportomatic transmission. Porsche felt that none of its customers would really want to give up complete control of their transmission, so instead of a total automatic, Porsche combined a torque converter, an automatic clutch, and a four-speed transmission. The torque converter was what could be considered a "loose" one, with a stall speed of 2,600 rpm. In operation, the clutch was

The dashboard of the original 911; note the wood dashboard insert and the wood-rimmed steering wheel.

disengaged by the vacuum servo when it received a signal from the microswitch on the shift linkage. When you grabbed the shift lever, the clutch would release, you could shift and when you let go of the shift lever the clutch would engage again. With the high stall-speed of the torque converter you could be a very lazy driver, starting out in second gear and shifting directly to fourth when the car came up to speed. Or if you wanted, the car could be driven quite aggressively using all four gears and it would give very little away to the 911s with their more conventional four- or five-speed manual transmissions.

Sportomatic transmissions were a good solution for people who still wanted a sporty Porsche but spent quite a bit of their driving time stuck in commuter traffic. Unfortunately for Porsche customers who liked their Porsche driving sans clutch, this transmission never really caught on in the United States. Ten years after its introduction Porsche ceased production of the Sportomatic.

There are people who swear by these transmissions saying that they offer the best of both worlds. It would be difficult to pin down exactly when Porsche quit building Sportomatic cars. The newest Sportomatic that I know of in the United States is a 1978 911SC. Nineteen-eighty was the last year that the Sportomatic transmission was listed as an option even in Europe. However, I did notice at Le Mans in 1985 that the Carrera Turbo-look Cabriolet that Wolfgang Porsche was driving had a four-speed Sportomatic installed. But then that is a very special case, isn't it?

1969

The most notable changes for 1969 were increased wheelbase length and fender flares. The 911S received Bosch's twin-row mechanical injection pump. The 911L also received a mechanical injection system and was renamed the 911E (the E stands for *Einspritzung*, German for injection). There was also more differentiation between the various models now with the 911S being the performance model, the 911T being the economy model, and the softer-riding 911E being the luxury model. The E's softer ride was provided by what Porsche called its "comfort group," which consisted of Boge hydropneumatic struts in front instead of torsion bars. These struts were self-leveling and offered a much softer ride than the conventional suspension. The comfort group cars also lacked a front sway bar and were fitted with 14x5 1/2-inch wheels with the high profile 185/78x14 tires. The comfort group was standard equipment on the 911E and optional on both the 911T and the 911S. The standard wheels on the 911T were 15x5 1/2 inches, while the 911E and 911S had 15x6-inchers.

All three 911 models were available to the world market for 1969. The mechanical injection allowed the 911E and 911S to comply with U.S. emission specifications, and the new-to-the-United-States 911T used a deceleration valve on its carburetors and a vacuum unit on its distributor to pass emission tests.

1970–1971

For 1970 and 1971, the 911 engines were increased to 2.2 liters (actually 2,195 cc), but the cars looked pretty much the same as they had in 1969, aside from some interior changes. The 1972 911s had yet another displacement increase to 2.4 liters (2,341 cc). The 1972 models also had the oil tank moved to in front of the right rear wheel like the tanks on the 911Rs. The oil tank returned to its previous location in 1973. Some said that it was because it had become an "attractive nuisance" and that gas stations occasionally put gas in the oil tanks. The wandering oil tank returned to its position in front of the rear wheel with the advent of the 964 platform in 1989. This is actually a good, out-of-the-way location, leaving the car's rear corners available for more important things like turbocharger intercoolers or mufflers, in the case of the 993.

In 1970 and 1971, several 2.2-liter 911s were specially built for road racing and rallying. These cars used some of

Porsche first showed its 911 Targa at the 1965 Frankfurt Motor Show. Porsche said it was its car with four personalities, the first of which was "Targa Spyder," a fully open car with the roof off and the rear window folded flat. Porsche AG

The 1967 911S introduced more power, better handling, and styling changes. With its "mag" wheels, it was one of the first production cars in the world with alloy wheels. Actually they were 4 1/2-inch-wide Fuchs forged aluminum-alloy wheels. The rubber trim strips on the sides and bumpers were made much larger and now had a square profile. The front bumper guards were left off altogether on the European version of the 911S. Porsche AG

the development work from the 911R such as lightweight bodywork and deletion of sound-deadening material. They had modified suspensions and an extensive selection of alternate gear ratios. There were different engines available for different applications, with the rally version usually employing a nearly stock 911S motor. For road racing there were special 2.2- and 2.3-liter versions and a 2.5-liter prototype based on the soon-to-be announced longer stroke crankshaft. Otherwise, these cars remained slightly modified production 911s in most other respects.

Some of the racing 911s that Porsche built during this period, however, were very specialized. One example was a car prepared for the 1970 Tour de France. Porsche reduced the weight of this car even further than that of the 911R to 1,720 pounds. The Tour de France car's powerplant was a 2.4-liter engine producing 245 hp. These extensive modifications were permitted because the car was raced as a prototype rather than as a GT car.

At the end of 1967 Porsche built a small series of very special 911s, the 911R. The "R" is for "rennsport," the German word for "racing." The 911Rs were extensively modified 911s with fiberglass bodywork, plexiglass windows, and a 210-hp Carrera 6 type engine. These Spartan 911Rs weighed only 1,830 lb. They were fitted with 6-inch-wide front wheels and 7-inch-wide rear wheels. Porsche AG

High-sided bucket seats were fitted to the 911R.

The 911R's doors were fiberglass replicas of the production-series steel doors, each with a fixed vent window and a leather strap to actuate the side window. The doors used on the later 935s were very similar to these doors.

The 911R had its oil tank mounted in front of the right rear wheel to better balance the car's weight. The 911R used a thin glass windshield, and all of the rest of the car's windows were plexiglass.

Specialized 911s were also developed for the East African Safari. The Safari cars were lighter in weight than the production cars, but the biggest difference was in the special preparation for the rigors of off-road racing, which included extra re-inforcement, raised suspension settings, and skid shields. Though the cars were successful in the East African Safari, they never won this event, one of the few in the world that a 911 or 911-based car has not been able to win.

The 1969 911T and 911S featured fender flares and a longer wheelbase. Note the Fuchs alloy wheels introduced in 1967 with a new paint scheme and a wider, 5 1/2-inch width. Most people felt that painting the background for the spokes flat black improved the appearance of the alloy wheels. Porsche AG

Porsche 914/6

Porsche also introduced the VW–Porsche 914 for the 1970 model year. This model was a joint venture between Porsche and Volkswagen and was marketed as such everywhere except in the United States. Stateside, the 914/6 was sold as a Porsche by the newly formed Porsche Audi distribution organization. The 914/6 was offered from 1970 to 1972, during which time 3,360 914/6s were built and 1,788 were sold in the United States.

A 914/6 GT version was produced to international Group 4 (GT class) rules for racing and rallying. It is impossible to speculate on the true number of 914/6 GTs that were produced because Porsche attempted to homologate the car into the Sports Car Club of America's B-production class. In an effort to comply with SCCA's requirement of 500 production cars, Porsche made some real 914/6 GTs, some look-alike GTs, and a lot of kits to convert production 914/6 models to the GT configuration. Porsche's efforts did not meet with SCCA's approval, and in July 1971 the 914/6 GT was thrown out of B-Production and placed instead in B-Sports Racing where it was not competitive.

The 914/6 was not as successful in sales or competition as Porsche had hoped. Even so, in 1970 a Porsche 914/6 GT won the GT class at Le Mans and placed sixth overall. Peter Gregg and Hurley Haywood won the IMSA GT championship in 1971 driving a 914/6 GT. In 1976 and 1977, Walt Maas successfully ran his 1971 914/6 GT in the IMSA GTU series, winning 12 races and the 1977 GTU championship.

The 916 was to have been the civilized street version of the 914/6 GT, but the project was killed by Porsche's accounting de-

The 914/6 roadster was powered by the 2.0-liter 911 engine with specifications that were nearly identical to the 1969 911T engine. The 914/6 was offered by Porsche from 1970 to 1972, during which time 3,360 were built and sold; 1,788 of these were the U.S. versions. Jeff Lateer

partment. Thirteen prototypes were built in 1971–1972. They were powered by a version of the 2.4-liter 911S engine, had 7-inch wheels, a steel welded-on roof, and deluxe appointments. Porsche kept half of them for family members and sold the rest to Porsche friends.

The 914's mid-engine layout was tailor-made for racing; here is Walt Maas' 914/6, the IMSA GTU champion in 1977. Note the overemphasized wheel arches, front air dam, and rear-deck spoiler mounted on the trunk lid of the car.

1972–1973

For 1972, Porsche used the new 2.4 liter as the basis for a 2.5-liter racing engine developed for GT racing. At the 1972 Paris show, Porsche introduced the 2.7-liter Carrera RS and planned to build 500 to homologate them as a series into Group 4 for GT racing. The RS actually came in three versions: (1) M471 RS Sport, the version of the Carrera RS that has become known as the "lightweight"; (2) M472 RS Touring, the most common version with more standard comfort options similar to the 911S; and (3) M491 RS Rennsport, the 2.8 RSR racing version of the Carrera. The Carrera RS was a much larger commercial success than Porsche expected, and by April 1973 1,000 had been produced, qualifying the Carrera for the Group 3 category of GT racing. By the end of 1973 more than 1,590 of the touring and lightweight 2.7 Carrera RS models had been built, including the first 10 prototypes.

The 1963–1968 911 with short wheelbase. Note the distance from the edge of the fender to the torsion-bar cover in the fender.

The 1969-and-later 911 with the longer wheelbase. Again, note the distance from the edge of the fender to the torsion-bar cover in the fender.

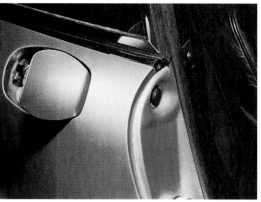

Opening the oil-filler hatch on the 1972 911. To check the oil level in any of the 911s it is necessary to run the engine to get it up to operating temperature, 176 deg F (80 deg C); the car should be level and running at idle speed when the oil level is checked. The level should be about halfway between the two marks on the dipstick. The dipstick should always be believed before the gauge. Perhaps the oil filler was too accessible when the filler was in the right rear fender, and most people don't have a clue as to how to check the oil level on a dry-sump system. Anyway, the filler only lasted one model year in the right rear fender. In 1973 it returned to the engine compartment, and the tank returned to the rear of the right rear wheel.

The 1970 911S-style dashboard; note the "factory air." Author

The 2.7 Carrera RS (lightweight option M 471) and 2.8 Carrera RSR (option M 491). The Carrera RS was the basis for the 2.8 RSR. The RSR was the car that Porsche wanted to build, so the Porsche staff determined what was required as a basis for homologation and reverse-engineered the required homologation car as the 2.7 Carrera RS. When Porsche built these cars, it incorporated a larger engine, several aerodynamic aids, larger wheels and fenders, and a lower weight. This new Carrera RS was also the first production Porsche with larger wheels on the rear than on the front. Conversions to RSR specifications were performed after production. Porsche AG

A view of the Carrera RS "lightweight" underhood area showing the 85-liter (22.5-gal) gas tank. The spare wheel is a 6x15-inch forged light-metal wheel with collapsible spare tire. Only one battery was used, instead of the normal two used in the other production 911s. James D. Newton

The Carrera RS "lightweights" had their interiors visibly stripped down to save weight. The sound-deadening material was left out, and the carpeting was replaced with rubber floormats. The emergency rear seats were also left out to save weight. The clock, passenger's visor, and glove-compartment lid were also left off in the interest of saving weight. Seats were simple, lightweight Recaro bucket seats with a thumbscrew adjustment for the backrest angle. The windshield and side glass were made of a special thinner, lighter Glaverbel safety glass, and the rear quarter windows were fixed. The Carrera RS was also the first production Porsche with larger rear fender flares to accommodate larger, 7-inch-wide rear wheels. James D. Newton

When Porsche built the Carrera RS, it incorporated a larger engine, several aerodynamic aids, larger wheels and fenders, and a lower weight. This new Carrera RS was also the first production Porsche with larger wheels on the rear than the front. The Carrera RS 2.7 be-came the basis for a successful racing version, the 2.8 Carrera RSR. Forty-nine 2.7 Carrera RS cars were rebuilt as the option 491 2.8 RSR models. Except for the 911R, this was the first real series of racing cars based on the 911 (others, such as the Tour de France car, were one-offs). The success of the RSR started even before it was homologated as a Group 4 car with its win at the Daytona 24-Hour race in 1973. By Sebring, the next race for the RSR, it had been ho-mologated for Group 4 and won GT class and overall honors.

The 911s remained basically un-changed for 1973. The fuel injection was changed from mechanical to CIS on the U.S. 911T for January 1973. The R.o.W. 911Ts used the Zenith carbure-tors until the end of production in 1973.

1974

For 1974, the displacement expand-ed to 2.7 liters for the base models. The 1974 models had a new simplified front sway bar (16 mm on the 911 and 911 S, and 20 mm on the Carrera which also had an 18-mm rear sway bar) which went under the front of the body and was mounted in rubber bushings to each of the front A-arms. The rear trailing arms were now stronger, lighter, cheap-er-to-produce aluminum castings. The 1974 U.S. Carrera also had larger wheels, fender flares, and a ducktail. Probably the most significant visual change to the 911 was its U.S.-legal bumpers. Nine-teen-seventy-four was the last year that steel wheels were standard equipment on the 911 as these created a misleading base price for the cars as no one bought their 911 with steel wheels.

A 3.0-liter Carrera RS was offered in Europe to take advantage of the FIA

The 1974 U.S. Carrera, with its larger wheels, fender flares, and ducktail. Model year 1974 brought what was probably the most significant visual change to the 911 over its whole production run, the U.S.-legal bumpers. When these were first introduced I can remember that everyone objected to their appearance, but by the time a year had passed we all thought that the earlier cars looked old-fashioned. Dale Miller evolution rules so that Porsche could make its racing version of the 911 more competitive and get it up to the class displacement limit. One hundred and nine were built for homologation purposes. Because it was an evolution of the original 1973 Group 3 2.7 Carrera RS, only 100 cars were required for 1974 homologation. Of the 109 built, 52 were the extremely desirable street version, while the remainder were prepared as race cars including 15 for the IROC series and the remaining 42 for factory and customer race cars. The resulting competition car was the familiar

3.0 RSR which was so successful in GT racing over the next several years. The 3.0 RSR was the first 911-based car built up from scratch as a race car, with some 57 3.0 RSR factory and customer race cars and 15 IROC cars having been produced. To add to the confusion, Porsche built additional 3.0 RSRs as both replacement and new cars as late as 1976.

In 1974, Porsche raced four extensively modified Carrera RSRs with turbocharged 911 engines in the prototype class. This was done as preparation for the upcoming "silhouette" formula

for Group 5. These highly modified GT cars were run in the prototype class and, as such, had to meet the 3.0-liter class limit which, with the 1.4 multiplier imposed on turbocharged cars, limited their displacement to 2,142 cc. The 2,142-cc engine Porsche developed for this car produced 480 hp at 8,000 rpm.

Several things were done in these cars that were to show up in later 911-based racing cars. A raised rear roof section with a raised rear window improved the aerodynamics at the rear of the car. Front and rear suspensions were lightweight fabrications, and coil-

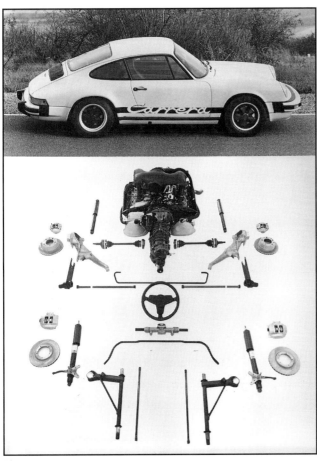

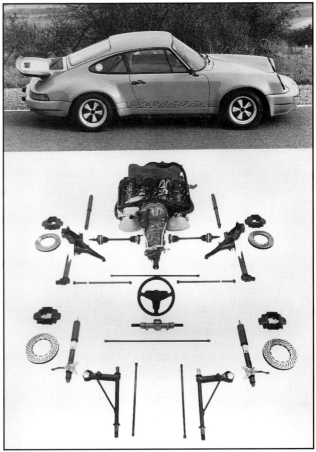

Above
The 1974 2.7 Carrera was the successor to the very successful limited-production series of 2.7 Carrera RSs. The 2.7 Carrera still featured its mechanical-fuel-injection engine with 210 hp, but otherwise it fit right into the standard R.o.W. 911 program with the 2.7 CIS 911 and 911S. The Carrera rear wing was an option.
Porsche AG

Above, right
The 1974 3.0 Carrera RS was an even more exciting model than its predecessor, the 2.7 Carrera RS, had been. The Carrera RS was built for homologation purposes as an evolution version of the original 1973 Group 3 2.7 Carrera RS. Only 100 cars were required for 1974 homologation, and actually 109 were built. Of the 109 cars, 44 were

the extremely desirable street version. The 3.0 Carrera RS was still a mechanically injected car with 230 hp, which was still just an extension of the 911S philosophy. Because Porsche was sure that most of these cars would be converted to race cars, all were delivered with 917 brakes and an oil pump with an external loop cooler for the transmission. They also had special shortened rear trailing arms with revised rear pickup points, 8-inch-wide front wheels, and 9-inch-wide rear wheels. The remainder of the 3.0 Carrera RSs were prepared as race cars with 15 for the IROC series and the remaining 50 for factory and customer race cars. The resulting competition car was the now-familiar 3.0 RSR that was so successful in GT racing over the next several years, both in Europe and in our IMSA GT classes. The 3.0 RSR was the first 911-based car built from scratch as a race car, and some 65 were produced. Porsche AG

15

over springs were used at both ends of the car.

1975

For the 1975 model year, there was a new exhaust system with new heat exchangers and a single-inlet muffler for the R.o.W. and the United States 49-state cars. California cars used another completely new exhaust system with different heat exchanges and thermal reactors with a dual-inlet muffler similar to those used on the earlier cars.

Only two models came to the United States for 1975: the 911S and the Carrera. Both shared the same engine—the standard 911 engine had been discontinued. In 49-state form, the engine was equipped an air injection pump to meet federal emissions standards and made 157 hp. The California engines were also fitted with Exhaust Gas Recycling (EGR) to comply with state laws, which further reduced the power output to 152 hp for the California cars. The transmission final drive ratios were raised on the U.S. 911s to reduce fuel consumption as well as engine emissions.

An additional electric heater blower motor was mounted on the engine to improve the flow of heated air from the engine to the passenger compartment. The engine's exhaust valve covers had a coating of black sound-absorbing material. A new vacuum-controlled warm up regulator was fitted to the fuel injection so that the throttle position valve was no longer needed.

Exterior changes included a return to standard-opening rear side windows on the coupe (they had been fixed in 1974). The rear edge of the rain gutter was rounded off instead of having a square edge—which is one way that you can tell the 1975 model from the 1974 model. A black finish was optionally available for the Targa's roll bar, and the duck-tail spoiler was replaced with a whale tail for the U.S. version of the Carrera. The Carrera's forged alloy wheels were changed to 7x17-inch in front and 8x15 in the rear. A new rubber front chin spoiler lip balanced aerodynamics front to rear to help offset the new, more-effective, rear whale-tail spoiler.

For the standard 1975 911S model, the 6-inch, cast, light-alloy ATS "cookie cutter" wheels replaced steel wheels as standard equipment. The ride height of the U.S. cars was set 25 to 30 mm higher than the Euro cars to help meet U.S. 5-mph bumper laws. The rubber bumper pads for U.S. cars also grew in size to better protect the paint on the bumper and the taillight assembly in the case of a minor collision. Nineteen-seventy-five also marked the last year of the small "911" script on engine lid.

A Porsche special factory Silver Anniversary Edition 911S was also offered in 1975. It featured Diamond Silver metallic paint and a gray/black all-tweed interior (except for the seat bolsters and headrests). These Silver Anniversary models had a special dash plaque with Ferry Porsche's signature and a special series number for each car. The Silver Anniversary edition cars were 911S models offered in both coupe and Targa bodies. Seven hundred and fifty were made for North America and a similar number for the R.o.W.

Porsche introduced the Type 930 Turbo as a 1975 model at the Paris Auto show in October 1974. In September 1973 at the Frankfurt auto show, Porsche had shown a prototype tur-

The 1974 Carrera RSR Turbo 2.1 engine lid and rear wing. Note the air inlet for the turbo on the left side from the scoop on the passenger side of the car. The big NACA duct in the center pulls the air into the intercooler, and the rectangular opening in the rear exits the air from the intercooler. The air inlet on the right is for cooling air for the engine.

Left
The 1974 3.0 Carrera RSR was basically the 3.0 Carrera RS modified for racing with wider fenders for the 10.5-inch-wide front wheels and the 14-inch-wide rear wheels. The engine was modified to produce 330 hp. Porsche AG

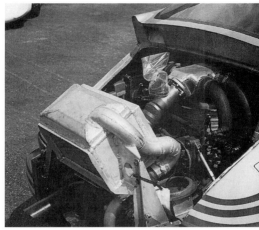

The 1974 Carrera RSR Turbo 2.1 fuel cell. Some versions of the Carrera RSR Turbo 2.1 had their fuel cell mounted inside the passenger compartment to shift more of the weight toward the rear.

The 1974 Carrera RSR Turbo 2.1. Note the outlet of the turbo goes directly to the inlet of the intercooler and the outlet of the intercooler goes directly to the intake plenum. Also note the flat engine cooling fan.

bocharged 911 show car to test the market potential. The type 930 was originally placed on the market in 1975 to gain homologation for the Group 4 and Group 5 cars that Porsche intended to race in 1976.

Porsche was very concerned about its ability to sell production cars as expensive as the 930s, so its original plan was to build only the necessary 400 required for homologation over a two-year period, 1975 and 1976. However, the 911 Turbo became such a success that it has been in production for most of the past 21 years. More than 23,341 Turbos were built between 1974, when production began, and 1989, when production of the original Turbo ceased. The Turbo became such a success that more than 20 years later one version or another has been in production almost continuously since 1975.

It took Porsche some time to realize that it was actually going to continue building these flare-fendered cars for an indefinite period of time. When it started to produce the 930, workers actually welded the fender flares on to the front and rear fender stampings as they produced the cars. Finally in 1986, the front and rear fenders for the Turbo were made as one-piece stampings without the welded-on flares.

The 1975 930 Turbo featured the change to a die-cast aluminum crankcase with a bore increase to 95 mm with the 70.4 mm stroke resulting in a 3.0-liter displacement. Porsche limited the boost to 0.8 bar (11.6 lb) which produced a peak power of 260 DIN hp. The

For 1975, the ducktail was replaced with the whaletail on the U.S. Carrera. Porsche Audi Division, VWoA

increased torque necessitated a larger four-speed transmission. The increased power also required an increase in clutch diameter from 225 mm to 240 mm. Unfortunately the brakes weren't upgraded from the standard 911S, and they had a hard time coping with the increased speed potential. In fact, in 1975, the brakes were not even power assisted.

Except for the much more powerful engine and the obvious body changes, there were really only minor differences between the 930 Turbo and the regular 911. The 930 Turbo had spoilers front and rear and modified suspension geometry. Its torsion bars measured 19 mm, front, and 26 mm, rear. The rear

trailing arms were special aluminum castings that were shorter to change the rear geometry and with much larger rear wheel bearings than the standard 911 arms. The standard tires were 185/70 VR 15, front, and 215/60 VR 15, rear, with 205/50 VR 15 and 225/50 VR 15 available as an option. A number of these early 930 Turbos had interiors that were a combination of leather and bright Scotch plaid cloth materials.

1976

The Group 5 "silhouette" formula and Group 4 GT rule changes finally came in 1976, and Porsche produced two new 911 race cars for the new classes: the 934 and 935. The 934 was homologated as a Group 4 car and sold to racing customers for GT racing. The 935 was a Group 5 car, and the Porsche factory raced the 935 itself and won the 1976 World Championship of Makes. The basis for the homologation of the 934 was the 930 Turbo Carrera and the requirement was for 400 to be produced in two model years. Because of the 1.4 multiplier for turbocharged cars, the 934 Turbo RSR could not be considered a lightweight model like its predecessor the 3.0 RSR. The multiplier placed the 934 in the 4,001–4,500-cc class, requiring the car's weight to be 2,469 lb. The 934s had power windows and still required 88 lb of lead in the front trunk to bring them up to weight. Thirty-one of these Group 4 934s were produced for Porsche's racing customers. Most of these cars remained in Europe and competed in the Group 4 category.

In the United States, IMSA had said "no" to the Porsche Turbos, preferring to encourage Porsche to continue to build and support the normally aspirated RSRs. SCCA, on the other hand, welcomed the Group 4 934s with open arms. Vasek Polak bought five and Al Holbert one to race in the popular SCCA Trans-Am series. Several drivers drove the Polak cars over the year, but George Follmer drove for Vasek most of the season and was rewarded for his efforts with a Trans-Am championship.

The Euro Carrera was continued into the beginning of the 1976 model year, but only 155 were built as 1976 models before they were replaced by the Carrera 3.0. The 3.0-liter Carrera was significant because it was the forerunner of the 911SC and the replacement for the Carrera as the top-of-the-line, normally aspirated Porsche 911 for the R.o.W. The Carrera engine was based on the same die-cast aluminum crankcase as the Turbo engine that had been introduced in 1975. The Carrera 3.0 also retained the larger fender flares of the earlier Carreras.

The U.S. version of the Carrera had been discontinued in 1976, and in addition to the normally aspirated 911S, the 911 Turbo was now available for the U.S. market. The 911's fuel pump was moved forward to the front axle carrier to combat problems with vapor lock that American cars had experienced.

The 1976 model carried a bolder "911" script on the engine lid than that used on the 1974 and 1975 models, making it easily identified. Power was up to 157 hp on the California version, which is what the 49-state version had in 1975. The 1976 models were the first 911s with an electronic speedometer. It was driven by an electronic signal generated by an inductive pick-up that plugged into the side of the transmission and picked up the magnetic impulses generated by a series of magnets mounted around the differential. The engines had an auxiliary air regulator added to make the engine idle fast when cold, replacing the hand throttle in the earlier CIS-injected cars. The 1976 911 had a single electrically controlled and heated exterior mirror. The engines had the five-blade engine-cooling fan that ran at a 1.8:1 ratio instead of the previously used 1.3:1 ratio. The pulley ratio was speeded up to increase the alternator output at the lower engine speeds and the five-blade fan decreased the fan noise caused by run-

Interior of the 935/77. This one has been modified to gain access to the engine from inside the passenger compartment, and the water tank for the intercooler has been moved inside the passenger compartment. The original Group 5 rules didn't allow any of the engine components to extend into the passenger compartment.

Left
Porsche introduced the Type 930 Turbo at the Paris Auto Show in October 1974. Porsche only planned to build 400 of the Type 930 Turbos over a two-year period to homologate the 934 and 935 race cars.

ning the fan at this faster speed. This latter change was necessary to comply with some European noise restrictions.

The 1976 911 used new cast-iron "A" brake calipers in place of the aluminum "S" caliper. The new calipers were the same dimensions as the aluminum "S" calipers, but used thinner brake pads. The Turbo's headlight washers were made optionally available for the standard 911 model as well. Padded and seamed door panels and color-matched dash upholstery replaced the black that had been used up until 1976. Cut pile carpeting was brought up to cover door storage compartments as well. For the first time Porsche offered a cruise control, called "Tempostat," in the 911.

Another limited-edition "Signature" 911S was available for 1976. This version came with special Platinum Metallic paint; cast-alloy wheels; beige tweed upholstery; a three-spoke, leather-covered steering wheel embossed with Ferry Porsche's signature; and black anodized trim. These cars were marketed in both North America and the R.o.W.

Few changes were made to the 930 Turbo in 1976, the biggest being a U.S. version available with 245 hp. The U.S. 930 used a more restrictive thermal reactor exhaust system to meet U.S. emissions laws. The power difference between the European and the U.S. 930 could be attributed largely to the U.S. exhaust. The 205/50 VR 15 and 225/50 VR 15 tires were standard equipment in 1976 for all 930 Turbos.

Porsche had started to experiment with advanced rust-proofing techniques as early as 1967 for its 911s, creating three cars with polished, unpainted, stainless steel bodywork. One of these cars was shown at the Frankfurt Auto Show in 1967. Two of the stainless-bodied cars were damaged in accidents and the third was retired to the Deutsches Museum in Munich in 1975 after seven years of extensive testing and 95,000 miles. The stainless had worked well and showed no signs of corrosion, but the process was too expensive for a production car, even a Porsche. The company's second choice was to galvanize the exposed portions of the car's underbody sheet metal, which it started to do to the 911s in the summer of 1970 for the 1971 2.2-liter models. At the 1975 Frankfurt Auto Show, Porsche introduced a fully rust-proofed body to go with its galvanized chassis. This new combination—rust-proof body and chassis—would enable Porsche to offer a six-year warranty for the 911. All of the body metal had a hot galvanized coat-

The 1976 Group 4 934 was based on the 1975 930, which had been produced for homologation purposes. The 934 had to have the same type of injection as the 930 did, so a special version of the CIS injection had to be developed to work with a racing version of the 930 engine. The fiberglass fender flare extensions—about 2 inches in front and 4 inches in the rear—brought the fender width out to the limit of the rules. The fuel tank was replaced with a 120-liter (32-gal) fuel cell. The 934 used a water-cooled intercooler system, and the two air inlets at the outer edge of the front air dam were for the water radiators that cooled the water in the intercooler system. The center opening in the air dam was the inlet to the oil cooler or radiator, and the two in between the oil cooler and the water radiators on each side were inlets for brake cooling air. Porsche AG

The 935 Baby. For a little additional excitement in 1977, Porsche took on BMW in the under-2-liter class of the German Group 5 series with the 935 Baby. The Baby was turbocharged, so the displacement had to be less than 1,425 cc because of the 1.4 multiplier. Porsche built a special 370-horsepower engine with air-to-air intercooling for this little engine because they were able to fit the smaller intercoolers under the engine lid. Baby looked very much like the 935/77 that the factory was racing in 1977, but it was a much lighter car. The Baby only weighed 1,600 pounds; they saved weight on the Baby by doing a number of different things including using aluminum subframes front and rear and by moving the oil cooler back to where the radiators were for the intercooler on 735/77. Porsche AG

ing on both the inside and outside of the sheet metal panels.

Beginning mid-year 1976, all of the 911s have been made of galvanized sheet metal. For the first few months after the introduction the roof section was not galvanized, but by the end of the production year the roof was galvanized as well. This process has proven so successful for reducing rust that the long-life warranty was increased first to seven years in 1981 for the world market and then to 10 years in 1986 for the U.S. market.

The 1977 Kremer K2 at the Daytona 24-hour race in February 1978. The Kremer K2 incorporated some aerodynamic improvements as well as some styling changes. The rear fenders were their own design, with a smoother leading edge for their rear fender and then fences to prevent air from spilling off the fenders. Note that the lower lip on the front spoiler is adjustable. Manfred and Erwin Kremer are shown near the rear of the car.

In addition to the galvanized body sheet metal, Porsche increased the use of corrosion-resistant aluminum components over the years; by 1976 they included the bumpers, the rear trailing arms, the front suspension cross-member, and the engine crankcase. The stainless steel exhaust system and Targa roll bar were also corrosion resistant. The exhaust system heater boxes had been aluminized, as had the dry sump oil tank to extend their useful lives.

1977

For the 1977 model year the U.S. Porsches had only one engine type for all 50 states and Canada. These engines had thermal reactors, EGR, and air injection to comply with U.S. emission standards. The specifications for these engines were the same as those for the 1976 California engines, and all of the United States, Canadian, and Japanese 911s shared the exhaust system with thermal reactors. The late-1977 911 engines used Dilavar studs for the bottom row of cylinder head retaining studs to help eliminate the head-stud-pulling problem that the 2.7-liter engines had experienced. Porsche also improved the valve guide material used for the valve guides in the 1977 models, changing to a silicone bronze alloy from the copper alloy used previously. This was a big improvement. With the 2.7-liter engine most of the exhaust valve guides would wear out between 30,000 and 60,000

miles because of the extra heat. The 911 engines with thermal reactors were, of course, the engines that had worn out guides at 30,000, but it is not at all uncommon to see one of the normal 2.7 911 engines with copper alloy guides with the guides worn out by the time the engine has turned 60,000 miles.

The 1977 911 had fresh air vents added to the dash; these vents were also used by the optional air conditioner. A brake failure warning light was also added to the dash. The center console contained air conditioner controls, cassette storage, and fittings to accommodate the microphone and memory button station tuner of the Blaupunkt Bamberg radio that was standard on the Turbo Carrera and available as an option on the 911S. The door locks were controlled by a rotating door-lock release knob, a unique-to-Porsche control. The 1977 911 Targa no longer had movable vent wings in the doors.

For 1977, adjustable rear spring plates were added for fine-tuning rear ride height and the suspension. All models were equipped with a power brake booster. An auxiliary spring was added to the clutch linkage on the transmission in addition to the over-center clutch helper spring on the pedal assembly. The new spring, called the "cuckoo clock spring," kept the cable tight while the clutch was released and assisted the force applied at the pedal. This "over-center" action reduced the effort needed to operate the clutch and worked well when properly adjusted.

There was also an optional comfort package for the 911S that included softer Bilstein shock absorbers, 185 HR14 tires mounted on 14-inch rims, electric windows, and a speed governor that limited the car's speed to 130 mph. The speed governor was necessary because of the use of the lower-speed-rated HR tires.

The 1977 930 Turbo was little changed from the 1976 model except that it had power-assisted brakes for the first time. The 1977 Turbo was the first model year to have the boost gauge built into the tachometer. The rear suspension spring plates were now made of two pieces and had eccentric adjusters to permit the two pieces to be moved in relation to one another like the regular 911 for 1977 (this feature was to be continued on all 911s until 1989). The fine tuning these plates allowed was actually more important on the Turbo with its wider track, wider wheels, and greater weight. The 930 Turbo received the new simpler front sway bar that had been used on the 911s since 1974 with

a 20 mm front bar and a 18 mm rear bar. Wheels and tires were changed to a 16-inch diameter with 205/55 VR 16s on 7x16 front wheels and 225/50 VR 16s on 8x16 rear wheels. The 1977 930 Turbo also had heated, electrically adjustable rear-view mirrors on both sides as standard equipment for the first time.

For a little additional excitement in 1977, Porsche took on BMW in the 2-liter class of the German Group 5 series with the 935 *Baby*. Because Porsche was running unopposed in its own class, it decided to go after the competition in the under-2-liter class. The *Baby* was turbocharged, so the displacement had to be less than 1,425 cc. Porsche built a special 370-hp engine with a 71x60-mm bore and stroke for the *Baby*. Porsche used air-to-air intercooling for this little engine because they were able to fit the smaller intercoolers under the engine lid.

The *Baby* was raced only twice, unsuccessfully the first time, but winning by more than half a lap in its second and last race. This was the first 935 to use an aluminum tube subframe, a technique later applied to the 937/78.

For 1977, Porsche produced a special series of 10 IMSA-legal 934s, which took full advantage of the more liberal IMSA rules and used many of the mechanicals from the 935. The IMSA cars were able to run with lighter weight, wider 15-inch wheels, larger Group 5 rear wing and the Bosch plunger-type mechanical injection instead of the CIS system. The mechanical change made the cars more pleasant to drive, more reliable, and able to produce close to the 600 hp of the 935 instead of the 500 hp of the Group 4 version.

In Europe, over the 1976 season, a number of Porsche's racing customers had been converting their Group 4 934 racers to Group 5 specifications, so for 1977 Porsche also produced a small series of 13 cars for its customers to race in Group 5. The cars were customer versions that were in effect replicas of the two 1976 factory single-turbo 935s.

Porsche built three additional 935s for the factory team's use in the 1977 season, taking full advantage of the liberalized Group 5 rules. The rules had been revised in an effort to help some other car makes be more competitive. The new rules let the competitors raise the floor up to the doorsills, move the bulkhead (firewall) between the engine and cockpit 20 cm (7.9 inches) into the cockpit, and redefined the body structure as the part between the front and rear bulkheads (firewalls). The true effect of these rule changes did not completely take effect until 1978 and later. The new factory cars had improved aerodynamic bodywork, made of fiberglass, which included a greatly revised rear section with a false plexiglass rear window over the existing stock window. The rules required the cars to retain the original rear window, but didn't state that a car couldn't have two. Porsche entered their factory team in eight of the nine races counting toward the 1977 World Championship of Makes. The factory team won three of the races they entered and private teams won the remainder, giving Porsche another championship.

The air inlets for the twin-turbo engine were at the rear edges of the rear vent windows and used a portion of the false roof. The front bodywork was changed to include a pair of front mirrors fared into each of the front fenders, and the cars had running boards under the doors and between the fenders on each side.

The engines were changed substantially on these 1977 factory cars and included twin turbochargers and an improved intercooler system. The use of twin turbos was not so much to increase horsepower as it was to improve throttle response. The twin-turbo system served to create a pair of smaller systems, each of which had half the inertia to start moving and get up to speed or to slow down and stop every time the engine was accelerated or decelerated. The new intercooler installation took advantage of the rule change that allowed the firewall between the engine and cockpit to extend 20 cm (7.9 inches) into the cockpit. The intercooler was moved around to the flywheel end of the engine and the plumbing from the turbochargers was routed forward.

In the mid-1970s, all of the new car models were having difficulties meeting the U.S. emissions and safety standards. Because the 911 is so different in concept from other cars, it was hit particularly hard by these drastic new laws. The majority of the cars in the world are front-engined and water-cooled, so the new emissions and safety legislation were written with this configuration in mind. With the 2.7-liter models, the 911 did not seem to be adapting gracefully to this new legislation. Consequently, most enthusiasts were anticipating its demise. The new generation transaxle Porsches were introduced in the mid-1970s, first the 924 in 1976 and then the 928 in 1977. Surely this spelled the end for the 911?

The 911SC was introduced for the 1978 model year and remained in production through 1983. Although visually little changed from the 1976 3.0-liter Carrera, the 911SC was the best 911 yet. The 911SC continued to be available in both a coupe and Targa model, with the Cabriolet becoming available as a 1983 model. Porsche Audi Division, VWoA

1978

With the introduction of the Turbo model in 1975, Porsche had the means to build a much stronger normally aspirated 911 engine. In fact, Porsche did just that in 1976 when it produced the Carrera 3.0 liter for the European market.

In 1978, the 3.0-liter 911SC replaced both the Carrera 3.0 in Europe and the 2.7-liter 911 models in both Europe and the United States to become the 911 for a world market. The 911SC engine, besides being larger at 3.0 liters and more powerful at 180 hp than the 2.7-liter engine, was essentially an all new engine—and the best 911 engine produced to that time. By adapting the 911 Turbo technology to the normally aspirated engine, Porsche had solved most of the problems caused by the engine's rapid growth in the 1970s. By developing more graceful emission control devices for these 1978 911SC engines, Porsche was able to make great progress toward meeting the world's ecological needs without making either the driver or the engine suffer. Even further progress was made in 1980 with the inclusion of the oxygen sensor system and three-way catalytic converter.

The body for the 911SC model was a fairly logical progression from the Carrera and continued to use larger rear fender flares with larger wheels in the rear than in the front. The standard wheel and tire combination was 6x15 with 185/70VR-15 tires in the front and 7x15 with 215/60VR-15 tires in the rear. Nineteen-seventy-eight was also the first year that the 16-inch wheels and tires were offered as an option with 6x16 rims with 205/55VR-16 tires in the front and 7x17 rims with 225/50VR-16 tires in the rear. The rear torsion bars were increased in diameter from 23.0 mm to 24.1 mm in 1980. The black window trim was also made standard in 1981. In 1981 the additional turn signal lights were added to the front fenders on the European model 911SC. The 911SC continued to be available in both a coupe and Targa model with the cabriolet becoming available as a 1983 model.

The capacity of the 930 Turbo's engine was increased to 3.3 liters by enlarging the bore to 97 mm and lengthening the stroke to 74.4 mm. The 3.3 Turbo was the first production car ever to use an intercooler. This device lowers intake charge temperature thus creating a higher density charge. The denser charge results in the same cylinder filling but at a lower boost pressure. It also reduces the final compression temperature, which allows the use of a higher compression ratio. The 3.3 Turbo compression ratio was increased from the 6.5:1 of the 3.0 liter to 7.0:1, which results in a theoretical overall effective compression ratio as high as 11.7:1. The power of the European 3.3 Turbo was 300 DIN hp, while the U.S. version with its thermal reactor exhaust system was up from the original 245 hp to 265 hp at the same 0.8 bar boost used by the earlier 3.0-liter 930 Turbo. The reduction of power from the Euro version was, again, a result of the emissions devices and the thermal reactor exhaust system.

A new rear spoiler was developed for the 930 Turbo, which was both more efficient aerodynamically and provided increased air flow into the engine

The 930 Turbo received a major revision in 1978. The engine was increased in displacement to 3.3 liters, and an intercooler was added to the engine for improved efficiency. The addition of the intercooler could be detected by the change in the rear wing. The 1978 and later Turbos have had the much larger and more efficient 917-type brakes. Porsche Audi Division, VWoA

The rear of a 935/78 customer 935 with its removable rear fenders. Pip pins retained the fenders. After removal of a few of these fasteners, the whole fender could be removed, which made it much easier to work on the cars. The 935/78 used twin turbochargers to improve the power and throttle response. The intercooler installation took advantage of the 1977 rule change that permitted engine components to protrude into the passenger compartment 20 cm (7.9 inches). Driver Paul Newman is shown with the car.

compartment for the large intercooler. This new, larger intercooler was a major feature of the new 3.3-liter Turbo engine. Brakes larger than those fitted to the standard 911 were used on the 930 Turbo for the first time with rotors that were both ventilated and cross-drilled. The rotors were clamped by calipers that were a production development of the four-piston calipers that had been used on the 917 Can-Am racing car. The fronts had larger pistons than the rears to provide correct brake proportioning front to rear.

On the competition front, Porsche built a series of 15 customer 935s and let its customers defend the World Championship of Makes for 1978. The cars looked very similar to the first series of customer cars, but featured some refinements including a twin-turbo version of the 935 engine. The bodywork was slightly altered for these cars in that the rear fenders were removable for the first time. This made the cars much easier to work on and repair. The rear wing was changed to a two-stage unit to provide improved rear downforce.

Porsche also drastically revised the concept of the Group 5 cars by taking advantage of the rule change that had been made in 1977. The 935/78 *Moby Dick* Porsche was created just to race at Le Mans—where the emphasis is more on straight line speeds rather than cornering speeds, but the results would have a great influence on the future of Group 5 racing. *Moby Dick* had a newly developed 3.2-liter version of the venerable 901 engine with four-valve, water-cooled heads and dual-overhead cams. In addition to the rules that were exploited in building the 1977 factory

The 935/78 customer 935 passenger compartment with intercooler installation that takes advantage of the rule change allowing engine components to protrude 20 cm into the passenger compartment. A new mount for the rear shock absorbers had to be made to take advantage of this 20-cm rule. An aluminum cover hid the new installation from the outside.

935s, the *Moby Dick* also took advantage of the bulkhead or firewall rule which stated that the car ends at the front and rear bulkheads. The *Moby Dick* was built with an aluminum roll cage/tube frame, the center section of the car was lowered, and the floor section was raised up to regain the ground clearance. All new bodywork with improved aerodynamics was developed to take advantage of the car's lower profile.

Moby Dick was 9 seconds-a-lap faster at Le Mans than the 935/77 had been, and the speed on the straight was increased from 205.7 mph to 222.0 mph. *Moby Dick* was raced four times, winning only at Silverstone, but the concept led the way for many innovative Group 5 cars.

1979

The 1979 model was essentially the same car as the 1978 model, and the 1979 930 was the last Turbo imported into the United States until 1986 when the Turbo was reintroduced. (A series of 80 1980 model Turbos that were basically the same as the 1978 and 1979 models were built before January 1980 and sold in the United States. The Turbo continued to be developed from 1980 through 1985, and a number of examples of these were imported to the United States as gray-market cars.)

Again in 1979, Porsche produced an updated version of the 935 for its customers to defend the World Championship of Makes title. The 935/79 incorporated some of the innovations from the 935/78 (*Moby Dick*) and was the basis from which private teams were able to develop their own more competitive versions. The result? Porsche again won the World Championship of Makes.

In 1982, the rules were changed, replacing Groups 4, 5, and 6 with Groups A, B, and C. Two-hundred cars had to be built to qualify for Group B, and once the 200 were built an "evolution" would be permitted with only 20 cars required for additional homologation. When the rules changed in 1982, Porsche homologated "evolution" models of both its 911SC and its 911 Turbo to help its customers with their racing efforts.

In 1982, Porsche homologated "evolution" models of its 911 Turbo to help its customers with their racing efforts. In 1982, Porsche included performance updates such as an aluminum roll cage, 100/120-liter safety fuel tank in the front luggage compartment, cross bar-braced front towers, an oil tank relocated to the front trunk, a reinforced suspension front and rear, improved brakes front and rear, dual master cylinder with balance beam, central locking wheel nuts, and reinforced axles. The engine modifications were restricted by the rules to minor changes, the most significant of which was the use of a larger intercooler, a camshaft with more overlap and duration (Group B cam), and boost increased by 0.1 bar.

1980

For 1980 the 911SC was further improved with the inclusion of an oxygen sensor system and a three-way catalytic converter. The European 911SC made 188 hp with 8.6:1 compression. The engine cooling fan was increased to the 245-mm diameter used on the Turbo and the speed was reduced to 1.68:1. The oil cooler on European cars was changed to a brass tube-type cooler, but for the United States the loop cooler remained standard. The SC and Turbo engines had new heavily reinforced exhaust valve covers, which were much stiffer and greatly reduced valve cover oil leaks.

Black window trim was made standard in 1980, as were power windows on the U.S. cars, the three spoke 380-mm diameter leather steering wheel, and the center console. An alarm system was made available as an option.

There was a limited-edition Weissach Coupe in 1980, option code M 439. This special edition consisted of 400 units offered in two exterior colors: Black Metallic or Platinum Metallic. The limited edition came with a special beige leather interior with contrasting burgundy seat piping and burgundy carpeting. The Weissach limited edition had forged-alloy Fuchs wheels, 7x15 in the front and 8x15 rear. Their centers were finished in Platinum Metallic. This limited-production model also came with front and rear spoilers to distinguish them from the standard 1980 911SC.

Gray-Market Turbos, 1980–1985

The 1980 930 Turbos had a new muffler featuring a twin outlet (the original had only one large outlet). This change was supposed to drop the noise from 82 dBA to 79 dBA without any power loss. Porsche also replaced the serpentine, remote, front-mounted oil cooler with a brass tube-type cooler for improved oil cooling. The 1981 930 Turbo was unchanged from the 1980, and the 1982 engine had an oil trap installed on the crankcase vent line. Fumes from the crankcase pass through the trap into an air filter. The vent line from the oil tank also feeds into the oil trap/air

filter line. The purpose of this trap was to prevent throwing oil out of the oil tank through the vent into the engine air filter during aggressive driving.

To improve the heating capacity two extra heater blowers were added to the heater ducts of the left and right footwells beginning in 1983. A three-speed switch next to the distribution control lever operates the extra blowers and greatly improves heater efficiency.

The exhaust system was revised again in 1983, and a separate muffler was added for the wastegate (previously the wastegate had dumped into the primary muffler). This change increased the maximum torque from 304 to 318 ft-lb. The CIS fuel injection was also revised with a different warm-up regulator and different fuel distributor. The distributor was also changed to one with a double vacuum unit and an altered advance curve.

There were no changes for the 1984 Turbo model. For the 1985 model year the front-mounted oil cooler was changed to a finned radiator-type cooler. A larger front bumper opening provided extra air flow. This change provided a reduction of about 20 deg (degrees) C while driving at full load. (Remember, any of these Turbo cars from 1980 through 1985, with the exception of those 80 1980 model cars brought to

the United States in 1979, are in the United States as gray-market cars.)

1981

To battle backfires that were causing blown airboxes, the 1981 911SC had a cold-start mixture distributor built into the air box. This change alone seems to have eliminated about 90 percent of the problem. Unfortunately, each year there are still a few engines that will backfire and blow their air boxes even with these changes. These are usually caused by an injection problem or big swings in climatic conditions.

All fuel and injector lines were changed to steel. The European 911SC had output increased to 204 hp, with 9.8:1 compression. The U.S. 911SC engine was also revised, with compression increasing to 9.3:1. Horsepower continued to be specified at the same 180, however. In 1981, additional turn signal lights were added to the front fenders just in front of the doors as on the European-model 911SC. The United States and Canadian models had halogen sealed-beam headlights. The Turbo was reintroduced in Canada as an R.o.W. model without thermal reactors.

1982

The 1982 911SC had an alternator with internal voltage regulator. Cam-

The factory team only raced one 935 in 1978, Moby Dick. Moby Dick was built with an aluminum roll cage/tube frame; in addition, the center section of the car was lowered and the floor section was raised to regain the ground clearance. All-new bodywork was developed to take advantage of the car's lower profile for improved aerodynamics. Moby Dick was created with the intention of doing well in just one race, Le Mans. At Le Mans, the emphasis is more on straightaway speeds rather than cornering speeds, so the car's aerodynamics were compromised toward high speed rather than downforce. Moby Dick only raced four times and only won at Silverstone, but the concepts it established had a great influence on the future of Group 5 racing and Group 5 racing cars. Porsche AG

The new 935/79 customer version had a great number of changes over its predecessors, using a lot of the technology gained from Moby Dick. *The 935/79 had the upside-down transmission and the new big brakes directly off of* Moby Dick. *The upside-down transmission allowed these cars to run revised suspension geometry and with a lower center of gravity without severe axle angles. The 19-inch rear wheels with their large tires had caused the axles to operate at some fairly extreme angles as the 935s were lowered. Note that more and more of the rear of the car was being cut away to accommodate these changes.*

shaft sprocket attachment was changed from a large nut to a bolt. The scale for the oil temperature gauge graduations were changed with the white field beginning at approximately 20 deg C (68 deg F) and running to 60 deg C (140 deg F). There were also marks for 90 deg C (194 deg F) and 120 deg C (248 deg F). The red field started at 150 deg C (302 deg F) and ran to 170 deg C (338 deg F).

The Cabriolet was introduced as a new 911 model for the 1983 model year. Porsche Audi Division VWoA

1983

With the addition of a Cabriolet to the model line in 1983, Porsche had six distinct body styles for the first time since 1961. The Cabriolet was a welcome addition to the 911 line, and Porsche's first true open car since the 356C Cabriolet was discontinued in 1965.

In 1983, U.S. bumper laws changed and the Porsche's ride height changed to be same as the R.o.W. The U.S. 911 oil coolers were finally changed to the same multiple-tube brass oil cooler as had been used since 1980 for the Rest of the World.

Perhaps the most dazzling Porsche event of 1983 was the introduction at the Frankfurt International Auto Show of the new 959 Group B car. The Type 959 was a technical exercise that was put into limited production. It incorporated technical advancements planned to keep the 911 concept current until the year 2000.

Even though the 959's relationship to the 911 was clear, it was an exciting, all-new car with totally new developments in engine, drivetrain, body, and chassis. Most of the visible parts of the new aerodynamic body were made of Kevlar mounted on a load-bearing steel-chassis structure. The front hood and doors were made of aluminum, and the

rear engine lid with integrated rear wing was made of Kevlar.

The 450-hp 2.85-liter engine was based on the 911 engine and used the four-cam, four-valve, water-cooled cylinder head design developed for the racing 935, 936, and 956 engines. Although the concept was the same, the 959 cylinder heads were single castings for each bank of three cylinders instead of individual cylinder and cylinder head assemblies. The engine was twin turbocharged for flexibility and also used the electronic performance optimization designs that were based on Porsche's 956 experience. Power reached the ground via a new electronic, program-controlled all-wheel-drive transaxle with six-speed transmission.

The 959's suspension was fully independent, using dual transverse arms front and rear with dual shock absorbers at each corner. The ride height and shock absorber stiffness were adjustable from the driver's seat while the car was underway.

The 959 was not only an exercise in high technology, but also a very attractive new car and the first of the new "supercars." Production of the 959 started in late spring 1987, and customer deliveries began in May 1987. In 1987 and 1988, 283 of the 959s were built. Two-hundred were required to comply with the Group B homologation requirements in effect when the car was conceived.

Originally Porsche had planned to produce an "evolution" version of the 959 in the form of the 961, but by the time it had completed its run of 200 cars the rules had been changed, and FISA no longer accepted cars like the 959 into Group B.

In addition to the rally versions of the 959 run in the Paris-Dakar event in 1986, Porsche also built a single racing version of the 961 that was raced three times as an IMSA GTX class car. The 961 first raced at the 1986 Le Mans 24-hour, where it placed seventh, and then later in 1986 at the Finale at Daytona. Unfortunately, it was crashed at the 1987 Le Mans and was badly damaged by the resulting fire. IMSA had agreed to accept the 961 into its GTO class after 200 were built for homologation. Porsche talked of building an evolution series of 25 961 customer racing cars, but because of their high price there was not much interest, and no 961 customer version was ever built.

Jacky Ickx had competed in the 1983 Paris-to-Dakar Rally and wanted Porsche to be the first sports car to compete in the event. Porsche took advantage of the opportunity to do some development work on the all-wheel-drive system that would be used in the 959. Porsche ran three all-wheel-drive 953s in the 1984 Paris Dakar Rally, winning the event on its first try. Porsche again entered the rally in 1985, this time with three 959 prototypes. The company was not so lucky this time out, and all cars eventually failed with different problems, some driver-induced. The cars Porsche ran in 1985 had the chassis and all-wheel drive of the 959, but used a 3.2-liter Carrera engine. For 1986, Porsche entered three rally versions of the 959 and again won. All three finished, the first two scoring first and second.

At one time there were plans for an Americanization of the 959, and Porsche even considered building another series of 200 cars to U.S. specifications. It even went so far as to crash one car in preparation for the conversion. Ultimately, Porsche decided that too much would have to be changed to make the car comply and that the changes would probably ruin the character of the car. Of the 283 959s built, three of these cars were brought into the United States before the federalization laws changed in June 1988; all have subsequently been legalized and licensed. Porsche had also planned to bring in a Sports version of the 959 and had actually brought eight into the country, but they got caught in a June 1988 law change, and all eight were sent back to Europe.

1984

In 1984, Porsche again used the Carrera name in its 911 product line. The 1984 Carrera was the best 911 to that date, with a new 3.2-liter engine and Digital Motor Electronics (DME)-controlled fuel and ignition system. At that time, the Carrera was the fastest road-going 911 ever offered in the United States.

Updates to the Carrera 3.2 included a new front spoiler with built-in fog lights, Carrera script on the engine lid, pressure fed chain tensioners, and additional heater blower fans. The Carrera 3.2 was available with optional front and rear spoilers. Porsche also offered the Turbo-look body, which it called "the 911 Carrera with 930 Performance Body/Chassis option." The Turbo-look coupe included the Turbo bodywork, the brakes, all of the suspension changes except the Turbo tie-rods, plus the larger Turbo wheels and tires. The front wheels and tires were 7x16 with 205/55

The 959 prototype shown at the 1983 Frankfurt Show. Porsche AG

The 911SC RS (Type 954) is an example of the evolution homologation procedure. The homologation was based on the standard 1983 3.0-liter 911SC. Twenty evolution cars were built and homologated on January 1, 1984. These cars embody all of the high-performance features necessary to win the European Rally Championship. The 911SC RS has an engine that has been modified to produce 250 hp. Other changes to the 911SC RS included Turbo brakes, aluminum hood and doors, and the use of fiberglass for the bumpers and rear engine lid. Porsche AG

VR 16, while at the rear were 8x16 with 225/50 VR 16.

The 1984 911SC RS (Type 954) was an example of the evolution homologation procedure. The homologation was based on the standard 1983 3.0-liter 911SC. Twenty evolution cars were built, then homologated, on January 1, 1984. These cars embodied all of the high-performance features then necessary to win the European Rally Championship. The 911SC RS engine was modi-

fied to produce 250 hp, Turbo brakes slowed it, aluminum hood and doors were fitted, and fiberglass was used for the bumpers and rear engine lid.

1985

For 1985, the Carrera's four-spoke steering wheel was made standard equipment and a windshield radio antenna replaced the front-fender automatic antenna. Electrically adjustable seats were fitted and the oil cooler was

Customer-Built 935s

Kremer K3 and K4

The outstanding examples of privately developed 935 racers were the Kremer Brothers' all-conquering K3s and K4s which won the Porsche Cup in 1979, 1980, and 1981. Other significant and successful 935 developments were the Joest *Moby Dick* copies, Akin's two cars, ANDIAL's *Moby Dick* copy, and John Paul's 935s. There was also a small series of three or four 935s made by Porsche for some of its special customers in 1980. However, by 1980 the Kremer K3 was the "in" customer car, and the private teams that did not buy a K3 made their own 935s. The K1 and K2 had been versions of the 935 that they had developed for World Endurance Championship racing and the German championship. The K1, built in 1976, was the original 935, which was based on a 934. The K2 was their 1977 car, which featured a different rear spoiler and rear fenders with fins on the top to hold more air atop the car. Both of these changes were made to increase downforce and improve handling. The Kremers had developed their K3 935 for their own use during the 1979 season, ultimately winning 11 of the 12 races in the German National Championship. They also won Le Mans with one of their K3s, the only 935 to ever to win that race.

The attractive K3 bodywork was designed as a collaboration with Ekkehard Zimmerman of Design Plastics. All of the bodywork was done in Kevlar instead of fiberglass to increase strength and reduce weight. The K3 had wings, or "fences," on both the front and rear fenders to trap air and improve downforce. The K3 also had a raised false rear roof section to clean up air flow over the car and a unique engine lid and rear wing. Both the front and rear of the chassis were reinforced with aluminum tubes, some of it replacing the original unit body construction.

The K3's main advantage over its predecessors and competition, however, was its air-to-air intercooler. This had been the Kremers' unfair advantage in 1979 and one of the main reasons the car had been so successful. The intercooler allowed the brothers to run with higher boost pressure for longer periods of time without overheating the engine's charge air.

In 1980, the Kremers built replicas of their winning K3 and sold them as customer cars to anyone who wanted to win for DM 350,000 to 375,000 depending upon the equipment supplied and parts prices. The Kremers built 13 racers from Porsche spare parts race chassis. Additionally, they converted three 935s to K3 specifications, two of them their own 1978 cars and the other shipped from

Japan by a customer. In addition to the K3s, they also sold several conversion kits so that 935 owners could convert their own 935s to K3 specifications. The K3 was so popular that several copies and K3 look-alikes were built in addition to the actual cars and conversion kits from the Kremers. The customer cars were almost as successful as the originals had been, and John Fitzpatrick won the IMSA championship and the Porsche Cup in K3 customer cars.

The Kremer Brothers also built a 935 they called the K4 based on information they gained from the factory's *Moby Dick* plans. *Moby Dick* had been built as a compromise for Le Mans with Porsche giving up some downforce and resulting cornering power in exchange for some extra speed down the long Mulsane straight. When the Kremers built their tube-framed *Moby Dick*-type car they changed the bodywork to get more downforce, as most of the tracks that the car would race at would place more demand on handling than sustained high speed. They also revised the suspension design, though their revision wasn't quite as successful as their body design. Even with its shortcomings, the K4 was successful enough for the Kremer's driver, Bob Wollek, to win the Porsche Cup in 1981.

The Kremers also built a second K4 for Interscope racing and Ted Field and Danny Ongias. Interscope did not like the K4 and never raced the car. John Fitzpatrick bought the Kremers' original K4 from them for use in the U.S. IMSA series. Fitzpatrick and his people modified the body and suspension extensively and won four IMSA races with it during the 1982 season. Fitzpatrick continued racing the K4 at the beginning of the 1983 IMSA season and then moved his operation to England to race a 956 team in the World Endurance Championship.

Joest *Moby Dick* Replicas

In 1981, Porsche gave two of the German private teams copies of the plans for its *Moby Dick* car so that they could build their own. Joest built its first *Moby Dick* replica for its own use in the German Championship and WEC races. The Joest team raced its *Moby Dick* replica three times in Germany with Jochen Mass as the driver. Mass won the Hockenheim race and then Joest sold the car to Gianpiero Moretti who brought the car and Mass to the Riverside, California, race in April 1981. Mass and Moretti were in contention until they dropped back with a rocker arm problem and ended up 14th. Dr. Moretti successfully raced the car in the IMSA series for a couple of years.

In 1982, John Fitzpatrick had Joest build him an additional copy of *Moby Dick*

for himself and David Hobbs to drive at Le Mans, where they placed fourth behind the three factory 956s. After racing his Joest *Moby Dick* car at Le Mans, he brought it to the United States and raced it in the IMSA series.

ANDIAL 935

In 1982, Glen Blakely and ANDIAL built another *Moby Dick* copy for Howard Meister. They raced the car at Riverside and sold it to Preston Henn. In 1983 Bob Wollek put the ANDIAL *Moby Dick* car on the pole and then he, Preston, Claud Ballot-Lena, and A. J. Foyt drove it to its first victory. Foyt and Hurley Haywood won again at Daytona in July. A. J. Foyt, Bob Wollek, and Derek Bell drove this copy to second place at Daytona in 1984, and the same trio placed third at Sebring. A. J. and Wollek placed fourth at Miami.

By 1984, these wonderful old beasts were not really competitive in IMSA against the always improving GTP cars, and the 935s only won at Sebring the entire season.

John Paul 935s

John Paul and John Paul, Jr., ran a series of cars that they either modified or had built for them. The first two, JLP1 and JLP2, were simply modified 935s with some tube frame modifications. Their JLP3 was the first car that was all of their own construction and was made for them by "Rabbit" Graham Bartills at Chuck Gaa's GAACO in Norcross, Georgia. The only Porsche body or chassis points used in its construction were the door frames, cowl, window frame, and roof section, which were from a crashed 1972 or 1973 911 salvaged from an Atlanta wrecking yard. The JLP3 was built along very conventional lines and still used all of the standard Porsche 935 suspension pickup points and suspension components.

The JLP3 car was new at Sebring in 1981, where it had some engine oil supply problems, so the race itself became a mere testing exercise.

The Pauls' next "Porsche 935" was the much more adventurous JLP4, which was designed by Lee Dykstra and built buy Dave Klym's FABCAR in Tucker, Georgia. JLP4 was built from scratch and featured a monocoque center section and tube frame front and rear sections. This was an extremely sophisticated car with fully independent suspension with inboard mounted coil-over shock absorbers. The JLP4 was a ground effects car and, like its predecessor the JLP3, it spent a great deal of time in the Lockheed wind tunnel in Marietta, Georgia. This complex car took 2,004 hours to build, and it was more difficult to maintain than the conventional 935s. As a result, the JLP3 stayed in service in the Pauls' team. During the 1981 and 1982 seasons, John Paul, Jr., won six poles and a total of nine races with these two cars and actually won five races in a row with the JLP3. In 1982, John Paul, Jr., won nine races of the 18-race IMSA series and the IMSA championship using these two Porsches and a Lola T-600.

Bob Akin 935s

Bob Akin had two 935s built in Georgia as well. Chuck Gaa of GAACO made Bob Akin's first Georgia 935, a mono-coque-chassised racer. The car looked like a cross between a Lola T-600 and a 935. Although this car was incredibly fast in a straight line, its handling could best be described as diabolical. The car went out after only two hours at Le Mans 1982, and Bob Akin was quoted as saying, "Good, I wasn't looking forward to driving it for 24 hours." The car was crashed at the end of the 1982 season and was never repaired. Bob Akin returned to racing his reliable Kremer K3 for the 1983 season.

But in summer 1983, Bob Akin had Dave Klym of FABCAR make "the Last 935" for him. There was nothing really new about "the Last 935"; in fact, it was fairly conventional. The chassis was a steel tube frame and it used all Porsche 935 suspension components. The goal with this car was strength and reliability, and they worked to optimize the suspension pickup points and get the car down to the IMSA weight limit of 2,060 lb. The body used an adaptation of the Kremer's K4 nose, and the rest was pretty much their own. The original bodywork was all done in aluminum and once they were happy with it a fiberglass mold was made from that.

The last 935 was completed and tested at Atlanta in October where it proved to be four seconds faster than Akin's K3. They tested again at Daytona and had it ready in time for its first race at the Daytona three-hour Finale, where Bob Akin and John O'Steen placed second to IMSA champion Al Holbert in his Porsche March 83G.

It's too bad that "the Last 935" was built so late; it was a marvelous 935. Nineteen-eighty-four was really the year of the GTP cars in IMSA. Brian Redman had won the 1981 IMSA championship in a GTP car, a Lola T-600. Then in 1982 John Paul, Jr., won the IMSA championship mostly with his JLP3 and JLP4, but with a little help from his Lola. The handwriting was on the wall in 1983, though, when Al Holbert won the IMSA championship with a Porsche March.

The 1984–1987 3.2-liter Carrera Cabriolet. Note the "Telephone Dial" cast wheels that became standard equipment in 1984 when the Carrera was introduced. Porsche AG

changed to a finned radiator type for both the Carrera and the Turbo. Porsche also began using Boge GZ, double-tube, gas pressure shock absorbers as an option to the Bilstein, single-tube, gas pressure shock absorbers.

Beginning with the 1985 models, the Turbo-look was also made available for both the Targa and Cabriolet in addition to the Coupe. The Turbo-look was also made optionally available without front and rear spoilers.

Porsche also introduced its short shifter in 1985. By shortening the shift travel about 10 percent, the shift lever no longer scraped the seat going into second gear when the car was fitted with sport seats.

1986

Nineteen-eighty-six was a year for great rejoicing among Porsche enthusiasts as the 911 Turbo (930) was reintroduced to the United States. Upon its re-entry to the United States, Porsche wanted to call it the 911 Turbo and drop its 930 designation.

To comply with the U.S. emissions laws, Porsche used a catalytic converter system with oxygen-sensor fuel control. Output of the new U.S.-version engine was up to 282 hp. All of the updates that had been made to the 911 Turbo since it was last available in the United States in 1979 were incorporated in the new 1986 U.S. version.

The 1986 911 Turbo and Turbo-look models had different rear wheel and tire sizes than the previous cars. The rim size was changed from 8Jx16 with a 10.3-mm offset with 225/50 VR 16 tires, to 9Jx16 with a 15-mm rim offset with 245/45 VR 16 tires. Turbo fender flares were now integrated into the front and

rear fenders instead of welded on as they had been previously.

Carreras for 1986 had their horsepower increased to 217 for the U.S. market by changing the DME ignition and fuel curves to take advantage of the 90 CLC (95 RON/85 MON) octane gasoline available in the United States. The dash was changed with new larger air vents added for fresh air and the air conditioner. The Carreras now had Boge, double-tube, low-pressure gas shock absorbers as standard equipment. The front sway bar diameter was increased from 20.0 mm to 22.0 mm, and the rear torsion bars were increased in diameter from 24.1 mm to 25.0 mm. The rear sway bar also increased in size from 18.0 mm to 21.0 mm. The additional third stoplight for the United States was also introduced in 1986. For the Cabriolet, the third stoplight is mounted on the engine lid, and for the

A number of changes had been made to the 911 Turbo since it was last available in 1980, and they have all been incorporated in the new U.S. version. Porsche AG

The Porsche 959. The technology for the future 911s will come from the 959. Porsche AG

A rear view of the 959's engine compartment. Porsche AG

The rally version, street version, and racing (961) version of the 959. Porsche AG

Coupe and Cabriolet it was mounted at the top of the rear window. The Cabriolet also had an optional electrically actuated Cabriolet top.

1987

In addition to the traditional 911 Turbo coupe, both the Targa and the Cabriolet were available as Turbo models in 1987.

The 961 race car, based on the 959, placed seventh at Le Mans in 1986. It also raced at the IMSA Finale at Daytona in 1986. The only 961 built was badly damaged by fire at the 1987 running of Le Mans. Porsche AG

The 1987 Carrera had a completely new five-speed transmission, Type Code G-50. The new five-speed had a different shift pattern with reverse out to the left of the standard "H" pattern and fifth out to the right of the "H." The clutch diameter was increased from 225 mm to 240 mm and was now activated by a hydraulic master and slave cylinder. The rear torsion bar tube had a bent center section to provide additional clearance for the new transmission and larger clutch. The 911 Carrera and 911 Turbo had new H5 headlights that were optically standard for R.o.W. and U.S. models. These looked like the Bosch H1s and H4s that had been used on R.o.W. cars for a decade. The U.S.-mandated central stop light was moved to the bottom of the rear window for all models except the Cabriolet, making the 1987 and newer 911s look different. The Carrera and Turbo were also equipped with catalytic converters and had an additional electric blower mounted on the oil cooler in the right front wheel housing to prevent excessive oil temperatures. The fan was controlled by a temperature switch mounted in the top of the oil cooler that switched on the fan when the oil temperature reached 118 deg C (244 deg F).

Cast-alloy "telephone-dial style" 7Jx15 wheels with 195/65VR 15 tires were used in front and 8Jx15 with 215/60VR 15 tires were used in the rear as standard equipment. Fuchs 6Jx16 forged alloy wheels with 205/55VR 16 tires in front and 7Jx16 with 225/50VR 16 in the rear were available as an option.

In addition to the standard production cars, Porsche had been performing custom work for its European customers at its customer service department in Werk I for several years. Porsche then started a program called the Sonderwunsche-Programm (Special Wishes Program) where it offered its customers a catalog of conversions, modifications, and customizing work. Starting with the slant-nose body option in 1987, Porsche Cars of North America (PCNA) offered a version of this program to its U.S. customers as the "Porsche Exclusive Program" until the end of the original Turbo production in 1989. The slant-nose was available for the Coupe, the Targa, and the Cabriolet. These slant-nosed cars were a little different than the previous Special Wishes versions in that they had to comply with U.S. bumper laws and didn't have front-mounted oil coolers.

In April 1987, Porsche offered a replica of the 953s it had entered in the 1984 Paris-Dakar Rally. Only one of these customer cars was ever built. The 953 had an engine derived from the production 3.2-liter Carrera engine which had 9.5:1 compression, 228 hp at 5,900 rpm, and peak torque of 195 ft-lb. The engine retained the Motronic management system and required a minimum of 95 RON octane fuel.

The 953 had full-time four-wheel drive using technology developed for the 959 and components from what would become Porsche's 911 FWD (the 964 C4). The transmission was a five-speed Type G-50 with multiple-clutch differential locking. An additional multiple-plate clutch locking-differential was used for the center differential to the front wheels as well. The front suspension was double control arm with two shock absorbers per wheel. Front torsion bars were 24.1 mm and the front sway bar was 22 mm. The rear suspension was semi-trailing-arm with torsion bar and coil spring. Rear torsion bars were 24.1 mm and the rear sway bar was 20 mm. Front wheels were 6x15 inch and the rears were 7x15 inch.

A reinforced Carrera coupe chassis was used and the car weighed in at 2,756 lb. The doors, fenders, and front hood were made from aluminum as were the front and rear bumpers. The windows were made out of thin glass. The car had racing seats and full harness safety belt.

1988

The wandering central stoplight returned to the top of the rear window for 1988, where it had been in 1986 when introduced. Fuchs forged-alloy 7Jx15 wheels with 195/65VR 15 tires were used in front, while 8Jx15 rims with 215/60VR 15 tires were used in the rear as standard equipment. Optional rims and tires were available: 6Jx16 Fuchs forged-alloy wheels with 205/55VR 16 tires in front and 7Jx16 rims with 225/50VR 16 tires in the rear.

The 911 Club Sport—a limited-edition model intended for sport and competition use—was introduced in 1987 for the R.o.W. and in 1988 as a U.S. model. To reduce the Club Sport's weight, luxury options that were normally standard equipment were deleted. Air conditioning, power windows, sound-absorbing material, radio, door pockets, and the right-side sun visor were all deleted. Performance was improved by blueprinting the engines, and hollow intake valves and a special DME control unit with a rev limiter increased from the standard redline from 6,250 rpm to 6,840 rpm. A total of 340 Club Sports were built from 1987 to 1989—81 cars in 1987, though none were imported to the United States, 169 in 1988 with 21 cars imported to the States, and 90 cars in 1989 with only seven brought stateside.

There was also a limited edition offered in the 1988 model year to commemorate "250,000 911s built." This series—built between July and September 1987—was painted Diamond Blue Metallic with a Silver Blue partial leather interior and wrinkled leather seat inserts. The wheels were painted to match the exterior color. There were Coupes, Targas, and Cabriolets, 325 for the United States, 250 for Germany, and 325 for the R.o.W. Of the total, there were 50 right-hand-drive models, 30 coupes, 10 Targas, and 10 Cabriolets. These cars are referred to by some as the "signature edition" because they have a Ferry Porsche-signed headrest.

The 1988 Turbo was essentially the same as the 1987 model.

1989

For the first time, the 16-inch forged-alloy wheels were made standard equipment for the U.S. market. Fronts were 6Jx16 with 205/55ZR 16 tires and the rears were 8Jx16 with 225/50ZR 16 tires. Light-emitting diodes (LED) enunciator lights in the door lock buttons

The 959's interior. Porsche AG

A 959 built for the Paris to Dakar race. Porsche AG

In 1987 Porsche made the Turbo available in Targa and Cabriolet versions, in addition to the traditional coupe version. Porsche AG

Porsche also produced the slope-nose as a limited series and for the first time made the factory slope-nose, or slant-nose, available in the United States through Porsche Car of North America's "Exclusive Program." Porsche AG

showed when the alarm was armed.

The 911 Speedster was added to the model line as a new open-top version of the 911. Porsche built 2,104 Speedsters—165 non-Turbo-look and the rest Turbo-look. Eight hundred Speedsters were brought into the United States. The Speedster had the same VIN number range as the 911 Cabriolet, but it did have different type-numbers as follows:

Type	911 730
R.o.W.	Left-hand drive
Type	911 731
R.o.W.	Right-hand drive
Type	911 740
United States	

The 911 Speedster was added to the model line as an additional open-top version of the 911. Porsche built 2,104 Speedsters total, and of those 165 were non-Turbo-look Speedsters; the rest were Turbo-look. These 800 Speedsters were imported into the United States. Porsche AG

The 911 Carrera 4 (Type 964) was also introduced in 1989 as an all-wheel-drive addition to the 911 line based on an all-new platform (Porsche said that 85 percent of the parts were new). The engine for this car was a development of the previous Carrera engine, increased in displacement to 3,600 cc by increasing the bore to 100 mm and the stroke to 76.4 mm. Porsche AG

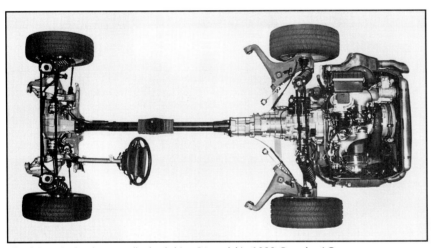

The drivetrain for the new all-wheel-drive C4 model in 1989. Porsche AG

In 1990 the regular 911 was replaced by the C2, and there were Coupes Cabriolets, and Targa models in both the C2 and C4 versions. This is a Carrera 2/4 Cabriolet. Porsche AG

The Turbo-look body option, which was standard for the United States, had option Code M491.

The 1989 911 Turbo had the G-50/50 five-speed manual transmission. This was essentially a stronger version of the G-50 transmission that had been used in the Carrera since 1987. Different gear ratios improved the Turbo's acceleration and driveability. The 1989 911 Turbo also had hydraulic clutch actuation like the Carrera and the corresponding bent center section in the rear torsion bar tube to provide clearance to accommodate the larger G50/50 transmission and clutch. The rear torsion bar size grew from 26 mm to 27 mm and the rear sway bar was reduced in diameter from 20 to 18 mm.

From 1987 to 1989, Porsche built 948 slant-nose 3.3 Turbos, 630 of which came to the United States—200 in 1987, 283 in 1988, and 147 in 1989.

The 911 Carrera 4 (Type 964) was introduced as an all-new, all-wheel-drive addition to the 911 line based on a brand-new platform. The engine for this car was a development of the previous Carrera engine now increased in displacement to 3,600 cc by increasing the bore and stroke to 100 mm and 76.4 mm, respectively. Porsche claimed that 85 percent of the parts in the car were all new.

The body for the Carrera 4 was revised while retaining the original 911 shape and appearance as the base. The new front and rear ends were made of thermoplastic and were integrated into the design, replacing the older 911 bumpers that had the tacked-on appearance common to many cars of the mid- to late-1970s because of the U.S. bumper laws. The new bumper design, together with the extending rear spoiler and smooth underside, greatly improved overall aerodynamics for the Carrera 4. The front fenders and headlight design were the same as the older 911 design, while the rear taillight assembly, including both taillights and rear fog lights, were angled on the 964.

The windshield was repositioned farther forward in the A-pillars to give it a more flush mounting and further improve aerodynamics. The rear window, though not mounted flush, was also mounted higher in the body to improve the aerodynamics.

The front suspension was changed to a type of independent MacPherson strut design using light, cast-alloy control arms and coil-over shock absorber springs. The rear was changed to independent suspension with light alloy, semi-trailing arms and coil-over shock absorber springs.

In addition to the all-wheel drive and new suspension, the Carrera 4 had all-wheel ABS and power steering.

A limited-edition Silver Anniversary model built to commemorate the twenty-fifth year of the 911 was also offered in 1989. Five-hundred were built, and they only came in Coupe and Cabriolet versions. Two-hundred-forty of the Coupes and 160 of the Cabriolets were Silver Metallic; 60 of the Coupes and 40 of the drop tops were Satin Black Metallic. They had leather interiors with seats in soft leather, and the wheel centers were painted to match the exterior color. These cars came with the following options as standard equipment: shorter gearshift lever, high intensity windshield washer, headlight washers, rear wiper (Coupe), electric Cabriolet top, cruise control, spoilers, Hi-Fi sound system, amplifier system, and sunroof.

1990

In 1990, the Carrera 2 was introduced as a two-wheel-drive version of the 964. The original 911 platform was discontinued and Carrera 2 and Carrera 4 replaced previous models of the 911. The Carrera 2 was very similar to the Carrera 4 and maintained many of the same features such as the new front and rear suspension designs, the four-wheel ABS, and power steering.

The Carrera 2 was offered with either the five-speed or a new four-speed automatic transmission called Tiptronic. This new sports transmission with integrated hypoid final drive was capable of both manual and automatic shifting. Carrera 2s and 4s with the manual five-speed transmission used the double-mass flywheel instead of a rubber-centered clutch to reduce transmission noise. The Carrera 4 had two switches in the center console, one to lock the rear differential in case you had one wheel on ice, and the other for raising the rear spoiler. The Carrera 2 only had the switch for raising the rear spoiler.

Both the Carrera 2 and Carrera 4 were available in Coupe, Targa, and Cabriolet. All Carrera 2s and 4s were standard with both driver's and passenger's air bags in the United States.

The 911 Carrera Cup replaced the 944 Turbo Cup series in 1990. These Carrera Cup cars were extensively modified Carrera 2 models with reduced weight and stripped interiors, which included a welded-in Wilfried Matter steel roll cage, a racing Recaro seat, six-point racing harness, and a fire extinguisher. Engine output was increased to 265 hp by changes to the exhaust and the engine management system. Interestingly, the Cup cars were fitted with a catalytic converter like the 944 Turbo had. Suspension was much stiffer with shorter springs, Bilstein shock absorbers, and a 50–55 mm lower ride height. Front sway bars were adjustable with five different positions and the rear sway bars were adjustable with three positions. The steering was more direct without servo assist, and the cars were shod

The 911 C2 Turbo was introduced as a worldwide model in 1991 as a coupe version only with flared front and rear fenders to accommodate the 7x17-inch front wheels with 205/55 ZR 17 tires and 9x17-inch rear wheels with 255/40 ZR 17 tires. Porsche AG

with 8x17-inch front wheels and 9.5x17-inch rears.

1991

The intake manifold system was changed from cast-aluminum to fiberglass-reinforced plastic in 1991. A "Check Engine" light was added to the dashboard. The rear seatbacks had a latch and pressure-release button added. The driver and front seat passenger airbag systems—standard equipment on U.S. Carrera 2/4 models—were offered as an option for left-hand-drive models worldwide.

The 911 C2 Turbo was introduced as a worldwide model in a coupe version only. Flared front and rear fenders accommodated the 7x17-inch front wheels with 205/55 ZR 7 tires and 9x17-inch rear wheels with 255/40 ZR 17 tires. The Turbo also had wider front and rear bumper panels to match with the flared fenders.

The new Turbo had running gear similar to the two-wheel-drive Carrera 2 and based on the new 964 platform. The new Turbo incorporated the Bosch hydraulic brake booster and ABS system and power steering was standard.

New, more-aerodynamic mirrors similar to those used on the 959 were fitted to the new 911 Turbo. (These mirrors were also used on the rest of the 911 models beginning in 1992.) Instead of the movable rear wing used by the C2/4 models, the familiar "whale tail" rear spoiler was used to accommodate the large, engine-mounted intercooler.

The 1992 911 Carrera RS was built to comply with the Group N for large series production touring cars and Group GT racing. Like the original 1973 Carrera RS, the new 911 Carrera RS is also very desirable for customers who want a more sports-oriented driving style. Many features of the Carrera RS were adopted from the Carrera Cup vehicles. The 911 Carrera RS was available in two versions—the touring version and the basic or lightweight version (which is about 10 percent lighter) for the export market. In Germany, only the basic version was offered. The Carrera RS was not available for the U.S. market. Porsche AG

The engine for the new 911 Turbo was essentially an updated version of the 3.3. Turbo with a K27.2 turbo and an intercooler with approximately 50 percent more surface area. The new Turbo was still equipped with the old CIS injection system, and the U.S. version had oxygen sensor control and a metal-matrix catalytic converter to clean emissions. The ignition system was electronically mapped like the ignition portion of the Motronic system used in the normally aspirated Carrera engines. The engine changes improved the performance of the old 3.3 Turbo engine and increased power output to 320 DIN hp. The Turbo used a dual-mass flywheel similar to those used on the C2/4 models. The Turbo was the first 911-derived production engine to use an oil filter in the oil system's pressure circuit. Porsche had used oil filters in the pressure circuit in its race cars since the 906, but never in a street car.

The ZF limited slip differential was changed to an asymmetrical design that had a lock-up factor of 20 percent under load and 100 percent under braking. Increasing the lock-up to 100 percent under braking stabilizes the handling by reducing trailing throttle yaw and the resulting oversteer effects. Porsche found that 20 percent under a load was a high enough ratio to provide adequate traction without disrupting the handling.

1992

For 1992, the Turbo-look Cabriolet was added as an R.o.W. model. This new model incorporated the running gear, brake system, 17-inch wheels, and flared fenders of the 911 Turbo model, while the engine clutch and transmission were the same as those used for the Carrera 2. This same model was also made available for the U.S. market and called the 911 Carrera 2 America Roadster.

The power steering was changed to a rotary-valve system instead of the piston system previously used for the Carrera 2/4 models. The 92 models had the same aerodynamic mirrors as the 911 Turbo from 1991. During the 1992 model year, the four-piston rear calipers were introduced on the rear wheel brakes of the Carrera 2. A proportioning valve was used to prevent rear wheel lock-up.

The 911 Carrera RS was built to comply with Group N rules for large, series-production touring cars and Group GT racing. Like the original 1973

Carrera RS, the new 911 Carrera RS is also very desirable for customers with a yen for a more sports-oriented driving style. Many features of the Carrera RS were adopted from the Carrera Cup vehicles. The 911 Carrera RS was available in two versions, the basic or lightweight version, which is about 10 percent lighter, and the touring version. In Germany only the basic version was offered, and in the export market both the basic and touring versions were offered. The Carrera RS was not available for the U.S. market.

The Carrera RS was available in the Carrera 2 coupe only with retractable rear spoiler. The cars were made without rear seats, that area instead filled with velour carpeting, and they were fitted with thin window glass, except in the windshield. The basic version came with undersealing omitted, passenger compartment sound deadening omitted, manual window lifts, plain door lining, and a pull-to-close handle and a

For 1992 the Turbo-look Cabriolet was added as an R.o.W. model. This new model incorporated the running gear, brake system, 17-inch wheels, and flared fenders of the 911 Turbo model, while the engine, clutch, and transmission were the same as those used for the Carrera 2. This same model was also made available for the U.S. market and called the 911 Carrera 2 America Roadster. Porsche AG

The Carrera RS 3.8 (Carrera RSR 3.8 street version) had 300 hp and cost $140,000. It had a sport clutch, 9x18-inch and 11x18-inch wheels, 235/40 ZR and 285/35 ZR tires, big brakes with ABS, adjustable sway bars front and rear, Turbo bodywork, an adjustable rear spoiler, air intakes in the front bumper for the front brakes, and a front spoiler. Porsche AG

The 911 Carrera 2 Speedster was added to the model lineup as an additional open-top 1994 model in late spring of the 1993 calendar year. The Speedster was introduced to the U.S. market at the Detroit Auto Show that year. This car had a normal body instead of the Turbo-look body style of the 1989 Speedster. Mechanically, the Speedster was identical to the Carrera 2, with either the five-speed or Tiptronic transmission. The Speedsters were delivered with the same Recaro racing-type bucket seats that came in the European RS model, and they were fitted with 17-inch wheels that were larger and wider than the standard wheels of the Carrera 2. Built as a 1994 model over the 1993 and 1994 calendar years, 930 were built and 409 of them were imported to the United States. There were 46 built with Tiptronic transmissions and nine of them were imported to the United States. Porsche AG

The interior of the 1993 964 Speedster with Recaro bucket seats like those used in the European RS model. Porsche AG

Porsche built a 911S Turbo Le Mans GT. Brumos Porsche debuted this car at Sebring in March 1993, and it won the Invitational FIA GT class with Hurley Haywood, Hans Stuck, and Walter Rohrl as drivers. Only one of these cars was ever built. Porsche AG

loop-type opener. The seats were racing-type bucket sports seats with provisions for a racing harness; sports seats like those in the touring version were available as an option. The cars came with an aluminum front trunk lid with a support rod to hold the lid up. New-generation Turbo-style mirrors were manually adjustable. Luggage compartment carpet was decreased to cover only a single section in the area of the spare wheel. The touring model had standard equipment in all of these areas except for the aluminum hood. The center section of the rear bumper was changed for these cars in both configurations, and they both had covers for the fog lights. A master kill switch is located above the battery in the luggage compartment.

The basic version had an engine modified with a sports flywheel and clutch in place of the double-mass flywheel used on the standard Carrera 2/4 and the touring version. The right camshaft of the basic version was without drive for the power steering. The engine power was up 10 hp to 260 from the 250 of the regular Carrera 2.

The transmission had modified shift sleeves and steel synchronizing rings on gears one through four to improve fast shifting. The gearshift was changed to a short shifter and moved to the left.

The suspension had different springs, shocks, and sway bars for improved handling. Front sway bars were 24 mm with five adjustment holes and the rear were 18 mm with three adjustment holes. Rubber suspension mounts were made stiffer for the Carrera RS models and the front strut mount was changed to a uniball ball joint. The Carrera RS was also 40 mm lower than the standard Carrera 2/4.

The steering was without power assist, except for the Carrera RS touring and right-hand-drive models. The 7 1/2-inch and 9-inch cast magnesium light-weight wheels were fitted with 205/50 ZR 17 front tires and 255/40 ZR 17 rear tires. The magnesium wheels were of the asymmetrical-hump, run-flat technology. Brakes on the Carrera RS were the same as the 911 Turbo brakes with vented and cross-drilled rotors. Front and rear brakes wore aluminum, four-piston calipers.

The 911 RS America was introduced in 1992 and sold that year as a 1993 model for the United States and Canada. Over the 1992–1994 model years, a total of 701 RS Americas were built: 297 in 1992, 328 in 1993, and 76 in 1994. The RS America had a standard Carrera 2 engine and transmission with the double-mass flywheel. A limited slip was available as an option. The curb weight was listed at 2,954 lb, which was down from the 3,031 lb of the standard Carrera 2. The America RS was built from a standard Carrera 2 chassis, which was then fitted with special M030 running gear with stronger rear Turbo springs and Turbo shocks front and rear.

The front sway bar grew in size to 22 mm from the standard 20 mm. The steering was manual without power assist.

The wheels were 17-inch light alloys of the cup design, with 7x17 wheels and 205/50 ZR17 tires in front and 8x17 wheels and 255/40 ZR17 tires in the rear. The body is identical to the Carrera 2 body with the exception of the fixed rear spoiler.

The RS America came in black, red, white, Polar Silver Metallic, or Midnight

The 911 Turbo 3.6 shares the bodywork with its predecessor, the 3.3 Turbo. Wheels were the 8x18-inch and 10x18-inch modular wheels like the Carrera Cup car's wheels. The Turbo 3.6 was the first Porsche with the larger red Brembo brake calipers and larger rotors. Porsche AG

Blue Metallic. The seats were upholstered with a black corduroy fabric. The door panels were adopted from the Carrera RS, but with switches for the power windows.

The three-point seat belts and the door opening straps were finished in Guards Red. The America RS had manually operated Turbo-style mirrors and offered optional air conditioning. The radio was also optional, and there was no cruise control. The RS America had a smaller 75 amp-hour battery, two fog lights, and a heated rear window. The cars came prepared for radio installation with two speakers, windshield antenna, antenna booster, and wiring. The Ameri-

For 1993, Porsche added the 911 Carrera 4 Coupe in Turbo-look to complement the Turbo-look version of the Carrera 2 Cabriolet. The Turbo-look coupe was offered as a 30-year anniversary model for the rest of the world and was not available as a 1993 model in the United States. The 30-year anniversary models were painted a violet metallic with a Rubicon gray interior. Porsche AG

The "new 911 Carrera," the 993, was introduced in the spring of 1994 as a 1995 model for the U.S. market. The 993 had been a 1994 model in Europe, introduced in the fall of 1993. The Cabriolet was introduced in March 1994 as a 1994 model for Europe and a 1995 model for the United States. Porsche AG

ca RS had as optional equipment a mechanical limited slip with 40 percent locking, sunroof, air conditioner, and a Porsche AM/FM stereo.

For the 1992 season the Carrera Cup cars were "tuned-up" and another 10 hp added for a total of 275 for an increase of a solid 25 hp over the standard Carrera 2/4. The 1992 version of the Carrera cup cars also rode on 18-inch, three-piece wheels, 8x18 inches in the front and 9.5x18 inches in the rear. Tires are 235-635/18 in the front and 635-645/18 in the rear. The tuned-up Carrera Cup cars used the RS body, with the thin glass in the doors and rear. They used the door pulls like the Carrera RS and also that car's aluminum front hubs. The Cup car also had brakes from the RS with disc diameter enlarged by an inch and the calipers moved out an inch to match.

For 1992, Porsche Motorsport North America had planned an IMSA Porsche Carrera Cup Series with cars nearly identical to those raced in the European Carrera Cup series. They brought in 45 cars as street legal vehicles. The cars were then shipped to ANDIAL in California and modified with more powerful engines, a lighter overall weight, stiffer chassis and suspension systems, and more powerful brakes than the standard Carrera 2.

The Carrera Cup cars were modified to increase the power from 247 hp to 271 with a racing exhaust system that retained the catalytic converter. The engines were tuned to produce maximum power on 98-octane unleaded gas.

The cars came with minimal comfort and convenience items to begin with, and then they were stripped when they got here so that they weighed 500 lb less than the standard U.S. version of the Carrera 2. The cup

cars also featured a more rigid chassis as a result of reinforcement welds, added cross-members and the installation of a welded-in roll cage.

The standard suspension was removed and Cup Car suspension was added, featuring stiffer springs and shock absorbers and larger adjustable sway bars. Porsche also replaced the brakes with the larger Turbo brakes in front and special Carrera Cup brakes in the rear.

The wheels were increased to 8x17 inches in the front and 9.5x17 inches in the rear as compared to the standard 6x16-inch front wheels and 8x16-inch rear wheels. The plans were to use Toyo F1-SR Z-speed-rated radial tires, 235/45/17 in the front and 255/40/17 in the rear.

The plan was to modify all 45 of the cars and sell them as turn-key Carrera Cup race cars that would not be legal for street use. The plans were to sell each Carrera Cup car for $100,000 plus a $10,000 performance bond promising to participate in the 1992 Carrera cup.

On May 8, 1992, Porsche Cars North America announced that it had postponed the Carrera Cup race series indefinitely. It converted the Carrera Cup cars that had been converted for racing back to the U.S. legal specifications, as when they were imported and sold them to collectors and enthusiasts as street-legal cars. Some of these Carrera Cup cars have been converted back to Carrera Cup racing specifications and are used for club racing and Porsche Club track events.

The 1992 911 Turbo was continued essentially unchanged from 1991. However, in addition to the regular C2 Turbo, Porsche also built 20 911 Turbo S2 models for the United States as a homologation basis for the Super Cars in the IMSA series. The 911 Turbo's 3.3-liter engine had more radical cams, a larger intercooler, and a different turbo with a larger compressor, which resulted in a power increase from the standard 315 hp to 322 hp and an increase of 22 ft-lb in torque to 354 ft-lb.

1993

For 1993 Porsche added a new model to the range, the 911 Carrera 4 Coupe in Turbo-look to complement the Turbo-look version of the Carrera 2 Cabriolet. The Turbo-look coupe was offered as a 30-year anniversary model for the R.o.W. and was not available as a 1993 model in the United States. The 30-year anniversary models were painted a violet metallic with a Rubicon Gray interior.

Also in 1993, the 911 Carrera 2 Speedster was added to the model line-up as an additional open-top model in spring of 1993 as a 1994 model. The Speedster was introduced to the U.S. market at the Detroit Auto Show in 1993. This Speedster was a normal body instead of the Turbo-look body style of the 1989 Speedster.

Mechanically, the Speedster was identical to the Carrera 2 with either the five-speed or Tiptronic transmissions. The Speedsters were delivered with the same Recaro racing-type bucket seats that came in the European RS model. The Speedster was fitted with 17-inch wheels, larger and wider than the standard wheels of the Carrera 2. The wheels were color-coordinated with the car's exterior color and were 7x17 front with 205/50 ZR-17 tires and the rears were 8x17 with 255/40 ZR-17 tires. Built only as a 1994 model year car over the 1993 and 1994 calendar years, 930 of the 1994 Speedsters were built and 409 of them were exported to the United States. There were 46 built with Tiptronic transmissions and nine of them were imported to the United States.

Porsche introduced its 3.6 version of the 911 Turbo in 1993 and sold it in the United States in 1993 and 1994 as a 1994 model. The engine in the C2 Turbo was replaced with a new 3.6 turbo engine based on the normally aspirated 964 engine. The 3.6 normally aspirated engine was modified with the CIS injection that had been used on the 3.3 Turbo in place of the Motronics system of the Carrera. The power output was increased from the 320 hp of the 3.3-liter version to 360 hp in its 3.6-liter configuration.

The 911 Turbo 3.6 shares the bodywork with the 3.3 Turbo that preceded the Turbo 3.6. Wheels were the 8 and 10x18-inch modular wheels like the Carrera Cup car's wheels.

The Turbo 3.6 was the first Porsche with the larger, red Brembo brake calipers and larger rotors.

At the end of the C2 3.6 Turbo production, Porsche built a special series of 88 slant-nose Turbo S models. These cars had the power increased to 385 hp and had modern-looking slant-nose bodywork. Forty-nine of these special Turbos were built for the U.S. market. There were 17 normal body 3.6 Turbo S models built, and these went only to the United States.

Starting in the summer of 1993 all cars produced at Stuttgart were filled with SAE 5W-40, fully synthetic, Shell TMO engine oil instead of the Shell mineral-based oil used previously.

The 1995 Supercup car. There was an improved version of the Supercup car for 1995 that had the larger rear wing and front spoiler of the RS Clubsport and the power increased to 310 hp. Porsche AG

To increase the driving range between refueling, a 92-liter (24.3-gal) optional fuel tank was made available in addition to the standard 77-liter (20.3-gal) tank. This tank was not available for right-hand-drive cars, Targa-top cars, or cars for the United States and Canadian markets.

For model year 1993, the brake systems in all Porsche models were filled with an improved brake fluid, ATE type 200. ATE Type 200 (also sold as ATE Blue) fluid was a new, improved DOT 4 fluid with a higher dry boiling point and a higher wet boiling point, which extended the life of the fluid and resulted in longer change intervals (every three years).

Also starting with 1993, all air conditioning systems were changed to CFC-free refrigerant R 134a.

Porsche also built a limited series of Carrera RS 3.8 and RSR 3.8-liter cars for 1993 that were based on the 964 platform with wide bodywork like the Turbo. They built 100 of these cars, 55 of the RS street version and 45 of the racing RSR version. These were built slightly differently depending on where they would be raced. They could be made to fit the Le Mans rules, the BPR rules, the Japanese GT rules, and IMSA rules as well as many national series. Different fuel tanks, different exhaust systems, and different intake restrictors were fitted for different racing series. The RSR 3.8s had essentially new engines, with a different crankcase; different pistons and cylinders; and a new, tuned intake plenum with six individual throttle butterflies. These engines developed 340–350 hp at Le Mans with the restrictors used there. The RSR was the first car to use the new ABS 5, which is much faster to react than the earlier systems. Prior to this new ABS, most drivers chose to turn the ABS off, but now they find that the ABS actually makes them

In January 1995 Porsche introduced the Carrera RS and RS Clubsport for the European market only. The Euro RS and Clubsport had 300-hp 3.8-liter engines. The bodywork was much more aggressive than the standard 993 bodywork, with aggressive front spoilers and a larger fixed rear wing. The Clubsport version had an even more aggressive front spoiler and a larger double-deck rear wing with side plates. Porsche AG

A GT2 car being built at Weissach. Porsche AG

faster. The RSRs won at their first outing at Le Mans in 1993.

The Carrera RS 3.8 (Carrera RSR 3.8 street version) made 300 hp and cost $140,000. It had a sport clutch, 9-inch and 11x18-inch wheels with 235/40 ZR and 285/35 ZR tires front and rear, respectively, big brakes with ABS, adjustable sway bars front and rear, Turbo bodywork, an adjustable rear spoiler, air intakes in the front bumper for the front brakes, and a front spoiler. Optional equipment included a radio, airbag, Clubsport package, roll bar, extinguisher system, belts, and reduced interior equipment.

The Carrera RSR 3.8 racing version had in excess of 325 hp, depending upon which air restrictor was used, and cost $140,000-plus. These cars were built to be eligible in the different GT classes of the world, from Le Mans to the Kärcher Global Endurance GT series (BPR), IMSA series, and Japanese GT series.

Air jacks added approximately $4,800 and center-lock wheel nuts another $4,000. The racing version of the

In time for Le Mans 1995, Porsche offered an evolutionary version of the 911 GT2 car that they called the 911 GT2 Evolution (Evo). The purpose of the Evo was to provide customers with a car that would be competitive in the Le Mans, BPR GT 1 class, and Japanese GT and IMSA championships when modified accordingly. The GT2 Evo racing version was raced for the first time in the Nürburgring BPR race in 1995 and then again at Le Mans. Porsche AG

For 1986 there was an updated version of the GT2 Evolution with revised bodywork and a stronger engine and transmission. Porsche AG

Carrera RSR 3.8 came with a racing clutch, 9-inch and 11x18-inch Speedline rims, racing suspension (unibal joints), big brakes with ABS and racing pads, adjustable sway bars front and rear, adjustable rear spoiler, air intakes in the front bumper for brake cooling, a front spoiler, racing seat, safety fuel tank, six-point safety belt, roll cage, fire system, reduced interior equipment, and hood latches. Optional equipment included an air jack system, center-lock wheels, and additional brake cooling.

Also for the 1993 racing season Porsche built a 911 S Turbo Le Mans GT. Brumos debuted this car at Sebring in March 1993 where it won the Invitational FIA GT class with Hurley Haywood, Hans Stuck, and Walter Rohrl driving.

Only one example of the 911 S Turbo Le Mans GT was built, and between Sebring and the Le Mans race, Frenchman Jack Leconte purchased this car and it was run thereafter by the French Labrare team. Labrare ran the car at Le Mans in 1993 with the same drivers who had run at Sebring and subsequent races under the Labrare banner with factory support. The car's best showing was at Daytona 1994 where it placed second overall and won the Invitational Le Mans GT 1 class.

This car, chassis number Le Mans GT 001, was specially-built as a challenger for the FIA GT class in 1993. The 911 S Turbo Le Mans GT weighed 2,300 lb and its 3.2-liter, twin-turbo engine produced 475 hp with the restrictors required by the Le Mans GT rules.

Also new for 1993 was the Porsche Supercup, which was run as a support series for the European Formula 1 series. In 1993, six of the eight races in the series were run in conjunction with F1 races. Thereafter, all races were support races for the F1 series.

1994

In the fall of 1993 Porsche introduced the 993, "The New 911 Carrera," which was sold in Europe and the rest of the world as the 1994 model. For the U.S. market, Porsche introduced the C4 "Turbo Look" Coupe as a 1994 model. They also sold the Speedster, the RS America, the 911 Turbo 3.6, the C2

Coupe, Targa, and Cabriolet unchanged from the 1993 model year, but now they were called 1994 models.

The "New 911 Carrera," the 993, was introduced in the spring of 1994 as a 1995 model for the U.S. market. The 993 had been a 1994 model in Europe, introduced in the fall of 1993. The Cabriolet was introduced in March 1994 as a 1994 model for Europe and a 1995 model for the United States.

The new 993-based Carrera was introduced in September 1993 with a claim of 30 percent new technology for the same or lower price, depending upon where it was sold. In the United States the 993 was actually priced lower than the C2 coupe that it replaced. The C2 coupe had sold for $64,990 and the 993 sold for $59,900 in 1994.

The 993 seemed to be more than just 30 percent new; it was a real step forward from the old 911. The 964, when it was introduced, was billed as 85 percent new parts, and though it was a radical departure from the old 911, it just looked like a warmed-over 911, and it was considered by most to be an evolutionary step. Well if the 964 was an evolutionary step, the 993 is an evolutionary leap. The new body style updated all of the old hallmarks of the 911 into a bright, new-looking car. The new bodywork creates the most significant appearance change in the history of the 911 while retaining the 911's classic identity. The 993 retained the pop-up rear spoiler, which not only improved the car's aerodynamics, but also enhanced engine cooling when it was up. The original prototypes were shown with the third stoplight integral with the rear roof molding at the top of the rear window. When the 993 showed up on our shores, instead of this integral stoplight they had a silly-looking picnic basket handle mounted on the engine lid with the brake light built in. It wasn't until the Turbo was introduced that the integral stop light showed up on the U.S. production cars. The 1996 Carrera coupe shared this much more attractive integral stoplight with the Turbo.

The 911's 3.6-liter, air-cooled engine for the 993 was further developed to produce 270 hp. The engine incorporated maintenance-free hydraulic valve lifters for the first time in 911 history. The engine management had been updated and the flapper box used for air flow measurement was replaced with a hot-film flow-sensing meter. A new three-into-two exhaust system was developed for the 993, the first major change in the exhaust since 1975. The outlet of this new exhaust merges into two catalytic converters and two separate mufflers. The engine changes produced more horsepower and more torque with improved emissions and fuel consumption and without increased weight.

A completely new, five-link, multilink rear suspension was developed for the 993, which improved the ride and handling. It was also much quieter than the early swingarm suspensions used on the 911. The multilink rear suspension used transverse A-arms with a toe-in link all contained on a subframe. The front suspension, was further developed and revised to work with the new rear suspension and new wheels were used on the 993-based Carrera.

The 993 had a new six-speed version of the G-50 transmission as well as a further-developed Tiptronic automatic transmission. Larger, cross-drilled front brake discs with larger front pads and cross-drilled rear discs improved the already unmatched braking of the 911. Because of the increased horsepower and torque, the 993-based version of the 911 had better acceleration and a higher top speed than its predecessor. The 993-based Carrera was quieter inside and out. The air conditioning and ventilation system was improved by the addition of particle filters. The seating was improved by redesigned seats. Driver and passenger safety were improved by the addition of upgraded driver and passenger air bags. The windshield wipers were redesigned to clear more of the windshield. New modular, ellipsoid, projection-type headlights were used for the first time for improved lighting.

At the same time that the 993 was introduced at the Frankfurt Auto Show, Porsche also introduced a 993-based Supercup car that looked essentially identical to the standard 993 but had a 3.8 engine that produced 300 hp. The chassis and suspension were also modified to enhance the Supercup Carrera's performance. The Supercup series was again held in conjunction with the Formula 1 series.

The Tiptronic S model was introduced in late August 1994. This new S version had additional shift controls on the steering wheel like some Formula 1 cars. You push up on a button on either side of the steering wheel to shift up, and you push down on the bottom side of either button to shift down.

Porsche introduced the 993-based turbocharged GT 2 model in time for the 1995 racing season. There was both a 430-hp street version and a 450-hp racing version. The racer was built to

The 1996 GT2 Evolution's interior. Porsche AG

comply with the Le Mans, BPR, Japanese, and IMSA rules.

The street version was rated at 430 hp. The cars had six-speed transmissions with sports clutch, limited-slip set-up at 40/65 percent, ABD (automatic braking differential), and rear-wheel drive. This was in contrast to the normal twin-turbo street car introduced that spring with four-wheel drive and 408 hp. The GT 2 street car had very aggressive bodywork with bolt-on, plastic fender flare extensions (40 mm front and 30 mm rear) and a large rear wing with the turbo inlets at the leading edge. The front spoiler had a large lip that curled at the edges. They were fitted with three-piece Speedline wheels, 9x18 inch in the front with 235/40 ZR/18 tires and 11x18 inch in the rear with 285/35 ZR/18 tires. These cars could be ordered with Club Sport options to equip them for competition or luxury options that would make them more pleasant grand touring cars, including such things as air bags, radios, tinted windows, and air conditioning.

The racing versions were set up to be competitive in the Le Mans GT 2 class, which resulted in the GT 2 name. When these cars raced in IMSA they raced in the GTS 1 class because IMSA did not allow turbocharged cars to compete in its GTS 2 class.

The standard brakes for the GT2 were 322 mm (12.67 inch) front and rear, but they also had a long-distance front brake option that included 380-mm (14.96-inch) diameter front rotors. Wheels were 10x18-inch front and 11x18-inch rear. The GT 2 cars used the new Bosch ABS 5 system.

Their first race outing was the IMSA Daytona 24-hour race at the beginning of the 1995 racing season, where both the Jochen Rohr and Champion teams ran them. The Rohr car came back after some mid-race difficulties to place second in the IMSA GTS 1 class and fourth overall.

Different racing organizations allowed these cars to compete with differ-

The new 1996 Targa. The 911 Targa probably should not have been called a Targa because it was a radical departure from what we have known as the Targa. The new 911 Targa is based on a Cabriolet with a roof assembly that features a sliding glass roof. The Targa is like having a car with an all-glass roof and a huge sunroof. The 911 Targa has a new 17-inch Targa Design Wheel. Porsche AG

ent-sized intake restrictors resulting in different power outputs. They were nominally rated at 450 hp. The cars had six-speed transmissions with a sports clutch. The weight was 1,150 kg (2,535 lb).

1995

The 1995 model year started out with existing 1995 models in the United States, the Carrera (993) Coupe and Cabriolet, and added the C4 Coupe and Cabriolet as well.

In January 1995, Porsche introduced the Carrera RS and RS Clubsport for the European market only. The Euro RS and Clubsport had 300-hp, 3.8-liter engines. The bodywork was much more competition-oriented than the standard 993 bodywork with aggressive front spoilers and a larger fixed rear wing. The Clubsport version had an even more aggressive front spoiler and a larger double-deck rear wing with side plates.

The Carrera RS and Clubsport wheels were the modular RS-Cup Design 8x18-inch with 225/40 ZR 18 tires in the front and 10x18-inch wheels with

New for 1996, the Carrera 4S was a new Turbo-look coupe. Just the rear fenders were enlarged on the Turbo and the Turbo-look car, but only by 25 mm. The wheels for the Carrera 4S are one-piece, pressure-cast replicas of the super-trick Turbo wheels with their hollow spokes. The Carrera 4S has the same awesome brakes, all-wheel drive, the same wheel and tire size, and same uprated suspension as the Turbo. The all-wheel drive in these cars is really nice. Unlike with the original C4, it is totally transparent until you need additional traction. The Carrera 4S was given all of the styling features of the Turbo except for the rear wing. The 4S retained the pop-up rear wing of the standard 993. Porsche AG

creased to 10x18-inch front and 12.5x18-inch rear. Weight was reduced to 1,100 kg (2,425 lb).

1996

The 1996 Porsche 911 Turbo was introduced in March 1995 at the Geneva Auto Show as the twin-turbo model that would last through both the 1995 and 1996 model years. This new Turbo was based on the 993 C4 platform and features a 408-hp, contemporary version of the venerable 911 Turbo engine. At long last the Turbo had the Motronic engine management—the first significant advancement in the Turbo's technology since 1978 when the intercooled 3.3 Turbo was introduced. The new engine management system and the twin turbos greatly improved the performance and throttle response.

The new twin turbo was based on the 993 C4 platform with four-wheel drive and a six-speed transmission. Porsche called this its supercar for everyday use. The new turbo had tremendous brakes that must be experienced to be believed. New wheels using hollow-spoke technology were developed for this new car. The wheel center and outer parts of the rim are inertia-welded together. The wheels are 18 inches in diameter with 8-inch wide front rims with 225/40 tire and 10-inch wide rear rims with 285/30 tires. The Turbo has new spoilers front and rear and rear fenders that are 25 mm wider than the standard 993 models. The rear spoiler is a fixed spoiler that is distinctive to the Turbo model.

For 1996 Porsche added two new models to the existing 993 line, a new 911 Targa and a 911 Carrera 4S. The 911 Targa probably should have been called something else because it is a radical departure from the traditional Targa. The new 911 Targa was based on a Cabriolet with a roof assembly that featured a sliding glass roof; it was like having a car with an all-glass roof and a huge sunroof. The 911 Targa wore new 17-inch Targa Design Wheels.

The Carrera 4S was a new Turbo-look coupe. The rear fenders were enlarged on the Turbo and the Turbo-look car, but only by 25 mm, not so much as to be disproportionate like the old Turbos and Turbo-look cars. The Carrera 4S wheels were one-piece, pressure-cast replicas of the super-trick, hollow-spoke Turbo wheels. The Carrera 4S had the same awesome brakes, four-wheel drive, wheel and tire sizes, and uprated suspension as the Turbo. The Carrera 4S used all of the styling features from the

The interior of the GT 2 street car. The GT 2 and RS models shared a sporty interior. Porsche AG

265/35 ZR 18 tires in the rear. Another new feature was a nice three-spoke Porsche Design Momo steering wheel.

The 911 Turbo C4 was introduced at the Geneva Auto Show in March 1995. Based on the 993 platform, it was powered by a contemporary version of the venerable 911 Turbo engine with twin turbos and Motronic engine management.

For 1995 a softer Touring Suspension and new version of the sport seat was offered for the Carrera.

A new version of the alarm system was introduced and called the "Porsche Electronic Immobilizer," which acted on the engine's DME control unit. The unit consisted of a control unit and two hand-held transmitters. The Immobilizer control unit mounted next to the DME unit under the left-hand seat. The two units were protected by a sheet metal cover attached by four shear bolts. To remove the cover for maintenance the

bolt heads must be drilled off. When the Immobilizer was activated it was impossible to start or operate the engine.

The 1995 C4 used a much simpler all-wheel-drive system than had been used on the 964-based 911. Power was transmitted to the front wheels by a viscous coupling and a central shaft to the front axle differential. The viscous coupling reacted to the difference in the speeds of rotation of the front and rear wheels so that the front wheels always received enough drive to ensure optimum traction. This system was much more transparent than the overly complicated computer-controlled system previously used, which always induced understeer and made the car feel as though it was front-wheel drive.

There was an improved version of the Supercup car for 1995 that had the larger rear wing and front spoiler of the RS Clubsport and a power increase to 310 hp.

In time for Le Mans 1995, Porsche offered an evolutionary version of the 911 GT 2 car that they called the 911 GT 2 Evo. The purpose of the Evo was to provide its customers with a car that would be competitive in the Le Mans, BPR GT 1 class, Japanese GT, and IMSA championships when modified accordingly. The GT2 Evo Racing version was raced for the first time in the Nürburgring BPR race in 1995 and then again at Le Mans. The Evo version had a new intake manifold, different turbochargers, rods, pistons, and camshafts that resulted in a power increase to 600 hp. A number of changes were made to reduce weight, and wider fenders were used so that fatter tires could be used in an effort to get the additional power to the ground. The front wheels were in-

Turbo except for the rear wing; the 4S retained the pop-up rear wing of the standard 993.

The performance of these new 993-based Carreras, with their Varioram induction system, was spectacular. Their specific power outputs were better than the 2.7 Carrera RS that was once so impressive. The 1996 993 with its 78.3 hp per liter was getting back to the same higher specific outputs that the old high-performance 911 engines had. The 1969 2.0-liter 911S engine had 86.4 hp per liter, the 2.4 911S had 81.2 hp per liter, and the Carrera RS was actually less than the 993 with its 77.8 hp per liter.

The big difference between the 1995 and 1996 standard 993s was the Varioram induction system. The Varioram increased midrange torque by 18 percent and peak horsepower rose from 270 to 282. All of this and they drive better, get better gas mileage, and meet all of the world's stricter noise and emission requirements.

Before the beginning of the 1996 racing season, the 911 GT 2 Evo was updated again. The new version was identifiable by the raised rear wing and modified front spoiler with additional intakes for the brake and oil coolers. The front wheels increased in size to 10.5x18 inch and the rear wheels remained the same at 12.5x18 inch. The first of these new GT 2 Evo cars was delivered to Franz Konrad, who raced it at the 1996 Daytona (the car went out with an electrical problem).

The Supercup car was further refined for 1996. The 3.8 engine had the valve gear altered, which resulted in a horsepower increase from 310 to 315 at 6,200 rpm. The maximum revs also increased from 6,700 rpm to 6,900 rpm. The suspension was revised to minimize bump toe-in and optimize the camber change at the front axle to make the steering more precise and stable on bumpy tracks. The spring and shock characteristics were also refined for the 1996 season. The sixth gear ratio was shortened to give more "punch" at very high speeds. New, stiff plastic bearings for the transmission mounting made the gear changes easier under racing loads.

For 1996 Porsche made a special version of its Supercup car for its U.S. customers so that they would have a contemporary car that was eligible for the IMSA GTS 2 class. In the rest of the world, Porsche's GT 2 cars were able to compete in the GT 2 classes, but because IMSA's GTS 2 class did not permit turbochargers—and the 964-based Carrera RSR 3.8s were getting old—U.S. customers needed a competitive GTS 2 car. The new car was called the 911 Cup RSR. It was essentially the current Supercup car with an RSR 3.8 engine.

The first one was delivered to Canadian Doug Trott in time for him to race it at the 1996 running of the Daytona 24-hour race in February of that year.

For Le Mans 1996 there was a new mid-engined 911 GT1 based on the single 911 GT 1 Road version that had been built prior to the 1996 Le Mans race as a basis for homologation of racing versions.

After the McLaren F1 GT cars won Le Mans overall in 1995, Porsche decided its conventional 911-based racing cars were no longer going to be competitive in the GT1 class. If Porsche wanted to be competitive it needed something new. Porsche felt that the GT1 class made the most sense for its needs, so it decided to build a new 911-based car to compete in the GT races of the world. Its new GT car would be competitive in the GT1 class with the potential for an overall win at Le Mans. The decision was made to build a 911 GT1 car on July 10, 1995, and in November Porsche announced its plans and showed the world photos of its one-fifth scale prototype. The rollout for the racer was March 14, 1996, with Jürgen Barth driving at the Weissach track, as he had when the 956 was introduced.

To qualify for Le Mans, the racing version of the Porsche 911 GT1 had to be based on a street-licensed version of the car. Porsche built a single example of the 911 GT1 car for the street. For its press photos, Porsche took pictures of this car painted white with a license plate affixed to each end. It then took this same car and applied the racing graphics that would be used and showed the same car as the race car. The racing version was not really seen

The C4 drivetrain. The 1995 C4 had a much simpler all-wheel-drive system than the one that had been used on the 964-based 911. Power is transmitted to the front wheels by a viscous coupling and a central shaft to the front-axle differential. The viscous coupling reacts to the difference in the speeds of rotation of the front and rear wheels. Porsche AG

The 1996 Porsche 911 Turbo was introduced in March 1995 at the Geneva Auto Show as the twin-turbo model that would last through both the 1995 and 1996 model years as a 1996 model. There was also a 1997 version. The new twin-turbo was based on the 993 C4 platform with all-wheel drive and a six-speed transmission. Porsche called this its supercar for everyday use. Porsche AG

The street version of Porsche's new 911 GT1 car. Porsche AG

by the public and press until the Le Mans Trials on April 28.

The racing version was more aggressive than the street car with added fender flares front and rear and a 600-hp turbocharged engine. The street version has a 300-hp normally aspirated engine. The world market for very expensive supercars such as the McLaren F1, Jaguar XK220, Ferrari F50, Bugatti EB110, and the new GT1 Porsche is said to be a total of something between 50 to 100 cars. Because of this limited market po-

tential, Porsche has said that if there is enough interest it will build street versions for sale. A street version would have around 500 hp and sell for around $750,000.

Porsche's real goal was not to sell street versions of the GT1, but to put customer versions of the GT1 race car in the hands of its racing customers in time for the 1997 GT racing season. As of Le Mans 1996, there were only four 911 GT1 cars: chassis 001, which was the test car; chassis 002 and 003, which were the Le Mans cars; and the street version.

Porsche's 911 GT1 used the front section from the current 993 welded to a box-steel section that makes up the front section that ends right behind the driver. This made 911 GT1 look very much like a production-based car when some of the front bodywork was removed.

To make the 911 competitive, Porsche designers felt that the 911 GT1 had to be a mid-engined car. This improved both the aerodynamics and the weight distribution. By moving the engine to the middle, the car's rear was cleaned up significantly and downforce was increased by using a diffuser under the rear of the car. From the bulkhead behind the driver on back, the 911 GT1 looked more like the mid-engined 962s of the 1980s than the 911. Aside from the steel monocoque front section, most of the car was made of carbon fiber.

Testing the new 911 GT1 car at Paul Ricard in April 1996. The car was unpainted and tested in the bare carbon bodywork with sponsor decals. Porsche AG

The windshield for the 911 GT1 was adapted from the 1994 Speedster to take advantage of its lower profile and more raked angle. The windshield was in a self-contained frame and could be removed easily and installed with a few Phillips screws around the periphery. The front bodywork was made to resemble the 993, as were the rears where the taillights mount. The roof section had a large inlet duct that provided air for both the twin-turbo inlets and the large air-to-air intercoolers mounted on top of the engine.

The 3.2-liter engine for the 911 GT1 was an adaptation of the tried and true, full water-cooled 962 engine that Porsche has used since 1986. However, instead of six individual heads like-fitted to all of the 911 engines and the 962 engines, the 911 GT1 engine uses the two one-piece, three-cylinder head castings from the 959 engine. The cylinders were electron-beam welded to the cylinder heads for the 962 and then the cylinders were enclosed in a water jacket. With the 959 cylinder heads, it would appear that the 911 GT1 engine has individual cylinders housed inside of the water jacket.

The camshafts were chain driven like the 959 instead of the gear driven dual-overhead camshafts normally used by the 962 engine. The engines were limited by a pair of 35.7-mm restrictors to about 600 hp. The engine used TAG 3.8 electronic engine management with multipoint, sequential fuel injection with Lambda control and cylinder selective knock control.

The suspension was double wishbone front and rear. The front suspension was mounted to the monocoque front chassis, while the rear suspension was mounted to the large casting that provided mounting points for the suspension as well as the six-speed 986-based transmission. The 986-based transmission was an evolution of the G50-based six-speed transmission used in the 993.

The 911 GT1 used one-piece BBS racing wheels, 11.5x18-inch front and 13x18-inch rear. Power steering eased driver input. Adjustable sway bars were fitted front and rear, but rules stipulated that these couldn't be driver adjustable; hence they are externally adjustable by the crew (the front sway bar had its adjustment in the radiator air outlet). The brakes were Bosch ABS with 380x37-mm carbon brake discs, front and rear, with Brembo, eight-piston, fixed front calipers with carbon pads and four-piston, fixed rear calipers with carbon pads.

Chapter 2

Buying a Used 911

Buying a previously owned Porsche 911 can be the beginning of a long, pleasurable relationship if you do your homework and select a good, sound car, or it can become a real nightmare if you aren't careful and select a dog. How do you prepare yourself to shop for a used Porsche? Well, a lot will depend upon what model and vintage Porsche you are looking for. If you are trying to buy a fairly new used 993 Carrera Cabriolet, for instance, you can and should be far more critical than if you were looking for a 1974 3.0 Carrera RS. There should be a very wide variety of 1985 Carrera Cabriolets from which to choose, whereas there may only be two or three 1974 3.0 Carrera RSs in the country and probably not more than 20 to 25 left in the whole world.

With any of the rare Porsche models you must decide what you are willing to accept in the way of flaws because the model you are pursuing is so rare. If you are not willing to accept an imperfect car, you may have to decide to get something else instead. However, if the 1995 Carrera is the car you want you shouldn't plan to accept anything but a premium condition 911. A 1995 Carrera is not at all rare, and since it is only two years old there is no acceptable reason for it not to be a near-perfect car.

Background Information

Start your selection process by narrowing the range of cars you will look at down to just a few models and years. Then start your search by learning as much as you can about the cars you have chosen. This is fairly easy to do if you select one of the production models, but it can be a real challenge if you select one of the rare Porsche models such as a 2.7 RS. Depending upon how rare the car is that you select, you may actually have to do a serious research project to learn anything about it.

A good place to start your research for any production model Porsche data is the Technical Spec books. These books are pocket size and have all of the information you will ever need to know. They are issued by model in a somewhat random manner, and there are 11

books covering the 911 from 1965 through 1995.

If you are interested in a 911 that is newer than 1995, which will be newer than the most current 911 spec books, or if you feel you need additional information on some of the earlier 911s, a reliable source is the *Service Information* booklets that Porsche publishes each year as the new models are introduced. Although these books are not pocket size, they are good, reliable sources for the type of information you will need to buy a used car. For instance, in 1994 when Porsche introduced the 993 version of the Carrera, the booklet described all of the differences between the 1993 964 version of the Carrera and the new 993 version and provided a

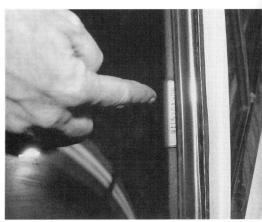

From 1969 on, the VIN number has been on the 911 windshield post. Check the VIN number and title to see if they agree.

A 911 ID sticker on the door jamb; the VIN number should match the numbers on the windshield post. This sticker also tells you where the car was made, when it was made, and the laws it complied with when made.

complete detailed list of the 1994 model's specifications.

Price Range?

Next, try to get a feel for the price range of the type of Porsche you are considering. How you go about this will depend upon how old and how rare the car is. If the car of your choice is fairly new, your bank is a good place to check the price range as they will have "blue books" that list wholesale and retail prices for used cars. Banks use these books to decide how much to loan their customers for the purchase of a used car.

Alternatively, you could purchase the newspapers from any large city in your area and compute your own low, high, and average prices. There are also people that do this type of thing on a national basis and publish newsletters listing price ranges. One such publication is *Porsche Market Letter*.

If you are planning to purchase a rare car, you will probably have to establish the price range yourself by calling owners and knowledgeable people in the field to get an idea of what you should expect to pay.

Taking a Look

Okay, let's go look at a used 911. You should start this phase of the process by prescreening the car yourself. When you find one you like, have it checked mechanically by the repair shop that will be doing your maintenance work for you. You should also have the body checked out at a quality body shop that specializes in Porsche repair and reconstruction. This is particularly true if the 911 of your choice has had recent body and paint work or any obvious body repair work—fresh paint can conceal a multitude of sins.

When you look at your first used 911 don't be intimidated by the seller. Remember the customer is always right, and you're the customer. Take control of the situation and make the seller show you everything necessary to prove to you that this is the car you are looking for. Don't be afraid to walk away from a car you are not comfortable with.

Cracking the Codes

You should develop a system for looking at used Porsches. Even if you are lucky enough to only have to look at one car before finding the 911 of your dreams, having a system will help you. Start by making sure that all of the serial numbers are what they should be. Check the VIN or chassis identification numbers. They are located on the driver's windshield post on 1970 and newer cars built for the U.S. market and in the driver's door jamb and under the hood. For 911s made before 1969, the chassis numbers are only under the hood. The numbers should all match and be the ones called out for the model you have selected in your spec booklet or other reference book. Next check the engine number and see if it matches the range of engines that should be in the car.

There are several good reasons for checking all of the numbers. First, you will want to make sure that the Porsche you are looking at is as it is represented. This will not be an easy task because the 911 has used six different chassis numbering schemes up until present. You will need your Spec Booklets or Service Information books for the cars you are looking for to make any sense of the VIN or serial numbers.

The first chassis number system was used from the beginning of the 911 production in September 1964 (1965 model year) through the 1967 model year. The chassis number system for these original 911s used a sequential, six-digit serial number starting with 300001 for the Porsche coupes built during the 1965 model year. When Karmann started producing coupe bodies for the 911 during the 1965 model year, Porsche differentiated them from the Porsche-built bodies by giving them a chassis number series that began with the number 450001. The Targa was added as a new body style during the 1967 model year, and Porsche differentiated these from the coupes by giving them a chassis number series that started with number 500001. The first digit (3, 4, or 5) in this numbering scheme was the only actual designator, and the remaining five digits served as a sequential serial number. When Porsche added the 911S it distinguished the new model just by simply adding an S to the end of the serial number.

In 1968, Porsche introduced a VIN or chassis-numbering system that was increased to eight digits (11860001); the first four digits had an encoded mean-

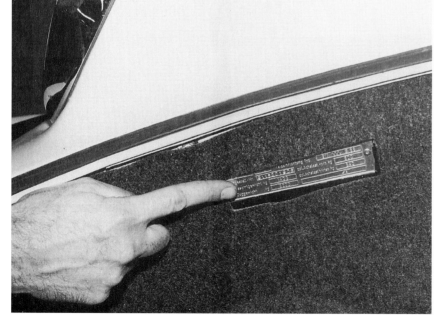

The location used for the ID plate on the later cars, after the bumper change in 1974. The ID plate under the hood on the passenger side gives the serial number, type, weight, and so on.

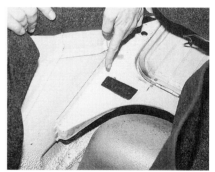

A 911 VIN number stamped under the carpet, up above the gas tank; all numbers should match.

ing, and the remaining four digits were a sequential chassis number. With this system the first two digits, "11," indicated that the car was a 911 ("12" if it was a 912), and the third digit, "8," indicated model year by giving the last digit of the model year. The fourth digit tried to tell everything else that there was to know about the car. (See Sample A.)

The remaining four digits were used as a sequential serial number. The first digit of this serial number was also used for further subcoding to differentiate between Karmann and Porsche bodies: 0 through 4=Porsche and 5 through 9=Karmann.

In 1969, the United States required that the VIN number be visible on the driver's side of the car from outside the car. In 1969, Porsche also increased its VIN or chassis numbers again, this time to nine digits (119210317) where the first *five* digits now had an encoded meaning. With this system the first two digits, "11," still indicated that the car was a 911, and the third digit, "9," indicated the model year by giving the last digit of that model year. The fourth digit, "2," now indicated the official engine type. The fifth digit, "1," was now used to indicate the body version. Again with this numbering scheme, the final four digits were a sequential serial number. (See Sample B.)

There was a minor revision to this scheme in 1970, the addition of a sixth digit to the encoded portion of the serial number bringing the total digit count to 10. A "9" was added in front of the "11" in the type number so that it now read 911 instead of 11 as before: i.e., 9119210001.

There was another minor revision in the system in 1972. The numbering scheme remained the same, but the engine types and body versions were changed. Porsche added some engine types and the body version was changed to just two types: 0=Coupe, and 1=Targa. (See Sample C.)

Some of these engine types probably require a little more explanation:
1=911T: Fuel injected, United States only.
5=911TV: The TV indicated that these engines were carbureted.
6=SC: This was the 2.7 RS Carrera engine with mechanical injection.

There was again a change in the engine types in 1974 with only three, otherwise the numbering system remained the same: i.e., 9114410125. (See Sample D.)

The 911 Turbo was introduced in 1975 and necessitated another change in the chassis number scheme. The first three digits still indicated the vehicle

The Codes

Sample A

Type	Last digit of model year	Model version code	Sequential serial number
11= 911	8=1968	0= Coupe, S-version	0001
12= 912	9=1969	1= Coupe, L-version	
		2= Coupe, T-version	
		3= Coupe, U.S. version	
		4= blank	
		5= Targa, S-version	
		6= Targa, L-version	
		7= Targa, T-version	
		8= Targa, U.S.-version	

Sample B

Type	Last digit of model year	Engine type	Body version	Sequential serial number
11=911	9=1969	1= 911T	0=Porsche body coupe	0317
911=911	0=1970	2= 911E	1=Targa	
	1=1971	3= 911S	2=Karmann body coupe	

Sample C

Type	Last digit of model year	Engine type	Body version	Sequential serial number
911=911	2=1972	1= 911T	0=Coupe	0317
	3=1973	2= 911E	1=Targa	
		3= 911S		
		4=blank		
		5= TV		
		6= SC		

Sample D

Type	Last digit of model year	Engine type	Body version	Sequential serial number
911=911	4=1974	1= 911	0=Coupe	0125
		3= 911S	1=Targa	
		4= 911 Carrera		

Sample E

Type	Last digit of model year	Engine type	Body version	Sequential serial number
911=911	5=1975	1= 911	0=Coupe	0047
930=Turbo		2= 911S U.S.		
		3= 911S	1=Targa	
		4= Carrera U.S.		
		6= Carrera		
		7= Turbo		

Sample F

Type	Last digit of model year	Engine type	Body version	Sequential serial number
911=911	6=1976	2= 911S U.S. 2.7 liter	0=Coupe	0047
930=Turbo	7=1977	3= 911/911S Japan 2.7 l	1=Targa	
		6= Carrera 3.0 liter		
		7= Turbo/Turbo Japan 3.0 liter		
		8= Turbo U.S. 3.0 liter		

Sample G

Type	Last digit of model year	Engine type	Body version	Sequential serial number
911=911	8=1978	2= 911SC U.S. 3.0 liter	0=Coupe	0047
930=Turbo	9=1979	3= 911SC R.o.W. & Japan	1=Targa	
		7= 930 Turbo R.o.W. & Japan 3.3 liter		
		8= 930 Turbo U.S. 3.3 liter		

Sample H

Type type	Model year	Manuf. Plant	Type supplement	Engine type	Sequential serial number
91=911	A=1980	0	3= 911SC	R.o.W 3.0 l.	0001
93=Turbo			4= 911SC	U.S. 3.0 l	
			7= 930	Turbo R.o.W.	

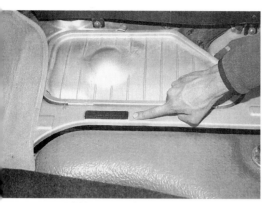

A 911 VIN number stamped under the carpet, up above the gas tank; this number moved over to the center in 1981, and the numbers no longer all match. This number will have the ZZZ characters, and the other plates will have letters and numbers specific to the U.S. market.

type, the fourth digit the model year, and the fifth digit the official engine types. To accommodate the turbo, another engine type code was added. The body version and consecutive serial number remain the same: i.e., 9115610047. (See Sample E.)

For model years 1976 and 1977 the only change was to the official engine type numbers: i.e., 9116300001. (See Sample F.)

For the model years 1978 and 1979 the only change was again to the official engine type numbers: 9118300001. (See Sample G.)

Another change was necessary in 1980 to prevent the possibility of repeating the chassis numbers from 10 years earlier. Porsche continued to use a 10-digit

chassis number (i.e., 91A0130001), but the encoding was changed. The first two digits, "91," indicated the model, type 91 = 911 and 93 = 930. The third digit, "A," was actually an alpha character, the A = 1980. The fourth digit, "0," indicates the manufacturing plant. The fifth digit, "1," was used as a supplemental type number: 1 = 911 and 0 = 930. The sixth digit, "3," indicated the engine version, and the remaining four digits continued to represent the sequential serial number: i.e., 91A0130001. (See Sample H.)

In 1981, a major change took place with the VIN numbering system. The new numbering system is international and uses 17 digits (1 2 3 4 5 6 7 8 9 10 11 12 13 14 15 16 17) The first three digits (1 2 3) are the world manufacturing code; Porsche's code is WPO.

The next three digits (4 5 6) are the VDS code for the United States and Canada. The VDS code consists of two letters and one number. The first letter (digit 4) indicates which series car it is. Letter A indicates a 911 coupe, the letter E indicates Targa Cabriolet or Speedster, and the character J indicates Turbo Coupe. The second letter (digit 5) indicates that the engine is for either Canada (A) or United States (B). The third character in this sequence (digit 6) indicates the type of restraint system: "0" stands for active and "1" stands for passive. These three digits are "ZZZ" for R.o.W. cars and are considered as fill-in digits or specific vehicle codes for United States and Canada. Note: On the VIN number stamped above the gas tank on U.S. cars, these three places are also stamped ZZZ.

The next two digits (7 8) are the first two digits of the Porsche model type, 91 is 911, 93 is 930, and 95 is 959. The next

digit (9) is used as a test digit. Digit 10 is a letter indicating the model year; i.e. 1981 was the letter B, and 1989 is the letter K. Digit 11 is a letter indicating the manufacturing site; S is Stuttgart. Digit 12 is the third digit of the Porsche model type; 1 indicates 911, 0 indicates 930, and 9 indicates 959. Digit 13 is the code for the body and engine. The remaining four digits, 14 15 16 17, make up the sequential serial number; i.e., 3173.

These numbers change every year for every model so you will need the spec books for the cars that you are interested in.

The different spec books also provide information about both the engine and transmission code numbers. For engine numbers, I prefer the internal Porsche Type numbers, which I have summarized in the engine section.

If you're looking at some of the rarer 911s, you may not be able to completely decode the chassis number with the information we have been given in these reference sources, and you may have to write Porsche for help.

A good example of a VIN for a rare car would be 9114600110. The first three digits, 911, indicate that the car is a 911, and the next digit, 4, indicates that it is a 1974 model; but our information sources do not decode the next digit, 6, which is the engine type. Looking at the engine number code itself, which in our example is 6840030, does not help much either. The first digit, 6, is the engine design and stands for six-cylinder engine; the second digit, 8, indicates the official engine type, but 8 is not listed so we cannot decode the engine type. The third digit, 4, is again the

The 911 engine serial number is on the vertical surface of the fan-housing support.

A 911 engine type number; this number is almost as important as the engine's serial number. The internal type number hides on the horizontal surface behind the serial number.

model year, which agrees with the chassis number that the car is a 1974 model.

The engine's internal type-number, Type 911/74, is not any help either because it, too, is not decoded in any of our references. Without additional information you cannot learn anymore about this car. In this case, the car happens to be one of the rare 1974 3.0 RS or RSRs, but without knowing what the engine number means, you cannot determine that.

Another good reason to check the VIN or chassis number is that one method of salvaging wrecked cars is to weld the pieces of two wrecked cars together to make one "good" car from the pieces. This is not necessarily bad if the work is done properly, but again, you shouldn't be able to tell that it was done. If you can tell that the car in question was made from two cars, the workmanship simply is not good enough. If you run into numbers that don't match or look like they have been altered this could be what happened.

Another possibility if the numbers have been altered is that the car of your dreams is a stolen car. If you find a car that has funny numbers or anything else suspicious, yet you feel the car is still interesting and you want to pursue it, check the VIN or chassis number with your local police department or Department of Motor Vehicles to make sure that the car was not stolen. If the car is not stolen, has a clear title, and you are still interested, have a quality body shop evaluate the car's condition and explain to you what they think has happened to the car.

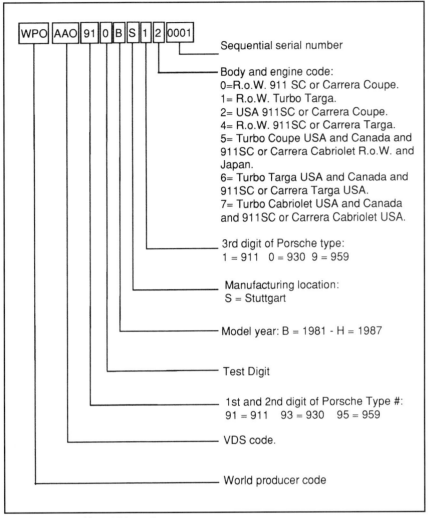

Sample 1981 and later VIN number

Inspection

With the number check done, you are ready to get down to some serious used Porsche shopping. Actually, while you were checking the numbers you were all over the car and you should have been giving it a quick once over. Even at this early stage, you may decide that from what you have seen that this is not the car for you. If so, don't waste anymore of your time or the seller's time, say good-bye and move on to the next car. Sometimes you will reject a car after just walking around it. Thank the owner and say good-bye. Do not waste your time with a car you do not like. There will be others, and even if there isn't, you're better off than with a car you don't care for.

If the car passes your preliminary inspection, it's time for a more serious look. Pretend you're a concours judge and that everything must be perfect or else you will be taking off points. The

big difference between this and a real concours is that the points you take off will be money you'll be subtracting from the asking price. Go over the interior with a fine-tooth comb looking for wear or stains on the carpeting or upholstery. Your job is to find everything that is wrong with the car and then decide what it's worth to you and whether or not you can live with it.

Check the paint and bodywork for condition and quality of workmanship. Look for any repairs or repaint work that has been done. If any body repair or paint work was done properly, and you cannot detect the work, then it is probably okay. However, keep an eye out for signs of rust damage, poor panel fit, or bad paint work.

There are some quick checks that you can make that will give you an idea of the overall condition of the Porsche you are looking at. Start with the front

because most crash damage will be there. Check for poorly repaired crash damage by lifting the carpets in the trunk and looking for wrinkles or gaps that haven't been repaired properly. If you suspect improper repair, have a quality body shop check the car.

One of the biggest enemies of any unit body car is rust. A good barometer for rust on the late-model 911s (1974–1989) is the flat rubber filler strip between the body and the front bumper. This rubber piece should lay flat and smooth over the rear edge of the bumper. If instead it has a bubbly or wavy look, the car may have a rust or corrosion problem. This rubber strip is bonded to a metal mounting strip, which is not galvanized, so it can rust, and if it rusts it causes the bubbly or wavy look where the rubber is separating from the metal strip. The fact that the rubber strip itself has deteriorated is not that important because it's easily replaced and is not too expensive, but it is a warning that there may be other rust or corrosion, so be careful. Check the front suspension pickups for rust—a common weakness on the early cars without galvanized bodies. Check around the headlights and taillights for signs of rust. You may need to take them out to see the rust as they are good at hiding the damage. While the headlights are out check the headlight bucket for squareness. The front surface should be flat and square. If there is a problem with the squareness of the headlight, it indicates improper crash or rust repair.

Another simple test that you can do on any Porsche built since 1969 is to run

A 911 headlight trim ring removed, revealing rust damage.

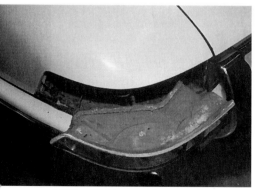

A 911 taillight assembly removed to expose possible damage underneath.

your finger along the fender lip. Porsche puts a textured finish on these fender lips to protect them from rock chips. If a fender or quarter panel has been replaced, the new part will come without this texturing and only a quality body shop will extend the extra effort to texture this area. If you find a fender lip without this texturing, look further, because it is surely an indication of collision repair work. And the body shop that did the work may not have been too careful elsewhere.

Another good rust check for these cars is to remove the floor mats and the wooden floor boards and inspect in the pedal assembly area. If this area is not kept clean during the car's lifetime, dirt and moisture will collect, followed by rust and corrosion. All of these places are fairly easy to check. If you find any rust in any of them, or have reason to believe that there has been recent rust or other body repair, or if you have any questions at all about the condition of the body, it would be a good idea to have a quality body shop that specializes in Porsches look over the car of your dreams. It never hurts to get a second opinion.

In addition to having the Porsche checked out by a quality body shop, you should consider getting professional help to have it checked out mechanically as well. You will likely save yourself some money and a great deal of grief in the long run. Some sellers will not be willing to have their used Porsche checked out. You should be very suspicious of these sellers; they probably have something to hide.

If you are buying the car in your home area, you should plan to take the car to the shop that will be doing your maintenance work. If you are buying the car from some other part of the country, check with your shop to see if its mechanics can recommend a shop in that area.

Some of the things the shop should check are oil leaks, the condition of suspension components (ball joints, tie rod ends, shocks, rubber bushings), the brakes, the wheels and tires, and the drivetrain and engine. If the mechanics find anything that they feel needs repair or replacement, have them give you a cost estimate for the repair and factor this into the price you are willing to pay for the car.

Most Porsche specialty shops will charge an extra fee for a compression test or a leak-down test on the air-cooled Porsches because some of the spark plugs are difficult to reach and they all should be removed to perform

either test. Spend the money and have the additional tests done.

The compression test is a good indication of general engine health, and it will pinpoint any weak cylinders. Compression readings on a healthy engine should be 130–170 psi, and all cylinders should be within 15 percent of each other.

If any weak cylinders showed up in the compression test, the leak-down test can be used to indicate how bad the problem is and to give you an indication of the source of the problem. Most people will tell you that 5 to 15 percent leakage is okay, but most good running, well maintained Porsche engines will be less than 3 to 5 percent.

The leak-down test measures each cylinder's ability to hold pressure. One cylinder at a time is turned to top dead center (TDC) and then pressurized. Most leak-down testers have two gauges, one gauge shows the fixed pressure being applied to the cylinder. This pressure is adjustable and should be set to 100 psi. The other gauge gives a direct reading of the pressure retained by the cylinder under test. As an example, the gauge may read 97 psi indicating the retained pressure. Subtracting this number from the 100 psi applied pressure indicated on the other gauge yields 3 psi or 3 percent leakage. (One hundred psi is used as the applied pressure so that when we subtract our leakage number we get our result directly in percent without any additional conversions.)

The source of the leak can be isolated by listening for the hissing noise made as the air from the pressurized cylinder leaks out. For example, if you put your ear to the tailpipe and you can hear the hissing there, the leakage source is probably an exhaust valve. You should also listen at the oil filler and the intake air cleaner. If the hiss is at the oil filler, the engine's problem is probably with its rings. If your hiss is at the air cleaner, the problem is likely with the intake valve. With small percentages this leakage sound is difficult to discern and it is hard to pinpoint the source. However, with larger leakages—15 percent and more—it is easy to hear the hissing and pinpoint the source.

Valve guide wear is another important item to have checked on your prospective 911. This check is particularly important for all 911s made before 1977 and particularly on the 2.7-liter and Carrera 3.2-liter 911s with their higher operating temperatures. A good indication of worn valve guides on these cars is noisy valves, the valves should be

A 911, with its firewall broken around the clutch tube; we are just starting to see this problem with the 911s now. This has been a problem that we have been dealing with on 914s for some time now.

A 911 with a crack under its door, by the jack receiver. The car is just old and tired.

Owners of 911s should always be on the watch for rust. This is rust peeking out from under the door.

quiet on a 911 after they have been adjusted. If your prospective 911 has noisy valves ask the mechanic to check guide wear by pushing the exhaust valves from side to side with a screwdriver with the valve lifted off the seat by about 10 mm. By pushing the valves from side to side, you will be able see the amount of valve guide movement and based on that judge the guide wear. You should also check the intake guide wear on the Carrera 3.2.

All Porsches up until 1977 used a copper material for the valve guides. As displacement grew and engines ran hotter, these guides started to fail earlier and earlier. Most 2.7 911s needed a top end overhaul by the time they had 30,000 to –60,000 miles on the odometer—30,000 for the thermal-reactor cars and as much as 60,000 for the 1974s without thermal reactors and the 1977s with improved guides.

During the 1977 model year, the guides were changed to a silicone-bronze material. These new guides are a brassy color, whereas the original guides were copper in color. The new valve material provides much better wear than the old copper material did, and I have seen some of the newer 911SCs with more than 250,000 miles that still have quiet valves, a sure indication that the guides are still in good shape.

The 2.7-liter 911s also have a problem with pulling cylinder-head studs. Unfortunately this is a difficult problem for a prospective buyer to assess when looking at used cars. If a 2.7 911 has more than 60,000 miles, it probably has had some major engine work performed to repair the worn valve guides. This may be a blessing in disguise because most Porsche repair shops have learned how to deal with the problems of the 2.7 engine in the years since its introduction. When experienced 911 mechanics have the 2.7 engines apart for a

top-end overhaul, they will usually repair the head studs and the rest of the engine's weaknesses. Check the repair orders from the previous owners to see if anything has been done to repair the head stud problem. Some type of case saver or time-cert should have been installed in the crankcase and the steel head studs should have been replaced with Dilavar studs. There are 24 of these studs, so you should see on the work order that all of them have been repaired and replaced.

The 1978 3.0-liter 911SC and newer engines have been remarkably reliable when compared to the 1974–1977 2.7-liter engines. Very few people have had to overhaul a 911SC engine because it has worn out. I have a friend in Seattle who used his 911SC to travel around the country and had over 200,000 miles on it, which at that time I considered very high mileage. One evening he called me up and said, "the 911 SC endurance test was over." He had missed a shift in a hill climb and bent valves and broken rocker arms and planned to rebuild the engine. That was the bad news. The good news was that his first run up the hill had held up for top time of the day.

At the time of his indiscretion his car had 222,000 miles on it and that was my high mileage mark for the SC. I have continued to look for high mileage 911s and I have a friend who does the service work on a car with over 455,000 miles on it that has never been apart. He said that he has a couple more high-mileage 911SCs and thinks that with a little luck we will see several of these cars exceed a half-million miles without requiring major engine work. This sort of reliability even exceeds the sort of reliability and mileage for which the 2.0-liter 911s and 911Ss were renowned.

Still, the 911SCs were not without a couple problems, though these were

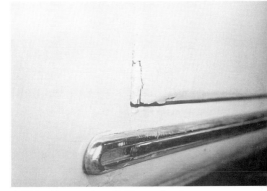

A 911 with poor door fit. The car has been damaged and poorly repaired.

solved during their lifetime. One is what I call the "exploding clutch syndrome" and the other was the dreaded chain tensioner failure. The rubber-centered (exploding) clutch was used from 1978 to 1983 when it was replaced with a spring-centered clutch. Check the repair orders for the car you're considering to see if the clutch has been replaced and if the replacement was a spring-centered clutch. If the clutch hasn't been replaced it will need to be, so budget for it.

The chain tensioners have been a problem throughout the life of the 911s. The failure of one of these tensioners can be expensive because of the additional damage it can do to the engine. In 1980, Porsche changed the major cause of tensioner failure, the chain's idler arms. Then with the 1984 Carrera, Porsche introduced what appears to be a bulletproof fix for all the 911s: the Carrera's pressure-fed tensioners. If you buy any used 911 up to the Carrera you should check the work orders or with the seller to see if the tensioners in the car you are looking at have been updated to the Carrera-style tensioners. If not, budget for their updating when you pur-

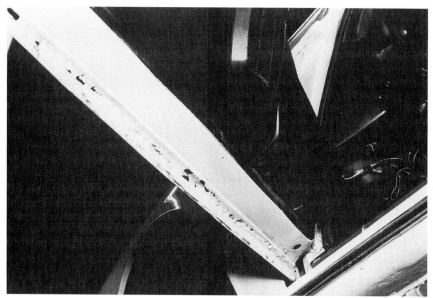

A 911 with poor rust repair work on the bottom of its door.

chase the car. Once the clutch and tensioners have been attended to, a good 911SC will run fine and last a long time.

The 911SC was the best of the 911s until the Carrera came out, and then the 3.2 Carrera was arguably a better car. The 964 is a much more modern 911 with 85 percent new parts, so surely it is a better car, and the 993 with its improved looks and performance is a still better car.

The 3.2 Carreras have had a few problems, but few have occurred with enough frequency to be considered epidemic. The one problem that we have seen enough of to be of some concern is random valve guide wear. There have been all sorts of plausible theories for the cause of this problem, but I am still not sure what the real cause is. The first car that I saw the problem on was a European Carrera 3.2 that we were converting to a 3.5. This engine had severely worn intake valves and valve guides when we took it apart. We thought maybe it had happened because it was a Euro car that had possibly been abused. My concern was that the valve stems were worn as bad as the valve guides themselves, and none of the intake valves were reusable. Even though the intake valves in most 911s have softer valve stems than the exhaust—you will often see wear on the intake valves—before this engine we had never seen what we would consider excess wear.

Since that original engine, I have seen and heard of several more Carrera 3.2 engines with worn-out valve guides, and I have heard a couple more theories

as to the cause. One theory held that something had gone wrong in the fuel injection for some period of time and that an extra-rich mixture had washed the lubricant out of the guides causing both the valves and guides to fail. Other Carrera 3.2 engines have had both the intake and exhaust guides worn, which seems to rule out the rich-mixture theory. Another theory suggests that this problem started when Porsche changed to the viton valve stem seals and that these seal too well and prevent the valve stem and guide from being properly lubricated. As a result, the valve stem and guide wear out, as does the stem seal, and the engines use excessive oil. Still another theory holds that there was a batch of bad valve guides and that it is just the engines with these guides that are failing. Even though there have been enough of these failures to make most Porsche mechanics aware of the problem, the problem is by no means an epidemic and most Carrera 3.2 owners will not see this problem.

There have also been a few problems with the 964 engines that are worth mentioning. One is a cylinder head leakage problem on some of the earlier cars. The cars built in 1989 (K), 1990 (L), and 1991 (M) had the engines that are susceptible to a cylinder head-to-cylinder leaking problem. The early cars were those built up to 62 M 06836, M64.01 for the manual transmission cars and 62 M 52757, M64.02 for the Tiptronic cars. During the model year 1991, Porsche fitted its 964 engines with a modified cylinder and cylinder

head gasket or seal. The original 964 engines did not have a head gasket and there was some oil leakage at the joint between the head and the cylinder. The way that the original heads and cylinders were machined there was a small gap left out at the edge where the head studs were. Distortion of the heads caused by the head torquing from the head studs was believed to be the source of this leak.

Actually only a small percentage of the cars had this leak, but while the cars were under warranty Porsche updated any of the cars found to be leaking. Leaking was defined as wet to the touch and not just showing signs of having leaked some time in the past. The update was to change the pistons and cylinders to cylinders that had a 32 mm larger (145 mm) diameter seating surface so that the heads would not be distorted by the head studs when the heads were torqued then expanded and contracted with heat. There was also a slot around the cylinder bore where they placed a seal ring. The original seal ring was made of pure graphite on an aluminum backing. Because of the larger, flush mating surfaces it was possible to change from Dilavar cylinder head studs to more reliable steel studs. The later engines with wider head contact surface and a head gasket seem to be much less likely to leak.

Another problem that some of the early 964s have experienced is a failure of the dual-mass flywheel. Many owners have interpreted this as a clutch failure, but it is not; the flywheel itself fails. The 964 clutches seem to be as reliable as any of the 911 clutches have been.

The dual-mass flywheels were introduced in 1990. The original Freudenberg dual-mass flywheel proved problematic in the 911, so it were replaced May 13, 1992, by the "LUK" dual-mass flywheel which seems to be much more reliable. The flywheel change was made with engine number 62 N 01738. The N in the serial number stands for model year 1993. The original Freudenberg flywheel was sprung rubber and was limited to 30 deg total travel. The Luk replacement was sprung by steel springs and had the travel limit increased to 50 deg.

So far the 993s seem to be free of any chronic bugs. Some of the early cars had a problem with the hydraulic lifters; there were a few engines that leaked oil and a few engines whose rings refused to seat. These are still pretty new cars and maybe some more serious problems will show with time, but to date the 993 looks to be a wonderful engine.

When buying an older Porsche be sure that it is either in good condition or that you know what you are getting yourself into. The cost for parts and labor for repair has gotten very expensive over the past 40-plus years. I was working on a 1972 911 project car while writing this book. I bought it for less than $4,000 as a running car that was straight but needed work. If I were to just restore this car as a stocker it would be easy to spend an additional $4,000 on paint and another $4,000 on upholstery. You could easily expect to spend $10,000 or more going through the engine, mechanical fuel injection, and intake manifolds, probably another $2,000 going through the gearbox, and probably close to that to go through the suspension and brakes. At this point we would have over $25,000 invested in a car that is probably only worth $10,000 to $15,000. I know that you will see restored cars advertised for more, but the sellers will seldom get these high asking prices. My point is that you have to be careful with any of the older Porsches, because you can easily get more money invested in them than they are worth. This is all right if you plan to keep the car in question; however, if it was considered an investment you may have a problem. This illustration also points out the importance of buying the best car that you can find so that you don't have to do everything on the car over again.

A word about gray-market cars. If you find one that you think you want to buy, *please* have it checked out. You should take it to whoever will be doing your Porsche service work and tell them, "I'm thinking of buying this gray-market 911, please check it over carefully and tell me if you think I should buy it. I will be bringing the car to you for service so please check over the service items, and the components or systems affected by the EPA conversion and let me know if you want me and this 911 gray-market car as one of your customers."

The problem with gray-market cars is not so much with the conversion itself, but the workmanship and corner cutting when it comes to the selection of components used for the conversions. I'm sure that a gray-market Porsche can be made to comply with both DOT and the EPA without destroying the car, but in truth not very many are.

It has also been difficult to make the gray-market 930/911 Turbo run properly while still meeting U.S. emissions laws. Basically, it has been an either/or choice with these cars: "either they run or they comply." Now that there is a U.S.-legal 911 Turbo again, this should be an easier problem to solve. Shops doing the conversion should just use the same components that Porsche has used to make the 1986s and newer Turbos comply.

If you are looking at gray-market cars that have been used in Europe, be forewarned that for the most part Europeans wear their cars out in very short order and that whatever they use on their roads to melt the snow does a great job on the cars as well. A two-year-old Euro car can be corroded so bad that it will be totally unacceptable by American standards.

I have a friend with a Euro car that has been converted and certified three times now. The first two companies were falsifying the conversions. The owner is responsible for making the car comply, so each time he or she has had to find someone else and have the conversion done again.

I recommend that unless you are looking for a special-interest Porsche,

Another example of poor repair work, this time on the fender lip.

such as a 356 or a Carrera RS, that you really should look for the best Porsche you can buy for your money. Plan to buy the newest Porsche (any model) that you can afford. For the past 20 years each new model has been an improvement over the preceding year's model.

All auto manufacturers had trouble with their cars in the early to mid-1970s because of their inability to come up with graceful solutions for the emissions laws, and Porsche was no exception. However, once Porsche solved the emissions problems it became a leader in the technology, and its cars have been just marvelous with excellent driveability, performance, and reliability.

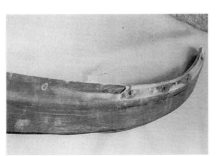

A front bumper filler strip. Note the ripples in its finish. These ripples are caused by rusting of the inner steel structure used for mounting the strip.

The front-bumper rubber filler strip, shown from the mounting side; note the rust.

Chapter 3

911 Engine Development

In the January 1985 issue of *Car and Driver* magazine, the editors selected the Porsche 911 engine as one of the 10 best engines of all time. When this issue came out, the first thing I did was turn to that article to see if the 911 made the list. I would have been disappointed if it had not. The 911 engine has become an extremely reliable high-performance engine. Even so there have been some times during the life of the 911 engine that its longevity and potential future may have been seriously in doubt. And, perhaps, despite the fact that some people still consider the Porsche 911 models to merely be hopped-up Volkswagens, the 911 engine has indeed become one of the great engines of all time.

Over the years Porsche has put a great deal of effort annually into winning the Le Mans 24-hour race. And after twenty years of trying, Porsche won Le Mans with the fabulous 917 in 1970. Another 917 won again in 1971, but 911-based engines have won that prestigious event for Porsche 12 times since then, including seven consecutive races in the 1980s. Le Mans is one of the world's most important races and Porsche has made the event its own. Thus the 911 engine has become one of the world's premier sporting powerplants both for road and track.

In its article about the 10 best engines, *Car and Driver* said, "In automotive history there have been many noteworthy cars whose distinction and fame have rested largely on their great engines. Conversely, there have been cars of great potential that have slipped into obscurity for lack of a decent powerplant." The editors said the engines honored in that issue had to be both innovative and successful in the marketplace to be selected. The other nine engines on the list were the 1901 35-hp Mercedes, 1909 Ford Model T, 1928 Alfa Romeo 6C 1500, 1932 Ford flathead V-8, 1945 Volkswagen flat four, 1947 Ferrari-Colombo V-12, 1949 Cadillac high-compression V-8, 1949 Jaguar XK Six, and 1955 Chevrolet small-block V-8.

During development in the early 1960s, a series of six-cylinder prototype engines led up to what became the 911 engine, or the 901 engine, as it was originally known. The Type 745 was a flat, opposed six-cylinder engine with two camshafts located down at the center of the engine—one above and the other below the crankshaft—driving the valves through pushrods. Probably even more significant was the Type 821 engine, which was the first of the prototypes that shared much of its technology with the final 911 design. In fact, this engine actually used the same Solex overflow-type carburetor design used on the first 901 engines when the car went into production in late 1964. The most significant differences between the Type 821 engine and the next prototype engine, the Type 901, was that the Type 821 was still a wet sump engine like the 356 pushrod engines. The near-hemispherical head design and the cam drives used to this day were originally used on this prototype engine.

The next prototype engine in this series was actually the prototype Type 901 engine, which used the more conventional triple-throat Solex downdraft carburetors. This prototype engine also had an exhaust system that was very similar to those used on the four-cylinder Carrera engines. In this setup, the exhaust gases first went forward to a pair of heat exchanger/expansion chamber premufflers, then went to the rear of the car to one large rear muffler with twin tailpipes. This was the version of the engine found in the 901 that was shown in the 1963 Frankfurt show. This prototype engine had the spark plugs angled upward at a very steep angle so they were nearly parallel to the intake ports. Because of the steep angle, the intake valve covers had a unique appearance; they were smaller and only had a pair of small notches in them to provide clearance for the spark plugs.

The 901/911 engine and car went into production in the fall of 1964 as a 1965 model 911. The engine was designed as a 2.0-liter (1,991 cc) with an 80-mm bore and a 66-mm stroke and room for expansion up to 2.5 liters. Professor Ferry Porsche later said that if he knew the engine had as much room for expansion (3.8 liters), he would have asked the engineers to redesign the engine as a smaller, lighter unit.

The Type 821 prototype engine, one of the early prototype engine designs for the 901. The Type 821 was actually similar to the first production engine except that it was still a wet-sump engine. Porsche AG

A Look at the 911 Engine

The basic layout of the 911 engine is a flat, opposed (boxer) six-cylinder engine with eight main bearings. The crankcase is split vertically along the crankshaft axis. The forged steel crankshaft has six rod throws spaced out at 120-deg intervals so that one of the cylinders fires for every 120 deg of crankshaft rotation, making it a very smooth-running engine. The crankshaft is nitrated, the early ones using the German Tenifer process and the later ones using more conventional processes. The Tenifer process was a surface treatment that was performed on the crankshaft by submerging it in a molten cyanide salt bath at elevated temperatures for extended periods of time. This is similar to a process used in the United States called Tufftriding. These processes increase the fatigue strength and improve the surface wear of the crankshaft journals. Although the two processes are very similar, they are performed at different temperatures and for different periods of time, so the results were not exactly the same.

Under the forged crankshaft is the layshaft, or counter rotating shaft, which is driven by a gear on the crankshaft. The layshaft uses a hunting system to reduce gear wear and noise by reducing the frequency that the same two gear teeth on the mating gears come together. This is not done by using the expected 1:2 gear ratio, but by using 28 teeth on the crankshaft and 48 teeth on the driven layshaft gear, thus requiring nine crankshaft revolutions before the same two teeth mesh. The layshaft has two drive sprockets for the camshaft chains. This is where the odd ratio of the layshaft is compensated for, by using a 24-tooth drive sprocket and a 28-tooth driven sprocket on the camshafts to achieve the required ratio of half the crankshaft at the camshafts. The layshaft also drives the dry sump oil system's tandem scavenge and pressure pumps through an internally splined interconnecting shaft between the layshaft and the oil pumps. The distributor is also driven at half-crankshaft speed by another drive gear on the crankshaft.

Six identical cylinder heads are mounted on the engine's six individual piston and cylinder sets. The 911 pistons were cast and used Biral cylinders. The Biral cylinder was a cast-iron cylinder with aluminum fins cast in place to improve the cooling. The heads have a near-hemispherical combustion chamber with one intake and one exhaust valve at an included angle of 59 deg from vertical.

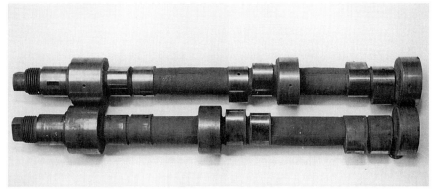

These are 901 Solex cams, with and without center-lubed cam lobes. Note the oil holes in the bearing journals and at the base circle of each lobe in the top cam.

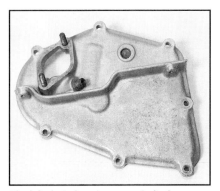

The left chain-housing cover (cylinders one through three) for the Type 901/01 engine, showing the mount for mechanical pumps for fuel recirculation and the fitting for an oil line for the center-lubed camshaft.

The inside of the left chain-housing cover for the Type 901/01 engine showing the axial sealing ring for supplying oil to the center-lubed camshaft.

With the final version of the Type 901 engine the spark plug angle was changed to one that puts the spark plug right in the center of the intake valve cover. This change was made because of the simultaneous development of the Carrera six (906) engine, which had twin-plug cylinder heads. To work out a symmetrical arrangement with the plugs centered in the combustion chamber for twin plugs, they changed the angle from the one used on the earlier Type 901 prototype engine. With this change the normal spark plugs come out spaced down the center of the intake valve covers. For racing engines the second plug for the twin ignition came out spaced down the center of the exhaust valve cover.

The engine is a single-overhead cam engine with the cams running directly in the aluminum cam housings mounted on each set of three cylinder heads. The cams are driven by a pair of duplex chains, each of which is guided by three guide ramps and tensioned by a spring-loaded hydraulic tensioner.

The left chain-housing cover for the Type 901/05 engine. Note that the casting still has provisions for a fuel pump and a center-lubed cam, but neither is used.

The cams operate the valves via rocker arms, which also mount in the cam housing in a unique manner. Each individual rocker arm is retained by an expansion shaft that also acts as an oil seal in the cam housing.

Lubrication in the engine is also unusual in that the main bearings are fed oil from the main oil gallery using the crankcase through-bolt holes as oil passages. The 11 crankcase through-bolts are used to hold the two crankcase halves together around the main bearing saddles and share their passageways through the case with the pressurized oil for the engine main bearings. Oil pressure is then fed through radial drillings in the bearings at the front and rear of the crankshaft (main bearing number one and number eight), and then through the drilled passage the entire length of the crankshaft to lubricate the connecting rod bearings.

In early production engines (up to engine number 903069), and in 911-derived racing engines, the lubrication was supplied to the camshafts from the end of the main oil circuit and fed to the end of the center-drilled camshafts by a special axial sealing ring. There are drillings to each of the cam's three journal bearings and the cam lobes to lubricate the cam running surfaces. Oil splashed from these points lubricated the rocker arms, rocker arm shafts, and the valve stems.

Early 901/01 Engines

The first production engines, Type 901/01, utilized permanent-mold aluminum sand castings for all major engine assemblies: crankcase, heads, cam housings, chain housings and covers,

and valve covers. These early engines had a pair of simple three-into-one exhaust systems that were enclosed in heat exchangers. Another oddity of these early engines it that they retained the 109-tooth 6-volt starter ring gear pattern that had been used on the 356 engines and all Volkswagens since the beginning of time rather than the later 12-volt 130-tooth pattern. The engine cooling fan used on the 911 engine is a 245-mm-diameter, 11-blade axial-flow fan which is driven at a 1.3:1 ratio from a pulley on the front of the crankshaft. The alternator for the 911 is mounted coaxially inside the 11-blade fan. The fan produced approximately 1,390 liters-per-second at 6,100 engine rpms.

After the first 3,069 engines had been built, Porsche replaced the center-

The left chain-housing cover for the Type 901/14 engine, with a seal for a camshaft-driven smog pump. This was only used in 1968 U.S. models.

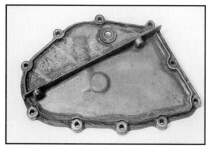

The left die-cast-magnesium chain-housing cover, as used on most engines from 1968 until late in 1977, when they were changed to aluminum die castings.

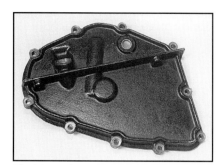

The left sand-cast-magnesium chain-housing cover, as used on most 911-derived racing engines, which retained center-lubed camshafts.

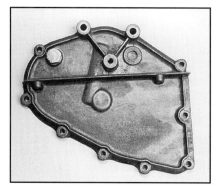

The left die-cast-aluminum chain-housing cover, as used from late in production year 1977 until 1984, when it was replaced by a cover with fittings for the pressurized chain tensioners.

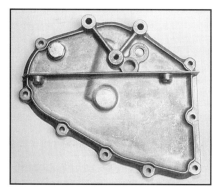

The left die-cast-aluminum chain-housing cover, as used from the introduction of the 1984 Carrera, which provides a hole and sealing boss for the oil-pressure-fed chain tensioners.

The sand-cast-aluminum crankcase used for engines from Type 901/01 until the crankcase was replaced in 1968.

Inside the sand-cast-aluminum crankcase, the layshaft runs in the crankcase without insert bearings. This particular layshaft was only used in these early crankcases.

The sand-cast-magnesium crankcase used for 906 and 910 racing engines only. The 906 engine was the first racing engine based on the 911 engine concept. The 906 engine used one of only two different special-built racing crankcases; all other Porsche racing engines adapted production crankcases.

Inside of the sand-cast-magnesium crankcase used for 906 and 910 engines.

The first in a series of cast-magnesium crankcases, first introduced in the spring of 1968 and used with changes and updates through the 1977 2.7-liter 911 production.

Inside the early magnesium crankcase, there is no provision for a rear lay-shaft bearing; the rear bearing journal of the layshaft ran in the magnesium, as it had in the aluminum crankcase. The magnesium did not prove to be durable enough in this application, so a shell insert bearing was installed in 1970.

By 1970 provisions had been made for a bearing insert for the rear lay-shaft bearing journal.

53

In 1971, case squirters were installed in the main-bearing webbing to provide additional cooling for the pistons. Note that the cylinder head studs have been removed and Time-Certs have been installed.

The strongest of the magnesium crankcases were the ones with casting number 901.101.101.7R. Note the extra reinforcement webs for main-bearing saddles. This version of the layshaft has been used in all of the production engines since the magnesium crankcase was introduced for the 1968 model year. The aluminum gear and the steel chain sprockets are replaceable.

The competition layshaft. The shaft and driven gear were a one-piece forging for high strength, while all of the chain sprockets, including the idler sprocket and the cam drive sprockets, were made of aluminum.

The competition layshaft with straight-cut gears. Straight-cut gears are noisier, but stronger and lose less power.

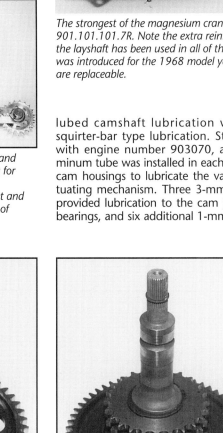

The 964 layshaft was the first production layshaft to use the steel-driven gear.

lubed camshaft lubrication with a squirter-bar type lubrication. Starting with engine number 903070, an aluminum tube was installed in each of the cam housings to lubricate the valve-actuating mechanism. Three 3-mm holes provided lubrication to the cam journal bearings, and six additional 1-mm holes sprayed lubricant for the cam lobes, rocker arms and shafts, and the valve stems. This change was made because the rocker arms and the valve stems were not getting adequate lubrication during low-rpm use. Oil for this new spray bar system was still derived from the end of the main oil circuit.

All type 901/01 engines had six individual Solex PI 40-mm overflow-type carburetors mounted on a pair of manifolds that contained overflow chambers (float bowls). A Bendix electric fuel pump supplied fuel to the overflow chambers, where a pair of mechanical pumps siamesed together took over the task of recirculating the fuel past the overflow carburetors. Each of the six carburetors had a fuel well with an overflow dam. The mechanical pumps supplied more fuel than was needed to these fuel wells, the excess ran over the dam, down the spillway, and back to the overflow chambers. The mechanical pumps were driven by the left-hand camshaft (cylinders 1-3) via a strange-looking wobble cam nut. These were pesky carburetors with their biggest problem being a severe flat spot in the 2,500-rpm to 3,000-rpm range, which was not satisfactorily solved until after use of the carburetors was discontinued. The Solex overflow-type carburetor had been successful in a side-draft version on the 1962 German-made Glas1004, and be-

The later 901.101.101.7R crankcases had additional reinforcement webs in the flywheel area.

An additional area in need of reinforcement was back in the flywheel area on the left side (cylinders one through three) of the engine. The early-style crankcases had little reinforcement.

During the 1975 model year, the main bearings were changed so that the locating tab moved from one side of the bearing saddle to the other. Because of this change, there were some crankcases with notches on both sides of the bearing saddle.

cause of this and Porsche's close relationship with Solex, engineers tried to make these carburetors work. The flat spot problem was more acute in the United States, probably because of differences in the fuel density of U.S. fuels and because of different driving styles and conditions. In the end, the problem was fairly simple to correct by changing the emulsion tubes and rejetting the carburetors. With the introduction of the Type 901/05 engine in February 1966, the Solex carburetors were replaced with Weber 40IDA-3C carburetors. The Weber carburetors were an existing model, having been designed for use on the Lancia V-6. Because the Webers were smaller, the two end tubes on each manifold were slightly inclined. An inexpensive update kit to change over to Weber carburetors was initially offered to all owners of Solex-carbureted 911s.

The first racing version of the 901 engine was actually developed in conjunction with the production engine, which benefited both projects. The 901 engine was first raced in 1965 in a 904. The engine was actually the Carrera Six, or 906 engine Type 901/20, which introduced many concepts that are still used in Porsche racing engines today. The Carrera Six engine differed from the production engine as the majority of the engine castings were made of magnesium instead of aluminum. The connecting rods and the rod bolts were made of titanium. Forged high-compression (10.3:1) pistons were used along with special Chromal cylinders, which were made of aluminum with a hard-chromed wear surface for the piston. The surface was lined with small indentations to help retain the oil film on the cylinder under the stress of racing. The engines used one-piece forged rocker arms and the valve clearance was set by valve lash adjusting caps. The heads had larger valves, larger ports, and dual spark plugs which were fired by the Marelli twin-plug distributor. The carburetors used on the Carrera Six engine were the 46 IDA-3C Webers. The Carrera Six engine also used a smaller 226-mm-diameter cooling fan driven at the same 1.3:-1 ratio as the fan used on the production cars. Because the racing engine would be run at consistently higher rpms, Porsche determined that the fan used on the production engine would produce more cooling air than was necessary if the fan was not changed. As a result, its diameter for street car use was reduced from 245 mm to 226 mm.

The 901/02 Engine

With the experience gained from the Carrera Six engine, Porsche developed the 911S model for street use. Introduced in late 1966 as a 1967 model, the 911S used the Type 901/02 engine.

These later 901.101.102.7R crankcases came with both the original 92-mm cylinder spigots and the later larger 97-mm spigots for the 2.7-liter engines. Note the thick cylinder base surface for the cylinders, which indicates that this is one of the 901.101.102.7R crankcases with 92-mm spigots. These are the best of the magnesium crankcases for use in building any 911 engine from 2.0 to 2.4 liters; the "7R mag cases" were the strongest of the magnesium crankcases.

The engine differed from the 911 Normal engine in that it had higher compression, larger valves and ports, and the cam timing was modified. Forged pistons were used rather than the cast units used in the 911 Normal, and the Biral cylinders were retained. The exhaust system had been greatly improved with two equal-length three-into-one header systems enclosed within heat exchangers.

The Weber carburetors for these first 911S engines were modified cast aluminum 40IDA-3Cs with an "S" stamped on the side after the cast-in 40IDA-3C and 3C1 designations. From engine serial number 960502 on, the 911S used Webers with a 40IDS-3C (right) and 40IDS-3C1 (left) designation. The 911S also used an aluminum pressure plate for lower inertia and better cooling. That contact surface of the pressure plate and the contact surface of the flywheel were coated with a thin layer of bronze to improve cooling and to provide a wearing surface for the aluminum pressure plate.

The header/heater system developed for the 911S was then used on the 911 Normal engine. The change in the exhaust system increased the horsepower, however, from 130 DIN hp to 140 DIN hp. Porsche felt that the difference between the S and the Normal would not be enough and took steps to reduce the engine's power to the original 130 DIN hp. To solve the problem initially, a restrictor ring was installed at the end of the header system where it joins to the muffler. For the 1967 models, in November 1966 new milder camshafts were introduced to provide a broader, more-elastic power curve and to restrict the power to its former value for advertising purposes, and the restrictor ring was removed from the exhaust system. The type number of this new engine was 901/06.

Rocker Arm Changes for 1967

During the 1967 model year the forged steel rocker arms were replaced with cast-iron rocker arms, which were less expensive to produce and had the side benefit of acting like a shear pin if there was a failure in the valvetrain. In earlier engines, which had used the forged rocker arms, if the camshaft lost its timing for any reason, the valves would be forced into the pistons, usually bending the valves, breaking the pistons, and sometimes bending the connecting rods. In the same situation, the cast-iron rocker arms usually break, resulting in much less damage.

These first cast rocker arms had no bronze bushings. Usually when two similar materials such as steel and cast iron are run together some form of bushing or bearing is used to prevent the mating surfaces from galling. Porsche tried a surface treating process on the rocker arm shafts in an attempt to cure this potential problem. Unfortunately, after a few thousand miles this surface treating wore through and the rocker arms started to gall both the rocker arm and the rocker arm shaft, leading to premature failure. These rocker arms without bushings were finally replaced in 1970 with a third version of the rocker arm, which was still made of cast iron, but had the bronze bushing again, eliminating the galling problem completely. Another change made in the 1967 model year was the addition of three more holes in each cam spray bar for a total of nine in each spray bar. The added holes sprayed up toward the intake valve covers and were added to ensure proper lubrication for the intake rocker arm.

The 930 crankcase of aluminum-silicon alloy (AlSi) was introduced for the Turbo, and a version derived from this crankcase is used for the later Turbo and Carrera engines.

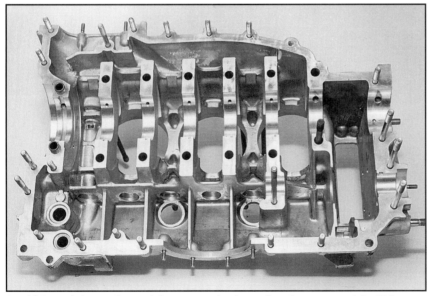
In addition to being made out of the stronger aluminum alloy, the structure of the 930 crankcase was also greatly reinforced.

1968: T Car is Introduced

In 1968, the 911T (T for Touring) was introduced for the European market with the Type 901/03 engine. This new engine was the economy model and as a result many of the changes were made to reduce the cost. Unlike its predecessors it had a cast, noncounterbalanced crankshaft, cast-iron cylinders, lower compression, and single-valve springs. The heads utilized the valves of the same size as the 911S but with smaller ports and milder cam timing for very tractable performance. A new version of the Weber carburetor, the 40IDT-3C, was developed for the 911T.

Several other changes were introduced in the 1968 model year to improve the growing 911 engine family. One change was to the one-piece rubber (soft plastic) chain guide ramps, which were later considered no improvement at all. These new ramps replaced the aluminum-backed plastic ramps that had been used in 1965 to 1967. New, sealed chain tensioners were used on all models, replacing the original open-reservoir type used previously. From engine number 4080733 on, the 40IDS-3C Weber carburetors used on the 911S had an added high-speed enrichment circuit for improved engine safety. The circuit provided an overly rich mixture at higher rpms to minimize the possibility of destructive detonation and offered no increase in performance. Another change was to the use of permanent-mold magnesium high-pressure castings in place of the sand-cast aluminum parts for all the major engine castings. This started after the beginning of the 1968 model year by replacing the castings of the chain housings, their covers, the engine breather, and the valve covers with magnesium castings. Along with the change to magnesium for the valve covers, the number of studs retaining the lower valve covers was increased from 6 to 11 in an attempt to solve the leaking problem. It didn't, but it was a nice try. In the spring of 1968 the crankcase itself was changed to a high-pressure magnesium casting. At the time, there were several advantages to this change: the pressure-cast magnesium crankcase was a more precise piece requiring less machining; magnesium machines more easily, saving on machining time; and the finished crankcase weighed 22 pounds less than the aluminum crankcase it replaced. In 1969, Mahle won a design award from the Magnesium Association for the Porsche crankcase, which at that time was the

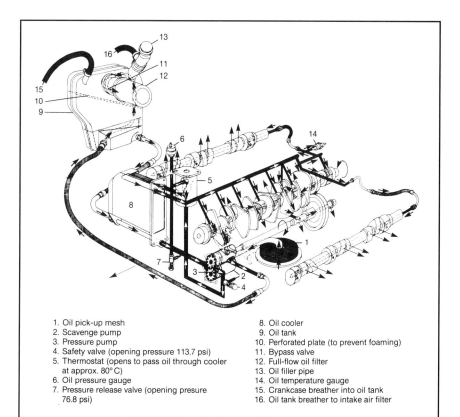

1. Oil pick-up mesh
2. Scavenge pump
3. Pressure pump
4. Safety valve (opening pressure 113.7 psi)
5. Thermostat (opens to pass oil through cooler at approx. 80°C)
6. Oil pressure gauge
7. Pressure release valve (opening presure 76.8 psi)
8. Oil cooler
9. Oil tank
10. Perforated plate (to prevent foaming)
11. Bypass valve
12. Full-flow oil filter
13. Oil filler pipe
14. Oil temperature gauge
15. Crankcase breather into oil tank
16. Oil tank breather to intake air filter

The oiling diagram for early 911 engines with center-lubed camshafts. The center-lubed-cam oiling scheme was always used for Porsche's racing engines because it provides better camshaft lubrication.

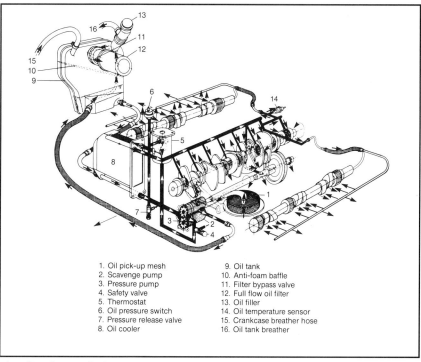

1. Oil pick-up mesh
2. Scavenge pump
3. Pressure pump
4. Safety valve
5. Thermostat
6. Oil pressure switch
7. Pressure release valve
8. Oil cooler
9. Oil tank
10. Anti-foam baffle
11. Filter bypass valve
12. Full flow oil filter
13. Oil filler
14. Oil temperature sensor
15. Crankcase breather hose
16. Oil tank breather

The oiling diagram for later 911 engines with spray-bar-lubricated camshaft.

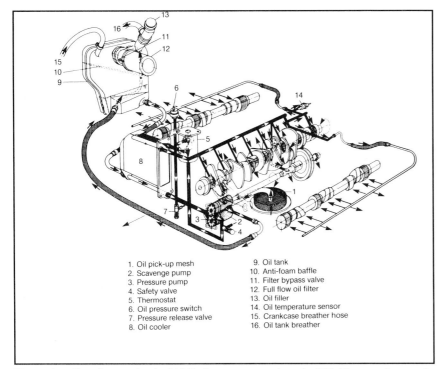

1. Oil pick-up mesh
2. Scavenge pump
3. Pressure pump
4. Safety valve
5. Thermostat
6. Oil pressure switch
7. Pressure release valve
8. Oil cooler
9. Oil tank
10. Anti-foam baffle
11. Filter bypass valve
12. Full flow oil filter
13. Oil filler
14. Oil temperature sensor
15. Crankcase breather hose
16. Oil tank breather

The engine oiling diagram for the 911 Turbo race cars, such as the 935. These engines used a combination of center-lubed and spray-bar cam lubrication, the center-lubed oiling system because of its superior cam lubrication and the spray-bar lubrication for enhanced cooling.

The 935 engines used both center-lubed and spray-bar cam lubrication, so the oil lines were modified to provide oil to both connections.

Porsche also changed the crankcase, which no longer had a removable sump plate and sump screen. The benefit of the new crankcase, for our purposes, was that it was stronger than its predecessor and less likely to leak oil along its bottom seam. This change was actually introduced on the 911SC production engines the previous April 1983 because the old molds had worn out. At the same time, the seal for the layshaft front

largest magnesium pressure die casting ever made.

A new series of engines was introduced to be compatible with the Sportomatic transmission. These engines were the Type 901/13 for the 911T, 901/07 for the 911 Normal, and 901/08 for the 911S. The new engines had all of the fittings, vacuum lines, and external oil pump to operate the Sportomatic transmissions. For the United States there were just two versions of the 911 Normal engine available in 1968: the Type 911/14 for standard transmissions and the Type 901/17 for Sportomatic transmissions. These engines differed from those sold in the rest of the world by having air-injection pumps, a distributor with a vacuum unit, and a throttle position valve to meet U.S. emissions regulations.

Fuel Injection for 1969

In 1969 Porsche introduced mechanical fuel injection to its street models with both the 911E and the 911S. In 1966, the 906E was produced with a fuel-injected version of the Carrera Six engine, Type 901/21. The Bosch mechanical injection system increased the power from 210 to 220 DIN hp. This

same technology was applied to the street cars in 1969, increasing their performance and allowing them to meet the 1969 U.S. emissions standards through more precise fuel metering. The basic concept of the fuel-injection system was similar to that used on the 906E engine but with a much-improved injection pump with an engine-speed-controlled space cam. With the space cam, the quantity of fuel is controlled by both the throttle position and the engine rpm, providing much better fuel economy and low-rpm throttle response.

The 911E engine, which replaced the midrange 911 Normal, had the same size intake and exhaust valves as the 1968 911S and 911T engines. The 911E's cam timing was the same as for the 911 Normal and 911L engines. The 911E cams were the same cams as those of the Type 901/06 engine—at least the right one was; Porsche had to make a new one for the left side with the mechanical fuel-injection belt drive. The larger valve size and the Bosch twin-row plunger fuel-injection pump increased the power from the 911 Normal's 130 DIN hp to the 911E's 140 DIN hp, and dramatically improved throttle response and low-rpm power. The basic engine produced for the world market was the Type 901/09 for the standard transmission and the Type 901/11 for the Sportomatic version.

For the fuel-injected 1969 911S engine, Porsche again increased its valve size, making them the same size as the valves of the 906 engine, Type 901/20. The larger valves, in conjunction with the Bosch twin-row plunger fuel-injection pump, increased the power from 160 to 170 DIN hp. Porsche changed the facing on the aluminum pressure plate to an iron coating; the bronze used on the contact surface of the 911S pressure plate and flywheel proved too fragile to provide adequate service life in

The 964 crankcase was changed to incorporate a number of small changes. The cylinder air deflectors bolted on, and the cylinder spigots were larger, as was the cylinder head stud spacing. The attachment for the fan shroud was also different.

Inside the 964 crankcase.

street car applications. The bronze surface was deleted from the flywheel at the same time. The Type 901/10 was the only 911S engine available for the world market.

The 911T engine was introduced to the U.S. market as the Type 901/16 for the standard transmission and 901/19 for the Sportomatic. The specifications were the same as those for the 1968 European 911T engine, Type 901/03, except for compliance with the U.S. emissions standards.

Other changes for 1969 included changing the valve springs on the 911T to the same double valve springs used on all other 911s; single springs were used in 1968 on European 911T engines. Both the 911E and the 911S engines had the more-efficient Bosch capacitor discharge (CD) ignition system. This system was such a big improvement in the 911E and 911S engines that Porsche later offered a CD update kit for the 911T owners. This system virtually eliminated the plug fouling problem that had plagued the 911 engines from the beginning. Because of the additional heat created by the added horsepower in the 911S, an external oil cooler was added in the right front fender. This cooler was thermostatically controlled to open at 83 deg C (182 deg F). On the various subsequent models, the thermostat operating temperature has varied from 83 deg to 87 deg C (182 deg to 189 deg F).

A Year of Changes: 1970

Nineteen-seventy was another year of big changes for the 911 engine. The displacement was increased to 2.2 liters (2,195 cc) by increasing the bore from 80 mm to 84 mm. The cylinder heads were standardized with 46-mm intake valves and 40-mm exhaust valves, with only the port sizes changing between the T, E, and S models. The contour of the near-hemispherical combustion chamber was changed to a more-shallow, larger-diameter, smaller-volume combustion chamber to accommodate the larger valves and larger bore. This change had the added benefit of eliminating all of the detonation problems that had existed previously. Split-shell bearing inserts were added to the crankshaft halves at the inner end of the layshaft because the magnesium had not proved as durable a bearing surface as had the original aluminum crankcase. The other end of the layshaft was already supported by split-shell bearing inserts because Porsche had changed it to a thrust bearing to establish the layshaft position and end play when it went to the magnesium crankcase. Previously, layshaft end play had been es-

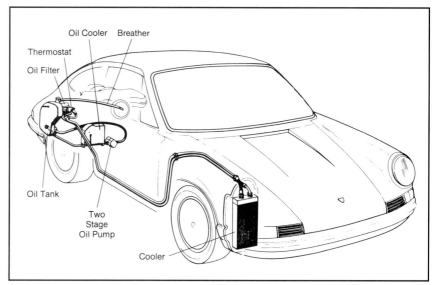

In 1969, because of the additional heat created by the added horsepower in the 911S, an external radiator-type oil cooler was added in the right front fender. Oil flow to this external cooler was controlled by a thermostat mounted in the engine compartment. The thermostat was in series with the scavenge return line to the oil tank. When the oil temperature reached 87 deg C (189 deg F) the oil was routed forward to this additional cooler before being returned to the oil tank. This version of the oil-cooler system was used from 1969 through 1971.

tablished by measuring the end play and setting it with shims. The spark plugs threaded directly into the aluminum rather than using Helicoil inserts; Porsche felt the insets caused inconsistent effective spark plug heat ranges. The clutch was changed from 215 mm to 225 mm diameter and changed to the stronger pull-type clutch, which permits the use of a larger-diameter clutch without increasing the overall diameter of the flywheel and bellhousing.

Another 1970 change was the use of CE-type head gaskets. The CE ring-type head gasket is a thin, metal C-shaped ring which encloses a tubular spring. This gasket fits in a groove in the upper cylinder flange. From 1970 on the CE ring-head gasket was used on all 911 street engines and most racing engines up to 3.0 liters in displacement. Starting in 1978, the 911 Turbo had no head gasket at all, and in 1984, when the 3.2-liter Carrera was introduced, it also used no head gasket.

In 1970 the power was increased for all three versions of the 911 engine, the T, E, and the S. The 911T had a new carburetor, the Zenith 40 TIN. The 911T also received as standard equipment the CD ignition used on both the 911E and 911S in 1969. All models received new reinforced connecting rods with a much more substantial bottom end and longer rod bolts. Engine type numbers were changed from 901 to 911 type numbers. The European 911T was the Type 911/03 for standard transmission and 911/06 for Sportomatic. The U.S.-emissions 911T engines were 911/07 for standard transmission and 911/08 for Sportomatic. The emission control on these engines consisted of a lean idle circuit and a deceleration idle fuel shut-off valve. The 911E and 911S engines were still suitable for a world market, with the 911E named the Type 911/01 for standard transmission and 911/04 for the Sportomatic transmission, and the 911S called the Type 911/02.

The 914/6 was introduced as a 1970 model with an engine that was identical in specifications to the 1969 911T engine. The 914/6 engine was the 901/36 for the European standard transmission and Type 901/37 for Sportomatic. The U.S. 914/6 engine was the Type 901/38, or Type 901/39 for the Sportomatic. This engine remained unchanged throughout the production life of the 914/6 with the exception of the addition of crankcase oil squirters to cool the pistons with the 1971 model change, but more about that later. A 2.4-liter version of the 911T engine (Type 911/58) was developed for use in the 914/6, but was never used in production.

Nineteen-seventy was also the beginning of larger engines for the racing 911s. Until 1970 there had been but two versions of the 2.0-liter 911 engines used in racing 911s: the small-valve Type 901/30 rally engine with 46IDA Webers and 911S cams (which produced 150 DIN hp), and the Type 901/22, called the 911R engine, which was very similar to the Carrera Six engine and produced 210 DIN hp at 8,000 rpm. The Type 916 engine was also used in the 911R racing cars. The Type 916 engine was a 911-based en-

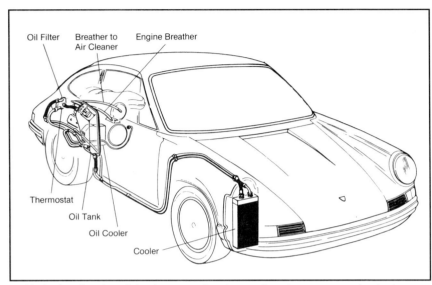

In 1972, the relocation of the dry-sump oil tank necessitated a new system for the front-mounted external oil cooler. Porsche designed a new oil filter housing that, in addition to providing the filter mount, had both the thermostat and an oil bypass valve built into it. This unit has fittings that permit remote mounting, which has made it popular for use by people building their own oil systems in racing and time-trial cars. The oil filler for these tanks was in the right rear fender, just behind the door, and the filter mount was in the engine compartment.

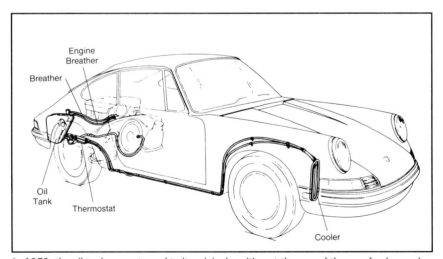

In 1973, the oil tank was returned to its original position at the rear of the rear fender, and again, Porsche designed a new front-mounted oil-cooler system. This oil cooler mounted on the oil tank under the car. The first year of the serpentine, or loop, oil cooler was 1973. These oil coolers were optional, unless the cars were ordered with an air conditioner. These same coolers were standard equipment on the new Carrera RS. These new loop coolers actually relied on the pipes running to and from the loop cooler to do most of the cooling, the loop itself just being a way to turn the oil around and start it back to the oil tank.

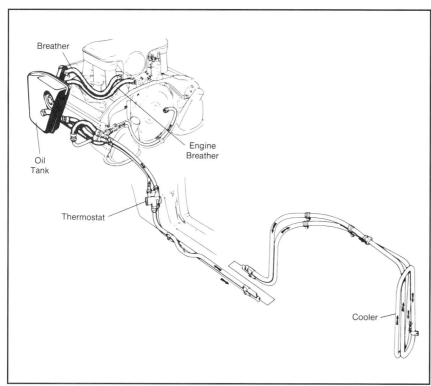

The best of the front-mounted oil-cooler systems was introduced in 1974 and used through 1989. The front-mounted cooler has changed several times since the 1974 introduction of this system, but the rest of the plumbing has remained the same. The system started with the loop cooler, then went to a brass-tube cooler in 1980, and finally to a radiator-type cooler in 1985.

The serpentine or loop-style cooler was introduced in 1973 for use on the 911S and Carrera RS. James D. Newton

The brass-tube cooler used from 1980 through July 1984 for the European cars and from 1983 through July 1984 for the U.S. cars. For U.S. driving purposes, the brass cooler was probably the best cooler; too bad we didn't have it on more cars. The earlier loop coolers relied on the lines to and from the loop to do most of the cooling. The brass-tube cooler worked well as a heat sink and wasn't too dependent on air flow. The radiator-type cooler that replaced the brass-tube cooler was very dependent on air flow and really didn't work well on the U.S. cars with our slow speed limits.

gine that had chain-driven dual overhead cams (for a total of four), which produced 230 DIN hp at 9,000 rpm, but was too peaky in use to be practical. There were also two versions of the 2.0-liter racing engines for the 914/6. Type 901/25 was a continuation of the Carrera Six type engine with 46IDA Webers; it produced 210 DIN hp at 7,800 rpm and maximum torque of 152 lb-ft at 6,200 rpm. The other engine was for rallying and produced 180 DIN hp at 6,800 rpm, with maximum torque of 132 lb-ft at 5,200 rpm. This engine utilized 911S cams and 40IDS Webers.

In 1970 the move to 2,195 cc for the production cars put the 911 in the 2.0-liter to 2.5-liter class for racing. Cars competing in this class were allowed to increase their displacement up to the class limit, provided it was done with a bore increase only. Thus began a series of larger-displacement 911 racing engines. The first was a small increase to 2,247 cc by increasing the bore 1 mm to 85 mm. These engines used Carrera Six Cams and retained the stock valve diameter. There were two versions of these engines, the Type 911/20 with mechanical injection and the Type

911/22 with 46IDA Webers carburetors. The power claimed for both versions of the engine was 230 DIN hp. The next step was the Type 911/21 with an 87-mm bore for a displacement of 2,380 cc with 250 DIN hp at 8,000 rpm. Other than the increased bore, this engine was unchanged from the Type 911/20. The final version of this series of engines was actually developed after the long-stroke engines came out and were used in racing; this was the Type 911/73 with an 89-mm bore, a 66-mm stroke and displacement of 2,466 cc. These Type 911/73 engines produced 275 DIN hp at 8,000 rpm. This large bore was achieved by using the newly developed thin-wall aluminum cylinders of Nikasil construction. The Nikasil cylinders are centrifugally cast finned aluminum with their bores electroplated with a very thin layer of nickel-silicon carbide. These new Nikasil cylinders provide several advantages over all the other types of cylinders Porsche used previously: the thin plating allowed larger bores within the same head stud spacing; they wear very well; and because of reduced friction and a better surface for ring sealing, they actually produced a small increase in horsepower. The Nikasil cylinders were originally developed in 1971 for 917 racing engines.

In 1971, production 911 engines remained unchanged except oil squirters were added for additional piston cooling. These were installed in the crankcase main bearing webbing and were fed from the main oil gallery to spray oil onto the bottom of each piston crown. The supply to the squirters was controlled by a check valve in each squirter which opened under pressure at 45 to 55 psi (pounds per square inch) oil pressure. The squirters reduce the operating temperatures at the crown of the pistons by 50 deg C (122 deg F).

1972: A Displacement Increase

The next big change was in 1972 with the increase to "2.4" liters, with 2,341 cc actual displacement, achieved by lengthening the stroke from 66 mm to 70.4 mm. Porsche increased the length of the stroke by decreasing the crankshaft rod-journal diameter off center and increasing the journal width to retain bearing capacity. The rod journal was decreased from 57 mm to 52 mm, and the rod journal width was increased from 22 to 24 mm. The connecting rods were changed because of the smaller crank journal, and they were shorter by half of the increase in stroke, 2.2 mm, allowing the wrist pin to remain at the same height in the piston. The cylinders were the same as those used on the 2.2-liter 911 engines while the pistons had material removed from the dome to reduce the compression, both to counter the effect of the longer stroke and to lower the overall compression and the required fuel octane. The noncounter-weighted cast crankshaft was discontinued for the 911T and all engines shared a common forged crankshaft. The valve diameters from the 2.2-liter engines (46 mm intake valves, 40 mm exhaust valves) were continued. The change to 2.4 liters occurred when Porsche finally changed the clutch shaft spline from 13/16x24 splines that had been used since the early VW days, to 7/8x20, which was used through the 1986 3.2 911 Carrera. At the same time the 901 transmission was replaced with the more substantial 915 transmission,

The 911 engine uses the through-bolt holes as part of the oiling system providing oil for the main bearings and the piston squirters. Note the pieces of crankcase shown with the through-bolt. These pieces were cut from a pair of damaged crankcase halves, up by the main-bearing saddles. Note the main-bearing oil holes in the crankcase main-bearing saddles. The main-bearing journals are lubricated from the right side of the crankcase (cylinders four through six).

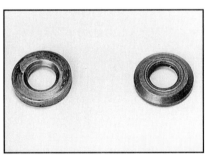

Through-bolt washers from production engines. The washer on the left was used on all production engines up until the 2.7-liter engines of 1973 and 1974. When the change to these larger-diameter cylinders for the 90-mm bore was made, it was found necessary to chamfer these washers to prevent them from interfering with the cylinder fit and holding up the base of the larger-diameter cylinders and causing them not to seat properly. The washer on the right has this chamfer and has been used on all of the 911 engines since the 2.7 liter.

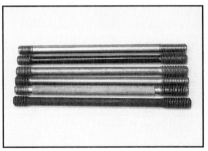

Various types of cylinder head studs used on the 911 engines. One of the original steel head studs is on the bottom. The next one up is an early Dilavar stud from a racing engine. These studs had fiberglass jackets that were supposed to keep them warm so that they would be able to expand at a similar rate to the aluminum cylinders. On later engines the cylinders themselves provided the jacket for these Dilavar studs. The next one up (third from bottom) was one of the shiny silver ones that were the style of Dilavar stud first used in production 930s in 1975 and later for the bottom row on 1977 911s. The next one up (fourth from bottom) was the next style Dilavar stud; it had a textured finish and was gold in color. There had been some problems with the studs fracturing because of corrosion, and the gold version was made to combat this problem. The next one up (fifth from bottom) is the latest style; it has a black epoxy finish that helps prevent corrosion pits and possible resulting fractures. The top one is a special stud for use on some Porsche racing engines. The difference between this and the other studs is that it is 9 mm in diameter and the others all neck down to 8 mm.

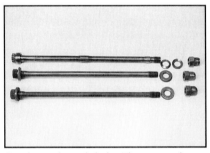

Crankcase through-bolts. The one on the bottom of this photo is as used in early-style street cars up until 1978 with the introduction of the 911SC. The middle bolt has a finer 1.25-mm thread pitch for more even torquing and was used on some of the racing 911 engines, such as the RSRs, and then on all production engines since the introduction of the 911SC in 1978. The top bolt is a special aircraft-quality bolt used in some of the more recent racing 911 engines. Porsche originally developed these bolts for use on the 917 as a weight-saving measure. These bolts use a pair of specially ground self-aligning spherical washers that fit inside each other at each end that, along with the special nut they used, will not introduce a bending stress on the bolt. The threaded portion of the stud and the nut are also designed to eliminate the notch effect of the threads. Porsche found that in many applications it could reduce the bolt by one unit size, so in some applications these bolts could be used as a weight-saving measure. When this type of bolt is used for the crankcase through-bolts, it is because the through-bolt holes are used as part of the main oil galleries. It is very critical that these bolts not break. The enlarged portion in the center of these special through-bolts is to stop, or at least limit, the travel, of any sympathetic harmonic vibrations that may be set up in these through-bolts.

which would also last through the 1986 model year 3.2 911 Carrera. There were still T, E, and S versions of the 2.4-liter engines. In Europe the 911T engine retained the Zenith 40 TIN carburetors as Type 911/57 for standard transmission and Type 911/61 for the Sportomatic. The U.S.-version 911T, with mechanical fuel injection to comply with emission standards, was the Type 911/51 for the standard transmission and Type 911/61 for the Sportomatic. The carbureted European version produced 130 DIN hp, while the mechanically injected U.S. version produced 140 DIN hp. The cams remained the same in the 911T engines; however, they were timed slightly differently. Both the 2.4-liter 911E and 911S engines retained their mechanical injection. The 911E engine had its cams timed differently as well and produced 165 DIN hp with Type 911/52 for the manual transmission and Type 911/62 for the Sportomatic. The 911S engine produced 190 DIN hp with the Type 911/53 for the standard transmission and Type 911/63 for the Sportomatic.

In 1972 Porsche moved the oil tank from its more normal location behind the right rear wheel to in front of the right rear wheel, between the wheel and the door jamb. This location offered the advantage of better weight distribution and freed-up space that might be put to

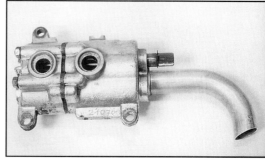

This is an early 911 engine tandem oil pump with sand-cast aluminum housing. The pressure pump is at the left end and the scavenge pump at right with the scavenge pickup.

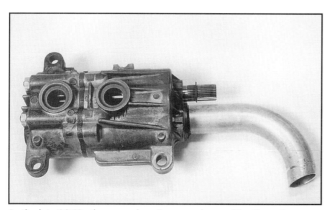

In the late 1960s the pump housing was changed to die-cast magnesium; the size of the pumps and the operation remained unchanged.

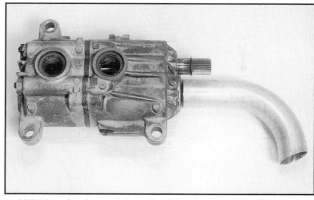

In 1976 Porsche changed the ratio of the oil pumps with the pressure pump section being made larger while the scavenge section was reduced in size while retaining the original overall dimensions. The oil bypass system in the engine was changed to compensate for this ratio change. This is essentially the same oil pump that was used through the 1989 Carrera model. The only difference was that in 1983 the oil pickup was changed to match the newer style crankcases without a removable sump cover; see the 3.3-liter Turbo oil pump.

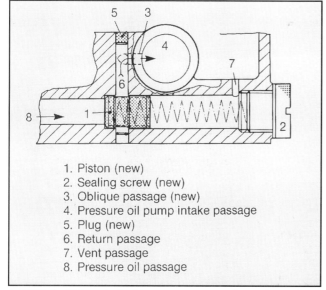

1. Piston (new)
2. Sealing screw (new)
3. Oblique passage (new)
4. Pressure oil pump intake passage
5. Plug (new)
6. Return passage
7. Vent passage
8. Pressure oil passage

In 1976 the 911 engine's oil bypass system was changed to make up for the different scavenge-to-pressure-pump ratio of the new-style oil pump. The bypassed oil is returned to the pressure pump inlet rather than being bypassed into the crankcase's sump.

The oil bypass pistons were changed when the oil pump and oil bypass circuit were changed in 1976. The piston on the left is necessary with the modified system. The piston on the right was used in the oil system from 1964 until the bypass circuit was changed in 1976. If the old-style pistons are accidentally used with the post-1976 bypass system, the engine will not produce oil pressure.

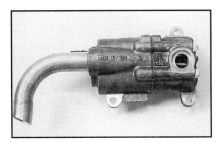

The larger 908 oil pump was used by Porsche in its racing 911 engines until the even larger 3.3 Turbo oil pump was introduced in 1978. The increased need for oil volume was because of Porsche's extended use of oil for cooling in their turbocharged racing engines.

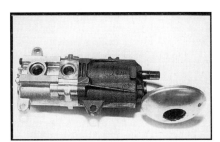

The "big" 930 oil pump was introduced with the 3.3-liter Turbo in 1978; it has much larger scavenge and pressure pumps. The pressure pump housing is made of aluminum, and the scavenge pump housing is made of cast iron to reduce thermal expansion to maintain closer tolerances. The venturi was built onto the oil pump pickup, but the screen was still a separate unit.

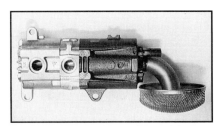

The crankcase was changed in model year 1983, and at that time a screen was built onto the venturi on the pump's oil pickup. This screen and pickup were to replace the one that was installed in 1980 to solve an oil pickup problem.

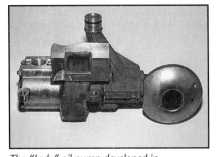

The "Indy" oil pump developed in 1979–1980 for the 911-based Indy engine that Porsche was working on with Interscope racing. Interscope found that the centrifugal forces threw the oil to the right rear of the crankcase, so Porsche added a second scavenge pump to scavenge for this area. Even though the Indy program was abandoned, some of these oil pumps were used to improve the scavenging in the 935 engines. This new racing pump had dual scavenge pumps to get more of the oil out of the engine. There are a couple of advantages to doing a more thorough job of oil scavenging. By getting the oil out of the engine more quickly, windage is reduced and frictional horsepower losses from the crankshaft operating in the oil are prevented. Without efficient scavenging, as much as a couple of quarts of oil can be in the engine at one time, and the crankshaft will whip this excess oil into a froth, introducing air into the oiling system. The added air in the oil makes it much more difficult to effectively cool the scavenged oil.

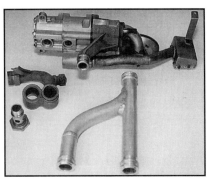

The 935 racing pumps required some additional modifications to fit the pump in the crankcase. Porsche siamesed the oil-return tubes so that they could utilize the oil-return-tube drain hole in the crankcase for the second scavenge outlet. A special adapter and bolt connected the normal scavenge line and the new scavenge line so that the oil could be returned to the tank.

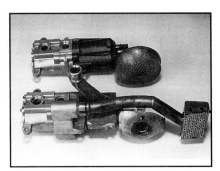

Here's a comparison of the standard 3.3 Turbo oil pump and the 935 racing oil pump introduced for use with the 935s in 1981. This version of the twin-scavenge oil pump placed the second pickup toward the front of the engine, where more of the used oil accumulated in these engines. There is a newer version of this pump used on the 956/962C engines that actually has three scavenge pumps and three different pickups, with the third pickup even farther forward to better scavenge the used oil from the cam drive gears.

The 959-style oil pump with three scavenge stages. This was the best of these big oil pumps, and it was also used in the Porsche racing engines from the mid-1980s on. It had a magnesium housing with bearings for all of the pump shafts. It was a very high-quality part.

The 964 pump is also a high-quality large-capacity pump made of magnesium, with bearings for the pump shafts. The pressure pump delivers 65 liters of oil per minute: 17 liters are used for the squirters to cool the pistons, around 35 liters are used to lubricate the main and con-rod bearings, and the oil flow to the camshaft housing was reduced by about 50 percent to the 13 liters necessary to lubricate the camshaft bearings, valve guides, and rocker arms. The scavenge pump has 1.84 times the capacity of the pressure pump to ensure a low oil level in the engine's crankcase.

good use. This installation used a new oil filter housing, which not only provided the filter mount but also had both the thermostat and an oil bypass valve built in. This unit's fittings permit remote mounting, which has made it popular for use by people building their own oil systems in racing and time trial cars. The oil filler for these tanks was in the right rear fender, just behind the door.

A special version of the 911S engine was produced for the limited series of 916s. The specifications were the same as those of the 2.4-liter 911S engine, but the exhaust and fittings were different for the midchassis installation in the 916. The type number for these engines was 911/56. The execution of the unique parts that were required for this installation indicate that Porsche intended to produce far more than the 13 916s that were actually built.

There was a racing version of the 2.4-liter-based engine with a larger 86.7-mm bore for a displacement of 2,492 cc, the Type 911/70. This engine produced 270 DIN hp at 8,000 rpm and a peak torque of 191.6 lb-ft at 5,300 rpm. This was the first 911 racing engine to reach the limit for the 2.5-liter GT racing class.

Emissions Addressed for 1973

For 1973 the 911E and 911S engine specifications remained unchanged for the world market. The 911T engine remained the same in Europe, but the U.S. version underwent changes. For the beginning of the 1973 production year the 911T was still sold with mechanical injection, offering the same specifications as for 1972. Starting with January production, Porsche introduced the Bosch CIS injection on the 911T, called K-Jetronic, or the KA Injection in Germany (K for continuous, A for non-powered). These engines had the compression increased from 7.5:1 to 8.0:1 and required new, very mild cam timing because the CIS injection is very sensitive to pulsations in the intake system; it requires cams with little or no overlap. This injection system

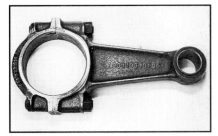

The 2.0-liter 911 connecting rod used in production cars.

The 2.0-liter 906 titanium connecting rod used in 2.0-liter racing engines, the 906 and 910.

The 2.2-liter 911 connecting rod with reinforced big end and longer rod bolts. Note that the black color indicates that this is a nitrated 911S connecting rod. Porsche nitrated the connecting rods for the 911S engines from the 2.0-liters in 1967 until the 2.4-liter 911S engines.

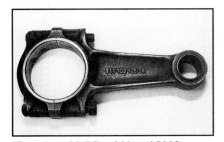

The 2.4- and 2.7-liter 911 and 911S connecting rod, redesigned for the longer-stroke engine.

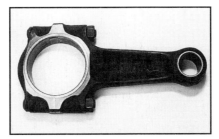

The 2.8- and 3.0-liter RSR connecting rods, balanced and polished before being soft nitrated.

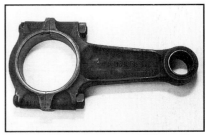

The 2.4-liter 911S connecting rod was also nitrated like the RSR connecting rod.

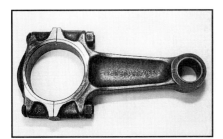

The 3.0-liter 911SC connecting rod was used from 1978 through 1983.

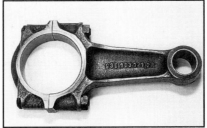

The 3.3-liter Turbo and 3.2-liter Carrera 964 and 993 rod.

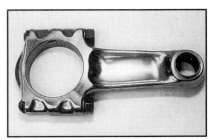

The titanium 935 connecting rod.

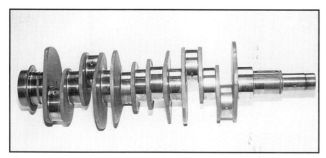

The crankshaft used with 2.0-liter through 2.2-liter engines.

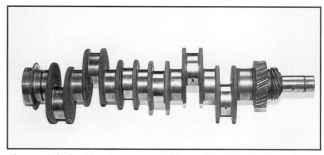

The crankshaft without counterweights used for 2.0-liter through 2.2-liter 911T engines only.

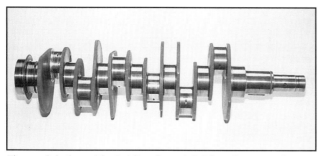

The crankshaft used for 2.4-liter through 3.0-liter Carrera engines.

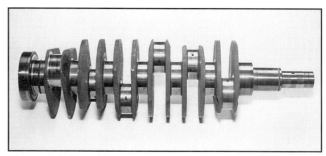

The crankshaft used for 3.3 Turbo and 3.2 Carrera engines.

was introduced on the 911T because Porsche could no longer meet the U.S. emission standards with carburetors, and the mechanical injection system was too costly for the low-priced car. The new 911T engine with CIS injection was Type 911/91 for the standard transmission and Type 911/96 for the Sportomatic version. The horsepower was claimed to be the same 140 DIN hp as the previous mechanically injected 911T engine.

For 1973 the oil cooler in the right front fender of the 911S was replaced with a serpentine (or loop) cooler. These oil coolers were now optional unless the cars were ordered with an air conditioner. These same coolers were standard equipment on the new Carrera RS. These new loop coolers actually relied on the pipe running to and from the loop cooler to do most of the cooling, the loop itself just being a way to turn the oil around and start it back to the oil tank. The more effective aluminum radiator-type oil coolers used since 1969 were deemed too fragile for general street use. One problem the aluminum radiator coolers had was that salt used to melt snow caused corrosion and deterioration of the cooler. A car could run all winter without getting warm enough to open the thermostat to the front cooler. When spring's warmer temperatures arrived, the thermostat to the front cooler would open and cause a bad oil leak. This was a problem particularly with the cars built in 1969 through 1971 because they did not have an oil bypass circuit built into the external cooler circuit.

The oil tank was also returned to its previous location behind the rear wheel in 1973, and the thermostat and plumbing for the front-mounted oil cooler were changed again. The thermostat was mounted on the oil tank where the oil return line is normally attached. This location made the thermostat and fittings vulnerable to the elements.

Limited-Edition Carrera RS

The big news for 1973 was the reintroduction of a car called the Carrera. The Carrera for 1973 was the Carrera RS with its 2.7-liter engine. The Carrera RS was not available in the United States. Since only a limited series was planned,

The cup-type flywheel and push-type pressure plate used on 911s from 1965 through 1969.

no effort was made to make the Carrera RS U.S.-emissions legal. Its 2,687-cc engine introduced the use of Nikasil cylinders on a production model Porsche. The displacement increase came from increasing the bore to 90 mm and retaining the 70.4-mm stroke. The crankcase was reinforced both internally at the base of the main bearing webs and at the base of the cylinders. The diameter of the cylinder spigots was increased from 92 mm (used for 2.0- to 2.4-liter engines) to 97 mm to accommodate the larger cylinders. There were actually two versions of this, with the final version of the magnesium crankcase casting number of 901.101.102.7R for both versions. One version is described here for the 2.7 engine, while the other version's spigot bore remains at 92 mm, making it suitable for all 2.0- through 2.4-liter engines. This 2.7 Carrera RS engine, Type 911/83, was identical to the Type 911/53 911S engine except for the 90-mm bore and a different space cam in the mechanical injection pump. Power output was 210 DIN hp at 6,300 rpm.

A racing version of this Carrera RS called the RSR was built in 1973 with a Type 911/72 engine. The bore was increased 2 mm to 92 mm for a displacement of 2,808 cc. The thin-wall Nikasil cylinders were used to achieve the 2.8-liter displacement with a 92-mm bore, which was deemed the safe limit for the magnesium crankcase with its 80-mm cylinder-head stud spacing and a 70.4-mm stroke. The RSR engines used pro-

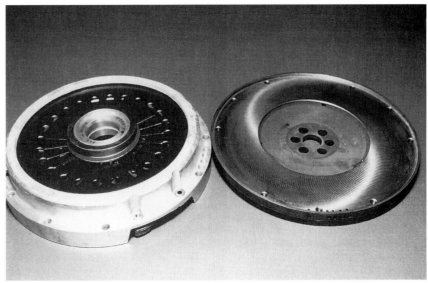

The flat-type flywheel and pull-type pressure plate used on all 911s since 1970.

Pilot bearings: at left is the type used from 1980-on, and at right is the type used in the flat-type flywheels from 1970 through 1979.

A crankshaft and flywheel showing how the 1980-and-newer pilot-bearing mounts.

The 911SC exploding clutch. These rubber-centered clutches were used to dampen the vibration noises of the transmissions. When the rubber fails, the drivetrain will vibrate. Often, a piece of rubber will jam between the clutch and the pressure plate and cause the clutch to cease operating. These clutches should be replaced with spring-centered clutches. The Carreras with G50 transmissions also used rubber-centered clutch, but it is a much larger, more substantial example.

The cylinders used on the original production model 911s were of biral construction, which was a cast-iron cylinder with aluminum fins cast around the cylinder.

The dual-mass flywheel used on 964 and 993 engines. Note both the starter ring gear and timing gear for the Digital Motor Electronics (DME).

At the same time Porsche was using the biral cylinder on its production engines, the company was using a cylinder that it called chromal on its 906 racing engine. These chromal cylinders consisted of an aluminum cylinder with a chrome-plated working surface. The chrome surface of these cylinders have what appears to be small indentations all around the cylinder to help retain an oil film on the working surface.

In 1973, Nikasil cylinders were used on the 2.7 Carrera RS. The Nikasil cylinders are made of a dense, centrifugally cast aluminum that then has its bore's working surface electroplated with a thin layer of nickel-silicon carbide. Nikasil cylinders provide several advantages over all of the other types of cylinders Porsche had previously used: the thin plating allowed larger bores within the same head-stud spacing, the wear properties are good, and because of reduced friction and a better surface for the rings to seal with, they actually produced a small increase in horsepower. The Nikasil cylinders were originally developed in 1971 for the 917 racing engines when they increased the displacement from 4,900 cc to 5,000 cc.

The 911Ts produced from 1968 through 1973 used a cast-iron cylinder to reduce the production expense.

In 1974, Alusil cylinders were used as an alternative to the more expensive Nikasil cylinders for some of the production 2.7-liter 911 engines. The Alusil cylinders are a special 390 eutectic aluminum silicon alloy and are used with a special iron-plated (ferrocoat) piston. The cylinders are electrically etched to leave a surface of exposed silicon particles protruding from the aluminum. This provides a durable surface for the piston and rings to wear on; the ferrocoat pistons prevent galling or excessive wear during break-in. The Alusil cylinders have some of the advantages of the Nikasil cylinders in that they had the same sort of thin wall construction as the Nikasil; however, it has been my experience that they do not provide as good service as the Nikasil cylinders do.

duction rods that were polished in the areas of high stress and soft-nitrated to make them more resistant to failure. The 2.0, 2.2, and some of the 2.4 911S connecting rods also used this soft-nitrating process for extra strength and added reliability. To strengthen the 70.4-mm crankshaft for the high-rpm racing applications, Porsche used a large, round and smooth radius for the transition between the crankshaft journal and the counterweight or cheek of the crankshaft. These larger-radius fillets on the RSR crankshaft necessitated special connecting rod bearings with clearance provided for these larger fillets. The 2.8 RSR engines had a new cylinder head with a larger-diameter, more-open, larger-volume combustion chamber and 49-mm intake and 41.5-mm exhaust valves. With this larger combustion chamber and the new larger valves, the valve angle was reduced to an included angle of 55 deg, 45 min (minutes), with an exhaust angle 30 deg, 15 min from vertical, and an intake angle 25 deg, 30 min from vertical. The 2.8-liter RSR used what is called high butterfly injection, with the throttle butterfly high up in the injection stacks. These Type 911/72 engines produced 308 DIN hp at 8,000 rpm.

There were some RSR engines built with 95-mm bores for 3.0-liter displacement using the magnesium cases with the old 80-mm cylinder-head stud spacing. These engines had some reliability problems because the metal separating and surrounding the cylinder spigots had become too thin to hold up under the rigors of racing. The new 3.0 RSR engine was introduced for the Riverside IROC race in September 1973 with engine Type 911/74. A new, more-substantial crankcase, which was made of aluminum, was introduced for this new

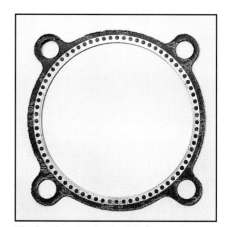

The head gasket for the 2.0-liter engine.

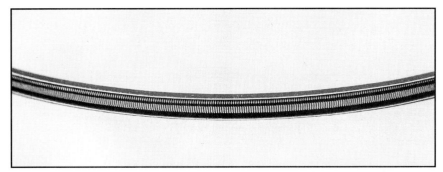

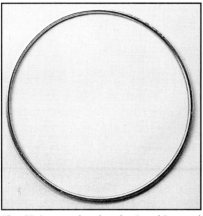

The CE-type head gasket of the type used on all 2.2- through 3.0-liter 911SC production engines and some of the racing engines.

The CE ring-type head gasket is a thin metal C-shaped ring that encloses a tubular spring.

3.0-liter engine. The new crankcase had larger 103-mm cylinder spigots as well as a wider 83-mm head stud spacing to accommodate the larger cylinders. The head stud spacing in all previous 911 engines had been 80 mm. New cylinder heads and pistons and cylinders were produced to match the new crankcase with its wider 83-mm head stud spacing. The 49-mm intake and 41.5-mm exhaust valve sizes and the large, open combustion chamber were carried over from the 2.8 RSR engine, but with the changed head stud spacing. The cams retained the same timing as the Carrera Six; however, the lift was increased from 12.1-mm on the intake to 12.2-mm, and the exhaust from 10.5-mm to 11.6-mm. These cams were referred to as "Sprint Cams." The 3.0 RSR also had a new Bosch breakerless capacitor dual ignition as used in the 917. The power for this new engine was 316 DIN hp at 8,000 rpm.

Late in the summer of 1973, an update "kit" was offered to some people racing the 2.8 RSRs which would allow them to update their 2.8 RSRs to 3.0-liter displacement. These kits consisted of a new crankcase, a new set of 95-mm pistons and cylinders, the cylinder heads that would fit on the new

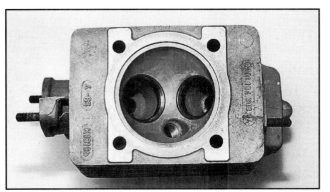

The 1965 911 cylinder head with 39-mm intake valves and 35-mm exhaust valves.

The 1969 911T cylinder head with 42-mm intake valves and 38-mm exhaust valves.

The 906E/910 cylinder head with 45-mm intake valves and 39-mm exhaust valves and twin plugs.

The 1969 911S cylinder head with 45-mm intake valves and 39-mm exhaust valves.

The 2.7-liter 911 cylinder head with 46-mm intake valves and 40-mm exhaust valves. All cylinder heads used from 1970 through 1977 were essentially the same, with the same combustion chamber and valve sizes, only the ports were changed for the various versions of the engines. The combustion chamber for the 2.2- to 2.7-liter heads were in the range of 68 cc.

The 2.8-liter RSR cylinder head with 49-mm intake valves and 41.5-mm exhaust valves. These heads had 43-mm ports and a larger combustion chamber with 80-mm stud spacing. With the 2.8 RSR head's more-open combustion chamber, the combustion volume increased to 76.0 cc.

The 3.0-liter RSR cylinder head with 49-mm intake valves and 41.5-mm exhaust valves. These heads had 43-mm ports and a larger combustion chamber with 83-mm stud spacing. These heads were very similar to the 2.8 RSR heads, with essentially the same size combustion chamber at 77.2 cc, and only the 3-mm-larger cylinder-head stud spacing making these heads unique to the 3.0-liter RS and RSR engines.

The 3.0-liter 911SC cylinder head with 49-mm intake valves and 41.5-mm exhaust valves. These 930-type cylinder heads have an even larger (90-cc) combustion chamber than the 2.8- and 3.0-liter RSR engines and the stud spacing was increased an additional 3 mm to 86 mm.

The 1980 935 cylinder head with 49-mm intake valves, 41.5-mm exhaust valves, and twin spark plugs. Note the groove machined in the cylinder sealing surface is for an interlocking-ring Nieresist head gasket.

The 962 cylinder head, with 49-mm intake valves, 41.5-mm exhaust valves, a single plug, and a special squish area to improve combustion in the absence of the second plug.

crankcase, and a set of the new high-performance camshafts.

1974: Carrera Reaches the United States

A revised version of the 3.0-liter RSR engine was built in 1974 as the Type 911/75, which was identical to its predecessor with the exception of the change to slide-valve fuel injection in place of the high butterfly type used previously. This new version of the engine produced 330 DIN hp at 8,000 rpm, with a peak torque of 231 lb-ft at 6,500 rpm.

The United States got the Carrera and the 2.7-liter engines. However, the U.S. Carrera was not the same as the world market Carrera. Only two engines were available to the United States for 1974, the 911 and the 911S. The U.S. Carrera shared engines with the 911S. To add salt to the wound, there was an additional 3.0 Carrera in Europe with a Type 911/77 engine. These engines were the basis for the 3.0-liter RSR engines that had the new 3.0-liter heads, crankcase, and cylinders with 83-mm head stud spacing. They had 9.8:1 compression, the 911S cams, and mechanical fuel injection. The world market Carrera produced 230 DIN hp at 6,200 rpm with a peak torque of 203 lb-ft at 5,000 rpm. To be fair, the 3.0 Carrera RS was a homologation special and few beyond the 100 required were ever produced. The purpose of the car was to make the 3.0-liter engine, parts, and chassis changes legal for GT racing.

In 1974 the emissions-legal U.S. engines for the 911 were 150-DIN-hp, Type 911/92 for the standard transmission and Type 911/97 for the Sportomatic. For the 911S and the U.S. Carrera there were the 175-DIN-hp 911S engines, Type 911/93 for the standard transmissions and Type 911/98 for the Sportomatic. The engines for the United States both had CIS fuel injection and consequently much milder cam timing. The U.S. engines had cast pistons rather than the forged pistons of the European 2.7- and 3.0-liter Carrera RS engines. Both Nikasil and Alusil cylinders were used on the U.S. engines. The Alusil cylinders are a special 390 eutectic aluminum silicon alloy, which are used with a special cast-iron-plated (ferrocoat) piston. The cylinders are electrically etched to leave a surface of exposed silicon particles protruding from the aluminum. This provides a durable surface for the piston and rings to wear on, with the ferrocoat pistons preventing galling or excessive wear during break-in. This is

The 935 featured specially modified cylinder heads with oil-cooled valve guides. The head on the left is a standard production 911 cylinder head with its valve guides (in front of the head), and the head on the right is the 935 head with its valve guides. The drilling that you can see on the 935 head provides a constant source of fresh oil to the exhaust guide about halfway down its length, and there is another drilling up in the finned area that provides additional oiling of the guide as well. This additional oil in the exhaust guide ensures that there is a path for the heat to be conducted from the exhaust valves to the guides and then out into the airstream. The finned guide also took advantage of the oil-spray mist created by the spray-bar cam lubrication to provide additional cooling.

a process originally used for the 1970 Vega, and it was used on all 928 and 924S/944/968 engines.

There was another oil system for the front-mounted external oil cooler for 1974. (This new thermostat and plumbing was then used until the end of 1989; the coolers themselves have changed several times since, but the plumbing remained the same.) The thermostat with its built-in oil over-pressure bypass circuit is mounted in front of the right rear wheel, where it is protected from physical damage, if not the elements.

Porsche breathed some new life into the old 911 engine in 1974 when it started developing the Carrera RSR Turbo in the sports prototype class of racing. This developmental program was done in preparation for the 1976 season and the new Group 5 Silhouette racing formula. There was a multiplier for sports racing cars which considered any turbocharged engine to be 1.4 times its actual size. To compete as a 3.0-liter proto-

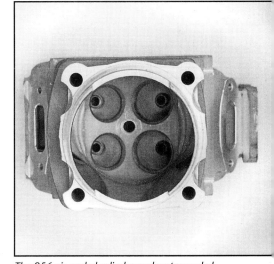

The 956 air-cooled cylinder and water-cooled cylinder head. These two units are welded together with an electron-beam welder to eliminate the blown-head-gasket problem that occurs with two 35 mm intake valves and two 30.5 mm exhaust valves.

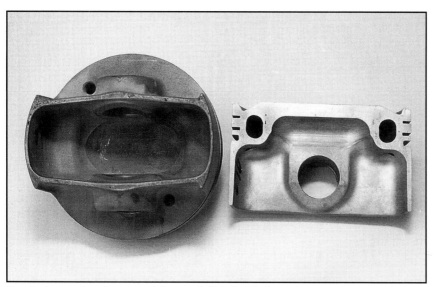

Porsche has continued to expand the use of oil cooling for its engines over the years. The piston oil squirters were first used on racing engines to provide additional cooling for the pistons and were then incorporated into all of the production 911 engines from 1971 on. The turbocharged racing engines further expanded the use of oil cooling by using an oil mist over the finned guides and using direct exhaust-guide oiling. The IMSA 962 engine uses a different form of oil cooling for the pistons. Instead of the squirters, a steady stream of oil is fed to a hole in the bottom of the piston crown so that there is a continuous supply of fresh oil to the gallery built into the piston's dome. This additional piston cooling relieves the top compression rings of one of its added-on jobs of cooling the piston crown, and lets it get down to its real job of sealing the piston to the cylinder for compression. By relieving this compression ring of its added cooling task, the designers were able to make the ring narrower, 1 mm instead of the normal 1.5 mm, and make the rings seal to the cylinder better, and increase the engine's performance. These pistons are made of multiple forgings that are electron-beam welded together.

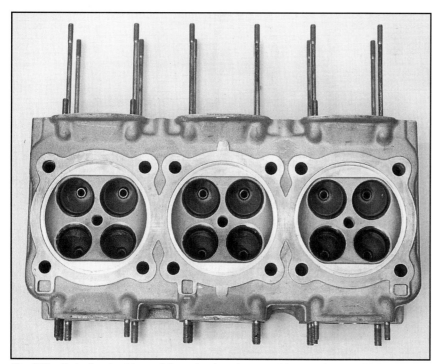

The 959 cylinder head, with two 35-mm intake valves, two 32-mm exhaust valves, and a pent-roof combustion chamber very similar to that used in the racing cars.

type, Porsche's engine could be no larger than 2,143 cc in displacement. The engine had an 83-mm bore and a 66-mm stroke for a displacement of 2,143 cc, and it was built using the old magnesium crankcase and 2.0-liter crankshaft and heads. The cam timing was changed for these engines and the lift reduced to 10.5-mm for both the intake and the exhaust valves. There were two versions of these engines: the Type 911/76, which was used in the Carrera RSR Turbo, and the Type 911/78, which was later used in the 936.

Focus of 1975: California Emissions

Nineteen-seventy-five was to be a year of little change for the production cars; however, this was the first year of the abominable thermal reactors and EGR (exhaust gas recirculation) for California cars (Type 911/44 for the standard transmissions and Type 911/49 for the Sportomatics). All U.S. engines were called 911S this year; the 49-state cars had an exhaust like the European engines with a primary muffler, and all the U.S. engines had air-injection pumps to meet U.S. emission standards. The 49-state engines were Type 911/43 for the standard transmissions and Type 911/48 for the Sportomatics.

The rest of the world had a nice selection of engines for the 1975 model year. The straight 911 was still available as Type 911/41 with 150 DIN hp at 5,700 rpm. The 911S was available as Type 911/42 with 175 DIN hp at 5,800 rpm. The 2.7 Carrera was still available as the Type 911/83 with mechanical injection and 210 DIN hp at 6,300 rpm. The R.o.W. engines and the U.S. 49-state engines received one new exhaust system, while California cars received another. The new R.o.W. exhaust system had a pair of new heat exchangers that merged into a single tube going back through a primary muffler to the final muffler. The beautiful three-into-one header-type heat exchangers were gone forever. The noise pollution laws had won out in Europe as had air pollution laws in the United States. The California exhaust also had two new heat exchangers, but they were each fed from a thermal reactor. Then from the heat exchangers the exhaust gases were fed back to a double inlet muffler like those used before with the three-into-one exhaust systems. There was an interesting midyear change during the 1975 model year: the main bearings were changed so the locating tab moved from one side of the bearing saddle to the other. Because of this change there were some crankcases with locating tab notches on both sides of the bearing saddle.

The 930 Turbo was introduced with the engine number Type 930/50. The 930 used another new aluminum-silicon alloy (Al/Si) crankcase with 86-mm cylinder-head stud spacing and 103-mm cylinder spigot diameter. These engines had new cylinder heads with 49-mm intake valves and 41.5-mm exhaust valves like 3.0 RSR engines, set at the new, more-shallow angle. The combustion chamber in these new cylinder heads was even larger and more open than the ones used by the 2.8 and 3.0 RSRs. The turbocharged engine still used CIS fuel injection, the unit being the one used on the Mercedes V-8 with two outlets

plugged. Four-bearing cam housings and camshafts were used for these engines. Bosch breakerless CD ignition was also a feature of the 930 engine. To transmit the extra power, the clutch was again increased in size from 225 mm to 240 mm in diameter and the splined hub in the center was increased in size again. To provide additional cooling for this new, higher performance, Porsche speeded up the fan ratio from 1.3:1 to 1.67:1, increasing the fan air transfer rate from approximately 1,390 liters per second to approximately 1,500 liters per second. The new "Turbo fan" had a smaller pulley, which in conjunction with a larger crankshaft pulley speeded up the fan. The new 930 engine produced 260 DIN hp at 5,500 rpm to be the most powerful road-going Porsche up to that time.

More Improvements for 1976

Nineteen-seventy-six was another good year for the 911. There were still two 911s for the United States, the U.S. engine and the California engine with identical power claimed for each, 165 DIN hp at 5,800 rpm. The 49-state engine was Type 911/82 for the standard transmission, the California version for the standard transmission was the Type 911/84, and the Type 911/89 was the engine for the Sportomatic for both 49-state and California cars. The engine-cooling fans were changed from 11-blade to 5-blade fans and the pulley ratio was speeded up from 1.3:1 to 1.8:1. The purpose of this change was to run the alternator at a higher speed for more efficient charging while reducing the fan noise. The 5-blade fans were

The original sand-cast-aluminum 911 valve covers; note the exhaust cover only uses six mounting studs.

The magnesium 911 valve covers used from 1968 until changed to die-cast aluminum in midyear 1977.

The die-cast-aluminum 911 valve covers introduced with the 930 Turbo in 1975 and phased into production on the 911s in midyear 1975. The top cover has remained unchanged since then, but the lower cover was changed again in 1980.

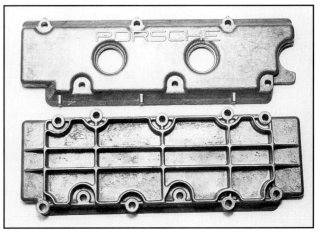

The die-cast-aluminum 911 valve covers, a 1980 update to the reinforced "Turbo" lower valve cover.

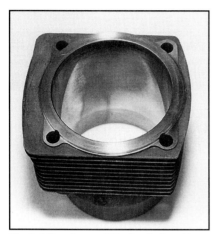

The 3.2-liter Carrera Nikasil cylinder with no head gasket.

The 964 Nikasil cylinder, early style with no head gasket.

The 964 Nikasil cylinder, late style with revised sealing surface and a groove for the head seal.

The 3.2-liter Carrera cylinder head. Note that the spigot for the intake manifold is shorter than on the 3.0-liter SC engines.

The early-style 964 cylinder head with no head gasket.

the same diameter (245 mm) as the 11-blade fans used on all previous 911 street engines. This 5-bladed fan worked fine on the cars in Europe, where they drove their cars at higher engine speeds, but proved to be inadequate for use in the United States, where at the time there was a strictly enforced 55-mph speed limit. The 2.7 engines with these fans generally ran too hot in most U.S. driving conditions.

There was also a U.S. version of the 930 Turbo with engine Type 930/51. The U.S. version had 245 DIN hp at 5,500 rpm, a loss of 15 hp from the European version through thermal reactors, air injection pumps, and different ignition timing used to comply with emission standards. A new car was introduced in Europe for the 1976 model year, a 3.0-liter Carrera with CIS fuel injection, engine Type 930/02 for standard transmission and Type 930/12 for the Sportomatic. This engine shared its crankcase, head design, and valve size

with the Turbo and was a forerunner of the 911SC engine. This Carrera engine produced 200 DIN hp at 6,000 rpm.

There was also a 911 Normal engine for Europe for 1976 which retained the specifications of the European 1975 911S. The 911 engine was Type 911/81 for standard transmission and Type 911/86 for the Sportomatic. All 911 engines now used the four-bearing camshaft housings, although the engines with the 911 Type numbers still used three-bearing camshafts. A new version of the chain tensioner and new, hard-plastic chain-guide ramps were used first on the Turbo engines and then phased into the rest of the 911 engine line. The oil pumps were changed in all engines for 1976 as was the oil bypass system. Porsche increased the size of the pressure portion of the pump and reduced the size of the scavenge portion of the pump while keeping the overall size the same. Because the scavenge section was reduced, the bypass was

changed to route the bypassed oil directly back to the oil pressure pump inlet rather than to the crankcase sump. This was done to minimize the work that the new smaller scavenge pump had to do, and to avoid filling the crankcase with oil.

The racing engines for 1976 were interesting with the 934, 935, and 936 all using the 911 engine as their base power source. All were turbocharged, with the 934 and 935 engines being based on the 930 engine while the 936 engine was based on the 911 engine. The 934 was a racing version of the production 930 homologated into Group 4 for GT racing. Four-hundred 930s had to be produced over a two-year period to allow a racing version to compete in the GT races as a Group 4 car.

The 1976 934 engine was Type 930/71, which was actually very little changed from the production 930 engine. To improve the performance, Porsche increased the ports to 41 mm, used different cam timing, and used a modified CIS fuel-injection system that utilized a metering cone rather than the normal sensor plate arrangement. Water intercooling was incorporated for these engines to cool the turbocharged air before it reached the engine, providing a denser charge and allowing higher boost pressure to be used. The intercooler system reduced the air charge temperature from 150 deg C to 50 deg C. The engine also used a horizontal (or flat) cooling fan for more cooling and more even distribution of cooling air over the engine. The flat fan puts out approximately 2,000 liters per second of cooling air at 7,000 rpm, but at the cost of approximately 35 hp to drive the fan as compared to about 5 hp to drive the street car fan. The flat fan runs at 13,800 rpm at 7,000 rpm engine speed. The street car fans put out between 1,100 to 1,500 liters per second of cooling air.

The 1976 935 engine was 2,857 cc in displacement which, with the 1.4 multiplier applied to turbocharged cars, made it a 3,999-cc engine for the 3.5- to 4.0-liter weight group in the Group 5 World Championship of Makes racing. The 1976 935 engine Type 930/72 used a production 930 crankcase, crankshaft, and heads although all were modified and the heads had larger 41-mm ports. The rest of the engine was typical of Porsche's racing tradition: titanium connecting rods, 908 oil pump, Bosch mechanical-plunger-pump fuel injection, and forged rocker arms with valve lash caps for valve adjustment. These forged rocker arms used no bushings, but instead the rocker arm shafts used a nitrating process similar to the one used on the crankshafts and some of the special connecting rods. This process worked much better than the one used on the production engines with cast-iron rocker arms in the late 1960s. The rocker arm shafts had special retainers to make sure that they could not slide out of place and let a rocker arm out. The rocker arm shafts also used a special seal at each end to prevent oil leaks in this area. The seals fit down into the compression grooves at each end of the shaft. When the rocker shaft is installed and the center pinch bolt is tightened, the seals are compressed and forced against the cam-housing rocker-arm-shaft bores, forming a good seal.

These engines used both the center-lubed racing cams and the spray-bar lubrication to ensure adequate lubrication, but more important, for additional cooling. In addition to the larger ports, the heads were also modified by the addition of a second spark plug and special guides with additional oiling provided to the finned exhaust guides. The flat fan was used both for more cooling and more even cooling of all six cylinders. The air flow from the normal vertical production fan does not like to make the abrupt turn necessary to provide adequate air flow over the front two cylinders (1 and 4).

Special crankcase through-bolts were used on these high-specific-output, turbocharged 935 engines. Porsche originally developed these bolts for use on

The 993 racing cylinder head. Porsche AG

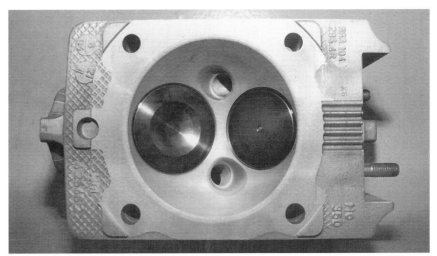

The 993 cylinder head with the large sealing surface. Joel Reiser

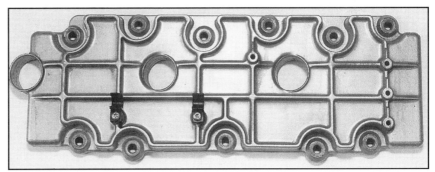

The die-cast-aluminum 964 valve covers.

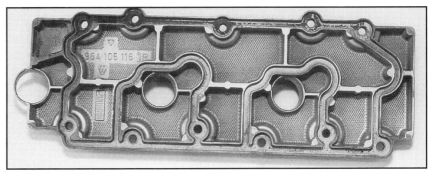

The die-cast-aluminum 964 valve covers with rubber seal.

the 917. These bolts use a pair of special-ground, self-aligning spherical washers at each end that fit inside each other with a special nut that will not introduce a bending stress on the bolt. The threaded portion of the stud and the nut were also designed to eliminate the notch effect of the threads. Porsche found that in many applications it could reduce the bolt by one unit size, so in some applications these bolts could be used as a weight-saving measure. When this type of bolt is used for the crankcase through-bolts, it is because the through-bolt holes are used as part of the main oil galleries and it is critical that these bolts not break. The

enlarged portion in the center of these special through-bolts is to stop, or at least limit the travel, of any sympathetic harmonic vibrations that may be set up in these through-bolts.

Initially, air-to-air intercooling was used on the 935s, but because of a reinterpretation of the rules, Porsche's placement of its intercooler was deemed illegal. FIA required that an original stock engine lid fit on the car, and with Porsche's air-to-air intercooler, it would not. A water intercooler system similar to the one used on the 934 was quickly developed midseason for use on the 935 engines. Fuel consumption for

these engines was 4.38 miles per gallon.

The 1976 936 engine was essentially the same engine that had been used in the 1974 Carrera RSR Turbo and carried the 911/78 Type number. The accessories and plumbing were changed to allow mounting in a mid-engined car, but the specifications remained the same as those for the Type 911/76 with the power increased to 540 DIN hp. The 936 was able to continue to use the more efficient air-to-air intercooling.

Single U.S. Engine for 1977

For 1977 the United States had only one type of engine for all 50

The fiberglass-reinforced-plastic 993 valve-cover gaskets use a rubber seal. Joel Reiser

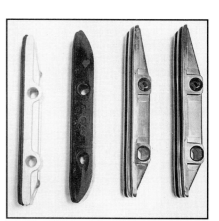

A comparison of chain ramps, from left to right: composite-aluminum-backed plastic ramps used in early 911 engines; black soft-plastic ramps used from 1968 to 1976/77; brown hard-plastic ramps introduced for the Turbo in 1976; and the taller, black hard-plastic ramps, five of which are used in conjunction with one of the earlier brown ramps for quieter operation.

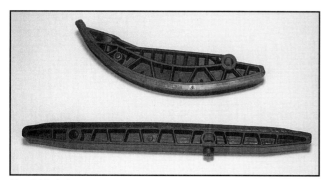

The 964 chain ramps.

Comparison of the various chain tensioners, left to right: early open-reservoir-style chain tensioner; early-style sealed-reservoir chain tensioner; late-style sealed-reservoir chain tensioner; and the superior 3.2 Carrera-style pressure-fed chain tensioners.

states, Type 911/85 for the standard five-speed transmission and Type 911/90 for the Sportomatic. These engines had thermal reactors, EGR, and air injection to comply with U.S. emission standards. These engines' specifications were the same as those for the 1976 California engines, and all of the United States, Canada, and Japan shared the exhaust system with thermal reactors that had been used for California since 1975. The late-1977 911 engines used Dilavar studs for the bottom row of cylinder head retaining studs. These studs were used to help eliminate the head stud pulling problem that the 2.7-liter engines had experienced. These Dilavar head studs had been used in racing engines from the early 1970s and also in the 930 Turbo engines. Dilavar is a steel alloy with a thermal expansion rate that is closer to that of the aluminum and magnesium used for the crankcase, cylinders, and cylinder heads. The effect is that the cold, or room temperature, stress is increased by different thermal expansion rates, resulting in the steel head studs being overly stressed at the higher operating temperatures. The result is that with time, many of the head studs would pull and deform the crankcase where the head stud screws in. Steel has an expansion coefficient of 11.5×10^{-6} per degree C, which is only about half of what the light alloys are at 22×10^{-6} to 24×10^{-6}. Dilavar has a heat expansion coefficient of about 20×10^{-6} and a tensile strength of 100-120 kp/mm^2. Specifications of Dilavar as manufactured by DEW, Krefeld, are as follows:

Carbon	0.065 percent
Silicon	0.200 percent
Manganese	5.000 percent
Chromium	3.500 percent
Nickel	12.000 percent
V+FE	78.650 percent

In 1977 there was also a reverse of the procedure seen in 1968 as the chain housings, chain housing covers, and valve covers were changed back to an aluminum alloy. These new castings were pressure-cast aluminum-silicon alloy (Al-Si).

The 1977 Turbo engine had some minor revisions in the fuel injection and the wastegate. The U.S. version received EGR to comply with the emission standards. The European engine became Type 930/52 while the U.S. version became the Type 930/53.

For 1977 there was even a U.S. version of the 934 engine, only this time

The 964 chain tensioner with ramps and chains installed.

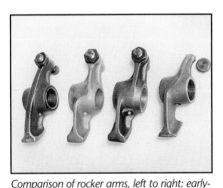

Comparison of rocker arms, left to right: early-style forged rocker arm with bushing; first-style cast rocker arm without bushing; current-style cast rocker arm with bushing; and the forged racing rocker arm without bushing or adjustment screw, shown with lash cap used for valve adjustment (these rockers have been used on most single overhead-cam racing 911 engines from 906 through the present IMSA 962 engine).

Comparison of various rocker-arm shafts. The shaft on the left is the early-style plain-steel rocker shaft; second from the left is a nitrated racing rocker shaft; third from the left is a surface-treated shaft used with nonbushed cast-iron rocker arms; and the one on the right is the plain-steel type. Note that the surface treatment on the treated shaft has worn through.

U.S. buyers came out ahead. The U.S. version of the 934 engine was built to what were then-looser IMSA GT rules. These cars were a blend of the Group 4 934 and the Group 5 935 and as such were called 934/5s. The engines were actually more like the 935 engine than the 934 engine, aside from the fact that they retained the single-plug ignition system from the Group 4 934 engine. The big change between these engines and the Group 4 934 engines was the Bosch mechanical twin-row plunger-type fuel-injector pump from the Group 5 935 engine. These engines were Type 930/73 and produced 590 DIN hp.

Porsche produced a customer version of the 935 for 1977 with the same engine used in the factory cars in 1976, engine Type 930/72. Most of these customer cars had their engines updated to a 3.0-liter configuration by increasing the bore to 95 mm. With the 1.4 multiplier applied, these cars fell into the 4.0- to 4.5-liter weight group for Group 5 racing, which required that the cars carry an additional 122 pounds. The 3.0-liter displacement version of the Type 930/72 engine produced 630 DIN hp at 8,000 rpm. Late in the year a second engine became available as the Type 930/76. This engine still had the 3.0-liter displacement and used the new twin-turbocharger intercooler system, but retained the single turbo. The Power for the Type 930/76 was 630 DIN hp at 7,800 rpm.

For 1977 the factory 935s retained their 2,857-cc displacement but had twin turbochargers and a new, more-efficient intercooler system. This engine was the Type 930/77. These changes not only increased the power to 630 DIN hp at 7,900 rpm but also greatly improved the throttle response. Throttle response is improved by the twin-turbocharger system because there is less inertia in each of the two smaller parallel systems than there is with one large system.

For a little additional excitement in 1977, Porsche took on BMW in the under-2.0-liter class of the German Group 5 series with the 935 *Baby*. Because Porsche was running unopposed in its own class, it decided to go after the competition in the under-2.0-liter class. The *Baby* was turbocharged, of course, so the displacement had to be smaller than 1,425 cc with the 1.4 multiplier. The car was called the 935-77-20 and it had engine Type 911/79. Development of an engine this small necessitated a new crankshaft with a 60-mm stroke and pistons with a 71-mm bore.

For this engine Porsche returned to the air-to-air intercooler system. The cooling effect of the air-to-air intercoolers was improved by using an exhaust gas-activated system called "Jet Cooling." This Jet Cooling system had originally been developed and tested for Porsche by an American company, Fletcher Aviation, in the early 1950s. Fletcher installed its Jet Cooling system on a then-new 1952 Cabriolet and sent it to Porsche for evaluation in 1953. The Jet Cooling was an interesting scheme that saved the power required to drive a cooling fan. Porsche did a great deal of development work with the cooling system for several years and even tried it on one of its racing spyders before concluding that the exhaust noise was excessive

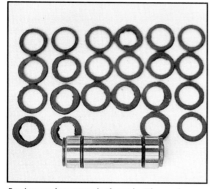

Racing rocker-arm shaft seals. The rocker-arm shafts also used a special seal at each end to prevent oil leaks in this area. The seals fit down into the compression grooves at each end of the shaft. When the rocker shaft is installed and the center pinch bolt is tightened, the seals are compressed and forced against the cam housing and rocker-arm shaft bores, forming a good seal. Note the seals shown in the production steel rocker-arm shaft in an effort to show contrast between the shaft and seal. These seals are available from Porsche or Wrightwood Racing.

A comparison of rocker-arm shafts: on the right is an early example with a 5-mm pinch bolt (used in 1965 and 1966 models), and on the left is an example of the later rocker-arm shafts with a 6-mm pinch bolt. The pinch bolts were too small in the originals and had to be overtorqued to retain the shaft in the cam housing. The small bolts used in these early shafts would often stretch, and the shafts would loosen up and work their way out of the cam housings.

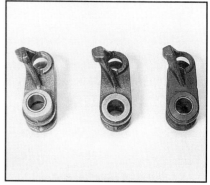

A comparison of the chain-sprocket idler arms, right to left: early 911 arm with bushing; arm without bushing used from the late 1960s until 1980; and 1980-and-later idler-sprocket arm with a broader stance and two bushings. This late style was introduced after Porsche had determined that the binding of these idler arms on the mounting spud was causing the majority of the premature chain-tensioner failures.

The 245-mm large-diameter 11-blade fan with small pulley as used on the Turbo.

The 245-mm five-blade fan used for 1976 and 1977 only.

The 226-mm 11-blade fan with a large pulley used for racing cars 906 and later.

and abandoning the program for jet cooling. It is interesting that Porsche tried this concept again for this project that was so important to them. However, this time it was not used for engine cooling, but instead more effective intercooling of the charge air. The power for the Type 911/79 was 370 DIN hp at 8,000 rpm. The *Baby* was only raced twice, unsuccessfully the first time, but winning by over a half a lap in its second and final race.

1978: Introducing the SC

For 1978 the 3.0-liter 911SC was introduced as the only 911 for the world market. Based on 930 components, the engine was Type 930/04 for the U.S. 49-state car, Type 930/06 for the California car, and Type 930/03 for the rest of the world. The differences between the engines were minor and the same specifications and performance were claimed for all. All of the engines had

The 11-blade 245-mm fan with a 1.3:1 drive ratio, as used in the production 911 from 1968 to 1975.

The 11-blade 226-mm fan with a 1.3:1 drive ratio, as used in race cars from the 906 through 956/962C engines with water-cooled cylinder heads. With the exception of Moby Dick, *all of the 934s and 935s used larger flat fans for additional cooling.*

The five-blade 245-mm fan with a 1.8:1 drive ratio, as used on 911s for 1976 and 1977.

The 11-blade 126-mm fan with a 1.8:1 drive ratio used on 1978 and 1979 911SCs.

The 11-blade 245-mm fan with a 1.67:1 drive ratio used on all Turbos and 1980-and-newer 911s.

The Solex 40 PI overflow carburetors used on the Type 901/01 engines. Note the wobble nut (used to drive the recirculating fuel pumps), tandem fuel pumps, and special chain housing cover with mounts for the fuel pumps.

air-injection pumps when the 911SC was introduced. The U.S. engine additionally had a catalytic converter and the California engines also had EGR to meet the various emission standards of the world. The engine cooling fans were changed again, this time to the smaller-diameter 226-mm 11-blade fan while retaining the higher speed 1.8:1 drive ratio of the 5-blade fan. The air delivery rate in this configuration is approximate-

Cam nuts: at left is the wobble nut used with Solex carburetors, at center is the normal street-car nut, and at right is the racing nut. The differences are that the street nuts have a 2-mm thread pitch and use a 46-mm wrench, and the racing nut has a 1.5-mm thread pitch and uses a 41-mm wrench. The current cars use a much simpler bolt.

ly 1,380 liters per second. These smaller-diameter fans had been used on most of the racing engines from the 906 on, but with the slower 1.3:1. pulley ratio. The front-mounted serpentine (loop) oil cooler became standard equipment on the 911SC.

The 1978 911SC introduced the Porsche clutch disc with a large rubber damper in the center. These rubber-centered clutches were to dampen out the vibration noises of the transmissions. The problem with these clutches was that the rubber dampers were prone to failure. Often when these clutches fail a piece of rubber will jam between the clutch and the pressure plate and cause the clutch to cease operating. Porsche used these clutches from 1978 until 1983 when they were replaced with a spring-centered clutch disc, and existing rubber-centered clutches should be replaced with spring-centered clutch discs.

The 1978 930 Turbo engine received some major changes, some of which were shared with the new 911SC engine. Both engines received new crankshafts with larger main-bearing journals; bearings 1-7 on both were increased from 57 to 60 mm, and number 8 on the Turbo was increased from 31 to 40 mm. This change required that

the crankcase bores be increased from 62 mm to 65 mm for both the 911SC and the Turbo. The flywheel mounting-bolt circle was increased from 44 to 70 mm and nine bolts were used to fasten the flywheel rather than the six used before. The flywheel seal was increased in size and the 928 seal was used. Both engines use the Bosch breakerless CD ignition system with distributors that rotate in a counter-clockwise direction instead of clockwise, which had always been the 911 tradition. These new-style pointless distributors were originally used on the racing 917s and the RSRs. They have a toothed rotor that causes a magnetic flux change and acts like a pulse generator. There are six little tabs on the rotor so that one turn of the distributor produces six pulses which drive the electronic capacitor discharge unit. The rev limiter was changed to a fuel-pump cut-off-type set for 6,850 rpms ± 150 rpms for the 911SC. The chain ramps were changed again in an effort to quiet the chains. One brown plastic ramp was retained while the other five were replaced with the new, taller black ramps.

Several other changes were unique to the Turbo engines, now Type 930/61 for the U.S. 49-state cars and Type 930/63 for the California cars. The displacement was increased on the Turbo by using both a longer 74.4-mm stroke and a larger 97-mm bore. New connecting rods, in addition to accommodating the larger journal diameter, were 0.7-mm shorter, and the wrist pin diameter was made 1-mm larger in diameter, 23-mm instead of the traditional 22 mm. The cylinders no longer used any type of head gasket at all for the first time on any 911-type engine. The cylinder cooling fins were drastically altered in an effort to even the cooling effect of the fan. The fins were completely left off the top of the cylinder (the side nearest the fan) and the fins were lengthened on the bottom of the cylinders, particularly at the end nearest the cylinder head. Both portions of the oil pumps were greatly increased in size to improve oil circulation. The new pumps were larger in size than the 908 pumps used in the 935 engines. The pressure pump is 51 mm long and the scavenge pump is 80 mm long. To improve the quality of the intake charge air, an air-to-air intercooler was added between the turbocharger and the engine. All Turbos had air-injection pumps. The U.S. engine had additional thermal reactors and the California engines had a distributor with a double vacuum unit to retard the timing at full load to meet the various emissions standards of the world. The power for the European Turbo was 300 DIN hp at 5,500 rpm while the emission controls reduced the U.S. models to 265 DIN hp at 5,500 rpm.

For 1978 the customer's 935 received the engine Type 930/78. This engine was similar to the Type 930/77 engine used by the factory cars in 1977, with twin turbochargers and an improved intercooler system. A pair of turbocharger scavenge pumps were driven off the end of the layshaft, scavenging oil from the turbochargers and returning it to the engine's sump The customer engines continued to be 3.0-liter engines. Power output was 720 DIN hp at 7,800 rpm.

An interesting change in these engines was that Porsche had replaced the CE ring head gasket with a solid-steel ring that fits in a groove in both the upper cylinder flange and the cylinder head, forming an interlocking seal. The ring was originally made of stainless steel and later made of Ni-Resist, a high-nickel-content alloy steel that is able to withstand very high temperatures. This is the same material that the turbocharger hot housings are made of.

Engines for both the factory 935 and 936 were greatly changed for 1978. They were both still based on 911 components but had new water-cooled four-valve heads with cog-gear-driven dual-overhead cams. These changes were made because of Porsche's desire to produce more reliable power from these engines. The forerunners were not at their mechanical limit, however; they were at their thermal limit. A good example of this thermal limit phenomenon was the 1979 Daytona 24-hour race where 10 of the 13 935s that entered failed, and the majority failed by exceeding the thermal limits of the engine—i.e., melted pistons, burned valves, and most commonly a blown head gasket or burned-out cylinder.

To obtain more power it was necessary to go from two valves to four valves, which, with air-cooled heads, would have been an additional thermal liability because the valves and their ports would severely reduce the cross section of the head used for cooling. Water cooling was essential if four-valve heads were to be used. In addition to offering a power increase, the four-valve layout reduces the thermal stress on the valves because of their smaller size. Experience gained from experiments with four-valve heads with water cooling for the 908 engine in 1970 and 1971 was applied to this project.

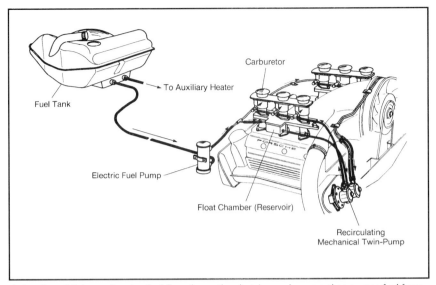

A drawing of Solex carburetor fuel flow shows the electric supply pump that pumps fuel from the tank to a pair of float chambers, one on each bank of three carburetors. A pair of mechanical fuel pumps, driven by the left camshaft, then recirculates the fuel past the jets in the overflow carburetors. The fuel level, which would normally be called the float level, is established by a spillway in each of the six carburetors. The fuel that runs over the spillway is returned to the float chambers to be recirculated again.

Cylinders were welded to the heads by an electron-beam-welding machine, eliminating the critical head gasket, an area where the thermal limit is often approached and sometimes exceeded in these turbocharged racing engines. The four-valve head used a very simple pent-roof-design combustion chamber with one centrally located spark plug. Spark plugs were fired by a high-tension distributor unit driven by the intake cam for cylinders 1-3, while the inductive driver for the electronic ignition unit was driven by the intake cam for cylinders 4-6. Camshafts were spur gear-driven

A Weber 40 IDA carburetor of the type used on 911 engines from midyear 1966 through 1969.

rather than by chains, and the valves were actuated by cup tappets.

Both the 935 and the 936 engines utilized twin turbochargers for improved throttle response. The 935 twin-turbo engine used water intercooling and twin wastegates. The smaller 936 twin-turbo engine retained the air-to-air intercooling and used one wastegate. The Type 935/73 936 engine had to remain under 2,146 cc because of the 1.4 multiplier and the 3.0-liter limit for the group 6 cars. The 60-mm stroke crankshaft from the 935 *Baby* was used in conjunction with an 87-mm bore to achieve 2,140 cc displacement. The

A Weber 40 IDS carburetor; note the high-speed enrichment tube. The high-speed enrichment circuit was added for improved engine safety. The circuit provided an overly rich mixture at higher rpm to minimize the possibility of destructive detonation and offered no increase in performance.

A Weber 40 IDA with no high-speed enrichment circuit. The carburetor design was essentially the same; they just didn't use the extra circuit.

Type 935/73 936 engine produced 580 DIN hp at 9,000 rpm.

The 935 engine was increased to 3,211 cc, which, with the 1.4 multiplier, brought the equivalent displacement to the 4.5-liter weight group limit with 4,495 cc. The displacement increase was achieved by using a new 74.4-mm crankshaft derived form the 3.3-liter street Turbo combined with the 95.7-mm pistons. The Type 935/71 engine was for the factory *Moby Dick* car, and power output was 750 DIN hp at 8,200 rpm.

Special U.S. 935 for 1979

Both the 911SC and the 930 Turbo engines remained unchanged for the world market in 1979. In 1979 a special version of the 935 was built for the United States and the IMSA multiplier for turbocharged cars. Single turbo cars had a 1.5 multiplier while twin-turbo cars had a 1.8 multiplier. As such, a 3.0-liter twin was required to weigh 88 pounds more than the 3.122-liter single-turbo cars that Porsche made especially to comply with the IMSA rules. Porsche chose the single-turbo approach with its Type 930/79 engine because Porsche felt it could make the engine as effective as the 3.0-liter twin-turbo engine by increasing the bore to 97 mm and developing a new, larger, more-efficient single turbocharger and using the same type intercooler it had used on the Type 930/78 engine. Porsche's solution to the IMSA rules was

not entirely effective, and only Peter Gregg won races with the Type 930/79 engine. Most of the other teams that had these Type 935/79 engines converted them back to the 3.0 Type 930/78 specifications because they felt that this configuration had better throttle response. The power output of the Type 930/79 was 715 DIN hp at 7,800 rpm.

Further SC Revisions for 1980

In 1980 the 911SC engine was revised for all markets. The U.S. version became the Type 930/07 with 9.3:1 compression, and it retained its 180 DIN hp. The emission-control devices consisted of a three-way catalytic converter with an oxygen sensor-controlled frequency valve to control the "control pressure" in the fuel distributor. This is the Lambda system that precisely controls the fuel/air mixture ratio of the engine to provide the correct combustion by-products to the critical three-way catalytic converter. The Lambda system was a great advancement in performance and driveability for emission-legal engines. The U.S. cars also used both vacuum-advance and vacuum-retard distributors. The R.o.W. cars retained their air-injection pump to comply with the emission laws.

The oil pump was fitted with a suction venturi surrounded by a cylindrical filter screen. This venturi pickup was added to eliminate an oil scavenge prob-

Zenith 40 TIN carburetors were used on the 1970 and 1971 U.S. 911T engines and 1970–1973 R.o.W. 911T.

lem that some 911SCs had when driven at sustained high-rpm. The lower valve covers received extra reinforcement to both help quiet the engine and provide a better oil seal. These new, reinforced "Turbo" valve covers actually solved the problem of leaking valve covers that had been with the 911 engine since its introduction. The pilot bearing was mounted onto the end of the crankshaft with three bolts rather than being pressed into the flywheel, as had been the case with all previous 911 engines. The fan size was increased back to the 245-mm diameter, and the pulley ratio was decreased to the 1.67:1 ratio of the Turbo. And because of the larger fan, the fan air-transfer rate was increased to approximately 1,500 liters per second.

The 911SC engine for the R.o.W., Type 930/09, had 8.6:1 compression and produced 188 hp at 5,500 rpm. All of the 1980 911 and 930 engines received revised chain tensioners. The tensioners were still hydraulic and, in fact, the internals had not changed. The body had been made thinner where it goes onto the support spud in the chain housing. This change was to provide room for the new chain sprocket carriers (chain idler arms), which were now wider and had two bronze bushings. These changes were made to relieve the binding stress and galling, which Porsche had determined was causing most of the premature chain tensioner failures. This problem was determined to be similar to the one they had with the change to the rocker arms without

bushings in 1967. Another change for the R.o.W. cars was the replacement of the front-fender-mounted loop oil cooler with a brass tube-type cooler for improved oil cooling. The U.S. cars retained the serpentine (loop) cooler, which had been standard equipment since the introduction of the 911SC. There was a limited series of 930 Turbos for the United States in 1980 built to 1979 specifications and delivered before January 1980, after which the Turbo was discontinued for the United States and Canadian markets.

The Porsche racing program for 1980 was to have been an Indy program with Interscope Racing. The engine for this car was the Type 935/72, a 2,650-cc development of the four-valve engines used in Group 5 and 6 racing in 1978. Porsche, as it turned out, attempted to enter U.S. Championship Car racing at the wrong time in history, right in the middle of the USAC vs. CART feud, and the rules were changed out from under it. Porsche had been told that it would be allowed to run with a boost of 54 inches of mercury, but on April 21, Porsche was told it would be limited to 48 inches of boost like the eight-cylinder cars. When the boost was reduced to 48 inches, Porsche withdrew, feeling that the reduction would require a complete redesign and there was not enough time left before the early May practice. Porsche was beaten before it started, not on the track but at the conference table.

The Type 935/72 was designed to run on methyl alcohol. The engine used

electronic injection with dual injectors. The compression ratio was 9.0:1 and the power output would depend on the boost it was allowed to run: at 60 inches boost (1.03 bar) the engine produced 630 DIN hp at 9,000 rpm, at 54 inches boost (0.83 bar) the engine produced 570 DIN hp at 9,000 rpm, and at 48 inches boost (0.63 bar)—we will never know, Porsche decided not to play.

The customer 935 engine for 1980 was the 930/80, an extension of the all-conquering version of the 935 engine the Kremer Brothers had developed for the 1979 season. In 1979, the Kremers won 11 of the 12 races in the German National Championship and they also won the prestigious Le Mans race with the only 935 to ever do so. The 930/80 had a bore of 95 mm and a stroke of 74.4 mm for a displacement of 3,163 cc with a Bosch-Kugelfischer injection pump with electronic regulation of fuel mixture and air-to-air intercooling. The Kugelfischer injection with its electronic regulation was Porsche's first real effort to reduce the fuel consumption on the racing turbocharged 911 engines. The engine with 7.2:1 compression and 1.7 bar boost would produce 800 DIN hp at 8,000 rpm. When run at a more conservative 1.4 boost, the Type 930/80 engine would produce 740 DIN hp at 7,800 rpm and was an extremely reliable endurance-racing engine. The intercoolers for the Type 930/80 were various forms of air-to-air intercooler systems. Porsche had one system, and several major teams developed their own

The belt drive for the 906E and 910 injection engine Type 901/21. Special cams were made for just this application. These cams featured an extension on the cam billet, which has a key-way drive for the Gilmer belt drive for the injection pump.

The Bosch mechanical injection for 906E and 910 engines, Type 901/21, was a simple in-line injection pump with simple speed and throttle-position control.

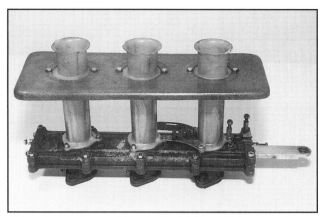

Slide-valve injection manifolds for the 906E and 910 engines, Type 901/21.

High butterfly injection manifolds as used on 2.8-liter RSR and early 3.0-liter RSR.

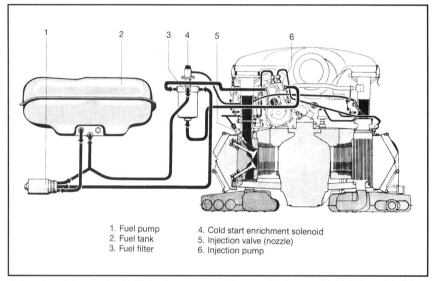

1. Fuel pump
2. Fuel tank
3. Fuel filter
4. Cold start enrichment solenoid
5. Injection valve (nozzle)
6. Injection pump

A drawing of the mechanical injection system used on production-model 911s from 1969 into 1976 with the R.o.W. 2.7-liter Carrera engine. Fuel was fed to the mechanical injection pump by an electric fuel pump with a pressure-regulating bypass circuit. The mechanical pump then supplied a timed mixture to each of the six cylinders. There was an auxiliary cold-start circuit that squirted fuel into the top of the intake stacks.

systems. One thing was sure, air-to-air was the way to go. No more heat build-up in the intercooler system, and with a cooler, denser charge the engines could produce more horsepower for extended periods of time.

1981: Injection System Reworked

In 1981 there were minor revisions in the 911SC engine for the U.S. market. Most of the changes were in the fuel-injection system. The fuel distributor was made nonadjustable to comply with the U.S. laws. A cold-start-mixture distributor was added inside the air box to give more uniform distribution of the cold-start mixture to all cylinders. Previously cold-start fuel was injected into the air distributor housing. Porsche had finally determined that a lean cold-start mixture was the cause of most of the backfires that were resulting in the blown air boxes. This change alone seems to have eliminated about 90 percent of the blown air boxes. Unfortunately, each year there are still a few engines that will backfire and blow their air boxes even with these latest changes. These are usually caused by an injection problem or big swings in climatic conditions. All fuel lines and injector lines on the engine were changed to steel. An acceleration enrichment circuit was added to the injection system to improve reliability when the engine or the oxygen sensor was cold. The engine type number was changed to Type 930/16 for the United States and Canada. Power remained unchanged at 180 DIN hp.

Nineteen-eighty-one also saw the return of the 930 Turbo to Canada with the Type 930/60 R.o.W. 300 DIN hp engine. The Canadian laws required that they use a U.S.-approved version of the car if there was one, and allowed them to import the R.o.W. version in the absence of a U.S.-approved car. The R.o.W. version of the 911SC engine was revised for 1981 as the Type 930/10. The compression ratio was increased to 9.8:1 and the effective combustion chamber was changed to improve the thermal efficiency and increase the hp to 204 DIN at 5,900 rpm.

The 1981 935 engine Type 930/81 had only minor revisions over the Type 930/80. The changes were an improved oil-scavenging system, improved cooling, and larger, 43-mm intake ports. The main changes to the cooling system were the use of a new drive system and higher drive ratio for the flat fan.

The change to the oil-scavenging system was more significant and there was a new 935 racing oil pump with dual scavenge pumps and oil pickups to get more of the used oil out of the engine. There are a couple of advantages to doing a more thorough job of oil scavenging. Getting the oil out of the engine more quickly can reduce the windage and prevent frictional horsepower losses from the crankshaft operating in the oil. Without efficient scavenging as much as a couple of quarts of oil can be in the engine at one time and the crankshaft will whip this excess oil into a fog by introducing air into the oiling system. The added air in the oil

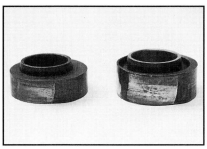

The three-dimension space cam used in Bosch twin-row mechanical injection pumps.

The twin-row Bosch injection pump used on the 911E and 911S. This was essentially the same technology Porsche had used on the 906E race car, but with a much-improved injection pump with an engine-speed-controlled space cam. With the space cam, the quantity of fuel is controlled by the throttle position, the engine rpm, and the space cam, providing much better fuel economy and low-rpm throttle response. This enabled Porsche to increase the performance of the 911S and 911E while allowing them to meet the 1969 U.S. emissions standards through more precise fuel metering.

makes it much more difficult to effectively cool the scavenged oil. There was a later version of this pump with three stages of scavenging and three oil pickups to even further improve the engine's oil scavenging.

These changes were made to allow the engines to run higher boost for longer periods of time, which meant they could produce more power with more reliability. Power for the Type 930/81 engine was increased to 760 DIN hp at 7,800 rpm, but in short races the boost was increased to the 1.7- to 1.8-bar range with more than 800 hp on tap.

The real excitement for 1981 was the good use that Peter Schutz and Porsche came up with for the Indy engine design. The Indy engine was converted to run on racing gas using a Bosch-Kugelfischer injection pump with twin turbochargers as the Type 935/75, and installed in the venerable 936 chassis to win again at Le Mans for Porsche's sixth win. When converted to gasoline, Porsche claimed a power output of 600 DIN hp at 8,200 rpm for the Type 935/75. The reason that these larger engines were now eligible in Group 6 is that the year before FIA had made an emergency change in an effort to give a car a place to compete. For 1981 the class limit had been increased up to 6.0 liters, so now almost anything could compete as a Group 6 car. There were weight penalties for the larger engine sizes, but obviously this didn't prove to be much of a handicap to Porsche.

1982: Another Le Mans Victory

Only minor changes were made in 1982 to the 911SC and the 930 Turbos. The largest change was that the camshaft drive gears were mounted to the cams with a bolt rather than the large nut always used previously. The alternators were changed to units that had a built-in voltage regulator rather than those used previously with remote-mounted voltage regulators. The 930 had an oil trap installed in the crankcase vent line to separate the fumes and return the oil to the oil tank. The type numbers remained the same for 1982: Type 930/10 for the R.o.W. 911SC, Type 930/16 for the U.S. 911SC, and Type 930/60 for the R.o.W. Turbo.

In 1982 the Indy engine was again pressed into service in the all-new 956 Group C car. The new Group C rules required a 100-liter fuel tank and limited overall fuel consumption to 55 liters per 100 km (5.14 mpg). The new fuel economy requirements were hard to meet with the Type 935/76 version of this engine with its Bosch-Kugelfischer injection. The Kugelfischer injection is a mechanical injection system with some limited electronic compensation devices to improve the fuel economy. Porsche did everything it could to improve the fuel economy, and its economy got better with each race. The fuel consumption had been its biggest problem at the beginning of the season and at Silverstone it actually had to race at a pace almost

10 seconds off its qualifying speed. Even so, Porsche was able to win at Le Mans in 1982 with this new car. As a result of its fuel conservation, the winning car went further for its win than 1981's winning 936, and in doing so consumed less fuel and won the Le Mans Index of Energy Consumption for the car that achieved the best ratio of fuel-used-to-distance-run.

Turbo Engine Reworked for 1983

The year 1983 was again one of little change for the 911SC. The engines had a modified acceleration control unit and a new oxygen sensor. Additionally, the California cars had a new oxygen-sensor control unit. These changes were made to improve throttle response while the engine was still cold and still comply with the various emissions laws. The U.S. cars received the brass, tube-type oil cooler.

The Turbo engine received enough changes to justify a new type number,

The auxiliary cam drive for the mechanical injection pump used on racing engines. This auxiliary cam drive was part of the camshaft on production cars with mechanical injection. Camshafts that did not have a pump drive can be modified using this drive piece.

during fast acceleration. The engines had a new distributor with a double vacuum unit with a temperature-controlled vacuum advance for emission control. The exhaust system was changed to bypass the wastegate exhaust through its own separate muffler. This change was made to reduce the noise level without restricting the power output, which was still 300 DIN hp at 5,500 rpm.

In 1983 Porsche produced a series of 11 956 race cars for its racing customers with essentially the same Type 935/76 engine that had been used in the factory team cars in 1982. Porsche then began to develop a new, more fuel-efficient version of the Indy engine for Group C as the Type 935/77. This new version produced 620 DIN hp at 8,200 rpm with 1.3-bar boost. A sophisticated electronic ignition and engine-fuel management system was used to cope with the changing conditions and provide more precise fuel control and timing. The system was developed by Bosch for Porsche and has some similarities to the DME (Digital Motor Electronics) used in the production Porsches. The system fed six input signals to the fuel injection and ignition control computer: current rpm, engine temperature, battery voltage, idling adjustment, inlet air temperature, and turbocharger boost pressure. This new car won at Le Mans in 1983.

New Carrera Engine for 1984

Nineteen-eighty-four marked the beginning of the third decade of the 911 and the introduction of the new-and-improved version of the Carrera engine. Its larger displacement produced more power and was more efficient, providing better fuel economy than the previous models. The basic engines for the world market were identical except for their emission-control devices and compression ratios. The high specific output is due mainly to the resonance-type intake system and the increased compression ratios.

In addition to the increased power there were several significant mechanical changes in the 1984 Carrera engines. The displacement was increased to 3.2 liters by using the 74.4-mm crankshaft and connecting rods from the 3.3 930 Turbo engine with the same 95-mm bore that had been used on the 911SC engines for a displacement of 3,164 cc. The cylinders for the 3.2-liter 911 Carrera engine did not have the groove for the CE ring-type head gasket that had been used on all other normally aspirated engines from 1970 until this change. Instead, the cylinder-sealing surface was cut at a slight angle and no head gasket was used. Porsche also changed the crankcase, which no longer had a removable sump plate and sump screen. The benefit of the new crankcase, for our purposes, was that it was stronger and less likely to leak oil along its bottom seam. This change was actually introduced on the 911SC production engines the previous April because the old molds had worn out. The change was made because some European countries were considering a law requiring that oil be removed by suction during an oil change and not gravity, as is common. The law was never passed, however.

Another major mechanical change in these engines was the all-new pressure-fed chain tensioner. This tensioner is actually best described as a spring tensioner that is hydraulically dampened. The chain tensioners are pressure fed from the engine's lubrication system through oil lines that "T" off the oil lines that provide lubrication to the cam and valve gear mechanism. These new tensioners proved to be a simple, reliable, trouble-free solution to an old problem.

The exhaust system remained the same in concept as the 911SC except for larger-diameter tubes for the larger-displacement engine. There are two identical heat exchangers that cross over at the rear of the engine (the flywheel end) and are combined and pass down the left side of the engine. The European (R.o.W.) cars had a new, larger-volume premuffler, while the U.S.-Japan version

The Kugelfischer injection pump used on 1980 and newer 935s and the original customer 956 race cars in 1983. The Kugelfischer injection system was also used on the 1984 911SC RS (Type 954).

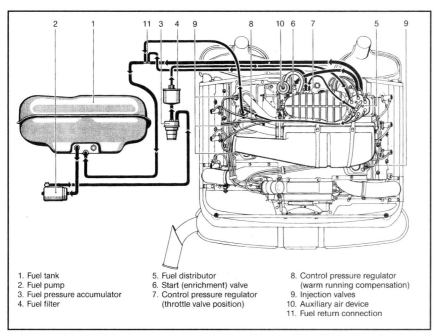

1. Fuel tank
2. Fuel pump
3. Fuel pressure accumulator
4. Fuel filter
5. Fuel distributor
6. Start (enrichment) valve
7. Control pressure regulator (throttle valve position)
8. Control pressure regulator (warm running compensation)
9. Injection valves
10. Auxiliary air device
11. Fuel return connection

A drawing of the CIS injection system shows the overall layout of the CIS fuel injection that was introduced on the 1973 U.S. 911T.

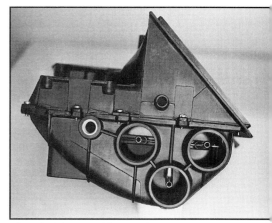

The CIS air box. A cold-start mixture distributor was added inside the air box to give more uniform distribution of the cold-start mixture to all cylinders. Previously, cold-start fuel was injected into the air-distributor housing.

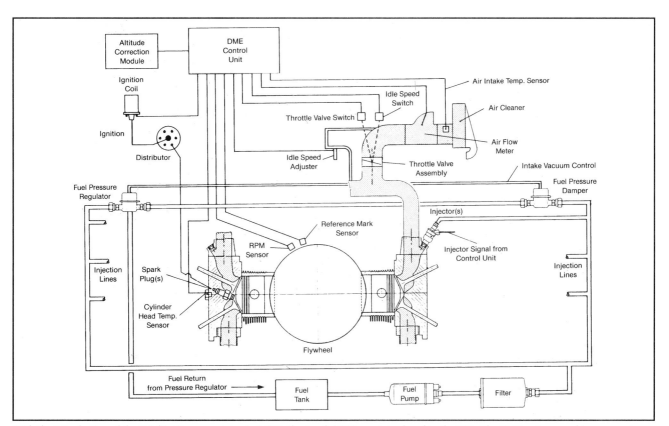

With the introduction of the 3.2-liter Carrera engine in 1984, the Bosch DME was introduced to the 911. The DME system combines separate ignition, fuel—and in the case of the U.S.-Japan car—oxygen-sensor systems into a single control system. The control system is a microcomputer with microprocessors. These microcomputers vary for different countries because of different emission regulations and fuel grades. Complete performance maps for both the ignition and electronic injection are stored within the DME control unit. Sensors on the engine provide the control system's microcomputer with instantaneous information and provides the engine with the correct amount of fuel and the optimum ignition timing for all engine operating conditions. The DME system allows the engine to be optimized for performance, economy, and exhaust emissions.

A Type 901/20 Carrera Six engine right-side view (cylinders four through six). Note: the tachometer drive at the rear of the camshaft and the oil-filter housing that mounts where the oil cooler is installed on production engines. Porsche AG

had a three-way catalytic converter in place of the premuffler. An oxygen sensor was installed at the input of the catalyst on these cars. The oxygen sensor was electrically preheated for faster response time. The exhaust from either the premuffler or the catalytic converter then went to the final muffler at the rear of the car as before. There was a new final muffler with a new interior with approximately 10 percent greater flow rate.

The big change for the 1984 3.2-liter Carrera was Porsche's use of the Bosch-Motronic-controlled fuel-injection and ignition system, which Porsche calls its DME system (Digital Motor Electronics). The DME system combined separate ignition, fuel, and—in the case of the U.S.-Japan model—oxygen sensor systems into a single control system. The control system is a microcomputer with microprocessors. These microcomputers were different for different countries because of different emission regulations and fuel grades. Complete performance maps for both the ignition and electronic injection were stored within the DME control unit. Sensors on the engine provided the control system's microcomputer with instantaneous information that then provided the engine with the correct amount of fuel and the optimum ignition timing for all engine-operating conditions. The DME system allowed the 911 engine to be optimized for performance, economy, and exhaust emissions without causing any driveability problems.

To achieve its goal of a high-specific-output, Porsche optimized the compression ratio for the R.o.W. cars at 10.5:1, and for the U.S. cars at 9.5:1. Porsche optimized the effective combustion chamber shape within the normal hemispherical combustion chamber with a squish hump on one side of the piston. Porsche continued to use the same camshafts that it had originally intro-

The racing oil-filter housing has a full-flow oil filter made up of a metal disc in its pressure circuit, whereas the production cars had their full-flow oil filter in the scavenge circuit only until 1991, when the C2 Turbo incorporated filters in both the scavenge and pressure circuits. This casting also incorporates an adjustable oil-pressure bypass for setting the operating oil pressure. This same casting has been used on all of Porsche's racing 911 engines from the 906 through the 956 and 962 engines.

The mechanical tachometer drive and cam drive used on the early 901-derived racing engines before Porsche grew to trust the electronic tachometers.

Disassembled here for cleaning, this is the oil-filter unit used in 911 racing engines.

duced with the 3.0 Carrera in 1976 and had used with all of the 911SC engines. When these cams were first used in the 3.0 Carrera engine they were timed to open the intake 1 deg BTDC and close it 53 deg ABDC; thus, they opened the exhaust valve at 43 deg BBDC and closed it 3 deg ATDC. In the various versions of the 911SC engines the cams were first advanced by 6 deg and then retarded again by the same 6 deg; sometimes the Euro version of the engine would be more advanced than the U.S. version, and at other times, vice versa. For the 3.2-liter Carrera engine the timing was a compromise between the two extremes and was 3 deg more advanced than the 911SC it replaced. The Carrera engine used resonance-type tuning for the intake system to optimize the power output. The R.o.W. version had 73 hp per liter, which was a higher power output than any of the other normally aspirated engines since the 1973 Carrera RS engine at 78.2 hp per liter. The R.o.W. engine had 231 hp, and the U.S. version had 207 hp.

There was another new 911 engine type for 1984, the type 930/18, which was the engine for the Type 954 911SC RS. This new engine was an evolution of the 3.0-liter 911SC engine for racing or rallying. The engine retained the 95x70.4 mm bore-and-stroke ratio of the 911SC for a displacement of 2,944 cc. The standard valve size of 49-mm intake and 41.5-mm exhaust was retained for these engines, and their ports were increased to 43 mm for both the intake and the exhaust.

These engines had a new sport camshaft that opened the intake valve at 82 deg BTDC and closed the intake valve at 82 deg ABDC. The cam opened the exhaust valve at 78 deg and closed the exhaust valve at 58 deg ATDC. The maximum valve lift for the intake valve was 11.70 mm, and the maximum lift for the exhaust valve was 10.25 mm. This engine used the Bosch-Kugelfischer mechanical fuel-injection pump and high-butterfly injection system. The power output for the Type 930/18 was 255 DIN hp at 7,000 rpm with a peak torque of 184 lb-ft at 6,500 rpm.

1986: Turbo Returns to United States

For 1986 the 911 Turbo was reintroduced to the U.S. market after a six-year absence. The new U.S. version with the Type 930/68 engine used a catalytic converter and oxygen sensor to meet U.S. emission laws. The engine was designed for operation on premium-grade

The 1968 916 2.0-liter four-cylinder OHC engine installed in the 911R. Sloniger photo, courtesy Porsche AG

The 1973 2.7-liter Carrera RS engine. The RS engine was the first of the 911 engines to use the then-new Nikasil cylinders, which allowed a larger bore within the same cylinder-head stud spacing. Aside from the larger 90-mm bore, the 2.7-liter Carrera RS engines were very much like the 2.4-liter 911S engines from 1972 and 1973 with 8.5:1 compression and mechanical fuel injection. James D. Newton

unleaded gasoline and met all U.S. laws as one version. The power output was 282 hp at 5,500 rpm with a peak torque of 287.4 ft-lb at 4,000 rpm.

In the first few years after its introduction in 1984, the 3.2 Carrera engine was relatively unchanged. In 1985 Porsche changed the front-mounted oil cooler to a finned-radiator-type heat exchanger, or cooler. This new finned cooler was mounted in the right front fender in place of the former brass-tube-type oil cooler. The change was actually made in July 1984 to both the Turbo and the Carrera. A notch in the lower portion of the front bumper was opened up to let more air-flow into the new radiator-style cooler. This type of cooler worked well at high-sustained speed—100-plus mph—such as you would enjoy on the autobahns, but was not necessarily an improvement over

The 1974 3.0 IROC RSR engine with high butterfly injection.

The 1976 934 engine for Group 4. Note the air-flow sensor for the CIS injection system and that this engine also uses the flat-fan cooling system from the Carrera RSR Turbo. Porsche AG

the tube-type cooler for U.S. driving, where there is not too much air-flow from that small hole or notch in the front bumper.

More Power for 1987

In 1987 Porsche installed a thermostatically controlled fan on the front-mounted radiator-type cooler on all catalyst cars to solve the cooling problems on the U.S. cars. The thermostat turned the fan on when the oil temperature reached 118 deg C (244 deg F).

Also for 1987 Porsche was able to wring a little more power out of the catalytic converter version of the engine, increasing it to 217 hp; the. R.o.W. version remained at 231 hp. There were two new versions of the. 3.2 Carrera engine, one for Australia, which still carried the same Type number as the U.S. version, but with a modified control unit that reduced the fuel-octane requirements by four points RON and also dropped the power back to 207 hp. The second version was Type 930/26, which had the same performance specifications as the. R.o.W. version, but with engine encasement to conform with the Swiss 75 dBA noise restrictions for 1987. A noise-reducing panel was mounted on the underside of the car and almost completely enclosed the engine compartment on the bottom. This was in addition to the special muffler that had already been installed for 1986.

There was also a new transmission for the Carrera for 1987, the G 50, replacing the 915 transmission that the 911s had used since 1972. A new development was the hydraulically operated, rubber-dampened clutch, which was increased in size from the 225 mm clutch of the 915 transmission to 240 mm for the G 50. This was a new, larger version of the rubber-damper unit which provided enough dampening action to absorb the torsional oscillation of a slow-running engine without the rattling noise in the transmission. In order to take pressure off the torsion damper's rubber package in high-torque applications, there were mechanical stops built in that restricted the torsional angle to 44 to 47 deg.

Porsche continued to develop its racing engines for the 956/962C as well as its engine for the U.S. IMSA version of the 962. The IMSA 962 engine was forced down in displacement from 3.2 liters to 3.0 liters for the 1987 season. At the same time Porsche increased the size of the WEC version up to 3.0 liters and added water cooling for the cylinders as well as the heads, which produced more power and increased the engine's reliability at the same time. Porsche ran a preliminary version of this engine in the German Super Cup in 1986. The water-cooled 962 engine was allowed for IMSA in 1988 with inlet-air restrictors, and it first ran at Columbus, Ohio, in 1988. Porsche's first win was Tampa at the end of the 1989 season, and it scored additional wins with the water-cooled version of the 962 at Daytona in 1991, Road America in 1993, and again at Daytona in 1995.

The Carreras for the United States and the R.o.W. were essentially the same for the 1988 and 1989 model years. For 1988 there was a special de-tuned version of the Carrera for Australia which provided only 207 DIN hp at 5,900 rpm. This was because the un-leaded fuel available in Australia in 1988 was 91/81 RON/MON, which was con-siderably below the 95/85 RON/MON octane unleaded fuels available in other markets where catalytic converters were required. Australian unleaded fuel would have been equivalent to the U.S. CLC rating of 86 octane, and the U.S. cars re-quired 90 CLC octane for the same peri-od. For 1989, the Australian version was discontinued since premium unleaded fuel with 96 RON octane was then avail-able in Australia.

New 3.6 Engine Debuts

There was an all-new 3.6-liter ver-sion of the 911 engine available for the new C4, the 964, in 1989. The engine's power output was increased almost 17 percent over the previous 3.2-liter Car-rera engine. The bore was 100 mm and the stroke 76.4 mm for 3,600 cc. The horsepower was 250 at 6,100 rpm with peak torque of 228 ft-lb at 4,800 rpm. This was the first 911 street car engine to use twin-spark-plug ignition. The twin plugs allowed it to run a higher com-pression ratio of 11.3:1, which improved emissions and gave it a power improve-ment of 2 to 3 percent plus a 3 percent reduction in fuel consumption. The idle-running and part-throttle performance was improved by approximately 20 per-cent, and the fuel consumption of the cold engine was improved by approxi-mately 20 percent. The addition of the second plug reduced the spark travel by about 17 percent and reduced the com-pression sensitivity by about one com-pression point.

There was a new, very-high-quality, larger oil pump for the 911's dry sump system, with a magnesium alloy casting with the shafts running in bearings. The pressure pump delivers 65 liters of oil

The 1974 Carrera RSR Turbo 2.1 engine. This is an early version of the Type 911/76 RSR Turbo engine, which still used the 226-mm vertical cooling fan that had been the standard for 911 racing engines up until this engine. The flat fan that was used on the later engines provided more even cooling to the hotter-running turbocharged engine. Porsche AG

The 1976 936 engine Type 911/78. This engine was essentially the same engine as the 911/76 that had been used in the Carrera RSR Turbo 2.1, but with all of the accessories turned around to facilitate the mid-engined position in the 936. Porsche AG

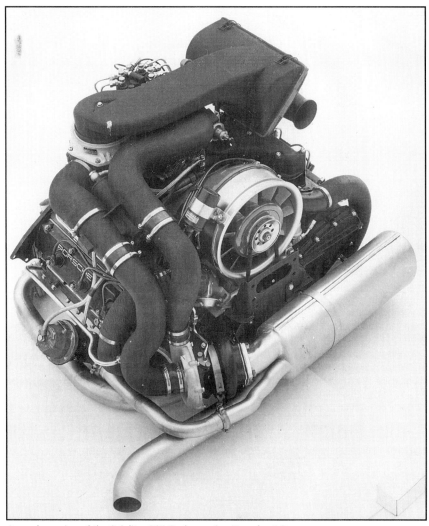

An early version of the 3.0-liter 911 Turbo engine. Porsche AG

A customer engine for the 935/77, engine Type 930/72, with bubble-type water intercooler. Porsche AG

per minute, of which 17 liters is used for the squirters to cool the pistons. Around 35 liters is used to lubricate the main and connecting rod bearings. The oil flow routed to the camshaft housing was reduced by about 50 percent from the earlier engines to the 13 liters necessary to lubricate the camshaft bearings, valve guides, and rocker arms.

The scavenge pump has 1.84 times the capacity of the pressure pump to ensure a low oil level in the engine's crankcase. The full-flow oil filter remained in the scavenge circuit, but was relocated in front of the right rear wheel, as was the dry sump oil tank. The thermostat is also located in front of the right rear wheel and still operates at about 188 deg F. (87 deg C), diverting the hot oil to the front-mounted oil cooler. There was fan mounted on the front-mounted oil cooler that was also controlled by a thermostat that would turn the fan on at 212 deg F (110 deg C) to improve the oil cooling. There was no engine-mounted oil cooler on the 964 engine, and in place of the engine-mounted thermostat is a cover with sensors for oil temperature, the oil pressure gauge, and the idiot light sender.

The traditional two-stud mounting flange for the intake manifold was changed and three studs were used. The twin ignition was used to achieve the same improved combustion provided by the central position of the single plug in a four-valve engine. In addition to adding the second spark plug the heads had been changed by increasing the cooling surfaces by 17 percent and casting in a ceramic port liner in the exhaust port to reduce the heat transfer and improve the heat flow. The ceramic liner helps to keep the cylinder head cooler and keeps the exhaust temperatures reaching the catalytic converter higher, increasing the scrubbing effect of the converter. The ceramic liners reduce the temperature in the cylinder heads by approximately 104 deg F (40 deg C) in that portion of the cylinder head. The 964 engine used a metallic matrix catalytic converter that improved the cleansing action of the converter while greatly increasing the exhaust flow. The metallic matrix had also proven to be very reliable in long-life tests.

The twin ignition allowed the use of a symmetrical, pent roof-shaped piston, which also helped the combustion process. The high-tension distributor had a pair of six-plug caps and rotors. One of the rotors was driven directly from the crankshaft and the other by a cog belt from the first rotor.

The cylinders had a tapered bore that was smaller up near the combustion chamber than down by the crankcase. This allowed the piston/cylinder clearance to run nearly the same top to bottom when the engine was at operating temperature with a piston-to-cylinder clearance of less than 0.0016 inch (0.04 mm). The tight clearances improve combustion sealing and reduce the engine noise.

The chain tensioning was improved by replacing the previous six ramps and idler wheel with four long fiberglass-reinforced plastic guide ramps, two on each side of the engine. One of these ramps on each side is fixed, and the other is tightened by a tensioner that is built in and is integrated into the engine's oiling system. The result is a tensioning system that seems to be totally reliable and is also quieter. The driven gear on the engine's layshaft was changed from aluminum to steel for improved durability.

To facilitate the high compression ratio of the 964 engine, the engine management system used a knock sensor that retards the spark when engine knocking is sensed. The knock sensor consists of a bridge mounted to the three cylinders on each side of the engine. Each of these bridges is then tied to a knock sensor on each side of the engine. The new, adaptive Motronic engine management system could retard the ignition on only the cylinder that was knocking or detonating.

Induction was via a two-stage system consisting of two resonance chambers, each on top of three of the pipes from the cylinders on each side of the engine. These resonance chambers then connect to one another by a pair of cross pipes with a different cross section. The intake air from the throttle housing goes to the larger of the two cross pipes, while the smaller pipe is included or excluded from the circuit by a flapper valve, which is opened and closed by a mechanical system that is controlled relative to engine speed. By opening and closing the flapper valve, the resonances in the induction could be optimized over the rpm range, taking advantage of these resonance charges to help fill the cylinders with an intake charge.

The exhaust system was an enlarged interpretation of the type of exhaust system that had been used since 1975. This new system was around 15 percent larger in volume and had an additional final muffler.

The cylinder-head stud spacing was moved out an additional 4 mm for a

The 1977 IMSA version of the 934 engine, Type 930/73. This was an interesting engine in that it retained the 934 intercooler system, but it used the mechanical injection of the 935 engine. Note that it still uses only single ignition. Porsche AG

The 1978 Type 930/60 300-hp 3.3-liter 911 Turbo engine for the 930. Porsche AG

The 1978 Type 930/78 twin-turbo 935 engine with water intercooler. Porsche AG

Side view of the 1979 Type 930/79 big single-turbo 935.

total of 90-mm center-to-center distance. A redesigned crankcase through-bolt was used with an improved O-ring sealing system at each end. The cylinder air deflectors were changed to a pair of one-piece magnesium castings that bolt onto both sides of the crankcase. The piston squirters were increased in size to 2 mm for improved piston cooling. The cylinders were changed so they were sealed at the bottom with an O-ring that fits into a groove machined at the bottom of the cylinder. The alternator and fan were changed to different drives via a concentric shaft arrangement. The fan has a larger-diameter pulley and runs at a slower rate than the alternator, which has a smaller pulley. The drive pulleys mounted on the crankshaft were now a vibration damper. The front of the crankshaft was tapered to improve the mounting of the damper with its increased mass.

New, more-modern camshafts were used with very fast ramps and increased lift: the intake was 11.9 mm and the exhaust was 10.9 mm. The intake opened 4 deg BTDC and closed 56 deg ABDC, and the exhaust opened 45 deg BBDC and closed 5 deg ATDC. The rockers and rocker shafts remained the same. The valve covers were changed to magnesium with grooves for rubber O-ring-type gaskets to eliminate leaking. The valve cover stud size was reduced to 6 mm. The chain housings and covers were also made of a magnesium alloy, and their covers sealed with a rubber O-ring-type gasket as well. In addition to improving the sealing, the new rubber gaskets help to reduce the engine noise. They also incorporated engine under-trays to reduce the engine's reflected noise; unfortunately this also increased the engine-operating temperature by restricting the air flow.

The engine-cooling fan was a new design with an air delivery rate of 1,010 liters per second. The curved blades of this new fan were used to reduce noise emissions. The combination of the new rear spoiler used by all of the C2/4 cars in conjunction with this new fan provided adequate cooling with reduced noise output.

Flywheel Revamped for 1990

In 1990 Porsche modified the dual throttle-valve assembly so the small valve moved toward open first in order to improve the engine pick-up transition during part-throttle slow acceleration. The larger throttle valve did not start to open until the small valve was open approximately 5 deg.

The Tiptronic transmission was available for the C2 version of the 964. The Tiptronic was an automatic four-speed sport transmission. This transmission can be left in its fully automatic mode in the left shift gate or shifted manually by putting the shifter toward the right and out of D into the second selection gate. Then you can shift up by pushing the lever forward, or down by pushing the lever toward the rear.

The C2 and C4 cars with the manual five-speed transmission received the new dual-mass (or double mass) flywheel. The purpose of the dual-mass flywheels was to dampen out the vibrations from the engine that were causing the rattling noise in the transmission. The dual-mass flywheel took the rubber out of the clutch plate itself and put it in the flywheel. The dual-mass flywheel allowed angles of deflection of up to 30 deg (up slightly from the 29 deg permitted by the SC rubber-centered clutch disc), and down from the 44 to 47 deg deflection allowed by the much-larger rubber-centered clutch used by the Carrera and Turbo with the G50 transmission. In addition to the rubber element in the dual-mass flywheel, there are eight damping elements whose movements are additionally damped by silicone grease contained within the dual-mass flywheel unit.

During the 1990 model year the pistons were modified by the addition of a groove between the top ring and the second ring down. The purpose of this groove was to improve oil consumption and blow-by, a trick sometimes used in racing engines.

Cylinder-Head Leaking Addressed

The cars built in 1989 (K), 1990 (L), and 1991 (M) had the engines that are susceptible to a cylinder head-to-cylinder leaking problem. The early cars were those built up to 62 M 06836, M64.01 for the manual transmission cars and 62 M 52757, M64.02 for the Tiptronic cars. During the model year 1991, Porsche fitted its 964 engines with a modified cylinder and cylinder-head gasket or seal. The original 964 engines did not have a head gasket and there has been some oil leakage at the joint between the head and the cylinder. The way the original heads and cylinders were machined, there was a small gap left out at the edge where the head studs were. Distortion of the heads caused by the head torquing from the head studs was believed to be the source of this leak.

Actually only a small percentage of the cars had this leak, but while the cars

The 1980 Type 930/80 3.2 twin-turbo 935 engine with air-to-air intercooler.

The 1981 Type 930/81 3.2 twin-turbo 935 engine with air-to-air intercooler, Kugelfischer injection pump, and upside-down transmission.

The 1981 Type 930/81 3.2 twin-turbo 935 engine with faster fan drive for improved cooling.

The Type 935/72 1980 Indy engine. Porsche AG

were still under warranty, Porsche would update any cars found to be leaking. Leaking was defined as wet to the touch and not just showing signs of having leaked sometime in the past. The update was to change the pistons and cylinders to cylinders with a 32-mm-larger, 145-mm-diameter seating surface. Then the heads would not be distorted by the cylinder-head studs when the heads were torqued and expanded and contracted with heat. A seal ring was also placed in a slot around the cylinder bore. The original seal ring was made of pure graphite on an aluminum backing. Because of the larger flush mating surfaces, it was possible to change from Dilavar cylinder-head studs to steel studs. The later engines with wider head-contact surface and a head gasket seem to be much less likely to leak.

Also in 1991 the cylinder-base O-ring was changed from the original black silicon O-ring to a green Viton O-ring. The driven gear on the intermediate shaft was changed from steel to a gray cast-iron material. The cast-iron gear was supposed to reduce the noise from the intermediate shaft.

The aluminum intake manifold system was changed to one that was cast out of fiberglass-reinforced plastic to both improve the performance and save weight. The smoother interior surface improved the flow at high rpms. At the same time Porsche replaced the double-flap throttle-valve assembly with an aluminum single-flap throttle valve. The throttle valve was mounted on a plastic connecting pipe that was held in place by sleeves between the two intake manifold halves. The idle-speed stabilizer was also replaced with a modified unit that incorporated a muffler to reduce noise.

For 1991 a 911 Turbo was also available. The engine was a modified 3.3 Turbo engine like the Type 930/68 used in 1989. The output was 320 hp at 5,750 rpm with peak torque of 332 ft-lb at 4,500 rpm. Many features of the 964 engine were incorporated in this new C2 Turbo engine. The cast bosses on the crankcase extend out to where they fully support the base of the cylinder around the head studs. The crankcase through-bolts were similar in design to the 964 through-bolts with the improved O-ring seals. The same 2-mm piston squirters were used for piston cooling as with the 964 engine. The squirters opened at approximately 3-bar oil pressure. There were fins around the full circumference of the cylinders to provide better cooling. The seal between the crankcase and cylinder was made by the same type of O-ring as used by the 964 engine. The bosses around the cylinder-head studs extend to where they match up with the crankcase, providing better support for the cylinder around the head studs.

The cylinder heads had new inlet guides made of a material that they called "Aeterna." There was a stainless-steel ring inserted between the cylinder and the cylinder head at the sealing surface. This ring is silicon-coated for additional sealing, and the stainless seal reduces the heat flow from the cylinder head into the cylinder.

The left-hand camshaft remained unchanged, but the right one had an additional drive boss for the power steering pump. The timing was unchanged from the previous Turbo version. The camshaft housing had additional support for mounting the power steering pump. The camshaft idler arms and hydraulic tensioners were carried over from the previous Turbo.

The engine lubrication for the C2 Turbo engine was similar to the 964 engine. As with the 964 engine, there was no engine-mounted oil cooler; on the Turbo engine, Porsche mounted an oil filter console where the oil cooler had been mounted on the earlier engines. This meant that the oil filtering was no longer part of the scavenge circuit but instead was a full-flow filter in the oil pressure circuit. As with the C2/4 cars, the oil cooler is mounted in the front of the right-hand front wheel arch with a cooling fan. The original hole for the engine-mounted thermostat is blocked with a separate cover where the oil pressure senders (for both the guage and the idiot light) are mounted, as well as a separate oil temperature sender unit for the digital spark-control unit. Oiling for the cam housings was the same as with the previous Turbo engine, except the oil flow was restricted to the camshaft housing by a 2.3-mm orifice in the fitting for the banjo bolt in the cam housing.

The cooling fan and the alternator were driven by different belts in a manner similar to that of the 964. A V-belt was used to drive the fan. There was a roller fitted with a contact switch to monitor the belt drive for the fan. The alternator and air conditioning (AC) compressor were driven by a poly V-belt. Tension was adjusted by shifting the position of the AC compressor.

The exhaust system was similar to the system used on the previous Turbo with a catalytic converter and the addition of a final rear muffler on the right

The Type 935/76 956 engine for 1983. Porsche AG

The Type 959 engine. Porsche AG

side of the engine. The engine had two tailpipes, one from the final muffler and the other from the wastegate muffler.

The C2 Turbo engine used CIS injection similar to what had been used on the previous Turbo. The engine was fitted with an improved digital-electronic-ignition system. The ignition system is crank-fired and gets its pulse from the flywheel.

The engine performance of the C2 Turbo engine was improved to 320 hp from the 282 hp of the previous U.S. engine by the use of the less-restrictive metal matrix catalytic converter, the larger intercooler size, and the digital ignition with improved mapping for dwell and timing.

The C2 Turbo engine used a dual-mass flywheel of similar design to those used on the C2/4.

The normally aspirated 964 engines were unchanged for the 1992 model year. The U.S. oxygen sensor from model year 1991 was adopted worldwide for the 1991 Turbo.

The Indy engine converted to gasoline as Type 935/76 in a prototype 956 for Group C racing for the World Endurance Championship. Porsche AG

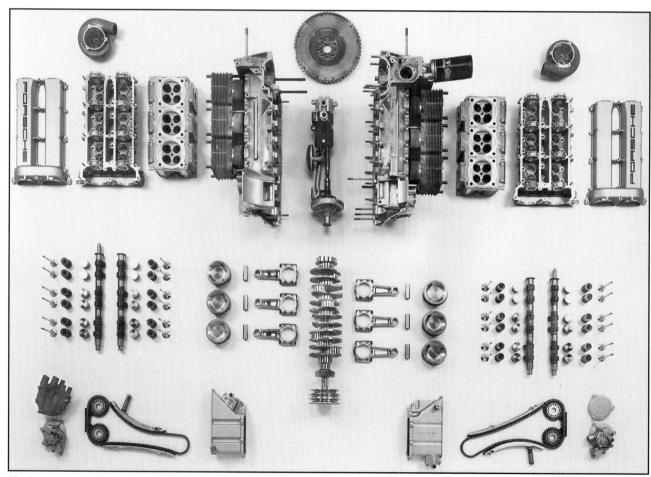

The Type 959 engine with its components laid out. Note three-stage scavenge oil pump with the standard pickup in the center, and additional pickup up front under the chain sprockets and the third pickup at the rear, near the pressure portion of the pump. Werkfoto

1992: 911 RS America Debuts

The 911 RS America was introduced in the spring of 1992, and the engine (M64/01) was the same standard 964 engine used in the C2/4 for the United States.

There was a 1992 model Carrera RS of the 964 with a special engine with power increased to 260 DIN hp. The Carrera RS engine had matched pistons and cylinders to enhance the power. The right camshaft was different on all but the touring version in that it had no drive for the power steering pump. The touring version used the standard 964 camshaft with drive for the power steering. Instead of the hydraulic motor mounts, rubber motor mounts were used for the RS version of the 964.

The basic-version 964 Carrera RS had a lightweight flywheel that was almost 15.5 lb (7 kg) lighter than the standard dual-mass flywheel at 29 lb (13.2 kg). The touring model retained the dual-mass flywheel. The fan drive was modified to be run by a single fan belt. The DME control unit was modified to provide more advance ignition timing to achieve the higher power output.

No engine changes were made for 1993. Starting with August 1992 Porsche started putting synthetic oil in all of its vehicles. The factory fill was Shell TMO synthetic engine oil, SAE 5W 40.

The dual-mass flywheels were introduced in 1990; the original Freudenberg dual-mass flywheel proved problematical in the 911 so it was replaced in May 1992 by the "LUK" dual-mass flywheel, which seems to be much more reliable. The flywheel change was made at engine number 62 N 01738. The N in the serial number stands for model year 1993. The original Freudenberg flywheel

The Porsche PFM 3200 aircraft engine. Porsche AG

was sprung rubber and was limited to 30 deg total travel; the LUK replacement was sprung by steel springs and had the travel limit increased to 50 deg

Porsche built Carrera RS 3.8 and Carrera RSR 3.8 versions of the 964 in 1993 for racing. The engines, type M64/04, had their bores increased to 102 mm for a total displacement of 3,746 cc. Porsche made new cylinder-head castings with larger 51.5-mm intake valves and 43.5-mm exhaust valves with new valve springs and retainers. These engines were able to develop 340 to 350 hp at Le Mans with the restrictors required there. (Each different race organization requires its own restrictor size.) The Carrera RS 3.8 street version produced 300 hp.

The engine used a new Motronic unit, the "Bosch 2.10," for engine management. This new unit had active knock regulation and further map optimization for improved power and fuel economy. A new resonance-tuned intake system was developed for the RS and RSR 3.8s with six individual throttle butterflies used in conjunction with sequential fuel injection.

1994: 3.6 Turbo Unveiled

For the 1994 model year Porsche offered the 3.6 Turbo as a replacement for the 1991 and 1992 C2 Turbo. To replace the 3.3 Turbo engine, Porsche built an engine that used many components based on the normally aspirated 964 engine with new pistons and camshafts, and the same CIS injection

The gear drive for the four-valve heads for the 956/962 engines.

The gear drive mounted on the crankcase for the four-valve heads for the 956/962 engines.

system optimized for the new 3.6-liter displacement Turbo. A modified version of the 964 crankshaft damper was also used. The bore size for the 100-mm cylinders were from the 964 and were Nikasil coated. They used the same viton cylinder-base O-ring. The boss for the knock sensor is not used for the 3.6 Turbo. Porsche continued to use the stainless-steel ring inserted in a groove at the top of the cylinder as a head gasket.

The cylinder heads for the 3.6 Turbo were adapted from the 964 engine with

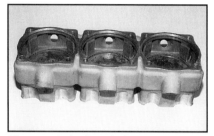

The water jacket for cylinders on the water-cooled engine with four-valve heads for the 962 engines.

the deletion on one of the spark plugs and the ceramic exhaust-port liner plus the addition of a threaded hole for secondary air injection. The intake valves were identical to the 3.3 Turbo valves, while the exhaust valves were increased to 42.5 mm and made of "P25" material. They were not sodium-filled. The rocker arms and rocker shafts were the same as the 3.3 Turbo. The 964 cylinder air deflectors were modified by the removal of the center section and used for the Turbo. New camshafts were made for the Turbo with 11.9-mm lift on the intake and 10.3-mm lift on the exhaust. The intake opened at 2 deg BTDC and closed at 54 deg ABDC; the exhaust opened at 43 deg BBDC and closed at 3 deg ATDC. The cam-housing castings are the same as on the 964 with the exception of the use of 8-mm studs for the exhaust valve covers. On the exhaust side the valve covers were the same Turbo valve covers used since 1980. The cam chain drive from the 964 naturally aspirated engine was used for the 3.6 Turbo.

The oiling remained essentially the same as for the C2 3.3 Turbo, with the

connection for the turbocharger lubrication provided by an additional connection to the left-hand tensioner connection. The fan belt and alternator AC belt arrangements were carried over from the 3.3 Turbo. The exhaust for the 3.6 Turbo is the same as for the 3.3 Turbo.

New 993 Engine

The 1994 993 M64/05 engine had many developments from the previous 964 engine plus increased power, easier maintenance, and improved fuel economy.

The crankshaft was made more substantial in the crank web area by making the crank cheeks or webs thicker; they were increased from 7.9 mm to 9.4 mm in thickness to increase the torsional stiffness. In doing this the weight of the crank increased by 2.2 lb to 33.95 lb (15.34 kg). The stiffer crankshaft eliminated the harmonic vibrations of the 964 crank so Porsche was able to do away with the crankshaft damper. The connecting rods were redesigned and reduced in weight. The lighter rods and the use of a belt pulley in place of the

Completed water-cooled four-valve 962 engine.

Jerry Woods timing cams on a water-cooled four-valve 962 engine.

964's crank damper made the total weight of the crankshaft assembly 1.8 lb (0.818 kg) lighter than the 964 crankshaft assembly.

The total weight of the 993 pistons was reduced by making the wall thickness thinner for the box-shaped piston-skirt area and by using a shorter wrist pin.

The 993 rocker arms have built-in hydraulic lash adjusters so it was no longer necessary to adjust the valves. In addition to reducing the required maintenance of the 911, the hydraulic valve adjusters also reduced exhaust gas emissions during the engine's warm-up running phase. The cam housings for the 993 engines were attached to the cylinder heads by cap-head screws instead of studs in the cylinder heads. The rocker shafts bolted onto the cam housing instead of being inserted in bores through the housing as they had before. The rocker shafts provided the oil supply for the rocker arms with their hydraulic valve lash adjusters. Oil was supplied to the rocker arms and to the hydraulic lifter via a peripheral groove on the front

camshaft bearing on the cam itself. The cams were new for the 993 engine with 12 mm of lift for the intake and 11 mm for the exhaust. The intake valve opened at 1 deg BTDC and closed 60 deg ABDC, and the exhaust opened 45 deg BBDC and closed 6 deg ATDC.

There were different rocker arms for both inlet and exhaust valves. These rockers with the hydraulic lash adjuster built in were lighter than the original rockers they replaced. The inlet rocker had an additional oil reservoir to ensure that it would not run out of oil. The cylinder heads for the U.S. cars had an auxiliary air port built into the cam housing and cylinder heads for emissions.

The engine oiling was essentially the same as it had been for the 964 engines with the exception of the addition of the full-flow filter in the pressure circuit similar to the one that had been used for the C2 Turbo and 3.6 Turbo. For the 993 engine, Porsche also retained the full-flow filter in the scavenge circuit. Porsche referred to the added filter in the pressure circuit as an auxiliary filter

to protect the hydraulic lash adjusters against contaminants in the oil. The recommended interval for replacement for both oil filters is 30,000 miles and the recommended oil change interval remained at 15,000 miles.

The engine management system was updated for the 993. The most significant of the changes was the replacement of the air-flow flapper valve for measuring air flow to the engine with a hot-film mass-air-flow sensor. Porsche continued to use the dual-resonance induction system to increase the performance of the 993 engine.

The exhaust flow was significantly improved for the first time since the original tuned system went away (the tuned, three-into-one header system, with heat exchangers, of the 1967–1974 911s). This new system also used three-into-one header systems, with heat exchangers, that dumped the exhaust into a common mixing chamber where the oxygen sensor was mounted, and then out toward each side to a pair of catalytic converters and

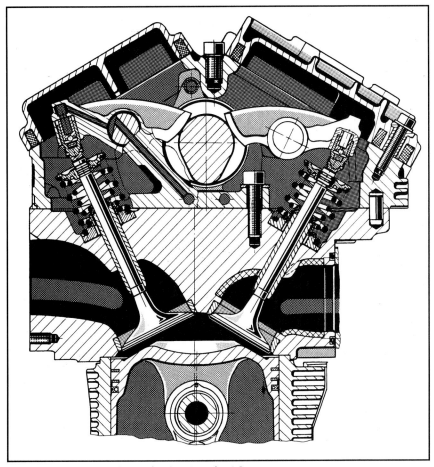

A drawing of the 993 valve mechanism. Porsche AG

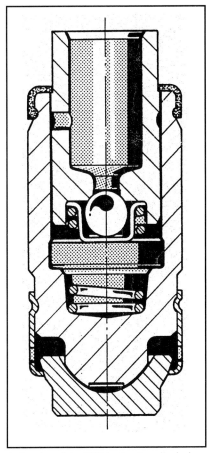

A drawing of the 993 hydraulic valve-lash adjuster. Porsche AG

The 993 rocker shaft (right) compared to traditional 911 rocker shaft (left). Joel Reiser

A comparison of a 993 rocker (left) to a traditional 911 rocker (right). Joel Reiser

A 993 Rocker with shaft. Joel Reiser

A 993 engine.

a pair of mufflers. The new, greatly improved exhaust system was responsible for most of the 22-hp increase from the 964 to the 993 engines. The power of the 1994–1995 993 engine was 272 hp at 6,100 rpm with peak torque of 243 ft-lb at 5,000 rpm.

There was also a Motor Kit 3.8 for the Porsche customers who wanted a little more performance from their 993. Porsche has decided to do a parallel program to its Exclusive Program, but for people who are interested in high performance. Based on the experience Porsche had with the Carrera RS 3.8 and RSR 3.8, it offered a motor kit for the

993 that gave increased performance while still meeting the strict European emissions codes that were due in 1996.

The motor kit consisted of: a set of 102-mm pistons and cylinders; different cylinder heads with larger 51.5-mm intake valves and 43.5-mm exhaust valves; different camshafts; and a Motronic control unit that was recalibrated to work with the kit and increase the rev limit to 6,900 rpm. This increased the displacement to 3,746 cc with a power increase of 10 percent to 299 DIN hp at 6,100 rpm and peak torque of 269 ft-lb at 5,250 rpm. The motor kit was only available for

the European market for the Type M64/05/06 engines.

1995: Varioram Induction Introduced

For 1995 there was a 911 Carrera RS with a 3.8-liter engine, Type M64/20. The RS engine differed from the regular engine in that it used 102-mm pistons and cylinders. The RS engine also used what Porsche called its Varioram induction system. This system combined the principles of ram-charge air tuning, or as Porsche called it, "vibrating tube intake system," with a resonating plenum system. Porsche used the ability to change the intake's tuned length to enhance the midrange power, and used the twin-resonance tuning to enhance the peak power of the engine. The peak power for this engine is 300 hp at 6,100 rpm with peak torque of 262 ft-lb at 5,400 rpm.

The ram tuning is like the older single-pipe ram-tuned intake systems such as the Weber carburetors and mechanical fuel injection. The resonance tuning is like what has been done with the CIS and the Carrera 3.2 with their single-stage resonance systems, and the 964 and the 993 with their two-stage resonance systems. The development of these induction systems has made it possible for the volumetric efficiency of the 911 engine to be greater than 1, meaning that the air inducted is greater than the cylinder volume.

The way it works is that each of the cylinders has its own ram-tuned induction pipe with what are effectively long, 18.7-inch (475 mm) intake stacks. Each of these pipes consists of two sections. One section is attached to the cylinder heads, and the other is attached to the rest of the intake manifold at two points. One of these points is at the end of the 18.7 inches, where it draws from one path through the intake and the throttle valve. The other point is halfway up the tuned stack where the connection is opened and closed by a vacuum-controlled sliding section. This sliding section connects the two halves of the tuned stack together, effectively doubling or halving the tuned intake length. Each of these vacuum-controlled sliding sections is controlled by diaphragm valves that are activated by vacuum from solenoid valves. At a certain rpm (5,160 rpm for the Carrera RS), and as long as the throttle is opened more than 50 deg, the engine management system opens the vacuum-controlled sliding section, which reduces the effective length by half to 9.44 inches (240 mm). When opened, the slides open into the large resonance-tuned intake plenum so that the engine can draw its air both from the original path plus a second path through the large resonance-intake plenum and throttle valve.

At first the system just uses the larger of the two resonance tubes, but with higher revs, the second resonance tube will be added to the volume. The resonance-induction optimizes the air flow to the short, tuned 9.44-inch ram-induction tubes. Then at 5,920 rpm, if the throttle valve is still more than 50 deg open, the tuning flap between the large and small resonance chambers is also opened and the air flows to both resonance chambers via all of the connecting pipes. The effect of all of this is to increase the power in the mid-rpm range and to increase peak power.

The Carrera RS engine also used new cylinder heads with larger 51.5-mm intake valves and 43-mm exhaust valves. Intake valve lift was increased to 12.5 mm and the exhaust lift to 11.1 mm. The intake valve opened at 5 deg BTDC and closed at 58 deg ABDC, while the exhaust valve opened at 50 deg BBDC and closed at 2 deg ATDC.

The crankcase had a 109-mm cylinder bore as compared to the normal 107-mm bore for the 964/993 engines. Porsche used what it called "profile seal rings" to seal the base of the cylinder to the crankcase. Whereas the standard 993 engines had an O-ring groove in the bottom of the cylinder where it mates to the crankcase, this O-ring seal fits a groove inside the crankcase spigot that seals with the portion that sticks down into the spigot bore.

The Clubsport version of the Carrera RS used a lightweight sports flywheel, and the basic version Carrera RS used the dual-mass flywheel. The pistons were grafal-coated. The grafal coating is ap-

A 1991–92 C2 3.3-liter Turbo engine. Porsche AG

A 1993 C2 3.6-liter Turbo engine. Porsche AG

plied by a silk-screen printing process and is 3 to 4 micromillimeters thick. The purpose of the coating is to reduce noise. The crankcase through-bolts used in the lower holes for bearing numbers 2, 3, 4, and 5 had large O-rings installed to prevent them from vibrating and reaching their resonance. The O-rings could not be used on the other through-bolts because the passageways for the bolts are also the main oil galleys.

The fan and the alternator are driven by one belt as they were with the previous Carrera RS, so the electric fan belt

monitoring system is not needed. Instead of the standard, hydraulic motor mounts, rubber mounts are used for the Carrera RS; these were the same as those used for the 964 Carrera RS.

1996 Twin Turbo

The Twin Turbo 911 C4 was introduced at the Geneva Auto show in March 1995 and marketed in the United States as a 1996 model year car. The engine, M64/60 was based on the 993 M64/05 normally aspirated engine. The complete crank drive assembly from the 993 engine was used with the connecting rods that were reinforced in the transition area between the big end and the rod beam. New grafal-coated pistons were used. This coating was silk-screened onto the piston skirts to help reduce piston slap noise caused by thrust loads. The pistons also have grooves forged into the top piston ring land to reduce the effect of combustion loads.

The cylinders were the same 100 mm size as the 993, but forged cylinders, rather than cast cylinders, were used. The forged cylinders offered the advantage of added strength; this was the first time forged cylinders were used for a production engine. They had been used in racing engines because of combustion sealing difficulties and problems caused by the severe rod angles of the long-stroke racing engines.

The intake ports were increased to 43 mm and the exhaust to 38 mm, and ceramic pot liners were used in the exhaust ports to reduce the cylinder head temperature. A spring-steel ring inserted into a groove in the top of the cylinder provided a seal for the cylinder head. The piston also traveled 5 mm farther into the combustion chamber to further reduce the combustion loads on the cylinders. (Extending the piston travel into the combustion chamber moves the point of extreme pressure away from the junction of the cylinder and cylinder head.) To improve cylinder head cooling, the fin area was made as large as possible and the cooling fins were made thinner to reduce air flow resistance. Smaller cylinder head nuts with a thinner cross section were used to further reduce any restriction to the cylinder head air flow. The cylinder head nuts also have a larger seating area to provide a more even pressure over a larger portion of the cylinder head.

The Turbo's valve mechanism is the same as the 993's, though a change to sodium-cooled exhaust valves improved cooling. The camshaft intake lift was changed to 11.6 mm and the exhaust lift was 10.5 mm. The intake opens 12 deg BTDC and closes 63 deg ABDC, and the exhaust opens 56 deg BBDC and closes 5 deg ATDC. The rockers and rocker shafts were unchanged.

Engine lubrication is the same as the 993 normally aspirated engine, and oil supply ports are provided from the left and right chain tensioners to supply oil to the turbochargers. A twin-stage oil pump was built into the air conditioning mount. It was driven by a gear on the end of the engine's layshaft; this twin-stage oil pump scavenges the oil from the turbochargers back to the oil tank.

The twin-turbo engine uses the same 245-mm, 11-blade cooling fan as the previous Turbo model. It's driven at a 1.8:1 ratio for an output of 1,210 liters per second at 6,100 rpm.

To reduce mass inertia two small turbochargers were used; each supplied a large, separate intercooler into a common intake plenum. The fuel needs and ignition timing and the electronic boost pressure control were all controlled by the M 5.2 version of the Motronic. This system was adaptive and operated over a wider ranger than the previous units.

The Twin Turbo had a completely revised exhaust system with a separate catalytic converter and muffler for each half of the motor. Each of the Turbos had vacuum-controlled wastegates. The engine used the new On Board Diagnostics

A C2 964 engine. Porsche AG

A C4 lightweight engine. Porsche AG

II (OBDII) system which required an oxygen sensor before and after each catalytic converter for a total of four sensors.

The Motronic system provided electronic control of boost pressure based on intake air mass. It has sequential injection, adaptive oxygen sensor regulation, adaptive knock control, adaptive boost charge control, and air mass metering with a hot-film mass air flow sensor.

Porsche also built the racing GT 2 car for worldwide GT racing in 1995. There was a GT 2 street car and the GT 2 race car. The twin-turbo engines for both were loosely based on the new twin-turbo 993, which had not yet been built when the GT 2 cars were introduced. The street version produced 430 hp and the racing version was rated at 450 hp with the appropriate 33.8-mm restrictors installed. With the larger restrictors allowed by IMSA, these original GT 2 engines produced around 550 hp. The GT 2 engine used turbochargers with built-in wastegates like the 993 street Turbo. The racing engine used the TAGtronic 3.8 engine management.

Later in 1995 there was a GT 2 Evolution version of the engine built to the Le Mans GT 1 regulations. With K27 Turbos and separate individual wastegates and larger 2x40.4-mm air-inlet restrictors, the power was increased to 600 hp.

1996 911 GT 1 Competition Engine

For the 1996 Le Mans race and subsequent sales to racing customers, Porsche developed a new 911-based GT 1 car for GT 1 racing. The 3.2-liter engine for the 911 GT1 is an adaptation of tried-and-true technology. Porsche used full water-cooling as it had with the 962 engines. However, instead of six individual heads like all of the 911 engines and the 962 engines used, the 911 GT1 engine uses the two one-piece, three-cylinder head castings from the 959 engine.

A Carrera RS 3.8-liter engine. Porsche AG

The cylinders were electron-beam welded to the cylinder heads for the 962, and then the cylinders were enclosed in a water jacket. For the 911 GT1 engine with the 959 cylinder heads, Porsche used individual cylinders housed inside the water jacket like those used on the 962 engines.

The 911 GT1 camshafts were chain driven like the 959 instead of the gear driven dual-overhead camshafts, as had been used in the 962 engines. The engines are limited by a pair of 35.7 mm restrictors to about 600 horsepower. The engine uses TAGtronic 3.8 electronic engine management with multipoint, sequential fuel injection with Lambda control and cylinder selective knock control.

Mid-1990s: Sound Levels Addressed

For 1995 and 1996 models Porsche had a sound option available for the 993. This was option 159, which changed the final mufflers and the intake housing. The final mufflers did less quieting and had large chrome tips on the tailpipes. The induction system had some added holes in the air cleaner cover and a chrome inlet tip. The idea was to increase the sounds of the engine inside the car to make it seem more sporty. No power increase was claimed for this modification and it was legal in all 50 states in the United States.

The 1996 version of the 993 engine also incorporated the Varioram induction system as had been used on the Carrera RS in 1995. The Varioram works just as it did with the 1995 Carrera RS, except that the switching speeds were changed for the 993. It ran on ram air up until 4,840 rpm, when the vacuum-controlled sliding section opened so the engine was run-

A Carrera RSR 3.8-liter engine. Porsche AG

A 911S Turbo Le Mans GT.

A 1996 911 Bi-Turbo engine. Porsche AG

ning on the short stacks and the large resonance chamber. Then, at 5,840 rpm, the flapper valve between the large and small resonance chambers is opened so that the engine is running on the short stack and both of the resonance chambers. Finally, at 6,640 rpm, the flapper valve closes again so that the engine is running on the short ram stacks and the large resonance chamber.

The specific power output for the 1996 993 is greater than the output of the 2.7 Carrera RS. The 1996 993 with its 79 hp per liter is really getting back up to the same sort of higher specific outputs of the really high-performance 911 engines. The old 1969 2.0-liter 911S engines had 86.4 hp per liter, the 2.4 911S had 81.2 hp per liter, and the Carrera RS was actually less than the 993 with its 77.8 hp per liter.

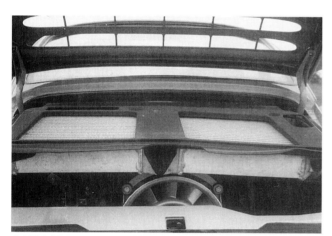

A 1995 GT 2 street engine. Porsche AG

A 1995 GT 2 race engine. Porsche AG

A 3.6-liter RS engine. Porsche AG

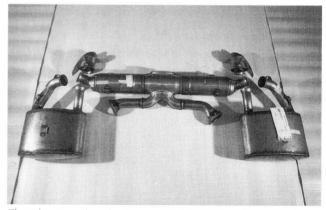

The exhaust used on the Carrera RSR 3.8 964 for a German series. Porsche AG

The exhaust used on the Carrera RSR 3.8 964 for a German series. Porsche AG

The 911 Carrera RS with its Varioram 3.8-liter engine did even better with its 80.08 hp per liter. This modern technology really is great; all of this and they drive better, get better gas mileage, and meet all of the world's stricter noise and emission requirements, too.

All of the things that Porsche has done over the years to quiet the noisy, air-cooled 911 have worked. One of the problems that Porsche has in trying to satisfy the noise restrictions of some countries it that all of the main noise sources, such as the engine itself, the engine fan, and the exhaust tailpipes, are located together in the back of the car. In spite of this, Porsche has been able to reduce the noise significantly from 84 dBa to 76 dBa with the 1996 993. They say that it would take five of today's 911s to make the same noise as one 911 that was made in 1966.

A GT 2 Evolution engine.

The exhaust used on the Carrera RSR 3.8-liter 964 for a German series. Porsche AG

A Carrera RS 3.8-liter engine. Porsche AG

Engine Type Summary

Type#	Year	Characteristics	Displacement bore x stroke in mm	valve size in mm	port size in mm	valve timing in degrees	Compression Power in DIN horsepower	peak torque
901/01	1965	911, Solex carbs	80x66,1991cc	I 39,E 35	I 32 , E 32	In opens 29 BTDC In closes 39 ABDC Ex opens 39 BBDC Ex closes 19 ATDC	9.0:1 130 hp @ 6100rpm	128 lb/ft @ 4200rpm
901/02	67/68	911S Weber carbs	80x66,1991cc	I 42, E 38	I 36 ,E 35	In opens 38 BTDC In closes 50 ABTD Ex opens 40 BBDC Ex closes 20 ATDC	9.8:1 160 hp @ 6600rpm	132flb/ft @ 5200rpm
901/03	68/69	911T Weber carbs European version	80x66,1991cc	I 42, E 38	I 32 , E 32	In opens 15 BTDC In closes 29 ABDC Ex opens 41 BBDC Ex closes 5 ATDC	8.6:1 110 hp @ 5800rpm	116 lb/ft @ 4200rpm
901/05	66/67	911 Weber carbs	80x66,1991cc	I 39,E 35	I 32 , E 32	same as 901/01	9.0:1 130 hp @ 6100rpm	128 lb/ft @ 4200rpm
901/06	67/68	911, revised cams & heat exchangers	80x66,1991cc	I 39,E 35	I 32 , E 32	In opens 20 BTDC In closes 34 ABDC Ex opens 40 BBDC Ex closes 6 ATDC	9.0:1 130 hp @ 6100rpm	128 lb/ft @ 4200rpm
901/07	67/68	911 for sportomatic specs same as 901/06						
901/08	67/68	911S for sportromatic specs same as 901/02						
901/09	69	911E mechanical injection	80x66,1991cc	I 42, E 38	I 32 , E 32	In opens 29 BTDC In closes 39 ABDC Ex opens 39 BBDC Ex closes 19 ATDC	9.1:1 140 hp @ 6500rpm	129 lb/ft @ 4500rpm
901/10	69	911S mechanical injection	80x66,1991cc	I 45, E 39	I 36,E 33 or 35	same as 901/02	9.9:1 170 hp @ 6500rpm	134 lb/ft @ 5500rpm
901/11	69	911E for sportomatic specs same as 901/09						
901/13	68/69	911T for sportomatic specs same as 901/03						
901/14	68	911 USA emissions specs same as 901/06						
901/16	69	911T USA emissions specs same as 901/03						
901/17	68	911 USA emissions for sportomatic specs same as 901/06						
901/19	69	911T USA emissions for sportomatic specs same as 901/03						
901/20	65	906 racing engine Weber 46 IDA carbs	80x66,1991cc	I 45, E 39	I 38 , E 38	In opems 104 BTDC In closes 104 ABDC Ex opens 100 BBDC Ex closes 80 ATDC	10.3:1 210 hp @ 8000rpm	152 lb/ft @ 6200rpm
901/21	66/67	906E racing engine slide valve mechanical injection	80x66,1991cc	I 45, E 39	I 38 , E 38	same as 901/20	10.3:1 220 hp @ 8000rpm	152 lb/ft @ 6200rpm
901/22	67/68	911R racing engine Weber 46 IDA carbs	80x66,1991cc	I 45, E 39	I 38 , E 38	same as 901/20	10.3:1 220 hp @ 8000rpm	
901/23		911 racing engine mechainical injection	80x66,1991cc				210 hp	
901/24		911 racing engine mechainical injection	80x66,1991cc				180 hp	
901/25	70	914/6 racing engine weber 46 IDA carbs	80x66,1991cc	I 45, E 39	I 38 , E 38	same as 901/20	10.3:1 220 hp @ 8000rpm	152 lb/ft @ 6200rpm
901/26	70	914/6 rally engine Weber 40 IDS carbs	80x66,1991cc	I 42, E 38	I 32 , E 32	same as 901/02	9.9:1 180 hp @ 6800rpm	132 lb/ft @ 5200rpm
901/30	67/68	911 rally engine Weber 46 IDA carbs	80x66,1991cc	I 39,E 35	I 32 , E 32	same as 901/02	9.8:1 150 hp	
901/36	70-72	914/6 engine European version	80x66,1991cc	I 42, E 38	I 32 , E 32	same as 901/03	8.6:1 110 hp @ 5800rpm	116 lb/ft @ 4200rpm
901/37	70-72	914/6 engine for Sportomatic specs same as 901/36						
901/38	70-72	914/6 engine USA emissions	80x66,1991cc	I 42, E 38	I 32 , E 32	same as 901/03	8.6:1 110 hp @ 5800rpm	116 lb/ft @ 4200rpm
901/39	70-72	914/6 engine for Sportomatic specs same as a 901, 901/38						
911/01	70/71	2.2 911E engine mechanical	84x66,2195cc	I 46,E 40	I 32 , E 32	same as 901/09	9.1:1 155 hp @ 6200rpm	141 lb/ft @ 4500rpm
911/02	70/71	2.2 911S engine mechanical injection	84x66,2195cc	I 46,E 40	I 36 , E 35	same as 901/02	9.8:1 180 hp @ 6500rpm	147 lb/ft @ 5200rpm
911/03	70/71	2.2 911T engine Europe Zenith 40 TIN carbs	84x66,2195cc	I 46,E 40	I 32 , E 32	same as 901/03	8.6:1 125 hp @ 5800rpm	130 lb/ft @ 4200rpm
911/04	70/71	2.2 911E engine for Sportomatic specs same as 911/01						

Type #	Year	Characteristics	Displacement bore x stroke in mm	valve size in mm	port size in mm	valve timing in degrees	Compression Power in DIN horsepower	peak torque
911/06	70/71	2.2 911T engine for Sportomatic specs same as 911/03						
911/07	70/71	2.2 911T engine for USA emissions specs same as 911/03						
911/08	70/71	2.2 911T engine for USA version for Sportomatic specs same as 911/03						
911/20	70	911 racing engine fuel injection	85x66,2247cc	I 46,E 40	I 38 , E 38	same as 901/20	10.3:1 230 hp @ 7800rpm	170 lb/ft @ 6200rpm
911/21	71/72	911 racing engine fuel injection	87.5x66,2380cc	I 46,E 40	I 38 , E 38	same as 901/20	10.3:1 250 hp @ 7800rpm	188 lb/ft @ 6200rpm
911/22	71	911 racing engine Weber 46 IDA carbs	85x66,2247cc	I 46,E 40	I 38 , E 38	same as 901/20	10.3:1 230 hp @ 7800rpm	170 lb/ft @ 6200rpm
911/41	75	2.7 911 engine CIS injection	90x70.4,2687cc	I 46,E 40	I 32 , E 32	In opens 1 ATDC In closes 35 ABDC Ex opens 20 BBDC Ex closes 7 BTDC	8.0:1 150 hp @ 5700rpm	173 lb/ft @ 3800rpm
911/42	75	2.7 911S engine CIS injection	90x70.4,2687cc	I 46,E 40	I 35 , E 35	In opens 6 ATDC In closes 50 ABDC Ex opens 24 BBDC Ex closes 2 BTDC	8.5:1 175 hp @ 5800rpm	175 lb/ft @ 4000rpm
911/43	75	2.7 911S engine for USA (49 state emissions) specs same as 911/42 but with reduced power					8.5:1 165 hp @5800rpm	167 lb/ft @ 4000rpm
911/44	75	2.7 911S engine for California specs same as 911/42 but with reduced power				8.5:1 160 hp @ 5800rpm		162 lb/ft @ 4000rpm
911/46	75	911 engine for Sportomatic specs same as 911/41						
911/47	75	911S engine for Sportomatic specs same as 911/42						
911/48	75	2.7 911S engine for Sportomatic for USA (49 state emissions) specs same as 911/43						
911/49	75	2.7 911S engine for Sportomatic for California specs same as 911/44						
911/50	73	2.4 911S engine mechanical injection	84x70.4,2341cc	I 46,E 40	I 36 , E 36	same as 901/02	8.5:1 190 hp @ 6500rpm	158 lb/ft @ 4000rpm
911/51	72/73	2.4 911T-E for USA mechanical injection	84x70.4,2341cc	I 46,E 40	I 32 , E 32	In opens 16 BTDC In closes 30 ABDC Ex opens 42 BBDC Ex closes 4 BTDC	7.5:1 140 hp @ 5600rpm	148 lb/ft @ 4000rpm
911/52	72/73	2.4 911E engine mechanical injection	84x70.4,2341cc	I 46,E 40	I 32 , E 32	In opens 18 BTDC In closes 36 ABDC Ex opens 38 BBDC Ex closes 8 ATDC	8.0:1 165 hp @ 6200rpm	151 lb/ft @ 4500rpm
911/53	72/73	2.4 911S engine mechanical injection	84x70.4,2341cc	I 46,E 40	I 36 , E 36	same as 901/02	8.5:1 190 hp @ 6500rpm	158 lb/ft @ 4000rpm
911/56	72	916 engine specs same as 911/53 with different exhaust and fittings for installation in the 916						
911/57	72/73	2.4 911T-V Europe Zenith 40 TIN carbs	84x70.4,2341cc	I 46,E 40	I&E 30or32	same as 911/51	7.5:1 130 hp @ 5600rpm	144 lb/ft @ 4000rpm
911/58		2.4 914/6 engine developed but never used	84x70.4,2341cc	I 46,E 40	I 32 , E 32	same as 911/51	7.5:1 130 hp @ 5600rpm	144 lb/ft @ 4000rpm
911/61	72/73	2.4 911T-E USA for Sportomatic specs same as 911/51						
911/62	72/73	2.4 911E for Sportomatic specs same as 911/52						
911/63	72/73	2.4 911S for Sportomatic specs same as 911/53						
911/67	72/73	2.4 911T-V Euro for Sportomatic specs same as 911/57						
911/70	71	911 racing engine mechanical injection	86.7x70.4,2492	I 46,E 40	I 41 , E 41	same as 901/20	10.3:1 270 hp @ 8000rpm	191.6 lb/ft @ 5300r
911/72	72	911 RSR racing engine mechanical injection	92x70.4,2808cc	I 49, E 41.5	I 43 , E 43	same as 901/20	10.3:1 308 hp @ 8000rpm	217 lb/ft @ 6200rpm
911/73	72	911 racing engine mechanical injection	89x66,2464cc	I 46, E 40	I 41 , E 41	same as 901/20	10.3:1 275 hp @ 8000rpm	
911/74	73	3.0 RSR racing engine mechanical injection	95x70.4,2994cc	I49,E 41.5	I 43 , E 43	same timing as 901/20 greater lift	10.3:1 315 hp @ 8000rpm	231 lb/ft @ 6500rpm,
911/75	74	3.0 RSR racing engine slide valve mechanical injection	95x70.4,2994cc	I49,E 41.5	I 43 , E 43	same as 911/74	10.3:1 130 hp @ 8000rpm	231 lb/ft @ 6500rpm,
911/76	74	2.1 Carrera RSR Turbo engine	83x66, 2143cc	I 47,E40.5	I 43 , E 43	In opens 80 BTDC In closes 100ABDC Ex opens 105 BBDC Ex closes 75 ATDC	6.5:1 480 hp @ 8000rpm (@1.4 bar boost,20 PSI)	340 lb/ft @ 5900rpm,
911/77	73/74	3.0 Carrera RS engine mechanical injection	95x70.4,2994cc	I 49, E 41.5		same as 901/02	9.8:1 230 hp @ 6200rpm	203 lb/ft @ 5000rpm

Type #	Year	Characteristics	Displacement bore x stroke in mm	valve size in mm	port size in mm	valve timing in degrees	Compression Power in DIN horsepower	peak torque
911/78	76/77	2.1 trurbocharged 936 engine	83x66, 2143cc	I 47,E40.5	I 43 , E 43	same as 911/76	6.5:1 540 hp @ 8000rpm (@1.4 bar boost,20 psi)	362 lb/ft @6000rpm
911/79	77	Baby 935 engine	71x60, 1425cc				6.5:1 370 hp @ 8000rpm (@1.4 bar boost,20 PSI)	
911/81	76/77	2.7 911 engine for rest of world	90x70.4,2687cc	I 46, E 40	I 35 , E 35	same as 911/42	8.5:1 165 hp @ 5800rpm	176 lb/ft @ 4000rpm,
911/82	76	2.7 911S USA 49 state CIS fuel injection	90x70.4,2687cc	I 46, E 40	I 35 , E 35	same as 911/42	8.5:1 165 hp @ 5800rpm	176 lb/ft @ 4000rpm,
911/83	73/75	2.7 Carrera RS engine mechanical injection	90x70.4,2687cc	I 46, E 40	I 36 , E 35	samd as 901/02	8.5:1 210 hp @ 6300rpm	188.4lb/ft @5100rpm
911/84	76	2.7 911S California	90x70.4,2687cc	I 46, E 40	I 35 , E 35	same as 911/42	8.5:1 165 hp @ 5800rpm	176 lb/ft @ 4000rpm,
911/85	77	2.7 911S USA 50 state engine	90x70.4,2687cc	I 46, E 40	I 35 , E 35	same as 911/42	8.5:1 165 hp @ 5800rpm	176 lb/ft @ 4000rpm,
911/86	76/77	2.7 911 engine for the rest of the world for S portomatic same specs as 911/81						
911/89	76	2.7 911 engine for California for Sportomatic same specs as 911/84						
911/90	77	2.7 911 engine for USA for Sportomatic specs same as 911/85						
911/91	73	2.4 911T-K USA 50 state engine K= K-Injection or CIS	84x70.4,2341cc	I 46, E 40	I 30 , E 33	In opens 0 at TDC In closes 32 ABDCV Ex opens 30 BBDC EX closes 10 BTDC	8.0:1 140 hp @ 5700rpm	148.5lb/ft @4000rpm
911/92	74	2.4 911 USA 50 state engine CIS injection, and for Rest of World	90x70.4,2687cc	I 46, E 40	I 30/32 , E 32/33	same as 911/41	8.0:1 150 hp @ 5700rpm	175 lb/ft @ 3800rpm
911/93	74	2.7 911S and Carrera USA 50 state engine CIS fuel injection and for Rest of World	90x70.4,2687cc	I 46, E 40	I 35 , E 35	same as 911/42	8.5:1 175 hp @ 5800rpm	167 lb/ft @ 4000rpm
911/94	77	2.7 911S engine Japan	90x70.4,2687cc	I 46, E 40	I 35 , E 35	same as 911/42	8.5:1 165 hp @ 5800rpm	176 lb/ft @ 4000rpm
911/96	73	2.4 911T-K USA 50 state engine for Sportomatic specs same as 911/91						
911/97	74	2.7 911 USA 50 state engine for Sportomatic specs aame as 911/92						
911/98	74	2.7 911S and Carrera USA 50 s state engine for Sportomatic specs same as 911/93	911/93					
911/99	77	2.7 911S engine Japan for Sportomatic specs same as 911/94						
916	68	2.0 twin overhead cam racing engine mechanical injection	80x66, 1991cc	I 46, E 40		In opens 104 BTDC In closes 104ABDC Ex opens 105 BBDC Ex closes 75 ATDC	10.3:1 230 hp @ 9000rpm	152 lb/ft @ 6800rpm
930/02	76/77	3.0 Carrera engine CIS fuel injection for rest of world	95x70.4,2994cc	I 49, E 41.5	I 39 , E 35	In opens 1 BTDC In closes 53 ABDC Ex opens 43 BBDC Ex closes 3 ATDC	8.5:1 200 hp @ 6000rpm	188 lb/ft @ 4200rpm
930/03	78/79	3.0 911SC engine rest of World	95x70.4,2994cc	I 49, E 41.5	I 39 , E 35	In opens 7 BTDC In closes 47 ABDC Ex opens 49 BBDC Ex closes 3 BTDC	8.5:1 180 hp @ 5500 rpm	165 lb/ft @ 4200rpm
930/04	78/79	3.0 911 SC engine USA 49 state	95x70.4,2994cc	I 49, E 41.5	I 39 , E 35	same as 930/02	8.5:1 180 hp @ 5500 rpm	175 lb/ft @ 4200rpm
930/05	78/79	3.0 911 SC engine Jajan	95x70.4,2994cc	I 49, E 41.5	I 39 , E 35	same as 930/02	8.5:1 180 hp @ 5500 rpm	175 lb/ft @ 4200rpm
930/06	78/79	3.0 911 SC engine California	95x70.4,2994cc	I 49, E 41.5	I 39 , E 35	same as 930/02	8.5:1 180 hp @ 5500 rpm	175 lb/ft @ 4200rpm
930/07	80	3.0 911 SC engine USA	95x70.4,2994cc	I 49, E 41.5	I 34 , E 35	same as 930/03	9.3:1 180 hp @ 5500 rpm	175 lb/ft @ 4200rpm
930/08	80	3.0 911 SC Japan	95x70.4,2994cc	I 49, E 41.5	I 34 , E 35	same as 930/03	9.3:1 180 hp @ 5500 rpm	175 lb/ft @ 4200rpm
930/09	80	3.0 911 SC rest of world	95x70.4,2994cc	I 49mm, E 41.5	I 34 , E 35	same as 930/03	8.6:1 188 hp @ 5500rpm 175 lb/ft @ 4200rpm	
930/10	81-83	3.0 911 SC rest of world	95x70.4,2994cc	I 49mm, E 41.5	I 34 , E 35	same as 930/02 189 lb/ft @ 4200rpm	9.8:1 204 hp @ 5900rpm	
930/12	76/77	3.0 Carrera for rest of world for Sportomatic specs same as 930/02						
930/13	78/79	3.0 911SC for rest of world for Sportomatic specs same as 930/03						
930/14	78	3.0 911SC for USA for Sportomatic specs same as 930/04						
930/15	78/79	3.0 911 SC Japan for Sportomatic specs same as 930/05						
930/16	81-83	3.0 911 SC engine USA	95x70.4,2994cc	I 49, E 41.5	I 34 , E 35	same as 930/02	9.3:1 180 hp @ 5500 rpm	175 lb/ft @ 4200rpm
930/17	81-83	3.0 911 SC engine Japan	95x70.4,2994cc	I 49, E 41.5	I 34 , E 35	same as 930/03	9.3:1 180 hp @ 5500 rpm	175 lb/ft @ 4200rpm
930/18	83	3.0 911 SC RS engines Kugelfischer mechanical injection	95x70.4,2994cc	I 49, E 41.5	I 43 , E 43	In opens 82 BTDC In closes 82 ABDC Ex opens 78 BBDC Ex closes 58 ATDC	10.3:1 255 hp @ 7000rpm	184 lb/ft @ 6500rpm
930/19	80	3.0 911 SC rest of world for Sportomatic specs same as 930/09						

Type#	Year	Characteristics	Displacement bore x stroke in mm	valve size in mm	port size in mm	valve timing in degrees	Compression Power in DIN horsepower	peak torque
930/20	84-86	3.2 911 Carrera engine rest of world	95x74.4,3164cc	I 49, E 41.5	I 40 , E 38	In opens 4 BTDC In closes 50 ABDC Ex opens 46 BBDC Ex closes 0 TDC	10.3:1 231 hp @ 5900rpm	209 lb/ft @ 4800rpm
930/21	84-86	3.2 911 Carrera USA	95x74.4,3164cc	I 49, E 41.5	I 40 , E 38	same as 930/20	9.5:1 207 hp @ 5900rpm	192 lb/ft @ 4800rpm
930/25	87-89	3.2 911 Carrera USA	95x74.4,3164cc	I 49, E 41.5	I 40 , E 38	same as 930/20	9.5:1 217 hp @ 5900rpm	195 lb/ft @ 4800rpm
930/26	87-89	3.2 911 Sweden	95x74.4,3164cc	I 49, E 41.5	I 40 , E 38	same as 930/20	9.5:1 231 hp @ 5900rpm	209 lb/ft @ 4800rpm
930/50	75/76	3.0 Turbo rest of world	95x70.4,2994cc	I 49, E 41.5	I 32 , E 36	In opens 3 ATDC In closes 27 ABDC Ex opens 29 BBDC Ex closes 3 BPDC	6.5:1 260 hp @ 5900rpm	253 lb/ft @ 4000rpm
930/51	76	3.0 Turbo USA engine	95x70.4,2994cc	I 49, E 41.5	I 32 , E 36	same as 930/50	6.5:1 245 hp @ 5500rpm	253 lb/ft @ 4000rpm
930/52	77	3.0 Turbo for rest of world	95x70.4,2994cc	I 49, E 41.5	I 32 , E 36	same as 930/50	6.5:1 260 hp @ 5500rpm	253 lb/ft @ 4000rpm
930/53	77	3.0 Turbo USA engine	95x70.4,2994cc	I 49, E 41.5	I 32 , E 36	same as 930/50	6.5:1 245 hp @ 5500rpm	253 lb/ft @ 4000rpm
930/54	77	3.0 Turbo Japan	95x70.4,2994cc	I 49, E 41.5	I 32 , E 36	same as 930/50	6.5:1 245 hp @ 5500rpm	253 lb/ft @ 4000rpm
930/60	78-82	3.3 Turbo for rest of world	97x74.4,3299cc	I 49, E 41.5	I 32 , E 34	same as 930/50	7.0:1 300 hp @ 5500rpm	304 lb/ft @ 4000rpm
930/61	78/79	3.3 Turbo USA 49 state engine	97x74.4,3299cc	I 49, E 41.5	I 32 , E 34	same as 930/50	7.0:1 265 hp @ 5500rpm	291 lb/ft @ 4000rpm
930/62	78/79	3.3 Turbo Japan	97x74.4,3299cc	I 49, E 41.5	I 32 , E 34	same as 930/50	7.0:1 265 hp @ 5500rpm	291 lb/ft @ 4000rpm
930/63	78/79	3.3 Turbo California	97x74.4,3299cc	I 49, E 41.5	I 32 , E 34	same as 930/50	7.0:1 265 hp @ 5500rpm	291 lb/ft @ 4000rpm
930/64	80-82	3.3 Turbo USA	97x74.4,3299cc	I 49, E 41.5	I 32 , E 34	same as 930/50	7.0:1 265 hp @ 5500rpm	291 lb/ft @ 4000rpm
930/65	80-82	3.3 Turbo Japan	97x74.4,3299cc	I 49, E 41.5	I 32 , E 34	same as 930/50	7.0:1 265 hp @ 5500rpm	291 lb/ft @ 4000rpm
930/66	83-86	3.3 Turbo for rest of world	97x74.4,3299cc	I 49, E 41.5	I 32 , E 34	same as 930/50	7.0:1 300 hp @ 5500rpm	321 lb/ft @ 4000rpm
930/68	86-89	3.3 Turbo for USA	97x74.4,3299cc	I 49, E 41.5	I 32 , E 34	same as 930/50	7.0:1 282 hp @ 5500rpm	287 lb/ft @ 4000rpm
930/71	76	3.0 934 Turbo engine CIS fuel injection	95x70.4,2994cc	I 49, E 41.5	I 41 , E 41	In opens 54 BTDC In closes 90 ABDC Ex opens 95 BBDC Ex closes 49 ATDC	6.5:1 530 hp @ 7000rpm @ 1.35 bar boost	434 lb/ft @ 5400rpm
930/72	76/77	2.8 935 Turbo engine factory 935 version	92.8x70.4,2856	I 49, E 41.5	I 41 , E 41	same as 911/76	6.5:1 590 hp @ 7900rpm	438 lb/ft @ 5400rpm
930/72	77	3.0 935 Turbo engine customer 935 version	95x70.4,2994cc	I 49, E 41.5	I 41 , E 41	same as 911/76	6.5:1 630 hp @ 8000rpm @ 1.45 bar boost	
930/73	77	3.0 934/5 Turbo engine mechanical injection	95x70.4,2994cc	I 49, E 41.5	I 41 , E 41	same as 911/76	6.5:1 590 hp @ 7500rpm @ 1.45 bar boost	
930/76	77	3.0 935 Turbo engine	95x70.4,2994cc	I 49, E 41.5	I 41 , E 41	same as 911/76	6.5:1 630 hp @ 7900rpm @ 1.45 bar boost	
930/77	77	2.8 935 Turbo engine	92.8x70.4,2875	I 49, E 41.5	I 41 , E 41	same as 911/76	6.5:1 590 hp @ 7900rpm @ 1.4 bar boost	
930/78	78/79	3.0 935 Turbo engine	95x70.4,2994cc	I 49, E 41.5	I 41 , E 41	same as 911/76	6.5:1 720 hp @ 7800rpm @ 1.4 bar boost	
930/79	79	3.12 935 IMSA engine	97x70.4,3121cc	I 49, E 41.5	I 41 , E 41	same as 911/76	6.5:1 715 hp @ 7800rpm @ 1.4 bar boost	
930/80	80	3.2 935 Turbo engine	95x74.4,3164cc	I 49, E 41.5	I 41 , E 41	same as 911/76	7.2:1 740 hp @ 7800rpm @ 1.4 bar boost	
930/81	81	3.2 935 Turbo engine	95x74.4,3164cc	I 49, E 41.5	I 43 , E 41	same as 911/76	7.2:1 760 hp @ 7800rpm @ 1.4 bar boost	
935/71	78	3.2 935/78 turbo engine	95.7x74.4,3211	2x I35, E30.5			7.0:1 750 hp @ 8200rpm @ 1.4 bar boost	
935/72	80	Indy Turbo Engine electronic injection	92.3x66,2650cc	2x I35, E30.5			7.0:1 630 @ 9000rpm @ 1.03 bar boost	
935/73	78/79	2.1 936 Turbo engine mechanical injection	87x60,2140cc	2x I35, E29			7.0:1 580 @ 9000rpm @ 1.4 bar boost	
935/75	81	2.7 936 Turbo engine mechanical injection	92.3x66,2650cc	2x I35, E30.5			7.0:1 600 hp @ 8200rpm @ 1.4 bar boost	
935/76	82	2.7 956 Turbo engine mechanical injection	92.3x66,2650cc	2x I35, E30.5			7.5:1 620 hp @ 8200rpm @ 1.3 bar boost	
935/77	83	2.7 956 Turbo engine D-Motronic injection	92.3x66,2650cc	2x I35, E30.5			7.5:1 620 hp @ 8200rpm	
959/	86	959 group B engine D-Motronic injection	95x67, 2849cc	2x I35, I32			8.0:1 450 hp @ 6500rpm	369 lb/ft @ 5500rpm
962/70	84	2.8 962 engine	93x70.4,2869cc	I 49, E 41.5	I 43 , E 41	same as 911/76	7.5:1 650 hp @ 7800rpm	
962/71	85	3.2 962 engine	95x74.4,3164cc	I 49, E 41.5	I 43 , E 41	same as 911/76	7.5:1 700 hp @ 7800rpm	
M64/01	89-	Carrera USA/Rest of World Manual transmission	100x76.4,3600cc	I 49 , E 42.5	I 41.5 ,E 38	In opens 4 BTDC In closes 56 ABDC Ex opens 45 BBDC Ex closes 5 ATDC	11.3:1 250 hp @ 6100 rpm	228 lb/ft @ 4800 rpm
M64/02	89-	Carrera USA/Rest of World Tiptronic transmission	100x76.4,3600cc	I 49 , E 42.5	I 41.5 ,E 38	same as M64/01	11.3:1 250 hp @ 6100 rpm	228 lb/ft @ 4800 rpm
M64/03	91-92	911 Carrera RS	100x76.4,3600cc	I 49 , E 42.5	I 41.5 ,E 38	same as M64/01	11.3:1 260 hp @ 6100 rpm	339.5 lb/ft @4800 rpm
M64/05	94-95	Carrera Rest of World (993) Manual transmission	100x76.4,3600cc	I 49 , E 42.5	I 43 , E39	In opens 1 BTDC In closes 60 ABDC Ex opens 45 BTDC Ex closes 5 ATDC	11.3:1 272 hp @ 6100 rpm	243.2 lb/ft @5000 rpm
M64/	93-	Carrera RS 3.8	102x76.4, 3746				11.0:1, 300 hp @6500 rpm	265 lb/ft @5250 rpm
M64/04	93-	Carrera RSR 3.8	102x76.4, 3746	I 51.5 , E 43.5			11.3:1, 350 @6900 rpm	284 lb/ft @5500 rpm
M64/06	95-	Carrera USA (993) Manual transmission	100x76.4,3600cc	I 49 , E 42.5	I 43 , E39	same as M64/05	11.3:1 272 hp @ 6100 rpm	243.2 lb/ft @5000 rpm
M64/07	94-95	Carrera Rest of World (993)	100x76.4,3600cc	I 49 , E 42.5	I 43 , E39	same as M64/05	11.3:1 272 hp @ 6100 rpm	243.2 lb/ft @5000 rpm

Type#	Year	Characteristics	Displacement bore x stroke in mm	valve size in mm	port size in mm	valve timing in degrees	Compression Power in DIN horsepower	peak torque
M64/08	95-	Tiptronic transmission Carrera USA (993) Tiptronic transmission	100x76.4,3600cc	I 49 , E 42.5	I 43 , E39	same as M64/05	11.3:1 272 hp @ 6100 rpm	243.2 lb/ft @5000 rpm
M64/20	96-	911 Carrera RS	102x76.4, 3746	I 51.5 , E 43.5		In opens 5 BTDC In closes 58 ABDC Ex opens 50 BBDC Ex closes 2 ATDC	11.3:1, 300hp @6500 rpm	261 lb/ft @5400 rpm
M64/21	96-	Carrera Rest of World (993) Manual transmission	100x76.4,3600cc	I 50 , E 43.5	I 43 , E39	In opens 0° BTDC in closes 59 ABDC Ex opens 47 BTDC Ex closes 5 ATDC	11.3:1, 285 hp @6100 rpm	250 lb/ft @ 5250 rpm
M64/22	96-	Carrera Rest of World (993) Increased output for manual transmission	100x76.4,3600cc	I 50 , E 43.5	I 43 , E39	same as M64/20	11.3:1 300 hp @ 6500 rpm	261.6 @5400 rpm
M64/22	96-	Carrera Rest of World (993) Tiptronic Transmission	100x76.4,3600cc	I 49 , E 42.5	I 43 , E39	same as M64/21	11.3:1 285 hp @ 6100 rpm	250 lb/ft @5250 rpm
M64/23	96-	Carrera USA (993) Manual Transmission	100x76.4,3600cc	I 49 , E 42.5	I 43 , E39	same as M64/21	11.3:1 285 hp @ 6100 rpm	2450 lb/ft @5250 rpm
M64/24	96-	Carrera USA (993) Tiptronic Transmission	100x76.4,3600cc	I 49 , E 42.5	I 43 , E39	same as M64/21	11.3:1 285 hp @ 6100 rpm	250 lb/ft @5250 rpm
M30/69	91-92	3.3 Turbo C2	97x74.4, 3299cc	I 49, E 41.5	I 32 , E 36	In opens 3 ATDC In closes 37 ABDC Ex opens 27 BBDC Ex closes 5 BPDC	7:1 320 hp @ 5750rpm	332 lb/ft @ 4500rpm
M64/50	94-	3.6 Turbo C2	100x76.4,3600cc	I 49, E 42.5	I 38, E 32	In opens 2 ATDC In closes 54 ABDC Ex opens 43 BBDC Ex closes 3 ATDC	7.5:1, 360 hp @5500 rpm	383 lb/ft @ 4500 rpm
M64/60	95-	Turbo (993)	100x76.4,3600cc	I 49, E 42.5	I 43, E 38	In opens 12 BTDC In closes 63 ABDC Ex opens 56 BBDC Ex closes 5 ATDC	8.0:1, 408hp @5700 rpm	400 lb/ft @4500 rpm
M64/81	95-	911 GT 2	100x76.4,3600cc	I 49,E42.5			8.0:1, 450hp @5000 rpm	479 lb/ft@5000 rpm
M64/83	95-	911 GT 2 Evo	100x76.4,3600cc	—			600hp @ 7000 rpm	479 lb/ft 4000-6500 rpm

Chapter 4

Engine Rebuild Fundamentals

When a 911 engine has high mileage it will require some form of major maintenance. And when it does, the decision must be made to either perform a top-end overhaul or a complete overhaul. So what is the difference between these two types of overhauls? Why should one be done instead of the other? Or why should either be done?

Those are good questions with any engine. This is a complicated decision with any engine, especially for the 911 engine, which isn't just any engine. The 911 engine has gone from having the extremely long life of the reliable 2.0-liter engine to the much shorter life of the not-so-reliable 2.7 liter engine. Over the past decade 911 engines have again returned to long life with the extremely reliable 3.0-liter 911SC and 3.2 Carrera engines.

Because of this wide range of experiences the rebuilding advice will have to be quite different for the different versions of the 911 engine. For the 2.0-liter engines, 2.2-liter, and 2.4-liter engines, for instance, the advice would be quite different than for the 2.7 911 engines. For the 2.4 and smaller engines, probably the best thing to do is a top-end overhaul at 60,000 to 70,000 miles when the exhaust guides wear out. Then, after the top-end overhaul, drive the car for another 50,000 miles or so, as 120,000 to 130,000 miles seems to be a nice, safe life expectancy for these engines.

However, with the 2.7-liter engines there are other complications that will make it more difficult to decide just what to do. The problem with the 2.7-liter 911 engine is that the Porsche engines had gotten just a little too big for their britches, and there are a few things about this engine that just will not last an acceptable period of time.

Head Studs Merit Attention

Magnesium is a wonderful material in some applications, and in fact it served us well for our 911 engine crankcases for a number of years when the engine was smaller in displacement (2.0- to 2.4-liter). As the engine grew in size and the power was increased, the heat produced also increased. While magnesium has a good strength-to-

Here is an example of valve failure caused by worn valve guides. The valve guide wore to the point that there was no longer adequate valve cooling, and the valve failed.

This valve failure was caused by excessively worn valve guides. Note the carbon trails up the valve stem of the failed valve and several others from the set of six exhaust valves. Failure necessitated a complete overhaul of the engine and ruined one cylinder head and one piston and cylinder.

weight ratio, strength alone is not really one of its main attributes. The Nikasil and Alusil cylinders that were such a big advantage for the future of the 911 when they were introduced for the 2.7, were also unfortunately among the things that taxed the strength margins of the magnesium crankcase. The thermal expansion of the aluminum alloy cylinders and cylinder heads put a tremendous strain on the steel cylinder-head studs. Porsche tried to solve this problem by changing the cylinder-head studs to a material called Dilavar, which is a steel alloy with a thermal expansion rate similar to that of aluminum and magnesium alloys. Unfortunately Porsche's change to Dilavar head studs did not start until 1977, when Porsche changed the lower row of head studs to studs made of Dilavar material. The 2.7-liter engines with steel cylinder-head studs commonly have one or more of these cylinder-head studs "pull." When the head studs "pull," they actually pull the threads out of the magnesium crankcase.

This is an example of cylinder-head damage caused by pulled head studs. Some of the magnesium crankcases used for 911 engines from 1968 through 1977 would experience the problem of pulled cylinder-head studs, particularly the 2.7-liter engines made from 1974 through 1977.

A cylinder damaged by pulled head studs.

Possible Problem: Valve Guides

Another problem that had become more acute with 2.7 engines because of their larger size and higher power output was the copper alloy valve guides that Porsche continued to use until 1977, when they were finally changed to a silicone bronze alloy. With the larger-displacement 2.7-liter engines, the exhaust valve guides would wear out at 30,000 to 60,000 miles because of the extra heat. The 911 engines with the thermal reactors were, of course, the engines that had worn-out guides at 30,000. But it is not at all uncommon to see one of the normal 2.7 911 engines, with copper alloy guides, whose guides are worn out by the time the engine has 60,000 miles on it.

Just what, then, is a top-end overhaul? Well, it actually means a lot of different things to a lot of different people. If someone is selling a car it may mean any work that person may have had performed on the top end of the engine. For instance, it could mean the replacement of one burned exhaust valve to make the engine run on six cylinders again. But then again it could be a proper top-end overhaul. I feel that a proper top-end overhaul is one that reconditions or certifies serviceable pistons and cylinders, valves, and as much of the valve actuating mechanism as possible.

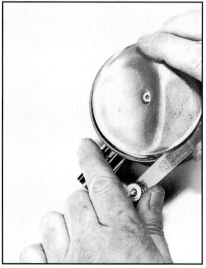

This is a look at checking top-ring side clearance, probably the most important piston measurement that can be made. Clearance should not exceed 0.004 inch. If the top-ring side clearance in the piston is excessive, the rings will break prematurely.

Loss of compression can be caused by a burned valve. Burned valves will usually have a pie-shaped notch burned out of them, as seen here. Generally speaking, the first indication of a burned valve will be rough running at idle and lower speeds that will smooth out as the engine speed is increased. In a 911 engine, a burned valve is most often caused by improper valve adjustment.

Overall low compression and excessive oil consumption can be caused by broken compression rings. Reringing is the most probable cause for the top piston ring to be broken. If a piston is reringed when the top ring groove has excessive clearance, the new ring with its better bite on the cylinder wall will beat up and down in the groove, making it even larger and finally breaking the ring.

Some mechanics will discourage top-end overhauls and instead recommend only a complete overhaul for an engine with top-end problems such as burned valves, low compression, high cylinder leakage, broken piston rings, or pulled head studs. However, a top-end overhaul is a legitimate solution for some specific engine problems under most conditions. The bottom end of the 911 engine has a safe life of at least 100,000 to 120,000 miles. Sometimes it is necessary to perform a top-end overhaul to give an engine the opportunity to last until it has enough mileage to require a complete overhaul. Any 911 engine with less than 60,000 to 70,000 miles that has top-end problems is a perfect candidate for a top-end overhaul. However, for engines with more than this mileage, top-end overhauls may be of questionable value since it is desirable to perform a complete overhaul on engines with 100,000 to 120,000 miles. If your engine has only a few miles to go before the complete overhaul, a top-end overhaul would be a waste of money. People planning to sell a car will often have a top-end overhaul performed when the engine has this kind of mileage on it so it will run well at the time of sale. Buyer beware!

With the 911 engine, the most common problem you are likely to have that would require a top-end overhaul is worn-out valves guides. This problem became more acute in the early to mid-1970s as, first, the engines became larger in displacement and then had to cope with the various emission-control devices. The basic problem was the soft copper valve guide material. When the engines were still 2.0 liters in displacement, they did not generate enough heat to cause excessive premature wear of these soft copper valve guides, so it took us quite a while to realize the extent of the problem. As the engine displacement became larger, the problem became more obvious.

The 2.0-liter engines wore out their exhaust guides as well, but usually not until the engines had at least 100,000 miles, so it was acceptable. When the engine size was increased to 2.2 and then 2.4 liters, the guides started to wear out at a lower mileage than was acceptable. When the displacement was increased to 2.7 liters, it was not at all uncommon for the guides to wear out at 50,000 to 60,000 miles. And finally, when the thermal reactors were used to help these engines meet emission laws in California in 1975 and 1976, then for all U.S. cars in 1977, it was not at all un-

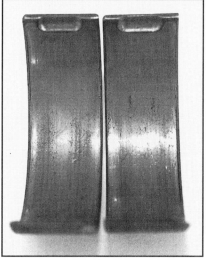

A connecting rod can be removed and the rod bearing can be inspected for wear and condition. I feel that a thorough inspection of all the top-end components should be performed any time the top end of a 911 engine is disassembled. These bearings show some wear but were holding up well.

These bearings show major wear, and in fact, the bearing on the right is "showing copper." If the car was driven much farther with bearings in this condition, the engine would fail.

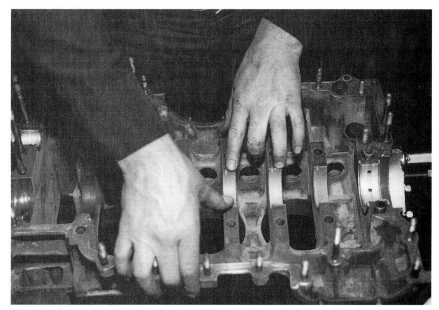

After the crankcase is cleaned and prepared, install the bearing inserts. Put a light coat of motor oil on each of the bearing surfaces.

common for the guides to be worn out at 30,000 miles.

Valve Guide Risk Underestimated

Worn valve guides can be a larger problem than most people realize, particularly in air-cooled 911 engines. All of the Porsche 911 engines up to the 964

have used sodium-cooled exhaust valves. Actually, the sodium cools the valves only inasmuch as it helps transfer heat from the valve head, down the valve stem to the valve guide, and into the cylinder head to be carried away in the airstream that flows past the fins on the cylinder head. For this heat transfer to work properly, the close proximity of the valve stem to the valve guide must be maintained so the heat can be transferred through the oil film between them as the stem slides up and down in the guide. Wear in the guide creates an air gap that acts like the air gap in a vacuum bottle, causing the heat to remain in the valve stem just below the head of the valve.

When the valves overheat, the metal is weakened, and the valve head can and will break off of the valve stem, allowing the head to fall into the combustion chamber. Unfortunately, there is not enough room in the combustion chamber for a loose valve head when the piston is at top dead center. I have seen several engines completely destroy themselves with this type of failure. I first became aware of how serious this problem was when I saw in one month two engines with exactly this problem. If the valve guides are ignored long enough, they can wear as much as 2-mm over size. I have seen valve guides so badly worn that there were black carbon trails all the way up the valve stem, and the valve spring and retainer were blackened with carbon with carbon trails from the engine combustion.

Other Top-End Problems

Other engine malfunctions that can necessitate a top-end overhaul are low compression, excessive oil consumption, or in the case of some magnesium crankcases used for some of the 911 engines (1968–1977), pulled cylinder-head studs. Compression loss or high cylinder leakage are usually caused by a burned valve, broken piston rings, or damaged pistons or cylinders. High oil consumption is usually caused by worn, broken, or sticking piston rings or worn cylinders.

Uneven cooling can cause the premature failure of one or two cylinders on an engine. I know of a 930 Turbo that required a top-end overhaul at an early mileage because rats had built a nest on top of one bank of cylinders, causing them to overheat. The overheating cylinders distorted and the rings lost their spring tension, causing both a loss of performance and excessive oil consumption. This was a Porsche with very low mileage, and initially the mechanic working on the car had difficulty diagnosing the source of the problem; that was until he found the dead baby rats. The rodents had gained access to the underside of the cooling shroud through the heater exhaust under the car. The heater works in this way: a flapper valve diverts the hot air into the car to warm its passengers or it exhausts the hot air under the car. So, with the heater in the "off" position, the flapper valves provide an open door to mice, rats, or other rodents into your engine cooling ducts.

Some mechanics advocate patching only the damage that necessitated the top-end overhaul. For example, if the problem is a burnt valve they will recommend replacing the burnt valve and reassembling the engine without inspecting the rest of the engine for any wear or damage. Once the top end of a 911 is torn down, it is easy to make a thorough inspection of the condition of all the top-end components. One of the cylinders of an air-cooled engine can be removed and the condition of both the piston and cylinder can be evaluated for condition. A connecting rod can be removed and the rod bearing inspected for wear and condition. I feel that a thorough inspection of all the top-end components should be performed anytime the top end of a 911 engine is disassembled. All of the components must be evaluated by someone with the experience to judge the engine's condition in its proper context, that is, considering the engine's mileage and its typical use. To put this in perspective, remember that

Assemble the connecting rods onto the crankshaft, and lightly oil the bearings with motor oil.

Torque the rod bolts. Use a mixture of motor oil and moly lube to ensure an even, accurate torquing. Remember, the 911 rod bolts are malleable, which means that they stretch, and they may only be torqued one time. You risk having them fail if you either reuse old bolts or for any reason retorque your new bolts.

while I said I would expect the bottom end on the 911 engine to last 100,000 to 120,000 miles, a high-revving racing 911 engine running in IMSA races would be expected to last something less than 40 hours before requiring a complete overhaul.

There are other conditions that can cause the top-end life to vary, such as cars that are driven infrequently. When the engine sits idle, the moisture and acids will corrode the engine's internal components. The only way to avoid this corrosion is to drive the car frequently so the engine heat will dry out the moisture. Frequent oil changes will also prolong the life of an engine that is not used as often as it should be. Regular operation also helps keep the rings free and will help avoid carbon buildup on the piston and combustion chamber. When an engine sits, the moisture will soften the carbon buildup and pieces of carbon can get caught between the valve and the valve seat, which can cause a burnt valve.

I have also seen an engine where all of the carbon mysteriously fell off of the piston and combustion chamber into a pile at the bottom of the cylinder and head. The carbon was piled up so thick that the engine would not turn over and acted like something mechanical was preventing its turning over. This type of problem would not occur in a normal in-line engine, but because the 911 is a flat, opposed engine, it could happen in the 911. The owner had the car towed into a repair shop because he could not get the engine to turn over and start. The mechanic assumed that the engine had a broken valve preventing its turning over. The mechanic could turn the engine over backwards until it would hit solid in the backward direction as well. He concluded that the problem must be mechanical and removed the cylinder heads only to find that the problem was just the carbon.

As with all Porsche maintenance work, the quality of the top-end overhaul work is vital. When you are looking at a used car that has had a top-end overhaul, ask to see the records and then check into the reputation of the Porsche repair shop that performed the maintenance work. Finally, call the repair shop that performed the work and ask the mechanics to review the records with you. Complete records of the work performed should be available, and they will let you feel more comfortable about your prospective purchase.

If you are considering having a top-end overhaul performed, make sure that you have the work done by a Porsche repair shop you feel you can trust. The top-end overhaul of a Porsche engine is not an inexpensive venture, so make sure you choose someone who has the experience and judgment to do proper, thorough, and complete maintenance on your Porsche. Many small Porsche repair shops perform excellent maintenance, but it is up to you to investigate and make sure that the repair shop you select will do the quality of work you expect and your Porsche 911 deserves. You may want to do the work yourself, but if you do so, please be sure that you take the time to learn enough about your 911 engine to ensure that you have the ability to do the job properly.

Choosing a Complete Overhaul

If you determine that your engine actually needs a complete overhaul instead of just a top-end overhaul, you should still be at least as careful in your selection of the repair shop that you

Install the oil pump and layshaft with chains in the crankcase half.

Install the assembled crankshaft in one crankcase half.

Check the layshaft gear clearance.

We prefer to use Dow Corning RTV 730 Fluorosilicone sealant for crankcase halves and cam housings. Put a small bead all around the crankcase. The Dow Corning RTV 730 is a one-part fluorosilicone Room Temperature Vulcanizing (RTV) silicone rubber. RTV cures from the exposure to moisture in the air.

Using the factory straps to hold up the chain and a couple of the connecting rods, assemble the other half of the crankcase.

have do the work. And if you decide that you want to do the work yourself, make sure that you know what you are doing. You should purchase both the factory workshop manuals and the Porsche technical specifications booklet for your specific 911 model. The factory workshop manuals are far from perfect, but they are vastly superior to any other manual you can buy. The manuals, like the car, have evolved over the years, and there are now five. The first manual (Porsche part number WKD 480 520) covers 1965 through 1971 and consists of two volumes. The second manual (part number WKD 481 021) consists of an additional four volumes and covers 1972 through 1983. This second manual is written as additional information to the first manual and relies on basic information and the tutorial information from the first manual. With the introduction of the Carrera in 1984, Porsche came out with an additional four-volume manual (part number WKD 482 020), which was written to cover the

1984–1989 911 Carreras. The fourth manual (part number WKD 482 520) consists of five volumes and covers the 1989–1994, 964 version of the 911. The fifth manual (part number WKD 482 121) consists of eight volumes and covers the latest 993 version of the 911. If you have a Turbo, there is also a specific manual for each version. Some of the aftermarket workshop manuals may seem to be written in an easier-to-use style; however, none of them are as complete or as accurate as the factory workshop manual.

Before you start your rebuild project, become thoroughly familiar with the organization and content of the engine section of the factory workshop manual. Read the engine section from beginning to end, supplements and all. Note any questions that you may have as you read through your manuals and resolve them before you proceed with the actual work.

As a do-it-yourself engine rebuilder your biggest problem will probably be in coordinating everything so that your overhaul will happen in a timely fashion. You will need to get everything organized and in order or your engine overhaul project can take forever. Make a list of all of the work that you are going to have to do, the work you will be sending out, and a list of all parts you are going to need.

Doing an Engine

Rebuild Yourself

Start your engine rebuild by removing and disassembling the engine. The condition of many components can be judged while you are taking the engine apart, so be sure to check and note the condition of all parts as you remove them; it will save you time later. Check for broken or damaged fasteners and studs, and check the rocker-arm shaft bores in the cam housing as you remove each shaft. Completely remove the bolts and taper cups from both ends of the rocker arm shafts before attempting to remove rocker shafts. Applying pressure to the shafts with the taper cups in place will expand the ends of the rocker shafts, making them very difficult to remove and damaging the cam housing.

Also you should only attempt to remove the rocker arms and shafts when the rocker is on the back, or heel, of the cam. Continue to rotate the engine as you are removing the rockers so that each one you remove is on the heel. If the cam housing rocker-arm shaft bores are damaged, your engine will leak oil when you put it back together. If you encounter an engine with damaged rocker-arm shaft bores in the cam housing, all is not lost. There were some special seals made for the 911 racing engines that can be used and may solve the oil leaking problem where the shafts are supposed to seal to the cam housing, if the housings aren't too badly damaged. The part number for the seal is 911.099.103.52.

Next, thoroughly clean all the engine components and check and measure the components for wear and condition. Compare your measurements with those in the Porsche spec book. The cylinder heads and crankcase are best cleaned in an aluminum-only type "hot tank," which will clean the grit, grime, and varnish deposits of age from your crankcase and heads more effectively than almost any other method. You must be careful when using a hot tank, however, since there are special hot tanks made for use with magnesium and aluminum alloys. Normal hot tanks for use with cast-iron engine blocks will melt the Porsche crankcase, so be careful when using hot tanks.

The hot tanks will soften, but not remove the carbon from the cylinder heads. The best way to finish cleaning the heads is with a walnut shell or glass bead blaster. These blasters are great for cleaning the carbon from cylinder heads, but should not be used on the crankcase because they can contaminate the oil passages in the crankcase. I prefer using the walnut shell blaster because it just cleans the aluminum surface without altering its finish, whereas the glass bead blasters will actually alter the metal's finish, much like a sand blaster would.

Now that you have cleaned and measured your parts, you can make your list of work that needs to be performed and parts that need to be ordered. On the following page is a work estimate sheet for a Porsche shop that regularly rebuilds Porsche engines. This estimate sheet should help you with a couple of things: first, if you wish, you can plug in your current local shop rates and generate your own estimate; the hourly labor rate used for the estimate is $70.00 and the sublets were priced at the going market rate at the time. Second, this worksheet will help you organize all of the operations necessary for rebuilding a 911 engine and will give you a list of parts needed for a rebuild.

Tending to the Crankshaft

Once you have made your list, you should plan to deal with the long-lead items first so everything will be ready when you are about to reassemble your engine.

Send the crankshaft and connecting rods out to someone you are sure you can trust to be magnaflux-inspected for cracks. If the crankshaft and connecting rods pass the crack test, you should have the crankshaft micropolished and the connecting rods reconditioned. I am not fond of regrinding Porsche 911 crank-

Install the crankcase through-bolts; remember, many of these through-bolt holes are main oil galleries for lubricating the engine's crankshaft, so it is important to seal up both ends. The sealing is done with the combination of the special washers with the internal chamfer, the O-rings at each end of the bolt, and the cap nut on the threaded end of the bolt. It is important to take care in installing these components, and particular attention should be paid to the O-rings at each end of the bolt to be sure they are seated properly. The O-rings should be lubricated with assembly lube or silicon compound to ensure that they seat properly and seal each end of the through-bolts.

With a torque wrench, tighten the crankcase through-bolts to the correct torque specifications.

Estimate Sheet

Work Needed	Time (est.) *(in hours)*	Price (est.)
R&R and rebuild engine	40.00	$2800.00
Magnaflux and polish crankshaft (sublet)		$70.00
Magnaflux and recondition rods (sublet)		$186.00
Regrind camshafts (sublet)		$350.00–500.00
Resurface and recondition rocker arms (sublet)		$325.00
Polish or replace rocker shafts	1.00	$70.00
Strip and paint sheet metal (sublet)		$420.00
Repair head studs	6.0	$420.00
Remove and replace head studs	2.25	$157.50
Install piston squirters on updates	5.8	$406.00
Modify oil bypass on oil pump updates	1.5	$105.00
Modify crankcase for layshaft bearings	2.6	$182.00
Install valve guides	2.5	$175.00
Grind valves	5.0	$350.00
Resurface cylinder heads	2.4	$168.00
Resurface flywheel	1.0	$70.00
Rebuild carburetors	6.0	$420.00
Remanufacture carburetor throttle bodies (sublet)		$500.00
Rebuild injection pump (sublet)		$700.00
Remanufacture FI throttle bodies (sublet)		$500.00
Clean crankcase and oil passages		$210.00
R&R and clean cam squirters		$150.00
Pressure-test oil cooler		$70.00
Check oil thermostat		70.00

Check List for Parts Needed

Motor oil
Gas
Paint
Sealant
Miscellaneous hardware
Complete gasket set, or gasket set (upper and lower)
Miscellaneous gaskets
Main bearings
#8 main bearing
Rod bearings
Layshaft bearings
Layshaft thrust bearings
Valve guides
Intake valves
Exhaust valves
Valve springs
Valve spring retainers
Valve spring keepers
Valve spring shims
Rocker arms
Rocker arm shafts
Elephant's feet valve adjusters
Upper valve covers
Lower valve covers
Cam drive chains
Black chain ramps (5)
Brown chain ramps (1)
Chain tensioners (early one not recommended)
Chain tensioners (1980-style) *or*
Left and right chain tensioner (1984-style)

Chain guards
Left idler arm (1980 and later)
Right idler arm (1980 and later)
Left cam-housing oil line
Right cam-housing oil line
Scavenge oil line
Supply oil line
Left camshaft (cylinders 1–3)
Right camshaft (cylinders 4–5)
Layshaft, complete
Layshaft sprockets, steel
Layshaft gear, aluminum
Pistons and cylinders
Cylinder heads
Dilavar head studs
Rod bolts
Rod nuts
Flywheel bolts
Oil pump
Oil cooler
Oil thermostat
Oil pressure switch
Oil gauge sender
Oil pump/layshaft lock tabs
Oil return tubes
Oil relief piston
Oil-pressure safety-valve piston
Fan belt
Air-conditioner belt
Smog-pump belt
Carburetors
Carburetor rebuild kits

FI pump belt
Injection pump pulley, upper
Injection pump pulley, lower
Injection preheat hose, rubber
Injection preheat hose, paper out
Injection preheat hose, paper in
Injector nozzles
Alternator
Alternator brushes
Spark plugs
Distributor
Distributor cap
Distributor rotor
Points
Condenser
Ignition coil
Spark plug wires
Spark plug connectors
Air filter
Oil filter
Smog-pump filter
Fuel filter
Miscellaneous gaskets
CV gaskets
Pressure plate
Driven disc
Throw-out bearing
Pilot bearing
Heater hoses (fresh air)
Heater hoses, orange
Any other forgotten parts

shafts. If your crankshaft is damaged and you feel it must be replaced or reground, try to replace the damaged crankshaft with a used crankshaft that is still in good condition. A good used crankshaft is better than a repaired damaged crankshaft.

Having said that, if you cannot find a good used crankshaft and you must have your crankshaft reground, there are people who can do a quality job. Carefully select a reliable, quality crankshaft grinder and have them repair, grind, and reharden your crankshaft. Most crank grinders now use a low-temperature gas nitriding process to reharden crankshafts. The original German Tenifer process and its U.S. equivalent Tufftriding are no longer used. In addition to environmental concerns (a molten cyanide salt bath was used in these processes), Tenifer and Tufftriding processes sometimes failed to harden the part properly.

Anytime a crankshaft has been ground, it is necessary to remove all of the plugs and properly clean it. Also, the nitriding process will damage the aluminum plugs, which will probably result in their falling out sometime after you put your engine back together. Have your machinist make new plugs to be used after you clean the crank.

If your crankshaft passed the magnaflux test and you had the journal surfaces micropolished, you must now thoroughly clean the crankshaft to remove any trapped dirt and grit. I don't

All magnesium crankcases should have Time-Certs installed the first time they are disassembled for any reason To install the head studs properly, measure from the crankcase's cylinder-base surface up 133–134mm (5 5/16 inches) to the top of the studs. These studs should be installed with high-strength red Loctite.

To remove and install these cylinder-head studs, either use one of these special collet-type removing tools or one of the threaded collet-type Snap On stud removers. These special stud-removal tools will prevent damaging the studs during removal or installation.

Install pistons onto connecting rods. The original pistons had a light press fit for the pin, so pistons had to be heated slightly to facilitate installation. The modern version of these pistons has a slight clearance so that the pins may be pressed in with a finger. It is a good idea to lay out all of the pistons, cylinders, wrist pins, and pin clips before you start assembly, to make sure that they are all there and that there are no extras. I have had the occasion to get all of the pistons assembled only to find that there was an extra wrist-pin clip, which meant that I had to remove all of the cylinders just to make sure that I hadn't left out a pin clip.

Lightly oil the piston rings and put a drop of oil on the piston skirt. Use your finger to spread that drop of oil around so that the same drop of oil is used to lubricate both the top and bottom piston skirts. I recommend aligning the rings so that the oil-ring gap is pointed straight up and the gaps for the two compression rings be spaced 120 deg apart. Use a quality ring compressor to ready each piston for installation in its cylinder.

Tap the cylinder over the compressed rings being sure to keep the cylinder square to the piston.

Cylinders installed on the engine. Note the cylinder holder screwed onto one stud for each cylinder. These are very handy to have because part of the process of installing all six pistons necessitates continually turning over the engine, which would cause the cylinders to go in and out with the pistons were it not for these cylinder holders.

Installing CE-style cylinder-head gaskets before installing cylinder heads.

Preparing oil-return tubes by lubricating O-rings with either grease or silicon paste. Dow Corning 111 compound works well here. The advantage of the silicon paste or grease over petroleum grease here is the fact that the silicon paste or grease will withstand very high temperatures and will not run off. The reason for lubricating these O-rings is so that they will reseal themselves anytime they have been disturbed by the thermal expansion of the engine. Do not use silicon sealer in this application. These O-rings, by design, must be free to move and work to do their job correctly.

recommend removing the plugs in the crankshaft to do this cleaning. I have seen more damage done by the improper replacement of these crankshaft oil passage plugs than I have seen caused by dirty crankshafts. I have, however, seen engines ruined within the first few hundred miles because they were put back together with dirt or polishing grit still in the crankshaft.

The best method of cleaning the oil passages is to use an aerosol-type carburetor cleaner with a long plastic nozzle. Thoroughly spray in each passage and then blow out with compressed air. Remember that the drillings in the crankshaft start from each end (number one and number eight main journal) and work their way toward the center, providing oil drillings for each connecting rod throw.

Connecting Rods, Heads, and More

Reconditioning of the connecting rods consists of: resizing of the big-end bores; installing new wrist pin bushings; boring the wrist pin bushing to re-establish the end-to-end length; and honing the pin bushing to size. All of the dimensions are critical, so this operation must be performed by a competent automotive machine shop. Specifications are given in the workshop manual and spec books. If any of the connecting rods require replacement, be sure to replace the damaged connecting rod with one from the correct weight group. Porsche recommends no derivation greater than 9 grams among the rod weights in an engine.

For the 911 you can usually match the rods up fairly well by weight into three pairs. Install the heaviest pair on cylinders 3 and 6, across from each other at the rear of the engine, the next-heaviest pair on cylinders 2 and 5, and the final (lightest) pair on cylinders 1 and 4. If the whole set of rods was originally balanced within factory specs, this sub-balancing will give the engine a nearly perfect balance.

You must also send your cylinder heads out to have the valves reground. Be prepared to have new valve guides installed, particularly the exhaust guides, because the exhaust valves are sodium-cooled and conduct more heat into their guides, resulting in greater guide wear. On high-mileage engines, the intake guides will also be worn and require replacement. Still, they should never be as worn as the exhaust guides; if they are, something strange is happening in your engine. Be sure the machine shop you have chosen knows how to install guides in 911 heads. The sizing is critical to a successful job. If the guides are improperly sized, they can fall out if too loose or crack the cylinder heads if too large.

Make sure that the machine shop doing your heads measures the valve stems for minimum size and taper. I recommend not letting the taper exceed .0005 inch (0.013 mm) over the valve stem length. The intake valves have softer stems and will often show more wear than the exhaust valves. If your valves are worn, replace them. Reusing them is like putting the engine back together with worn-out valve guides. Also, you should probably have your cylinder heads resurfaced so they will seal to the cylinder properly.

You're not done with the heads and valve mechanism yet. If your camshafts show any signs of wear or pitting, you should either have them reground or replace them with new or serviceable used camshafts. Check your rocker arms. The bushings are usually worn out of tolerance in a high-mileage engine. If so, you can have them reconditioned or replaced with new rocker arms. You should check the "elephant's feet" adjusters for excessive wear and replace them also, if necessary. The valve spring condition should also be checked with a spring tester to ensure that they are still within specifications. Again, replace if necessary.

Check all the chain sprockets and idler arms for wear. If excessive, replace the offending sprockets. Check the condition of the intermediate (lay) shaft aluminum gear. These gears, as well as the chain sprockets, are now available as separate replacement parts for the later-version layshaft used since 1968. There are no replacement aluminum gears for the early style layshaft as used in the original aluminum crankcase. Check the backlash of the aluminum gear on the intermediate shaft before you remove the crankshaft and intermediate shaft from the crankcase half while disassembling the engine. The chains should be replaced as a matter of course while the engine is apart.

Replace All Chain Tensioners

Now we come to the chain tensioners. If you are rebuilding a 1964–1983 engine, you should replace the tensioner no matter what style your engine is. Either use the 1980-and-later type with the updated idler arms or the new pressurized type used on the 1984 911 Carrera. The pressure-fed chain tensioner should last forever and be a mainte-

A proper valve job is a necessary part of any top-end or complete engine overhaul. The valves and guides should be measured and replaced as necessary, and then a three-angle valve job performed. The seat is ground at 45 deg, and 75 deg and 30 deg are used as the topping and throating angles to narrow the seats.

nance-free component. However, the sealed-type chain tensioner (1968–1983) probably should be replaced every 40,000 miles as preventive maintenance.

If you are rebuilding a 911 engine with a magnesium crankcase (1968–1977), you should remove the cylinder-head studs and install timed threaded inserts. If you will be using either Nikasil or Alusil cylinders, you should also replace the steel cylinder-head studs with the later-style Dilavar head studs. This is particularly true for the 2.7-liter engines, whose crankcases were a little over-stressed. Here's the reason for tending to this while the engine is apart, even though everything may look all right: Once the studs have been disturbed by the process of rebuilding the engine, they will very likely pull soon after the rebuild. While on the subject of repairing potential future problems, the 8x1.25-mm stud that holds the case halves together at the inner layshaft bearing also has been known to pull and should have a timed insert installed while the case is apart. I know of no way to repair this stud if it has pulled after the engine is assembled other than disassembling the crankcase again.

The main-bearing bores should be measured while you have the engine disassembled for the rebuild. If the crankcase bores are too tight, they should be reamed or honed to size. If the crankcase bores are too large, they should be reamed or line-bored for the first oversize bearings. If the crankcase shows any other signs of damage, perhaps the crankcase should be replaced. Nothing lasts forever. Check the crankcase mating surfaces for any nicks or damage, and if they are found, carefully dress them down with a file.

Clean all oil passages in the crankcase with solvent and compressed air. While you are blowing compressed air through the passages, make sure that the air passes freely through every passage. Note that the through-bolt holes are used as part of the main oil system with the main bearings receiving their oil through drillings from these holes. Be sure that you remove both the oil-pressure relief valve and the oil-pressure safety valve from the crankcase prior to cleaning the crankcase.

Examine both the pistons and their bores for any damage. If the pistons are damaged, replace them. Make sure that the replacements are the same type as you removed. If you mix up the types of bypass pistons, you will create oil-pressure mysteries for yourself. Damaged bores can usually be repaired by polishing any score marks with fine crocus

Check all of the valve springs before installing them. First, check the spring pressure at 30.5–31.0 mm (1.201–1.220 inch), which will simulate the spring in the valve-open condition; the pressure should be 80 kp (176.4 lb). Next, check the spring pressure at 42.0–42.5 mm (1.6535–1.6731 inch), which will simulate the seat pressure; the pressure should be 20 kp (44.09 lb). The 911 valve springs are high quality and will usually last the life of the car. With the exception of some special applications, none of the aftermarket valve springs are nearly as good as the original equipment, so do not replace them unless it is absolutely necessary. There was apparently a bad batch of springs in the late 1977 to mid-1978 time frame because I have seen several cars built during that time frame with broken intake valve springs. You can check for broken valve springs when you are adjusting the valves: press on the intake rocker arms; if you can move the rocker arms by hand, you must have a broken valve spring. The springs can be replaced in the car by pressurizing the cylinder with compressed air and using the 906 valve adjusting tool to compress the valve springs.

Resurfacing of 911 cylinder heads creates a special challenge because of the counter bore in the cylinder head to accept the mating cylinders. For this reason, the 911 cylinder heads cannot be machined by conventional means. It is essential that the heads be machined square to the cam housing mounting surface and all six cylinder heads must be machined the same amount so that they will not put the camshaft in a bind. The best way to machine a set of these 911 cylinder heads is with a lathe, which requires a special mounting fixture.

cloth. Inspect the oil pump; it should be replaced if any wear or damage is found.

Before reassembly of the engine, check for worn or damaged parts, washers, spring washers, nuts, studs, and so on, and replace if necessary. All elastic lock-type nuts, aluminum crush washers, and seals should be replaced. These aluminum crush washers are actually a silicon-magnesium alloy and not dead-soft aluminum. As with many of the parts you will purchase for your rebuild, you will have to make sure that you get the real thing. There are a number of after-market parts available for use in the rebuild and some of those parts are just not up to the job. This is one area where you can actually test the part yourself. Take a nut and a bolt and a couple of these crush washers and assemble them together. Then take your torque wrench and torque the nut to 15 ft-lb. The washers should hold their shape. If they don't hold their shape and they squish out, you clearly did not get the right stuff.

In purchasing all your rebuild parts, you will have to be careful to get the real thing. Almost everyone will try to sell you aftermarket parts wherever they can because they make more money on them. Unfortunately, I don't have a nice simple test like the one for the crush washers for all parts. You will just have to use your own judgment. Be careful; most aftermarket parts are not as good as the real thing.

Gaskets, Sealants, and O-Rings

When reassembling your engine, be sure that you use either the graphite-coated or the new green-style gaskets and either Loctite 574 (orange; a European product) or Dow Corning RTV 730 (a U.S. product) sealants. The sealant is only used on the crankcase halves and where the heads are sealed to the cam housing. All other joints are sealed by using the graphited or green-coated gaskets on a clean, dry surface with no sealant. The sealant can cause these treated gaskets to slip, causing leaks. There are some very good aftermarket suppliers of these treated gaskets. This is one area where you can get the real thing in the aftermarket.

There are several O-ring-type seals used on the 911 engine in various applications. To help seal the O-rings used on the oil return tubes the camshaft O-ring seals, the thermostat O-ring, and the number 8 main-bearing O-ring lubricate the O-rings with a silicon paste or grease-type lubricant. Dow Corning 111 compound works well here. The advantage of the silicon paste or grease over petroleum grease is the fact that the silicon paste or grease will withstand very high temperatures and will not run off. The reason for lubricating these O-rings is so they will reseal themselves anytime they have been disturbed by the thermal expansion of the engine. Do not use silicon sealer in this application. These O-rings, by design, must be free to move and work to do their job correctly.

For assembling the engine, an assembly lubricant should be made by mixing engine oil and molybdenum disulfide compound (not moly grease). Molybdenum disulfide (moly) is a sulfide of molybdenum MoS_2. Pure molybdenum disulfide is a soft, black solid with many interesting uses. The only use we are really interested in is here is its ability to act as an effective lubricant under severe operating conditions. When used as a lubricant, moly can withstand extremely high temperatures and extremely high pressures. This is important here because the camshaft and rocker arms will see their most severe wear when the engine is first started. Proper lubrication during the first start-up procedure will go a long way toward extending the life of any engine.

The assembly lube should be used on the camshafts and cam thrust plates. Use engine oil for the connecting-rod bearings and main bearings and the pistons and cylinders. Lightly oil the rings and the pistons with engine oil. If you make them too slippery, your rings will not seal. Your mixture of assembly lube should also be used on the rod bolts and any other bolts or studs where the torque is critical. Exceptions would be the studs where elastic stop-type lock nuts are used (which are best assembled dry or with a light coat of engine oil), and the flywheel bolts where I recommend using red Loctite.

Cam Timing is Vitally Important

When people are assembling 911 engines, they always worry about the cam timing. It's a shame they don't have the same concern for some of the other more subtle pitfalls of building 911 engines. There are several other things that must be done correctly. These are carefully explained in the workshop manual, but are often not correctly performed. The cam timing is a fairly simple, straightforward procedure that is described well in the workshop manual. For most engines you will need to refer to the Porsche spec books to determine the intake valve lift at overlap TDC for your engine.

It is doubly important to install the rocker arms and rocker arm shafts properly because in addition to carrying the rocker arms, the rocker shafts also seal in the camshaft housing to prevent oil leakage. The rocker-arm shafts must be centered in the rocker arms to avoid damage to the rocker-arm bushings and camshaft housings and to ensure proper sealing in the camshaft housing. The rocker shafts are made so they expand at the ends when the Allen-head bolt is tightened. One end has a tapered, threaded cap and the other has a tapered cap through which the bolt fits. When the Allen-head bolt is tightened, these tapered ends expand the ends of the rocker-arm shaft, sealing

and retaining the rocker-arm shaft in the housing. If the shafts are off center, this wedging action will occur in the rocker-arm bushing and both loosen the rocker shafts and ruin the rocker-arm bushing. The rocker shafts should also be installed so they can be removed later if necessary for maintenance. All of this is carefully explained in the workshop manual, but somehow is often overlooked.

It is important to be able to tell the left cam from the right. Proper cam identification can be done by looking at the camshafts from the nose, or drive end, by looking at the relationship of the first two lobes on each cam. There is a little trick for remembering which is which. The left cam has the front two lobes spread out and it looks like an "L," while the right cam has the lobes close together and it looks like a pair of rabbit ears; the first letter in rabbit is "R," as is the first letter in right. The reason it is so important to make sure you install them correctly is that if you don't, you may not catch it as you go through the remainder of the cam timing and valve adjustment procedure, but when you get done, the engine will try to run backwards.

Another common error is to install

Apply a small bead of Dow Corning RTV 730 Fluorosilicone sealant around all of the areas where you need to seal the oil from the rocker arms.

Install the cam housing onto the cylinder heads.

Camshaft Timing

The 911 is powered by a four-stroke engine. The four strokes are:

1—INDUCTION the down stroke on the first revolution where the cylinder draws in the fresh air/fuel mixture;

2—COMPRESSION the up stroke where the air/fuel mixture is compressed;

3—POWER ignition starts the combustion (or power) stroke and the down stroke on the second revolution;

4—EXHAUST the up stroke where exhaust gases are expelled. The timing of this cycle is described in degrees of crankshaft rotation. Each stroke requires 180 deg of crankshaft rotation—a total of 720 deg to complete the four cycles. The camshafts are directly timed to the crankshaft in a 1:2 ratio so that the camshaft rotates at one-half of the crankshaft speed.

Timing the camshafts is performed to synchronize the camshafts with crankshaft rotation. The accompanying illustration shows both the exhaust valve travel and the intake valve travel for the number one cylinder through two complete crankshaft rotations. Since the camshaft runs at half the crankshaft's speed, it takes two complete revolutions to complete one cycle. The exhaust cam profile is shown to give a total picture of what happens with both of the valves opening and closing, but for

cam timing we are actually only interested in the intake profile. However, showing both the intake and exhaust profiles clearly illustrates why this point is called TDC overlap; it's the point where the exhaust valve is still open and the intake valve has just started to open.

When the crankshaft is rotated 360 deg from 0 deg to TDC overlap, you reach a point where the camshaft is just starting to lift the intake valve. I call this point the "timing point." At this timing point, the valve lift should be what is specified as the "Intake Valve Lift at Overlap TDC with 0.1 mm (0.004 inch) valve clearance" for the camshafts being used. If you are using any of the factory camshafts, this checking value will be given in the Technical Specification booklets. If you are using a special camshaft grind, the manufacturer of the cam should provide the lift specifications at overlap TDC.

If the reading is too high the camshaft is advanced, and if it is too low the camshaft is retarded. There is usually a range given for this check; for example, for the 911 SC engine in this illustration the range is 0.9–1.1 mm (0.035–0.043 inches). This timing specification is only one of three timings that have been used for these camshafts since they were first introduced as the 3.0 Carrera cams in 1976.

Originally these cams were set for 0.9–1.1 mm (0.035–0.043 inches) for the 1976 and 1977 3.0-liter Carrera. When the 911 SC was introduced in 1978 Porsche advanced the camshaft timing 6 deg for the R.o.W. version and checking clearance increased to 1.4–1.7 mm (0.055–0.067 inches). The camshaft timing for the 1978 U.S. version of the 911 SC remained the same as it had been for the 1976–77 R.o.W. 3.0 Carrera. The cam timing for the 1980 U.S. version of the 911 SC was advanced to the same timing that had been used for the R.o.W version since 1978. In 1981, the R.o.W. 911 SC had its timing retarded to what had been the original cam timing for the 1976–77 3.0 Carrera. The cam timing was changed again when the 3.2 Carrera engine was introduced in 1984 when Porsche split the difference and set the timing halfway between the two settings that it had used before—3 deg more advanced than the original 1976–77 3.0 Carrera with a checking height of 1.1–1.4 mm (0.043–0.055 inches).

Some people believe that if you advance the cams you will improve bottom-end performance, and if you retard the cams you will improve the top-end performance. We have experimented with various timings for these "SC cams" and have found that it seems to make little difference in the engine's performance.

Recommended Torque Settings

Component	Ft-Lb of Torque
Crankcase and cam housing, 8 mm	18
Connecting-rod bolts	37 to 40.5
Nuts for through-bolts and studs, 10 mm	25
Oil-screen-cover nuts	7
Cylinder head nuts (steel)	25
Cylinder head nuts (Dilavar)	29
Rocker-shaft Allen pinch bolts	13.2
Nut for fan and pulley	29
Flywheel retaining bolts (six)	110
Flywheel retaining bolts (nine)	66
1980-and-later pilot bearing	7
Nut for camshaft drive sprocket	110
Bolt for camshaft drive sprocket	88
Covers for camshaft housing	6
Crankshaft pulley	59
Crankshaft pulley, double-belt AC	125
Pressure-relief and bypass pistons plugs	44
Oil-drain plugs	31
Air injectors in cylinder heads	11
Exhaust-to-cylinder head	15 to 17
Spark plugs	18 to 21

the cam chain sprockets incorrectly. This error would be caught if the whole procedure for setting up the chain sprockets were followed. The camshaft sprockets are identical and are interchangeable. They are offset and the left-hand sprocket is installed with the offset toward you, and the right-hand sprocket is installed with the offset away from you. There is a procedure that allows you to measure the alignment of both sprockets so any misalignment can be adjusted out. If this procedure is followed, it is impossible to end up with the sprockets installed incorrectly. While on the subject of chain sprockets, there is one other thing I have seen done that is equally inexcusable. I have seen an engine assembled with only one row of the duplex chain on the layshaft sprocket; the other half was flapping in the breeze.

The importance of the O-rings on the crankcase through-bolts is so often overlooked. Because the through-bolt holes in the crankcase are used as part of the main oil system, feeding oil from the main oil gallery to the main bearings, it is important that the through-bolts are properly sealed. When you install the crankcase through-bolts, you must be sure that the O-rings and chamfer washer are installed on each end of the through-bolts to ensure sealing. The later-model 911s with their larger cylinders also have an external chamfer on these washers to provide clearance for the larger cylinders. The O-rings should be lubricated with assembly lube or silicon compound to ensure that they seat properly and seal each end of the through-bolts.

The rod bolts are another often-overlooked potential problem. The stock factory rod bolts used in the 911 engines are malleable and must be replaced whenever the engine is disassembled. "Malleable," in this instance, means the stretch bolts take a stretch when they are torqued, and if they are reused, they will not torque properly. Be sure that when you send your rods out for reconditioning, you send them out with the old bolts. In the course of reconditioning the rods, the machine shop will torque your rod bolts, which would ruin your new rod bolts. When you are installing the connecting rod, lubricate the threads of the rod bolts with a mixture of oil and moly lube. This ensures that when you torque the rod bolts, you will get a proper torque value.

I recommend having the rod bolts and nuts magnafluxed to check them for cracks. This is a worthwhile procedure since over the years I have found a few of them with flaws. Rod bolts are another area in which to be wary of aftermarket parts suppliers. There are some aftermarket rod bolts in circulation that do not have the correct locating diameter. Beware! On the other hand, there are also some aftermarket rod bolts that I consider to be an upgrade, such as Raceware and ARP.

Avoid Mistakes of Inexperience

There are a few other things that I have seen the inexperienced 911 en-

All of the cam-housing nuts are installed and tightened to their proper torque. There are 18 nuts retaining the cam housing to the three cylinder heads, six per head. Note that the three special, round Allen nuts are used where there isn't adequate room for a conventional socket wrench.

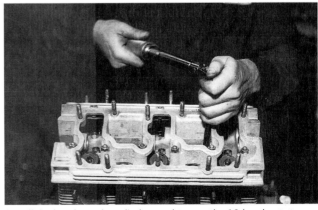

Install the heads on the cylinders and torque the 12 head nuts to their proper torque. The steel studs should be torqued to 25 ft-lb.

gine builder inflict on the 911 engine. Pistons installed upside-down, for example, so that the intake valve lines up with the exhaust valve pockets in the piston. The result was that the intake valves hit and cracked the pistons and bent the valves. I have also seen the cylinders installed upside-down so that the longer cooling fins were up rather than down. This caused unequal cooling and resulted in the pistons seizing in the cylinders. I've seen the air-deflector plates installed upside-down so that rather than channeling the air under the cylinders for even cooling, they deflected the air away from the cylinders, again causing the engines to overheat and ruin the pistons and cylinders.

Be sure that you lubricate the pilot bearing before installing the engine to the transmission. They will fail if not properly lubricated. Use a moly grease; a good one is SWEPCO 101. When a pilot bearing fails, the symptom is that the clutch will not release. What is actually happening is that the remains of the pilot bearing are grinding away on the end of the transmission mainshaft, trying to friction weld the mainshaft to the crankshaft.

When you clean the chain housing, it will usually disturb the epoxy used to seal the pins that mount the chain ramp and tensioner in the chain housing. It is a good idea to clean them off and re-apply a new coat of epoxy. .

Here's a look at installing camshafts in their respective cam housings. It is important that you make sure that you get the correct camshaft in the correct housing. The housings are identical, so either cam will fit in either cam housing.

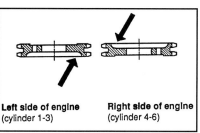

To time the cams, it is necessary to measure the valve travel relative to the crankshaft's rotation. To keep track of the crankshaft rotation, we will use the crankshaft pulley with its markings at TDC and each 120 deg of rotation. The illustration shows the crankshaft pulley with the "Z" TDC mark lined up with the seam in the crankcase. The crankshaft has its throws at 120-deg intervals, and the firing order is: 1, 6, 2, 4, 3, and finally 5. In our example, the crank pulley is marked with "1" and "4" at "Z1," and then at 120 deg "3" and "6" and again after another 120 deg "2" and "5." At TDC and each of these 120 deg marks, two of the engine's pistons will be at TDC. Before the camshafts are installed and timed, it does not matter which TDC is number "1" and which is number "4"; it is actually the cam timing that makes this determination.

An example of measuring the fixed offset to the front chain sprocket on the layshaft on a 1968–1983 mid-year engine. Use Porsche's method for checking sprocket alignment by first measuring the position of the front chain sprocket and then measuring from a straight edge the right camshaft (cylinders four through six) drive sprocket. The cam drive sprocket should have the same reading as the chain sprocket on the layshaft; the maximum permissible difference is 0.25 mm. The shims for adjusting sprocket position are 0.20 mm thick.

Left side of engine
(cylinder 1-3)

Right side of engine
(cylinder 4-6)

Camshaft sprockets. First install a thrust washer and the same number of shims as was removed in cam housing. Place half-round Woodruff key into the camshaft and install the sprocket wheel flange. The sprocket wheel flange is the same for both sides of the engine. Next install the sprocket on each of the camshafts. The sprockets are identical, interchangeable, and offset. The left-hand sprocket is installed with the offset and the left-hand sprocket is installed with the offset towards you, and the right-hand sprocket is installed with the offset away from you.

Recommended Tools

- Open-end wrenches of these sizes: 6 mm, 8 mm, 9 mm, 10 mm, 11 mm, 12 mm, 13 mm, 14 mm, 15 mm, 17 mm, 19 mm, and 22 mm
- Socket wrenches of these sizes: 8 mm, 10 mm, 13 mm, 14 mm, and 15 mm
- Needle-nose pliers, 90 deg, piston circlips
- Screwdrivers
- Allen wrench, 5 mm and 8 mm, rocker shafts
- Allen wrench, long 8 mm, exhaust Allen nuts
- Allen wrench, long 10 mm, Allen head nuts
- Allen wrench, short 12 mm, 12-point star wrench, flywheel
- Plastic hammer
- Steel hammer
- Depth gauge, minimum length 150 mm (3 inch)
- Vernier calipers
- Straight edge, minimum length 50 cm (20 inch)
- 3/8 drive ratchet
- 3/8 drive extension
- 1/8 drive universal sockets, 12 mm, 13 mm, and 14 mm
- Dowel-pin remover for cam sprocket (spark plug)
- Engine stand
- P202 camshaft-holding wrench
- P203 camshaft-nut wrench
- P207 dial-gauge holder
- P221 connecting-rod props
- P222 timing-chain props
- Engine TDC indicator
- Dial gauge
- V-belt pulley holder
- Torque wrench
- Feeler gauge, 0.004-inch valve clearance
- Chain-tensioner holder (holds tensioner collapsed)
- Solid tensioner (holds chain tight while adjusting right camshaft, cylinders 4–6)
- "C" clamp (holds chain tight while adjusting left camshaft, cylinders 1–3)
- Exhaust-manifold wrench
- Pliers, piston-ring expanding
- Piston-ring compressor
- Valve-spring tester
- Valve-spring gauge (for measuring installed length)
- Piston-pin drift (for installing piston pins)
- Liquid graduate glass (for measuring cubic centimeters; combustion chamber, and piston dome)
- Clutch centering tool

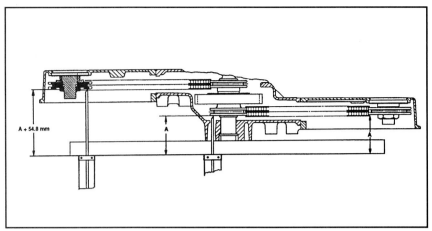

Checking parallel of chain sprockets. The following is a procedure that allows you to measure the alignment of both sprockets so that any misalignment can be adjusted out. If this procedure is followed it is impossible to end up with sprockets installed incorrectly. The deviation in parallel between the driving sprocket on the intermediate shaft (lay shaft) and the camshaft must not exceed 0.25 mm (0.001 in). Prior to measuring, slide the layshaft and camshaft towards the flywheel until they hit the end of their travel. The sprockets are adjusted by adding or removing shims (Porsche part number 901.105.561-00). The shims' thickness is 0.5 mm (0.0197 in). Normally three shims will be required under the left sprocket (cylinders 1-3) and four shims underneath the right sprocket (cylinders 4-6). Measure distance "A" to the front edge of the driving sprocket on the layshaft. This is the fixed offset to the front chain sprocket on the layshaft. Measure the distance "A" to the front edge of the right-hand camshaft (cylinders 4-6) sprocket wheel.

Example: measured fixed offset distance "A" + 78.7 (3.098 in).

Measured distance from straight edge to the face of the front edge of the right-hand (cylinders 4-6) camshaft sprocket wheel. If this dimension is off by more than 0.25 mm (0.001 in) in or out it must be altered by changing the shims.

The left-hand (cylinders 1-4) chain sprocket measurement is more difficult because there is an offset value 54.8 mm (2.157 in) that must be added to the measured fixed offset "A." The reason for this is that we are unable to actually measure the distance that this gear is back from the front of the engine because the layshaft-driven gear is in the way, so we use the offset value provided by Porsche.

Example: measured fixed offset distance "A" + 78.7 mm (3.098 in) plus the 54.8 mm (2.157 in) gives a value of 133.5 mm (5.2565 in). When we measure from the straight edge to the face of the front edge of the left-hand (cylinders 1-3) sprocket wheel we should get this 133.5 mm (5.256 in) number, if we do not and this dimension is off by more than 0.25 mm (0.001 in) in or out it must be altered by changing the shims.

This measurement was further complicated in mid-year 1983 when the crankcase was modified. After the change you could no longer reach the front gear to measure what was previously considered dimension "A" and you had to assume a new offset or "Design" value provided by Porsche for that dimension as well. The new "A" dimension was now the distance from the straight edge to the face of the end of the layshaft. The new "Design" dimensions for the offset distances from "A" are:

- *From the face of the layshaft to the face of the front intermediate shaft sprocket (cylinders 4-6) the "Design dimension" is 43.27 mm (1.7 in).*
- *From the face of the layshaft to the face of the rear intermediate shaft sprocket (cylinders 1-3) the "Design dimension" is 98.07 mm (3.86 in).*

Example for the right sprocket: measured distance "A" to the face of the layshaft is 35.5 mm (1.4 in) plus the "Design dimension" for the right-drive sprocket (cylinders 4-6) is given as 43.27 mm (1.7 in) which equals a total of 78.77 mm (3.1 in). When we measure to the face of the right-hand (cylinders 4-6) camshaft sprocket wheel we should get 78.77 mm (3.1 in). If we do not and this dimension is off by more than 0.25 mm (0.001 in) in or out, it must be altered by changing the shims.

Example for the left sprocket: measured distance "A" to the face of the layshaft is 35.5 mm (1.4 in) plus the "Design dimension" for the left-drive sprocket (cylinders 1-3) is given as 98.07 mm (3.86 in) which equals a total of 133.57 mm (5.26 in). If we do not and this dimension is off by more than 0.25 mm (0.001 in) in or out, it must be altered by changing the shims.

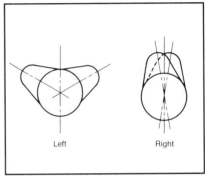

Measuring sprocket alignment for the chain sprocket on the left side (cylinders one through three) is a little more difficult because you can't actually measure the position of the layshaft drive sprocket for that bank, so you have to calculate its position using the offset provided in the spec book. After the offset has been checked and adjusted, rotate both cams until the punch marks stamped in the faces point straight up, which will provide an initial rough setting and establish which is the number one cylinder and which is the number four cylinder at TDC. Note that some camshafts may not have the punch mark to indicate this rough setting, but you can use the key way for the Woodruff key as an indication of which direction to point the camshafts; the key way should point up. Next, find the hole in the camshaft sprocket that is in alignment with the hole in the camshaft sprocket mounting flange and install the dowel pin through the aligned holes. Be sure that when you install the dowel pin that you face the threaded portion outward so that it can be removed again. There is a special tool available for pulling this pin out, but the threaded end of a spark plug will work just as well. Install the washers and nuts on each of the cams and tighten to the specified torque.

A camshaft identification drawing. There is a little trick for remembering which cam is which. When you look at the cams from the nose or nut end, the left cam has the first two lobes that you see spread out like a wide "V" or "L." The "L" stands for left; this is the left cam. The right camshaft, when viewed from the front, will have its lobes closer together so that it looks like a rabbit with its ears up in the air, and the first letter in rabbit is an "R," and the "R" stands for right. It is important that you catch this when you install the camshafts because there is nothing that will alert you to your error once the cams are in their housings, except that when you try to start the engine it will try to run backwards.

This photo shows the mechanic setting the camshaft timing for cylinders four through six. The cam nuts must be torqued and the chain and chain-tensioner idler arms installed. You may want to use something other than the tensioners to hold the chains tight during this process. The tensioner on the left side will get in your way while you are trying to tighten the cam nut, so I recommend a mechanical tensioner for the right side and a C-clamp for the left side. The C-clamp reaches over the top of the chain housing so that the idler arm can be pulled tight against the chain. The mechanical tensioner can be used on the right side to tighten the chain. For the timing procedure, set the chains a little tighter than normal so that timing is accurate. Install the rocker arm for the number one intake valve and adjust the valve lash for 0.004 inch (0.10 mm). A dial indicator with a feeler pin is needed to measure the valve travel in relationship to the rotation of the crankshaft. Using a wrench, rotate the engine 360 deg until you align "Z1" with the seam in the crankcase. The dial indicator should indicate the inlet valve lift specified for the camshaft you are timing. If the reading is not correct, readjust the cam and try again. After you have adjusted the camshaft for the number one intake valve, you can install the rocker arm for the number four intake valve and repeat the procedure for that camshaft.

A rocker-arm shaft. When installing the rocker-arm shafts, be sure that the shafts are centered in the rocker arms. There is a procedure in the workshop manual for installing these shafts, but it may be easier, and just as accurate, to visualize where the shaft will be when it is installed relative to one end or the other of its bore in the cam housing. When torquing the shafts in the housing it is essential that you make sure that they are tight in the housing; otherwise, they can work their way out of the housing. To make sure that they are tight in the housing, use a torque wrench on the 5-mm bolt end and just hold the 8-mm nut end enough for it to start to tighten in the housing. Then torque the 5-mm bolt end up to the 15 lb-ft of torque specified. If they tighten up in the housing without requiring the 8-mm end to be held before the 15 lb-ft of torque is reached, they will probably be all right. However, if they turn in the housing you may have a problem with the shafts working their way out it.

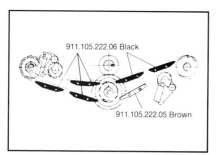

A chain ramp identification and installation diagram. The 911 engines use five black 911.105.222.06 chain ramps and one brown 911.105.222.05 chain ramp. The brown ramp goes in the lower right side of the engine. Also note that the longer end of each of the ramps points toward the nearest chain sprocket. The four ramps that actually mount in the crankcase halves point toward the sprockets on the layshaft, while the remaining two ramps point toward the cam drive sprockets.

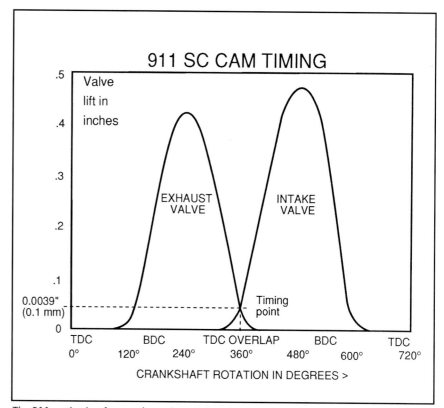

The 911 engine is a four-stroke engine. Each stroke takes 180 deg of crankshaft rotation, and a total of 720 deg for the four cycles to be completed. The camshafts are directly timed to the crankshaft in a 1:2 ratio so that the camshaft rotates at one-half of the crankshaft speed. The process of timing the camshafts is performed to synchronize the camshafts with the rotation of the crankshaft. This illustration shows both the exhaust-valve travel and the intake-valve travel for the number one cylinder through two complete rotations of the crankshaft. Since the camshaft runs at half the crankshaft speed, it takes two complete revolutions to complete one complete cycle. The exhaust-cam profile is shown to give the complete picture of what happens with both of the valves opening and closing, but for the cam timing we are only interested in the intake profile. However, showing both the intake and exhaust profile does clearly illustrate why this point is called TDC overlap; this point is where the exhaust valve is still open and the intake valve has already started to open. When the crankshaft is rotated 360 deg from 0 deg to TDC overlap, you reach a point where the camshaft is just starting to lift the intake valve; I call this point the "timing point." At this timing point, the valve lift should be what is specified as the "Intake Valve Lift at Overlap TDC with 0.1-mm (0.004-inch) valve clearance" for the camshafts being used. If you are using any of the factory camshafts, this checking value will be given in the technical specification booklets. If you are using a special camshaft grind, the manufacturer of the cam should be able to provide the lift specifications. If the reading is too high, the camshaft is advanced, and if it is too low, the camshaft is retarded.

A completed long block with pressure-fed chain tensioners.

Engine Builder's Checklist

Customer: _____ Build Date _____
Engine Type _____ Type # _____ Engine Number _____
Engine's Purpose: _____
Special Conditions or Remarks: _____

Operation
1. Disassemble and check the following:
_ Condition of clutch assembly and flywheel; recondition or replace as necessary
_ Condition of induction system
_ Condition of valve covers; early bottom covers probably should be updated
_ Condition of cam chain housing, idler arms, and gears; update idler arms to 1980-style
_ Condition of rocker arms, rocker-arm shafts, and adjusters
_ Condition of camshaft for wear
_ Condition of camshaft-housing cam bores and rocker-shaft bores for wear, burrs, and scoring
_ Condition of cylinder heads for breakage or damage
_ Condition of pistons and cylinders
_ Condition of crankshaft
_ Condition of connecting rods
_ Condition of oil pump
_ Condition of intermediate shaft
_ Intermediate shaft backlash in crankcase
_ Condition of crankcase
_ Condition of crankcase oil bypass and pressure-relief pistons and crankcase bores
_ Each piston-cooling spray valve with compressed air and solvent

2. Clean all engine parts.

3. Magnaflux or Zyglo the following:
• Crankshaft
• Connecting rods
• New connecting rod bolts and nuts
• Pistons
• Piston pins
• Camshafts
• Rocker arms

4. Measure crankcase line bore
2.0–2.7 liter: 62.000–62.019 mm (2.4409–2.4416 inch)
3.0–3.6 liter: 65.000–65.019 mm (2.5590–2.5598 inch)
Bearing #: 8____ 7____ 6____ 5____ 4____ 3____ 2____ 1____

5. Measure crankshaft main-bearing journals
2.0–2.7 liter: 56.971–56.990 mm (2.2429–2.2437 inch); wear limit 56.960 mm (2.2425 inch)
3.0–3.6 liter: 59.971–59.990 mm (2.3610–2.3618 inch); wear limit 59.960 mm (2.3606 inch)
Journal #: 8____ 7____ 6____ 5____ 4____ 3____ 2____ 1____

6. Measure crankshaft rod-bearing journals
2.0–2.2 liter: 56.971–56.990 mm (2.2429–2.2437 inch); wear limit 56.960 mm (2.2425 inch)
2.4–2.7 liter: 51.971–51.990 mm (2.0461–2.0468 inch); wear limit 51.960 mm (2.0456 inch)
3.0 liter: 52.971–52.990 mm (2.0854–2.0862 inch); wear limit 52.960 mm (2.08504 inch)
3.2–3.6 liter: 54.971–54.990 mm (2.1642–2.1649 inch); wear limit 54.960 mm (2.1637 inch)
Journal #: 6 ____ 5 ____ 4 ____ 3 ____ 2 ____ 1 ____

7. Measure connecting-rod big-end diameters
2.0–2.2 liter: 61.000–61.019 mm (2.4015–2.4023 inch); wear limit
2.4–3.0 liter: 56.000–56.019 mm (2.2047–2.2054 inch); wear limit
3.2–3.6 liter: 58.000–58.019 mm (2.2834–2.2842 inch); wear limit
Rod #: 6 ____ 5 ____ 4 ____ 3 ____ 2 ____ 1 ____

8. Measure connecting-rod small-end diameters
2.0–3.0 liter: 22.020–22.033 mm (.8669–.8974 inch); wear limit 0.055 mm (0.002 inch)
3.2–3.6 liter: 23.020–23.033 mm (.9063–.9068 inch); wear limit 0.055 mm (0.002 inch)
Rod # 6 ____ 5 ____ 4 ____ 3 ____ 2 ____ 1 ____

9. Measure intermediate-shaft backlash with dial indicator
Intermediate-shaft backlash: 0.016–0.049 mm (0.0006–0.0019 inch)_____.

10. Measure valve guide
Intake and exhaust guide inside diameter: 9.000–9.015 mm (.3543–.3549 inch) check by using pilot as go/no-go gauge
#1I__ &E__ 2I__ &E__ 3I__ &E__ 4I__ &E__ 5I__ &E__ 6I__ &E__

11. Measure valve stem diameters
Intake valve stem: 8.97–0.012 mm (0.3531–0.0005 inch)
Exhaust valve stem: 8.95–0.012 mm (0.3523–0.0005 inch)
Valve stem taper and out-of-roundness: 0.01 mm (0.00039 inch)
#1I__ &E__ 2I__ &E__ 3I__ &E __ 4I__ &E __ 5I__ &E __ 6I__ &E __

12. Measure valve springs
Spring pressure at 30.5–31.0 mm = 80 kp (1.201–1.220 inch = 176.4 lb)
Spring pressure at 42.0–42.5 mm = 20 kp (1.6535–1.6731 inch = 44.09 lb)
#1I__ &E__ 2I__ &E__ 3I__ &E __ 4I__ &E __ 5I__ &E __ 6I__ &E __

13. Compression ratio:
• Swept volume, 1 cylinder = V1
• Deck-height volume = V2
• Cylinder-head volume = V3
• Piston-dome volume = V4

• V1 + V2 + V3-V4 ÷ V2 + V3 - V4 = Compression ratio

14. Remove and reinstall injection tube (spray bar) from cam housing
• Remove plug, loosen centering screws, and slide injection tube out.
• Install injection tube, make sure bores are located correctly. Separate bores must face upward toward intake-valve covers; double bores face cam lobe's surface.
• Install new plug with epoxy about 0.3 mm (0.012 inch) deeper than sealing surface.

15. Measure pistons and cylinders
• Measure vertical clearance of rings in ring grooves with a feeler gauge. Experience indicates the top ring-groove clearance is the most critical and excessive clearance will cause the compression rings to prematurely break.
Compression rings, numbers I and II: wear limit 0.115 mm (0.0045 inch).
• Oil-control ring, number III: wear limit is 0.1 mm (0.0039 inch)
• Top compression-ring groove; cylinder #1 __ 2 __ 3 __ 4 __ 5 __ 6 __
• Second compression-ring groove; cylinder #1 __ 2 __ 3 __ 4 __ 5 __ 6 __
• Bottom oil-ring groove; cylinder # 1 __ 2 __ 3 __ 4 __ 5 __ 6 __
• If ring grooves are not excessively worn, make other piston and cylinder measurements as specified for each different type of engine (see spec book)
• Piston diameter; piston # 1 __ 2 __ 3 __ 4 __ 5 __ 6 __
• Cylinder diameter; cylinder # 1 __ 2 __ 3 __ 4 __ 5 __ 6 __
• Clearance between piston and cylinder, set # 1 __ 2 __ 3 __ 4 __ 5 __ 6 __

16. Piston-ring end gap
- Compression ring I: 0.1–0.2 mm (0.0039–0.0078 inch); wear limit 0.8 mm (0.0314 inch)
- Compression ring II 0.1–0.2 mm (0.0039–0.0078 inch); wear limit 0.8 mm (0.0314 inch)
- Oil control ring III 0.15–0.3 mm (0.0059–0.0118 inch); wear limit 1.0 mm (0.0393 inch)

17. Assemble crankshaft
- Install gears on crankshaft
- Install connecting rods on crankshaft

18. Assemble crankcase
a. Mount right side (cylinders 4–6) of crankcase on engine stand.
b. Place oil-seal-ring groove in oil-suction passage in right side of crankcase.
c. Install oil pump and intermediate shaft in right side of crankcase; fasten oil pump and bend lock tabs into place.
d. Install crankshaft in crankcase.
e. Install connecting rod and chain props.
f. Install seal rings between oil pump and left crankcase half, and seal ring connecting the oil passage between the left and right crankcase halves.
g. Coat outer perimeter of crankcase with sealing compound.
h. Place flywheel seal into right side of crankcase, flush with outer end.
i. Install left side of crankcase onto the right.
j. Pre-assemble through-bolts. First place the double-chamfer washer onto the bolt and then slide the O-ring in place. Install the through-bolts and slide O-rings and chamfer washers onto the nut end of the through-bolts and hand tighten the cap nuts. These O-rings are very important as many of the through-bolt holes are used as oil passages.
k. In addition to the 13 through-bolts there are three additional 10-mm studs that serve the same function. The two under the oil cooler receive the same treatment with the O-ring and cap nut; the third is inside the chain housing on left-hand side of the crankcase.
l. Torque the through-bolts to 25 ft-lb, proceeding evenly in a crosswise order.
m. Place 8-mm magnesium crush washers onto all of the crankcase retaining studs and bolts, install nuts and torque to 18 ft-lb.

19. Install pistons and cylinders.

20. Install air deflectors (if air deflectors are early style, update).

21. Install cylinder heads.

22. Coat camshaft housing with sealing compound.

23. Install oil-return tubes.

24. Install camshaft housings.

25. Torque camshaft-housing nuts progressively in a crosswise order to 18 ft-lb.

26. Install camshafts in camshaft housings.

27. Torque cylinder heads to 24 ft-lb; keep checking the camshafts for binding during the tightening procedure.

28. Install chains, sprockets, and idlers.

29. Measure parallel of the chain-drive sprockets with straight edge.
- Intermediate shaft measurement (drive sprocket for chain to cylinders 4–6). Using a straight edge and a depth gauge, measure the distance from straight edge to front intermediate-shaft sprocket face: =A.
Measure "A" and record: _____.
- Measure the distance from straight edge to camshaft sprocket for cylinders 4–6. Measure and record: _____. This distance should also be equal to "A." Note: maximum permissible deviation = ±0.25 mm (0.0098 inch)
- Measure the distance from straight edge to camshaft sprocket for cylinders 1–4. Measure and record: _____. Note: There is a fixed offset from the front intermediate-shaft gear (cylinders 4–6) to the rear intermediate-shaft gear (cylinders 1–3) of 54.8 mm (2.1575 inch). The resulting measurement should equal "A" +54.8 mm (2.1575 inch). Note: maximum permissible deviation = ±0.25 mm (0.0098 inch).

30. Install distributor, point rotor at 45 deg angle toward air inlet to blower housing with cylinder #1 at TDC.

31. Install rocker arm for # 1 intake valve.

32. Adjust camshaft timing for cylinders 1 to 3. See spec books for timing data.
    #1 intake at overlap TDC _____.

33. Install rocker arm for #4 intake valve.

34. Adjust camshaft timing for cylinders 4 to 6.
    #4 intake at Overlap TDC_____.

35. Install remainder of rocker arms and adjust valves.

36. Install chain housing and valve covers.

37. Install alternator, blower, and engine sheet metal.

38. Install induction system; induction system type _____.

39. Install exhaust system; exhaust system type _____.

40. Run-in engine.

Chapter 5

Engine Performance Modifications

Modifying Porsches in general and 911s in particular is quite a bit different than modifying other makes of automobiles. You probably bought your Porsche because you thought it was the best car you could buy for your money. Porsche has selected the best quality components for most applications, which makes it difficult to improve on what it has done. For example, you will often see the term "blueprinting" used to describe the process of modifying a stock engine for stock use in racing, such as Showroom Stock Racing. The term "blueprinting" was coined for engines that did not resemble the original engineers' design for the engine. When they said that they were blueprinting an engine, it meant that they were remaking the engine like the designer had originally drawn it in his blueprints and not as it was built in manufacturing. We have been cheated out of this fun by Porsche; the tolerances and the quality control are such that only minimal improvements may be made using any of these so-called blueprinting techniques.

You will have to be careful when you modify or change any of the components that Porsche has used in one of its engines. Before you change anything, make sure you are sure you will get the results you want. Don't forget that almost all of the alternative components are of lesser quality than the original Porsche components. If you are not careful with your modifications, you can actually do your Porsche more harm than good.

The best way to improve the performance of most of the 911 engines is by increasing their displacement: the 2.0-liter engines can be increased to 2.2 liters, the 2.4-liter engines can be increased to 2.7-liter engines, the 3.0-liters can be increased to 3.2-liter engines, the 3.2-liters can be increased to 3.4- or 3.5-liter engines, and the 3.6-liters can be increased to 3.8-liter engines. If you are careful and use the correct components, you can increase the performance of most 911 engines without sacrificing the reliability. With some of the engines, you'll find you can even improve their reliability while you have them apart for performance work.

2.0-Liter 911 Modifications

Any of the 2.0-liter 911 engines can quite easily be converted to 2.2-liter 911 engines during a routine overhaul. It doesn't matter if you have one of the early sand-cast aluminum-crankcase engines or one of the later 2.0-liters with a magnesium crankcase; when you need the engine rebuilt it can be easily increased in size to 2.2 liters by changing the pistons and cylinders to the 84-mm size used on the 2.2 engines of 1970 and 1971.

The heads will require machining to accept the larger bore and the different-style head gasket used on the 2.2-liter cylinders. You can use the pistons from the 2.2-liter 911 T, E, or S. You will not have a problem with too much compression with these conversions because the combustion chamber was slightly larger for the 2.0-liter engines so the effective compression ratio will actually be reduced by about 4/10 of a point of compression.

If you are converting a 1969 911 E or S to a 2.2 liter, you will have a bit more of a problem with the conversion because of the mechanical-injection pump. The pump will have to be converted to the 2.2-liter specifications, but even then you will not have a perfect match because of the difference in combustion chamber sizes and resulting difference in compression ratios and slightly different combustion characteristics.

When you rebuild one of the 2.0-liter engines with a magnesium crankcase, whether you plan to increase the performance or not, you should plan to install threaded inserts to repair and strengthen the crankcase where the head studs screw in. You should not use the Dilavar head studs if you limit your displacement to 2.2 liters because the cylinders in this size are either cast iron or biral and do not cause the thermal expansion problem the all-aluminum cylinders cause. If you have one of the 1968 or 1969 magnesium crankcases where the inner-bearing surface of the layshaft ran directly in the magnesium, you will need to modify the crankcase to accept a layshaft-bearing insert.

If you need to replace the oil pump, I recommend that you update it to one of the 1976-and-later-style pumps with a larger pressure pump. If you do re-

The early (1968 and 1969) crankcases can be modified to accept the inboard bearing insert using reamers and a fixture for driving the reamers in a vertical mill.

place the pump, be sure that you remember to modify the oil bypass circuit and change to the newer style oil bypass pistons. The oil bypass circuit modification is a good idea even if you don't change the pump, because reducing the effort required by the scavenge pump keeps the oil level lower in the crankcase and reduces wasted horsepower.

2.2-Liter 911 Modifications (also applicable for 2.0-liter engines)

It is difficult to do much with the 2.2-liter engine inexpensively. You can put 2.2 911 S pistons on a 2.2 911T engine, raising the compression and resulting performance. But to do much else becomes difficult and necessitates replacing the crankshaft and rods to increase the displacement. There is, however, one conversion that, on the surface, looks attractive. That consists of using a set of the European Carrera 90-mm (2.7 Carrera RS) pistons and cylinders on one of these 2.2-liter engines—or for that matter, a 2.0-liter engine as well. The European Carrera pistons have been imported in fairly large quantities, which has kept the price relatively low and makes this conversion even more attractive. I have built several of these conversions myself. The 90-mm bore and 66-mm stroke give a displacement of 2,519 cc.

The one problem with this conversion is that the pistons provided only 8.5:1 compression when installed on their 70.4-mm-stroke crankshaft in the 2.7-liter application, so when you reduce the stroke to 66 mm, you reduce the compression to something slightly less than 7.0:1. You can sneak the compression back up to about 7.5:1 by machining about 0.040 inch (1 mm maximum) off the cylinder heads' cylinder sealing surface. You will have to machine your heads in any case to work with the 2.7 cylinders with their CE-ring head gasket, and the heads will have to be angle-cut to accommodate the larger pistons. If you do machine your heads, be sure to take a like amount off of the chain housings where they seal to the crankcase. This is important because otherwise you will have problems with the cam being off-center in the housing, and the O-ring seal for the cam-to-housing seal will fail.

The effect of moving the heads closer to the centerline of the crankshaft is to make the chain a little too long, but a little too long we can live with. When you reassemble the engine be sure to

An early magnesium crankcase that has been modified to accept bearing inserts.

The 901.101.102.7R magnesium crankcase is the best crankcase to use when building any of the engine displacements up to 2.7 liters—and 2.8 liters if you insist. It was stronger than all but the first sand-cast-aluminum crankcases, and it enjoyed all of the updates that came from evolution. There were two versions of the 901.101.102.7R crankcase—one with 92-mm cylinder spigots used for 2.0-, 2.2-, and 2.4-liter engines, and one with 97-mm cylinder spigots for the 2.7 engines.

use new cam chains to minimize this problem. This is why this modification is limited to 0.040 inch (1 mm) to try to minimize the potential of this chain-tensioning problem. Even though you limit the modification to 0.040 inch, you may run into a problem on the left side of the engine (cylinders 1 through 3) when the engine has high mileage (80,000 to 100,000 miles) and the chains stretch or

wear at the links and get longer. The problem will be that the idler arm will ride too high in its travel and will actually start to hit the chain housing itself.

Because of the low compression of this configuration, I recommend that you use the 911 T camshaft grind. I have done this conversion with both the 911 T cams and the 911 E cams. The 911 E cams do produce more peak

The 901.101.102.7R magnesium crankcase with the 92-mm cylinder spigots was introduced for use with the 2.4-liter engines in midproduction. I recommend them for use with any of the smaller engines—2.0, 2.2, or 2.4 liters—because of their additional strength. Note how thick the cylinder spigot bases are; they could be increased to 97 mm for use with the larger-bore 2.7-liter engines.

The 901.101.102.7R magnesium crankcase with the 97-mm cylinder spigots for the 1973 2.7-liter 911 Carrera RS. The combination of the larger spigot base and bore in the crankcase and the Nikasil cylinders permitted Porsche to expand what had originally been a 2.0-liter engine to 2.7 liters. Note that the cylinder-head studs have been removed and Time-Certs have been installed.

When you modify any of the crankcases that used the 92-mm cylinder spigot bore to the larger 97-mm diameter, make sure that you check the clearance for the skirt of the pistons into the crankcase. Note the step-bore at the base of the cylinder spigot bores; the outside diameter provides clearance for the cylinder, while the inner diameter step-bore provides clearance for the piston skirt.

horsepower, as you would expect. The 911 T cams, however, provide a much broader torque curve. The subjective, seat-of-the-pants results definitely favor the 911 T cams. As a result, I also recommend using the small 32-mm ports from the 911 T engine as well.

My recommendations for the Weber carburetors in this application is to set them up as follows:
• 32 mm venturi
• Tall pre-atomizers (secondary venturi) from the 46IDA Webers
• Main jet: 120-125
• Air-correction jet: 180
• Idle jet: 60-65
• Emulsion tube: F3
• Injection quantity: stock 0.5-cc per stroke

The idle circuit in the Webers in this application leaves quite a bit to be desired, so you will have to run fairly rich at idle to avoid low-speed surging. For idle jets you may have to run 60 to 65 idle jets to get rid of the low-speed, part-throttle surge problems caused by the idle-circuit difficulties with these carburetors. To test for this condition, drive around on part throttle between 2,000 rpm and 3,000 rpm until you have eliminated the problem. Just keep trying larger idle jets until there is no longer a surge problem in the 2,000 rpm to 3,000 rpm range. You will want to run the idle circuit just rich enough to eliminate the lean surge but as lean as you possibly can for the best possible fuel economy.

Drivers actually find that with a street car they spend most of their driving time on the idle circuit in the

You can determine how far the piston skirt will stick out the bottom of the cylinder and then make sure that there is adequate clearance for the piston's skirt when the piston is at BDC. When checking the clearance, you can push the piston down into the cylinder the depth of the stroke plus 2 mm to make sure you have adequate clearance. Trial-fit the cylinder with the piston extended out the bottom into each cylinder spigot hole to make sure that the clearance is adequate.

In racing applications where greater than 250 hp is anticipated, Dowel pinning (or shuffle pinning) the magnesium crankcases will extend the life of the crankcase and the crankshaft by reducing the flexing and moving. The modification consists of installing 10 dowel pins, one on each side of each main bearing.

Weber carburetors. A street car spends about 85 percent of its entire life near one-third load, which has the engine still running on the idle circuit. Because of the low compression and the problem with the idle circuit in the carburetors, this conversion does not provide good fuel economy.

There is another conversion approach that allows us to take advantage of the reduction of compression caused by using pistons made for the 70.4-mm stroke on a 66-mm-stroke engine. If we use the 92-mm pistons and cylinders from the 2.8 RSR engine on a 2.0- or 2.2-liter engine, the compression ratio will be reduced by about one point for a 2.2 engine and about one-and-a-half on a 2.0-liter engine; this will reduce the compression to a point where these pistons and cylinders are usable with the available gasoline.

The 92-mm pistons used on a 66-mm stroke will result in a displacement of 2,634.15 cc. If you use any of these larger-bore pistons and cylinders it will be necessary to increase the cylinder spigot bore from 92 mm to 97 mm to accommodate the larger cylinders; you must also modify the base of the crankcase main-bearing webs to provide clearance for the wider skirts of the pistons.

If either the 2.0-liter or the 1970 2.2-liter engines are converted to accept either the 90-mm 2.7-liter Carrera RS pistons and cylinders, or the 92-mm 2.8-liter RSR pistons and cylinders, a set of the case squirters should be installed in the crankcase. In 1971 Porsche added these case squirters to provide additional piston cooling by installing six oil jets fed from the main oil gallery, which spray oil onto the bottom of the pistons. These jets reduce the operating temperatures at the crown of the piston by 50 deg C (122 deg F). The jets can be installed in any of the other earlier crankcases where a high-performance application is anticipated. If the Nikasil (or Alusil) cylinders are going to be used on one of these earlier engines, this

An oil-bypass modification. Porsche made this change in 1976 so that they could reduce the size of the scavenge pump while they increased the size of the pressure pump. This modification should be made in any car that will be used in competition, to reduce the task of the oil pump and to ensure that there are no windage problems. The modification consists of plugging the original bypass hole with a 1/4-inch pipe plug and drilling a new bypass hole into the inlet passage for the pressure pump.

If the oil-bypass modification is performed, it is essential that you use the updated oil-bypass pistons as well. The original-style bypass piston is shown on the right, and the late-style piston, which works with the oil-bypass modification, is on the left.

A comparison of the 2.7- and 2.8-liter combustion chambers. The 2.8 RSR cylinder heads were unique in that they were the only cylinder heads made with the small cylinder head stud spacing (80 mm for 2.0–2.8-liter engines) and the larger-diameter, more-open combustion chamber. The volume of the 2.8 RSR combustion chamber was about 76 cc, whereas the 2.7 combustion chamber was a much smaller 68.1 cc.

modification is a must because the piston-to-cylinder operating clearance is based on the use of these case squirters.

Also, since the engine is going to be modified to accept the 2.7-liter or 2.8-liter cylinders, the crankcase should be treated like a 2.7-liter engine's crankcase. Time-Cert (threaded inserts) should be installed for the cylinder-head studs and you should be concerned with the difference in thermal expansion rate between the stock, steel cylinder-head studs and the all-aluminum cylinders.

There was a 2.5-liter racing version of the short-stroke engine, which is a nice combination if there is a class where you need a racing engine under 2,500 cc. It uses the 66-mm stroke and a set of Mahle 89-mm pistons and cylinders for 2,463.57-cc displacement. These engines were very popular in the IMSA GTU class when the class limit was 2.5 liters. These 2.5-liter engines were very driveable and had good throttle response and a nice, broad power curve.

You can also increase the displacement of either a 2.0-liter or 2.2-liter engine up to 2.7 liters by replacing the crankshaft and connecting rods with the 70.4-mm crankshaft and a set of matching connecting rods from a 2.4- or 2.7-liter engine. However, with the expense involved you should consider replacing your engine with a 2.4 or a 2.7 to begin with.

2.4-Liter 911 Engine Modifications

Because they use the 70.4-mm-stroke crankshaft and rods, it is fairly easy to make one of these 2.4-liter engines into a 2.7-liter engine. The crankcase spigots have to be bored out from 92 mm to 97 mm to accept the larger 2.7-liter cylinders. The cylinder heads must be angle-cut to accommodate the larger-diameter pistons. In addition to the angle-cut, the conversion to larger pistons and cylinder sets often requires that additional clearance be provided in the crankcase for the piston's wider skirt at the bottom of its travel.

We have been spoiled by 911 engines in general; there are so many combinations of the 911 engine that will just bolt together and work, and work well at that, that we seldom run into combinations that will not work. However, it is always good practice to do a trial assembly to check clearances before you do the final assembly on any combinations with which you're not totally familiar. The consequences of failing to check the clearances can be a damaged engine. It is common practice when building most engines to check both the piston-to-cylinder-head clearance and the valve-to-piston clearance and either make pockets in the pistons or deepen the existing pockets to provide adequate valve-to-piston clearance.

The piston-to-cylinder-head clearance should be a minimum of 0.89 mm (0.035 inch). The only place that I have seen Porsche refer to the required valve-to-piston clearance is in the original 911 workshop manual. There, in referring to a very early 2.0 engine, it says the valve-head-to-piston clearance must not be less than 0.8 mm (0.0314 inch). I don't feel this is adequate clearance and would recommend a minimum clearance of 1.5 mm (0.060 inch) for safety's sake. Simply determine the existing clearance and if it is inadequate, have the pockets deepened to provide adequate clearance. It is possible to get the piston top too thin; 0.200 inch should be the minimum thickness (Mahle says that the dome thickness should be a minimum of 5 mm thick).

To check the clearance, lay a strip of modeling clay, at least 3/16-inch thick, on top of one of the pistons, across the valve pockets, in the partially assembled engine. Note it is only necessary to check one cylinder. Install the head assembly, torque the head, set the cam timing, install intake and exhaust rocker arm, and adjust the valve lash to 0. Rotate the crankshaft through two complete revolutions. The minimum valve clearance will not be at top dead center, but somewhere before top dead center, depending upon the cam timing of the camshaft you are using. Rotating the engine through two complete cycles will allow both intake and exhaust valves to open and close once. After rotating the crank, carefully disassemble the head. If the valves make an impression, cut the clay in half with a sharp knife and measure its thickness at the thinnest point with a vernier caliper.

Another measuring media preferred by many mechanics is solder in place of the modeling clay. If you use this method, use solder with an uncrushed diameter of 2.54 mm (0.100 inch). You can also judge the clearance between the valves and pistons by screwing the valve-adjustment screws in easily identified amounts. The thread pitch on the valve-adjusting screws is 1 mm, so one complete rotation of the valve-adjusting screw is 1 mm (0.040 inch); a half-turn would be .5 mm (0.020 inch), and a quarter-turn would be .25 mm (0.010 inch). Using any one or a combination of these measurement techniques will allow you to accurately determine the valve-to-piston clearance.

The minimum clearance for the intake and exhaust valves should be 0.060 inch. If there is not adequate clearance, up to a point you can increase the depth of the valve relief in the pistons by fly-cutting for clearance, but remember you should not get the piston dome any thinner than 0.200 inch.

To raise the compression in 2.4-liter engines, people have been replacing the 2.4-liter pistons with pistons from the 2.2-liter engines. This modification is usually performed on the 2.4-liter 911 S to take advantage of various club rules that allow cars a compression increase and still let them run in the stock class. When Porsche went to the longer-stroke 2.4-liter engines, one of the things it did was lower the compression ratio of all of the models so they all could run on regular gasoline. Where the 2.2-liter 911 S had compression of 9.8:1, the 2.4-liter 911 S had its compression reduced to 8.5:1. Using the higher-compression pistons from the shorter-stroke 2.2-liter 911 S engine on one of the 2.4 911S engines would significantly improve the engine's performance. The change in stroke will increase the compression ratio by about 0.55 points above what it would have been when used on the shorter-stroke engine. But don't be alarmed, for some reason it comes out to only 9.66 when measured and calculated out, not the expected 10.35:1, which still makes a fine-running engine of the 2.4 911S.

Again, all of the clearances will need to be checked to make sure that you have no interference when the engine is assembled. Be aware of a potential problem with the deck height that some owners have experienced, while others said they had a problem with the bottom of the piston skirt hitting the main-bearing webs in the crankcase. A 3.2-liter 935 engine we bought new from

the factory had that problem just when we thought we had an unfair advantage on the competition. We didn't find the problem until qualifying, when one of the pistons broke and we were forced to use a 3.0-liter engine for the race. So much for our unfair advantage.

2.7 911 Modifications

The 2.7-liter 911 engine has always been a popular engine to modify. Early on, one of the most popular modifications for this engine was to fit the 2.8-liter RSR's 92 mm pistons and cylinders. The only problem with this was that most people making this conversion didn't realize what they were doing to the compression. The only quality pistons and cylinders available for the conversion are the Mahles made for the 2.8 RSR engine. The RSR cylinder heads were unique in that they were made with the small cylinder-head-stud spacing (80 mm for 2.0-2.8 liter engines) and the larger diameter, more open combustion chamber required by the larger 49 mm intake and 41.5 mm exhaust valves. The larger valves necessitated a reduced included valve angle of 55 deg, 45 min, exhaust angle; 30 deg, 15 min from vertical, and the intake 25 deg, 30 min from vertical.

The effect of all of this was to create a combustion chamber that had greater

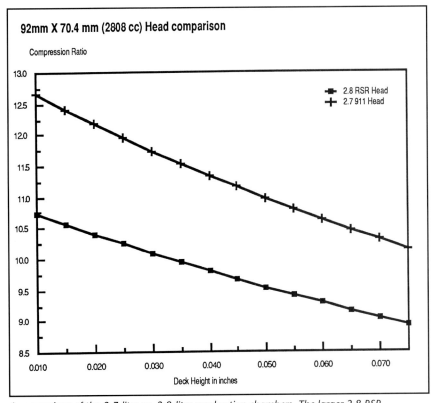

A comparison of the 2.7-liter vs. 2.8-liter combustion chambers. The larger 2.8 RSR combustion chamber was required by the larger 49-mm intake and 41.5-mm exhaust valves. The larger valves necessitated a reduced included valve angle of 55 deg, 45 minutes from vertical; an exhaust-valve angle of 30 deg, 15 minutes from vertical; and an intake-valve angle of 25 deg, 30 minutes from vertical. The effect of all of this was to create a combustion chamber that had a significantly larger volume than any of the earlier (2.0 through 2.7) engines had. The 92-mm Mahle pistons were then made to work with this larger combustion chamber and still provide the nominal 10.3:1 compression ratio of the normally aspirated Porsche racing engines. For this comparison, I measured the volume of a 2.8-liter RSR head and a 2.7-liter 911 head. The RSR head had a volume of 76 cc and the 911 head had a volume of 68.1 cc. The effect of these volumes on the compression ratio of the engine when used with the Mahle 92-mm pistons is shown in this graph. The deck height in the 911 engines is usually in the 0.030 to 0.040-inch range. You can see from the graph that the range of deck heights shown would give us a range of compression ratios of 9.8:1 to 10.1:1 for the RSR head and a whopping 11.3:1 to 11.75:1 for the 911 cylinder head. Note that the compression ratio of the 2.8 RSR actually works out to be lower than the expected 10.3:1. In our example, the dome of the piston is slightly too small to actually achieve the 10.3:1 ratio.

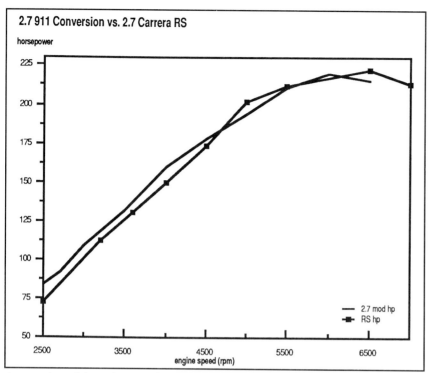

A comparison of the performance between the 2.7-liter Carrera RS engine and the 2.7-liter 911 engine using 2.7-liter Carrera RS pistons and cylinders, 911 E camshafts, and Weber carburetors. Performance data provided by Jerry Woods.

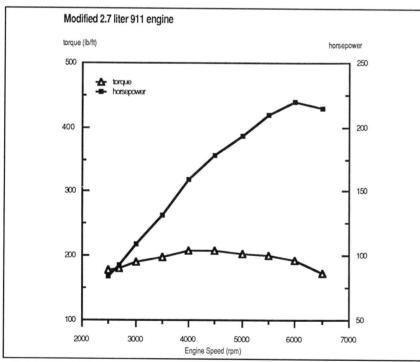

Here's a look at the performance of an excellent 2.7-liter engine conversion for a street-driven 911, one that uses the 95-mm European Carrera RS pistons and cylinders, 911 E camshafts, a set of Weber 40IDA carburetors, and an early-style (1974 or earlier) exhaust system with a sport muffler. If you are using a 1974 2.7-liter engine, it will already have the early style exhaust, but you will need to replace the CIS fuel injection system with carburetors to get the horsepower. Performance data provided by Jerry Woods.

volume than any of the earlier (2.0 through 2.7) engines. The 92-mm Mahle pistons were then made to work with this larger combustion chamber while still providing a compression ratio in the 10.3:1 range—common to most of Porsche's normally aspirated racing engines. The RSR head has a volume of 76 cc and the stock 2.7 911 head has a volume of 68.1 cc (I have measured other stock 2.7 heads ranging 66.0 to 70.0 cc). The effect of these volumes on the compression ratio of the engine when used with the Mahle 92-mm pistons is shown in the Head Comparison graph.

The deck height in 911 engines is usually in the 0.030–0.040-inch range. You can see from the graph that the deck heights shown would give us a range of compression ratios of 9.8:1 to 10.1:1 for the RSR head and a whopping 11.3:1 to 11.75:1 for the stock 2.7 cylinder head. Notice that the compression ratio of the 2.8 RSR actually worked out to be lower than the expected 10.3:1. In our example the dome of the piston is slightly too small to actually achieve the 10.3:1 ratio. If the dome were larger just think what it would have done to the compression ratio of the engine using the stock 2.7 cylinder head. You might think that the alternative would be to build a 2.8 engine from your 2.7 by using the pistons, cylinders, and cylinder heads from the 2.8 RSR. The problem with that choice is that the 2.8 RSR cylinder heads used 43 mm ports, which are much too large for a street engine of this displacement. Additionally the 2.8 RSR cylinder heads are difficult to find.

I don't recommend altering the deck height on the 911 engine to alter the compression ratio. When you raise the compression by changing the deck height, it requires machining the heads or cylinders and the chain housings and chain housing covers to realign the chain housing with the camshafts. Conversely, when you want to reduce the compression ratio you need to add spacers under the cylinders and then under the chain housing to get the chain housing realigned with the camshafts. Changing the deck height can also put the chain tensioning system out of its proper operating range, or at best compromise its reliability. (Different diameter sprockets are available for the chain sprocket idler which will allow you to compensate for any unusual deck heights you may create by using various parts combinations.) The most you can practically change the deck height in the 911 engine is about 1 mm. You can see on the graph that by increasing the deck height by a full millimeter the compression will still be about 10.2:1 with the stock 2.7 cylinder head. This is probably still too high for today's gasoline unless you convert your engine to a twin-plug ignition system. Considering all we have discussed, I recommend against using the 2.8 conversion for a street car.

There was also a special cylinder made that would allow the use of the 3.0-liter RSR pistons on a 2.7 911 engine case. Unfortunately, these 95-mm pistons and cylinders compounded the weaknesses of the 2.8 conversion. The 3.0 modification meant the crankcase had to be bored out even more, further weakening the material in the area of the spigot bases. Larger crankcase spigot bores also weaken the base material for the cylinder-head studs. The area at the top of the cylinder was too thin to reliably support a CE-type cylinder head gasket even though it used one. And finally, because 3.0 RSR combustion chamber is virtually identical to the 2.8 RSR, the high-compression-ratio problems were carried over to this conversion as well.

ANDIAL has a more modern 2.9- and 3.0-liter conversion for the 2.7-liter engines. It is made by Mahle and addresses all of the problems discussed earlier. ANDIAL offers two versions of this conversion, one for CIS-injected engines and another for carbureted or mechanically injected engines. The ANDIAL 3.0-liter CIS conversion has special Mahle pistons made to work with the CIS fuel-injection system. Its 3.0 conversion for the carbureted or mechanically injected engines has special Mahle pistons that provide adequate valve-to-piston clearance to clear 911 S camshafts. ANDIAL's conversion has special Dilavar cylinder-head studs that have a longer threaded portion at the bottom so that they do not require the use of a threaded insert for additional strength. The compression ratio has been lowered to 9.5:1 for the CIS conversion and 10.5:1 for the conversion for the carbureted or injected racing engines. Like the 3.2 Carrera, the cylinders use no head gasket.

If your enlarged 2.7-liter engine is destined for street use, then my favorite conversion is to use the 95 mm European Carrera RS pistons and cylinders, 911 E camshafts, a set of Weber 40IDA carburetors, and an early-style (1974 or earlier) exhaust system and sport muffler. If you are using a 1974 2.7-liter engine, it will already have the early-style exhaust, but you will need to replace

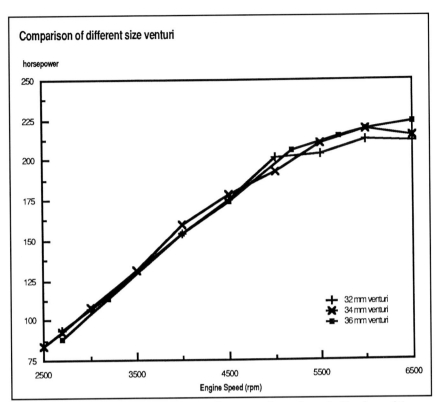

A comparison to aid in venturi size selection. Tests were also performed with a larger 36-mm venturi and a smaller 32-mm venturi, but the 34-mm seemed to be the optimum compromise. Furthermore, the performance difference between the 32-mm and the 36-mm was so small that it is doubtful that you would be able to perceive the difference in a driving test. Performance data provided by Jerry Woods.

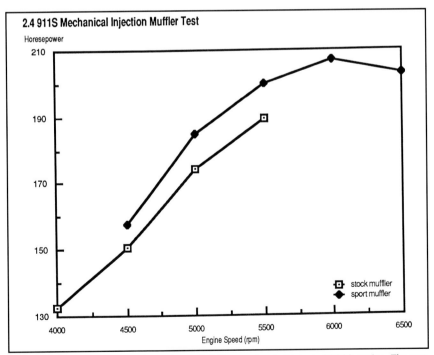

A muffler comparison test performed on a 2.4-liter mechanical-injected 911S engine. The test compared a stock muffler and a twin-pipe sport muffler; the sport muffler showed a significant increase in power, particularly in the upper rpm. Performance data by Paul Schenk.

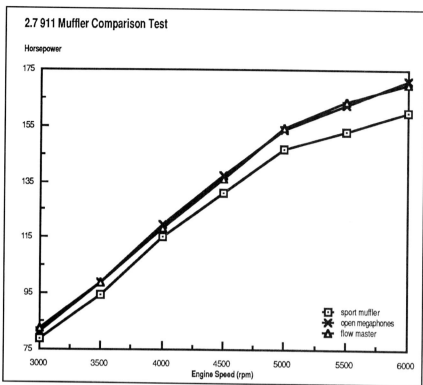

2.7 911 Muffler Comparison Test

Horsepower

Legend:
- □ sport muffler
- ✕ open megaphones
- △ flow master

Engine Speed (rpm)

A 2.7-liter muffler comparison test. This engine is used for track events where there are noise restrictions. The idea of the comparison test is to look for a muffler or silencer that will actually improve the performance while meeting the noise restriction. You can see by the results that the test was successful and the Flow Master racing muffler actually came very close to matching the performance of the open megaphones. Performance data by Paul Schenk.

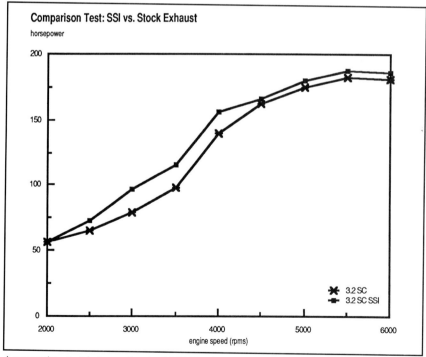

Comparison Test: SSI vs. Stock Exhaust

horsepower

Legend:
- ✕ 3.2 SC
- ■ 3.2 SC SSI

engine speed (rpms)

A comparison test between the stock 911SC exhaust system and the SSI heat exchangers and a stock early muffler system. The engine used for this comparison was a 911SC with a bolt-on 98-mm 3.2-liter conversion. Performance data provided by SSI.

the CIS fuel-injection system with carburetors to get the horsepower you want. There are two reasons that I recommend replacing the CIS system with carburetors for this conversion: The first is that the CIS system is not particularly performance-oriented. It was used instead as a means of meeting the emissions standards of the early 1970s. The only racing car that Porsche ever built that used CIS injection was the 934 Group 4 car, and this because the rules required it. The air-flow metering unit used by the CIS system is intolerant of pulsations in the intake system, so relatively mild camshafts must be used in engines with CIS injection to avoid affecting low-rpm running.

So, if we are going to make a hot rod of the 2.7 engine we must replace the CIS-injection system with either Weber carburetors, mechanical injection, or one of the more modern aftermarket electronic-injection systems. Keep in mind that the Webers are readily available and probably a more practical solution to the problem on this particular engine combination.

If the 2.7 liter being converted is a 1975–77 with either of the two later style exhaust systems, it will need to have the exhaust system back-dated to the 1974 version. The engine pictured uses a twin-pipe sport muffler. The remainder of the conversion is a fairly simple matter. In addition to the carburetors and exhaust system, all that is needed to complete the conversion is a set of European Carrera RS pistons and cylinders and a pair of 911E camshafts. The heads will have to have the ports increased to 36 mm in diameter. It is particularly important to increase the port size if the engine being modified was a standard 911 with its 32-mm ports and not one of the 911 S or Carrera engines with their 35-mm ports.

To carburet this modified 2.7-liter engine use a set of 40 IDA-3C Webers with 34-mm venturi, F3 emulsion tubes, 135 main jets, and 145 air correction jets. Comparison testing with a larger and smaller venturi was performed, but the 34 mm seemed to provide the optimum compromise.

These modifications make for a wonderful, fun-to-drive engine, so if you are wondering what to do with your stock 2.7-liter this might be the answer. The only down side to this conversion is a loss in fuel economy as compared to what is available with the CIS injection-system. The carbureted engine will return mileage of 16–19 mpg, whereas the CIS-injected engine will get 22–25 mpg.

A really nice alternative to the carbureted 2.7 with 911 E cams is a replica of the 2.7 RS engine—if you can round up all of the appropriate injection-system parts. You'll also need 911 S cams to match the needs of the mechanical injection-system. The Carrera RS engine offers a little more power, improved low-speed throttle response, improved fuel economy, and legality in some states where the carbureted conversion will not be.

3.0 911SC Engine Modifications

There are a few fairly simple but very effective things that can be done to the 911SC engines.

Many enthusiasts have experimented with the camshaft timing on their SCs, either advancing the timing to improve the bottom-end performance or retarding the timing in an effort to improve the top-end performance, but I have found that it actually makes little difference in the overall performance. I agree with what Porsche finally did with the timing for the Carrera 3.2 engines, which was to split the difference between the two extremes. The camshafts used in the 3.2 were introduced in 3.0 Carrera in 1976. Porsche has advanced and retarded these cams several times over the years; and finally with the introduction of the 3.2-liter Carrera in 1984, it struck the midpoint compromise mentioned above.

Another very popular and successful modification is to replace the exhaust system with that from a 1974 or earlier 911. The early-style exhaust system—made by SSI—can be installed on any of the 911SC engines for a performance gain of 17–22 hp depending on the year of the engine and the dynamometer used. I have no specific test data on an SC engine, but we did get 13 hp on a Carrera 3.2 engine with the SSI heat exchangers and a dual outlet muffler. The change requires a pair of SSI heat exchangers, muffler, different scavenge oil line, and some pieces to adapt the heater system.

Michael Bavaro of Bodymotion, Inc., modified a stock 1984–89 911 Carrera crossover tube to work with the SSI heat exchangers. His modified crossover allows you to fit the SSI heat exchangers and retain the modern heater updates for plenty of cold weather heat.

The next change is to replace the CIS fuel injection with a pair of Weber 40 IDA-3C carburetors. The conversion to carburetors is good for an additional 10 hp for a total increase of 20–30 hp—but the greatly improved throttle re-

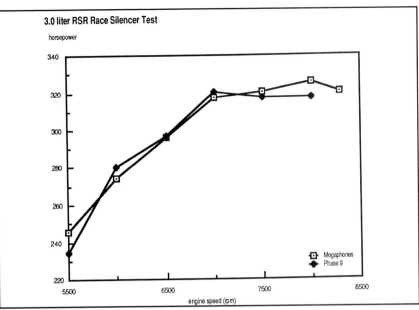

Here are the results of a 3.0-liter RSR race silencer test. The consequences of this test were more severe than for the muffler comparison test for the 2.7-liter engine. In that test, the objective was improved performance, whereas in this test the objective is to quiet a racing car so it can compete at a race track that has noise restrictions with a minimal loss in performance. More and more race tracks are imposing noise restrictions on cars in competitions. At a recent race in Oregon, IMSA black-flagged one of the GTO race leaders and had him put his car on the trailer because of excessive noise. If you bolted on a stock 911 muffler on the 3.0-liter RSR engine, it would run poorly because of the camshaft timing. The choices are either to detune the engine until it will run with a stock muffler or find a muffler that will make it quiet enough to pass the noise restrictions without altering the engine's performance too much. The Phase 9 race silencers were able to bring the noise of the RSR engine within the 105 dBa noise limits that most tracks require, and you can see from the results of this test that it had minimal effect on this racing engine's performance. Performance data provided by Jerry Woods.

Carrera 3.0–3.6 liters 1976–1996

911 Model	Cam timing	Checking height at TDC Overlap
1976/77 3.0 Carrera	Intake open 1 deg BTDC Intake close 53 deg ABDC Exh. open 43 deg BBDC Exh. close 3 deg ATDC	0.9 to 1.1 mm (0.035–0.043. inch)
1978–80 R.o.W. 911SC	Intake open 7 deg BTDC Intake close 47 deg ABDC Exh. open 49 deg BBDC Exh. close 3 deg BTDC	1.4 to 1.7 mm (0.055–0.067. inch)
1978–79 U.S. 911SC	same as 1976–77 3.0	0.9 to 1.1 mm (0.035–0.043. inch) Carrera
1980–83 U.S. 911SC	same as 1978–80 R.o.W.	1.4 to 1.7 mm (0.055–0.067. inch) 911SC
1981–83 R.o.W. 911SC	same as 1976–77 3.0	0.9 to 1.1 mm (0.035–0.043. inch) Carrera
1984–89 3.2 Carrera	Intake open 4 deg BTDC Intake close 50 deg ABDC Exh. open 46 deg BBDC Exh. close 0 deg TDC	1.1 to 1.4 mm (0.043–0.055. inch)
1989–94 3.6 Carrera (964)	Intake open 4 deg BTDC Intake close 65 deg ABDC Exh. open 44 deg BBDC Exh. close 4 deg ATDC	1.26 ± 0.1 mm (0.045–0.54 inch)
1994–96 3.6 Carrera (993)	Intake open 1 deg BTDC Intake close 60 deg ABDC Exh. open 45 deg BBDC Exh. close 5 deg ATDC	0.9 to 1.1 mm (0.055–0.067 inch)

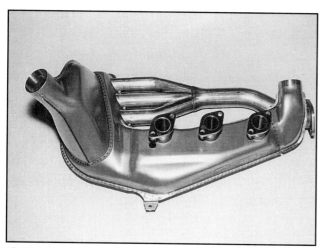

The SSI all-stainless-steel heat exchanger.

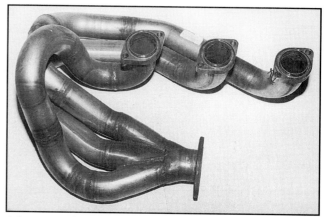

A factory equal-length three-into-one racing header for the 3.0-liter 911SC engine. Left side: part number 911.111.049.00, as used on the 911SC RS (Type 954). The inside diameter of the pipe is 42-mm (about 1 5/8 inches). Porsche AG

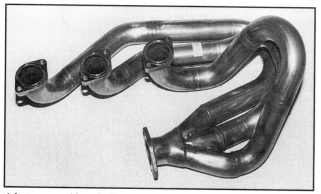

A factory equal-length three-into-one racing header for the 3.0-liter 911SC engine. Right side: part number 911.111.050.00, as used on 911SC RS (Type 954). Pipe inside diameter is 42-mm (about 1 5/8 inches). Porsche AG

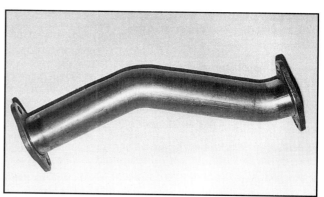

Adapters for adapting a stock muffler or a sport muffler to a set of factory racing headers: part numbers 911.111.053.00 for the left side and 911.111.054.00 for the right side. Porsche AG.

sponse feels more like 50 hp. The 34-mm venturi will be correct for this engine size. Use F3 emulsion tubes, 160 main jets, and 175 air correction jets as a starting setup. The engine should be tested on a dynamometer to optimize the carburetor settings. Idle jets are best selected with a driving test. You will probably need to run with 60, 65, or maybe even larger idle jets. The idle jets have to be rich enough to eliminate the part-throttle lean surge, but as lean as possible for the best fuel economy.

The distributor used with the 1978 and 1979 engines will work fine with the carburetors, but when the vacuum unit is discarded the mechanical advance curve from the 1980 and later 911SCs' distributor is too short for use with carburetors. For the later engines your options are use the distributor from a 1978 or 1979 911SC, have your dis-

tributor recurved, or use the "European" distributor. If you need your distributor recurved, Barry Hershon IAE (International Auto Electric) in Detroit, Michigan, has all of the parts and equipment needed to do the job.

A really nice conversion for the 3.0 911SC engine is a small increase in displacement to 3.2 liters (3,186 cc) using 98-mm pistons and cylinders. I first heard of this conversion in 1979. German customers were picking up their new 911SCs at the factory and then taking them to either Werk I, the customer repair center, or to one of the independent German tuners (like Kremer Brothers or Max Moritz) to have the engine modified. The only changes made in these conversions were a new set of pistons and cylinders and resetting the fuel mixture, yet 220 hp was claimed as the output.

Mahle made the piston sets for all of these conversions. The piston sets that Max Moritz had Mahle make have a wedge-shaped dome that improves combustion chamber efficiency. The Moritz pistons and cylinders have finally become a fairly popular conversion here in the United States. Because this conversion retains all of the stock emission-control devices, it has the advantage of offering a significant performance increase without violating emissions laws.

This displacement modification would have been a natural for the 2.7 911s because almost all of them required some form of major maintenance before they reached 100,000 miles. "Unfortunately" for the 911SC hot rodder, the 3.0 engine is much too reliable and seems to want to last forever. You may have to take a perfectly healthy 911SC engine apart just to perform this

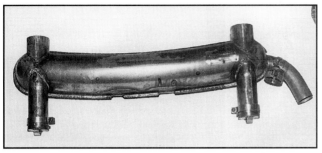

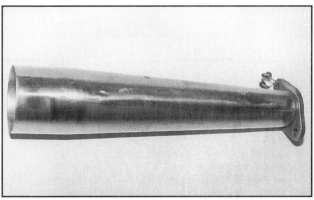

A rally silencer for use with racing megaphones, part number 911.111.010.00. With the megaphone outlets uncapped, these mufflers are probably not quiet enough for our track events. These mufflers are used for European rallies where they use public roads and have special stages. For the special stages, the megaphone outlets are uncapped, and then for the road portions, the megaphone outlets are capped so that the cars will be quiet enough to meet the noise laws of the various European countries. Porsche AG

The factory racing megaphone diffuser, part number 911.111.043.75. Porsche AG

modification. I have been bragging about some friends who have more than 200,000 miles on their 911SCs for some time now, and I just recently talked with shop owner Bob Grigsby who maintains a 911SC that has more than 400,000 miles on it and it still runs great. Neither of us has ever rebuilt a 911SC engine because it wore out.

For even more horsepower fun, the Max Moritz pistons can be combined with a carburetion change, exhaust system backdating, and a mild cam, like a GE40 or a 911 S cam, for a truly wonderful power increase. Additional valve clearance will be necessary because of the increased overlap and duration of the 911 S camshafts. I still recommend using the Weber 40 IDA-3C carburetors for this conversion. Again, I used the formula for sizing the carburetors as follows:

The 3.2 Carrera engine produces its 231 hp at 5,900 rpm, so 5,900 was again selected as the rpm. Displacement for one cylinder is 527 cc

$$\text{Venturi size in mm} = 20\sqrt{\frac{527}{1000} \times \frac{5900}{1000}}$$

Venturi size in mm = 35.26 (35) mm

The calculated venturi size has increased from 34 mm to 35 mm. Using Weber's throttle-bore-to-venturi-size recommendations (throttle bore should be 10 to 25 percent larger than the venturi size) in this example, the throttle bore should be between 38.5 mm and 43.75 mm, proving that even for the 3.2 conversion, the Weber 40 IDA-3C carburetors are probably still the best compromise.

There are also racing pistons available for these engines that have been made to work with the more aggressive racing

camshafts. There are 3.0-liter pistons available from Porsche which were made by Mahle for the 954 engines and their compression ratio of 10.3:1. There is also a 9.0:1, 3.2 piston/cylinder combination available for these engines with the traditional rounded dome piston with adequate valve-to-piston clearance for racing camshafts. The Max Moritz CIS pistons have a higher 9.8:1 compression ratio, but were not designed with adequate valve clearance for racing cams.

One thing that you must watch for when you attempt to build racing engines based on the 911SC engine is that there are also RSR 3.0- and 3.2-liter pistons that can be matched to the 3.0 911SC engine's cylinders, and they just aren't the same thing. The problem encountered is that the combustion chambers in the cylinder heads from the RSR engines were considerably smaller than those in the 911SC heads. The RSR heads had combustion chambers that were about 76–77 ccs in volume, whereas the 911SC's combustion chamber is about 90 cc. The result of all of this is that it is hard to get a decent compression ratio out of the RSR pistons when used in the 911SC-based engines.

3.2 Carrera Engine Modifications
Bosch DME Background

When the Carrera 3.2 was introduced it came with a new more reliable and more efficient engine management system, the Bosch DME (Digital Motor Electronics) or Motronics. At first this seemed to mark the end of engine modifications. It appeared that there would be no way to modify the engine's fuel mixture or advance curves to match the changed needs of a modified engine.

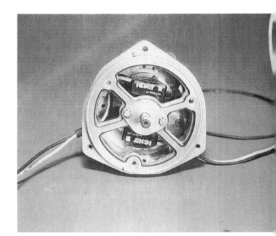

A Marelli twin-plug distributor with a pair of Ignitor units installed in place of the four sets of points normally used. The Ignitor units are self-contained units with an inductive pickup and Hall-effect transistors used as a switching devices. These Ignitor units also solve a problem that the Marelli twin-plug distributors had with point bounce at high rpm.

This new electronic trickery replaced the carburetors, simpler fuel-injection systems, and ignition distributors previously used and understood by mechanics with a computer, which most mechanics didn't understand and didn't like. There were no simple screwdriver adjustments that a mechanic could make to modify either the fuel mixture or the ignition timing or advance curve.

The DME system combined the basic functions of ignition and fuel injection into a single, computer-controlled system. Other functions such as Lambda control, knock sensor control, and boost control can also be incorporated into the same basic system. Engine sensors provide the control signals to the central unit, which then directs all fuel delivery and ignition timing based on the engine's needs by sensing the rpm, load, engine crank position relative to Z1, and temperature. This computerized control of the engine uses these control signals to select and manipulate maps stored in the PROMs or E-PROMs (programmable read-only memory and erasable programmable read-only memory) for fuel mixture and ignition advance.

Almost as soon as the DME system was introduced, computer hackers started to modify the PROMs to change the maps and the manner in which the computer used them to alter ignition timing, fuel mixture, and maximum rpm for the rev limiter. Unfortunately,

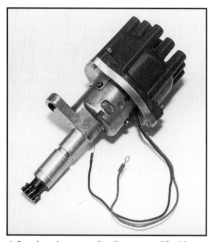

A Bosch point-type distributor modified by Jerry Woods to be pointless, with Hall-effect Ignitor units, and to have a twin-plug rotor and cap. Woods also performed the same modification to the later inductive distributors used on the SC and Turbo.

though a lot of the early hackers and programmers understood the electronics and programming, they didn't really understand the engine's needs—some of the first aftermarket chips were pretty crude. On the other hand, many of the best engine developers were not the best software writers so many of their early chips were really no better. Time, however, has rectified this situation, with knowledgeable people decoding the computer logic of the Bosch system and modifying the chips to both enhance the performance of stock engines and to meet the changed needs of modified engines.

There are chips available now that will reliably enhance Porsche performance. I did some testing of modified chips fairly early on to see what improvements they really made. Initially I was interested because some end users were making some pretty impressive claims about performance improvements they had experienced.

I have been trying to get more power out of Porsche engines for most of my adult life, so I really did not expect much performance improvement just by changing the engine's timing and fuel mixture. The internal combustion engine is really nothing more than an air pump with heat exchange capability, and the only way to make it produce more power is to make it a more efficient air pump. Considering that perspective, no amount of fiddling or tweaking with the fuel mixture or ignition advance is really going to greatly improve its efficiency as an air pump.

Before modern engine management systems controlled fuel mixture and ignition advance, we had carburetors to

meter the engine's fuel mixture and distributors to establish the ignition advance curve. No one really expected to be able to make significant power improvements by changing carburetor jets or the ignition advance curve on stock engines. You can only set the optimum spark for a given condition and the optimum fuel mixture for a given condition. The real advantage of the DME system was that you could optimize the fuel mixture and the ignition curve for all points of engine operation over a wider range of operating conditions by changing the software. However, in order to improve a Porsche's performance by modifying the computer software one must assume that the original software program was incorrect or that Porsche had been too conservative in its settings.

Early on in the development of DME, the manufacturers were very conservative and assumed the worst operating conditions using the worst fuel. Now with well over a decade of experience, Porsche and other manufacturers are not as conservative, and there is much less to be gained with the modified chips.

To really make a Porsche engine into a better air pump we must improve its ability to get the air in or out by improving the intake and the exhaust. We can also make it pump more air by increasing the displacement. Turbocharged engines can be made into better air pumps by increasing the boost and

A 2.4-liter 911T CIS piston. The CIS pistons had offset domes to alter the effective combustion chamber and ensure more complete combustion. These pistons have little practical use in a modified engine because of the lack of adequate clearance for the valves if one of the more aggressive camshafts is used.

Updated piston and cylinder for a 906 or 910 racing engine. Note the tall dome and large valve cut-outs for valve-to-piston clearance. The cylinder is a Nikasil made with a CE ring head gasket.

A 2.0-liter 911S piston. The piston was forged and had a high dome to achieve a 9.8:1 compression ratio.

blowing more air into the pump. You can also make your engine a more efficient air pump by improving the thermal efficiency so that the engine produces more power for less energy input. This is where small improvements might be made by tweaking the fuel mixture and ignition advance curves.

Sometimes we want to run an overly rich mixture at full-throttle low-speed conditions where knock occurs. This is done so that we can run a higher compression ratio, which proves beneficial over the whole operating speed range. For the same reasons, it is sometimes beneficial to use high compression ratios and retard the ignition timing at full throttle. This has the effect of improving the economy at part throttle where the engine really spends most of its time. It would be possible to make some gains here by changing the compromises and perhaps running more advance and more fuel.

Of course, it is important to fire the spark plugs at the right instant for every engine operating condition. The right timing for one operating condition will not be the correct timing for another condition. For instance, the ignition timing requirements for light-throttle and light-load conditions—such as driving down the freeway—are quite different than the full-throttle full-load conditions that would exist under heavy acceleration for the same range of engine rpms. All engines also require more ignition advance at higher engine speeds than at lower engine speeds. Engines will run better with more ignition advance in a part throttle condition than they will be able to tolerate at a full-throttle full-load condition. This is why conventional distributors use a vacuum advance unit.

The DME system used by Porsche allows the engine designers to set the ignition advance curve accurately for varying engine operating conditions. It is hard to improve on what these engine management systems do; essentially if the spark plug is fired at the right time and this spark successfully ignites the combustion at the right time and in the right place, nothing more can be done.

The engine needs a different fuel mixture for different engine speeds at different throttle openings and engine loads. The engine needs a richer mixture for cold conditions, but a different mixture for normal running conditions. In theory the perfect mixture for complete combustion is a 14:1 ratio (14 parts air to 1 part fuel). This is called the Stoichiometric mixture or Lambda=1. However, mixture requirements can vary from a low of 10 percent or more lean (a 16:1 ratio) for maximum fuel economy to a mixture that is 10 percent or more rich (a 12:1 ratio) for maximum torque. Before auto manufacturers were forced to be as concerned with emissions and fuel economy as they are today, the 14:1 ratio was good enough, but now much more accurate control is a must.

One of the real advantages of the Motronic engine management system is its ability to accurately control the fuel mixture and to quickly respond to changing engine requirements. The designers at Porsche and Bosch have mapped these systems to optimize the engine's best overall performance for all operating conditions. This is, of course, a compromise that takes into consideration such things as emissions, fuel economy, performance,

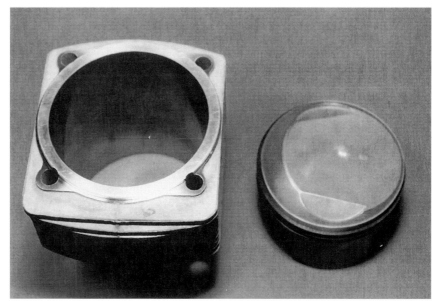

Here is a Max Moritz 3.2-liter conversion for the 911SC engines. This is a really nice conversion for the 3.0-liter 911SC engine. In addition to the increase in displacement, the piston has a nice wedge-shaped dome that improves the overall combustion chamber shape.

A series of pistons cut in half to show their construction. On the left is a 95-mm piston for a 962 racing engine; second from left is an 89-mm piston from a short-stroke 2.5-liter engine; next is a 82-mm piston from a 2.8-liter RSR engine; and on the right is a piston from a 2.0-liter 906 engine.

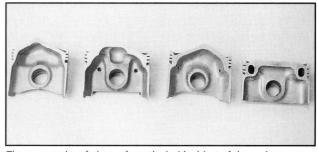

The same series of pistons from the inside. Most of these pistons were cut in half so that the valve-clearance pockets could be observed.

A 911SC cylinder with a groove for the CE ring head gasket.

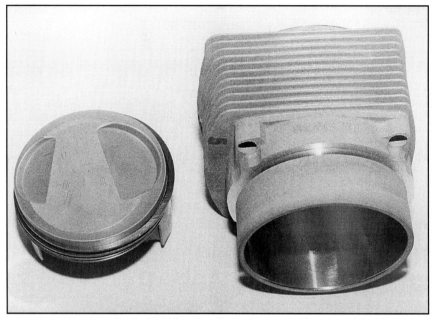

A Porsche racing piston for the 911SC engine. These pistons are 95 mm, retaining the engine's 3.0-liter displacement, and they have a 10.3:1 compression ratio. They have a wedge-shaped dome similar to the one used by the Max Moritz pistons. Porsche AG

A 935 cylinder with interlocking Ni-Resist sealing ring. Both the cylinder and the cylinder head must be machined to accept this interlocking ring. You must start with new cylinders that do not use the CE ring head gasket because the CE ring groove is larger than the groove for the interlocking ring.

and driveability. Surely it is possible to change these compromises and alter the engine's performance.

Tuning the DME System

So what is engine tuning? We tune up an engine to make it run properly and we tune it to make it produce more power. In Europe, high-performance shops are called tuners. This is probably a British term, but German Porsche performance shops such as Ruf and Kremer Brothers are also considered tuners. What we want to do with the high-performance chips for the engine management system is "tune" the engine and make it perform better under some operating conditions.

Emissions requirements are only applicable to engine manufacturers under normal driving conditions, and they are allowed to disregard them entirely when the cars are driven under wide open throttle. Consequently, wide open throttle is where the chip makers make most of their changes. Some makers have altered some of the part-throttle maps for some improved driveability, but the real performance gains are at wide open throttle.

A few years ago Jerry Woods and I did some testing of all of the chips that we could get our hands on. We tested Autothority, Hypertech, Z Industries, Keno, and Knightech. At the time, each chip that we tested offered some improvement over the stock chip at some rpm range. The largest horsepower improvement that we saw was 9 percent, and at peak horsepower the greatest improvement was 4 percent, or an increase in power from 217 DIN hp to 226 DIN hp. The average improvement of the best of the best was 3.4 percent. That is picking the best performance of the best chip for each given rpm of the test.

At the same time we also tested different exhaust systems and concluded that the best chip change was probably an exhaust system change, because it gave the best overall improvement above 2,500 rpm. The exhaust system change (using SSI heat exchangers with a twin-pipe sport-type muffler) produced a peak increase of 13 hp compared to a 9 hp increase for the best chip. The muffler was a stock-type with a second tail pipe added to the right end like the muffler that Performance Products sells.

More Displacement

There are several, nice, large-displacement options available for the 3.2 Carrera already. There was actually a 3.5-liter normally aspirated combination available before the Carrera 3.2 was introduced. This was a bit of an odd ball engine that used the "3.2-liter 935" (74.4-mm stroke) crankshaft and either titanium 935 connecting rods or 911SC connecting rods and 100-mm Mahle pistons and cylinders (these are the 100-mm pistons that you see listed for sale with the 22-mm wrist pins). The pioneers that attempted to build these original 3.5-liter engines had a great deal of difficulty because of the funny pistons that resulted from the original combination. In addition to having the wrong diameter wrist pin, the wrist pin was also located wrong in the piston because it was made for the 0.8 mm (0.0315 inch) longer Titanium/911SC connecting rods. The result was that even after the wrist pin diameter problem was solved, you still had about 0.8 mm more deck height than you would have liked.

Fortunately, or perhaps unfortunately for some of the pioneers, this original combination stimulated a great deal of interest in these large-displacement 3.5-liter engines and now pistons are available with the correct 23-mm wrist pins and pin locations so it's fairly easy to build one of these 3.5 engines. When you build a 3.5-liter engine you will need to bore out the spigots in the crankcase from 103 mm to 105 mm to accept the larger-diameter cylinders.

Another popular size modification for these 3.2 Carrera engines is the 3.4-liter conversion using 98-mm piston and cylinder sets. There is both a racing version and Ruf's street version. The advantage to the 3.4-liter conversions over the 3.5-liter conversions is that no machining is required—they are true bolt-on conversions.

We will use the formula again for sizing the carburetors for our 3.4 hot-rod engine. Let us assume it produces 250 hp at 5,900 rpm and the displacement for one cylinder is 561 cc.

$$\text{Venturi size in mm} = 20\sqrt{\frac{561}{1000} \times \frac{5900}{1000}}$$

Venturi size in mm = 36.38 (36) mm

The calculated venturi size has increased from 34 mm for the 3.0 911SC engine to 35 mm for the 3.2 liter Carrera engine and finally to 36 mm for the 3.4-liter version of the Carrera engine. Using Weber's throttle-bore-to-venturi-size recommendations (throttle bore 10–25 percent larger than venturi size) in this example, the throttle bore should be between 39.6 mm and 45 mm. Hence, for the 3.4-liter conversion the Weber 46 IDA carburetors are probably the correct choice.

Some Case Studies

Gary Bohrman of Exclusive Motorcars also did some testing on a 3.2 Carrera engine. First he ran a baseline test of the stock engine on the dyno and got 213 hp, then he tried a set of SSI heat exchangers with an early-style muffler with a chip matched to the exhaust and got 226 hp. Next he tried the Autothority A.P.E. mass air flow sensor with the SSI heat exchangers and stock muffler and got 236 hp. Finally he tested the mass air flow sensor with the W&W exhaust system designed and built by Jerry Woods and Peter Weber for a peak horsepower of 240.7.

A modification for the Weber float bowl. Weber supplies its carburetors with a little stand-off around the main jet well in the bottom of the float bowl chamber. This is done to prevent the main circuit from picking up dirt from the bottom of the float bowl. Unfortunately, there are also some heavy cornering conditions where this stand-off prevents the main jet from picking up fuel.

The modification to improve the Weber's fuel pickup consists of either milling away the stand-off with an end mill or grinding it away with a rotary file in a die grinder. It must be ground or milled down so that the fuel can be picked up off the bottom of the float bowl.

To finish the Weber main-jet pickup modification, a small sheet-aluminum dam is made to fit into the float chamber and sit on top of the main-jet bores and stand-off tubes. This dam is then glued into place with epoxy. The dam's purpose is to trap fuel around the main-jet pickup to prevent momentary fuel starvation.

Additional Weber float venting. Unfortunately, the volatility of U.S. gasoline has greatly increased in just the past few years. Prior to 1983 there was a period of about 20 years when the fuel had an average Reid vapor pressure (RVP) of 9–9.5 psi. Since 1983, the RVP has increased to 11.5 psi (industry standard specification) and above. This increased RVP causes excessive volatility, which results in vapor lock and the fuel foaming, hot starting problems, poor low-speed driveability, and boiling in the carburetors. The high RVP causes the fuel in the Weber float bowls to boil and percolate the fuel out through the secondary venturi. Once this process starts, it can siphon all of the fuel out of the float chamber into the throttle bore and intake port, which creates a high risk of fire when the engine is restarted. To fix this problem, PMO offers the fixture shown in this photo for drilling additional venting holes in the carburetor top cover. The fixture aims the drill into the vent chamber for the idle air correction jet. This vent chamber then is vented into the carburetor throat via the little square slots visible in the photo. This extra venting seems to solve most of the problems caused by the excessive volatility of the fuel.

You can see from these results that Bohrman was successful in boosting the engine power by 27.7 hp—a 13-plus percent increase—just by using external modifications. These sorts of modifications would have no effect on an engine's longevity, and my experience has been that this type of modification actually improves the driveability of these cars.

Another way to increase the engine's efficiency as an air pump is to make it bigger by increasing displacement. If you just increase the engine's displacement and do nothing to improve the engine's intake and exhaust efficiencies, the most that you can hope to increase the engine's output will be equivalent to the displacement increase, but the performance characteristics will be similar to the engine's stock configuration. The U.S. version of the Carrera 3.2 produces 217 hp, so if you increase its displacement to 3.5 liters, which is 10.8 percent, and maintain the same compression ratio, you should increase the power by nearly 10.8 percent to 240.5 hp. The Euro engine had a higher compression ratio and different DME, and it was rated at 231 hp; so if you increase its displacement by that same 10.8 percent to 3.5 liters and maintain its stock compression ratio with the same efficiencies you end up with 256 hp.

I had the opportunity to test a Carrera 3.2 engine that had been modified from the standard 3,164.1-cc displacement to 3,506 cc by changing the pistons and cylinders to a set with a 100-mm bore. The engine also had a twin-ignition setup, but the pistons did not provide the high-compression ratio of the European engine. Consequently, the performance did not match our hypothetical peak of 265 hp, instead making only 252.1 hp. Though this does not exceed the potential European horsepower, it does exceed by quite a bit the 240.5 hp potential of an engine with the U.S. compression.

The reasons for the increased efficiency are that the 3.5 version that we tested used a twin-plug ignition, a modified chip, and had a modified dual-outlet muffler. Because of the twin ignition, the ignition map was reprogrammed—retarded about 5 to 8 deg—to work with the twin ignition. (The stock two-valve 911 engine has its spark plug squeezed to the side by the large valves, creating a combustion problem. This problem is alleviated in Porsche's four-valve heads, which permit the optimum, central location for the spark plug. The problem had been diminished in the two-valve heads of the Carrera 2/4 engines by using dual plugs.) The twin ignition is so much more effective at igniting the mixture that the engine will detonate if the advance curve is not retarded to compensate.

The second plug gives better combustion by starting the fire in two places instead of one. This helps reduce the longer flame travel time inevitable with a single plug that is squeezed off to one side of the combustion chamber as in the earlier 911s The improved combustion of the twin-ignition system reduces the engine's sensitivity to octane, and you can usually get away with a compression ratio about one point higher. The twin plugs also make the engine run crisper and cleaner.

The following table shows how the 3.5-liter Carrera engine with twin ignition is improved over the stock U.S. version of the 3.2 Carrera engine.

Engine Speed (rpm)	Modified 3.5-Liter Carrera
1,000	6.3%
1,500	21.59
2,000	19.90
2,500	19.90
3,000	22.21
3,500	21.60
4,000	25.82
4,500	23.09
5,000	18.41
5,500	18.06
6,000	16.18

The displacement increase from 3.2 to 3.5 liters was 10.8 percent, so you can see that the engine under test was able to exceed the displacement increase thanks to its dual-plug setup. The reasons for this increased efficiency is that the 3.5 version of the engine used the twin-plug ignition, a modified chip and a muffler change. So it was not really a direct comparison, but it does show the potential for changes of this kind.

I also tested another 3.2 Carrera engine that had been made into a more efficient air pump by making improvements to the induction and exhaust systems. In this case, the engine was destined for a race car owned by a friend who wanted to spend neither the time nor the money to build a proper racing engine. All changes made to this engine were exter-

Right
A modified 3.2-liter 911SC engine. Originally a 3.0-liter 911SC engine, it has been modified by the addition of larger-bore 98-mm pistons and cylinders, special high-performance camshafts, 40 IDA-3C carburetors, and an SSI exhaust system.

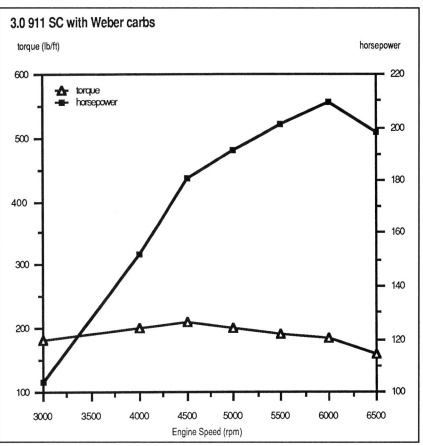

A 3.0-liter 911SC engine with Weber carburetors. This engine has been modified by the addition of a set of 40 IDA-3C carburetors and an early-style exhaust system with a stock muffler.

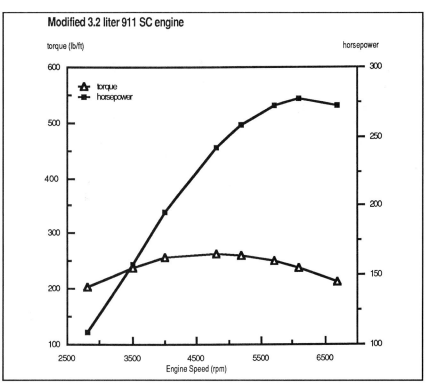

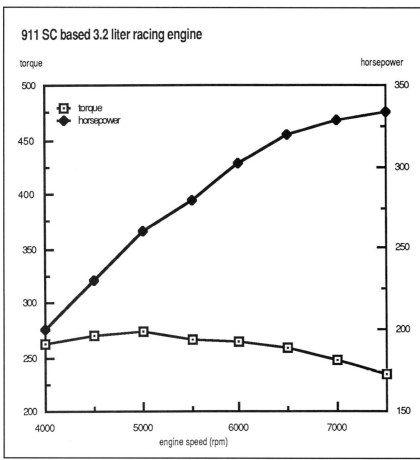

911 SC based 3.2 liter racing engine

A 911SC-based 3.2-liter racing engine. This 3.0-liter 911SC engine has been modified extensively with larger ports, Jerry Woods Enterprises GE 80 camshafts, Carrera RSR racing headers, and a set of 46 IDA Weber carburetors.

An intercooler kit for the 1975–1977 3.0-liter 911 Turbo. This Fred Garretson intercooler kit and a later-style rear wing allow you to adapt an intercooler to one of these pre-intercooler cars. This larger intercooler is more efficient than the factory 911 Turbo intercooler.

nal. The induction system was replaced with a set of 46 IDA Webers, and the exhaust system was replaced by a set of properly designed racing headers. The engine retained the DME control but only for the ignition portion of the engine management. The ignition advance curve was optimized to match the changes in exhaust and induction systems.

We tested the engine with both the racing header system with megaphones and the racing header system with a set of Phase 9 silencers (these make the car quiet enough for most track events, but not really quiet enough for street use). These changes in exhaust and induction system alone increased the peak horsepower to 265.5 at 7,000 rpm from the stock 217 hp at 6,000 rpm—a better than 22 percent increase over stock.

So, despite initial concerns about diminished hop-up opportunities for DME engines, it is clear we will be able to continue making major changes to the engines that will improve the volumetric efficiencies. Of course these must be accompanied by altered chips to match the spark and fuel needs of these modified engines.

3.6 Carrera Engine Modifications

As of this writing, 3.6 Carrera engines are the correct size for IMSA GTS 2 racing and have become very popular engines to modify. Depending upon the chassis, IMSA allows Porsche air-cooled engines of 3.2, 3.6, and 3.8 into this class. The 3.2 engines are required for mid-engined, tube framed 911s; the 3.6 versions for tube-framed, rear-engined cars or cars with altered suspension or relocated suspension pickups; and the 3.8s are for full-monocoque chassis with stock suspension pick-ups. As a result of these diverse requirements there are engines of all of these sizes based on the 3.6 964/993 engines running in the IMSA GTS 2 class. Porsche makes a lot of racing parts available for these engines, including all of the components necessary to build a Carrera RSR 3.8 engine. The RSR has special pistons, cylinders, and cylinder heads, and a special intake system with a tuned resonance intake chamber and six individual throttle butterflies.

A number of tuners—Alex Job Racing, Jack Lewis, Perfect Power, Jerry Woods Enterprises, Larry Schumacher Racing and others—have built engines to run in this IMSA class. Most of these are the 3.6-liter engines required for the modified chassis or tube-framed cars.

Jack Lewis has built his engines using Cosworth pistons in Mahle cylinders with cams of his own design and mechanical fuel-injection. Of the private tuners, Alex Job has probably created the most different combinations. He has one that uses the factory induction-system and another with slide-valve injection stacks. Both of these engines use Motech fuel injection. Job uses pistons of his own design made by JE and cams from Dema Elgin. Saul Sneiderman of Perfect Power uses the factory racing cylinder heads with their larger valves and different valve springs. Sneiderman uses his own injection system. Jerry Woods uses a variety of injection manifolds, GE 100 cams of his own design, and Motec fuel-injection.

The factory claims 350 hp for its RSR engine with the proper inlet restrictors, but most of the private tuners claim more like 400 hp for their 3.6-liter versions, which are not required to use restrictors.

When you consider the numbers, it is obvious that the 964 engines can use some serious induction and exhaust system improvements. The major difference between the current, 1996, 993 with its 285 hp and the 964 with 250 hp are the induction and exhaust systems. The first version of the 993 in 1994–95 had the improved three-into-one exhaust header and output increased 22 hp from 250 to 272 horsepower. Very little else was changed between the 964 and the 993 with the exception of the mass air-flow sensor. Then in 1995 the whole induction system was changed to the Vario-ram induction system, matching the intake tuning to the exhaust tuning and increasing the horsepower another 13 from 272 to 285. Essentially just by modifying the induction and exhaust systems Porsche increased the 3.6 liter's output by 35 hp—a 14 percent increase.

Jerry Woods modified one 3.6-liter 964 engine for competition by just replacing the induction system with 46 IDA Webers, adding a set of racing headers, and installing a mild cam that would still provide adequate valve-to-piston clearance. He also runs a pair of Perma-Tune CD units with a programmable crankfire unit that he makes. With these modest changes he was able to increase the output by 69 hp from the stock 250 to 319.3—a better than 27 percent improvement in peak power.

Carburetor Sizing

Since there are only two carburetor sizes that work with the 911, you would think that the choice would be a simple matter. Unfortunately, it's not. Ultimately, the choice must be made between slightly better peak power or better dri-

A larger, more efficient Fred Garretson intercooler conversion for the 1978–1987 3.3-liter 911 Turbo (930). These larger intercoolers will allow you to safely use higher boost levels and produce more horsepower.

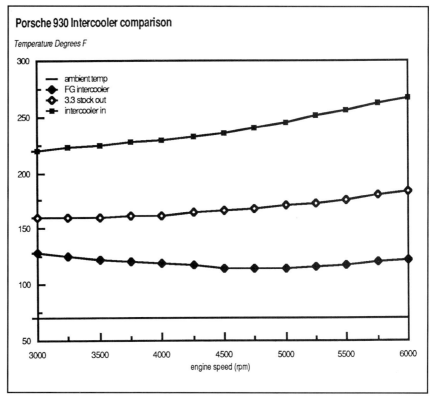

A Porsche 930 intercooler comparison. This chart shows how much more effective the Garretson intercooler is than the stock cooler. Performance data provided by Fred Garretson.

A Ruf intercooler kit. The Ruf intercooler is designed by Laengerer & Reich Kuehlerfabrik GmbH, which is the same company that makes the original equipment intercooler for Porsche. The Ruf intercooler has 66 percent more surface area than the stock intercooler. A well-designed intercooler, like Ruf's, will provide a cool, dense charge to the engine, which will result in an increase of about 30 hp. The intercoolers make an even greater difference when incorporated along with other modifications. Exclusive Motorcars, Inc.

veability. PMO (a company that sells Webers) is currently building its own carburetors—which will be a replacement for the Webers—and it will offer them in 40-mm, 46-mm, and 50-mm sizes. PMO has incorporated a number of improvements that should make them better than the Webers that they replace.

Even though larger carburetors may produce more peak horsepower on a dynamometer they may not be the best

choice for day-to-day driveability. If the carburetors are too small there is potential power loss; on the other hand, if they are too large low-rpm torque and driveability may suffer. At best, carburetor selection is a compromise. Street-driven engines will spend about 85 percent of their entire life near one-third load, a point at which they are still operating in their idle circuit range. Consequently, any carburetor you choose for street use must have

an efficient idle circuit and be matched to both the engine and your driving needs. When choosing a carburetor for any application you must be honest with yourself. The incorrect compromise can be quite unpleasant to drive and expensive to own. In the case of the 3.0-liter 911SC engine, the 40 IDA-3C Weber is probably the correct compromise.

Remember when choosing carburetors that the venturi size is responsible for the main circuit metering signal, and the throttle bore size is important for the idle metering signal strength. If it is driveability you want, always choose the smaller throttle bore for a street application. After all, what percentage of the time is really spent with the foot to the floor?

The formula for selecting carburetor venturi size provided in Colin Campbell's *The Sports Car Engine* used in conjunction with Weber's recommendations for the relationship of venturi size to throttle bore works well for sizing carburetors for a wide range of engine applications. Colin Campbell's venturi size formula is as follows:

$$\text{Venturi size in mm} = 20\sqrt{\frac{V}{1000} \times \frac{N}{1000}}$$

where:
V= cylinder volume of one cylinder in cc
N= rpm where engine reaches peak hp in rpms

Weber suggests that the throttle bores of its carburetors should be between 10 and 25 percent larger than the selected venturi. The highest powered version of the 3.0-liter 911SC engine (Type 930/10)) with stock camshafts develops its peak 204 hp at 5,900 rpm. The displacement for one cylinder is 499 cc, so now we can solve the equation to determine the venturi size and resulting choke size.

$$\text{Venturi size in mm} = 20\sqrt{\frac{499}{1000} \times \frac{5900}{1000}}$$
$$\text{Venturi size in mm} = 34.31\ (34)\ \text{mm}$$

Using Weber's throttle-bore-to-venturi-size recommendations in this example, the throttle bore should be between 37.4 mm and 42.5 mm showing that for the 3.0 911SC engine, the Weber 40 IDA-3C carburetors are a perfect choice for the best compromise.

Using the larger 46 IDA Webers with the 3.0 SC engine instead of their 40 IDA counterpart would only induce problems. Because the 46 IDAs have larger throttle bores, the idle and transition metering signal is weaker. The available signal goes as a fourth power of the diame-

A Kremer intercooler kit. The Kremer intercooler kit is very large and requires installing a larger rear wing.

ter, hence changing from a 40 IDA to a 46 IDA carburetor leads to a 75 percent reduction in the metering signal. Simply stated, there will be less control and larger flat spots in the low-speed driving range. Additionally, earlier versions of the 46 IDA carburetors had idle progression, or transition ports that were not at all optimized for use on 911 street engines. In all fairness, this objection has been more or less eliminated by the Weber importer's efforts on behalf of the end user. Weber has drastically altered the idle progression ports in the current version of the 46 IDA and greatly improved its match to street-driven 911s.

Turbocharging and Modifying Turbocharged Porsches

It seems that everyone who owns a turbocharged Porsche wants it to be faster than it is in stock form. There are obviously things that can be done quite easily with these cars to make them faster, the easiest simply being to increase the boost.

All of our turbocharged Porsches come with the boost set at a pressure that, in the opinion of those at Porsche, will give reasonable performance and reliability. On the typical street-driven 911 Turbo you can increase the boost a little for added performance without causing any damage because the cars are driven at full boost for only short periods of time. I recommend that the boost never be run in excess of 1.0 bar (14.5 lb/in^2) on an otherwise stock car. Running boost above 1.0 bar puts the engine close to its thermal limits in stock configuration. It also exceeds the fuel injection's ability to provide a proper mixture, which may cause detonation and can result in extensive engine damage.

The correct method of modifying the preset boost is to install a pressure regulator across the diaphragm in the wastegate, in a manner similar to the system used on the 935 race cars, or to use an electronic control unit such as the HKS. If you use a manual regulator I recommend locating the regulator back by the wastegate and using it as an adjustable preset device rather than locating it up in the cockpit where the driver might be tempted to play race car driver. At the same time you will have to modify the boost-sensitive fuel pump cut-off switch so that it operates in the 1.35–1.4 bar range. This modification has to be made because when the turbo first comes up to boost it will overshoot, which will cause a normally set cut-off switch to turn off the fuel pump. Some people just bypass the fuel

This larger rear wing will accommodate the Kremer intercooler.

cut-off switch. I don't feel this is a good idea; the cut-off switch will act as a conscience for those drivers who may need a little reminding. I also do not recommend shimming up the wastegate. Before you get the desired boost you run the risk of having the spring so tight

that it will be in "coil bind," which will confuse both you and your car. (Coil bind occurs when the coils of the spring are binding up before the valve achieves the lift that you desire.) One further note on playing with the boost setting: I recommend that before you

Here is Protomotive Engineering's (PE) very large intercooler. The manufacturer claims that its intercooler is 98 percent efficient compared to the original factory intercooler, which PE claims is 17 percent efficient.

modify the boost you install an accurate boost gauge.

The stock CIS injection has a fuel capacity limit of about 400 hp. On any turbocharged car you should always use the highest octane fuel you can obtain when you plan to run the car hard. Owners of pre-1978 911 Turbos (930s) should consider the installation of an efficient intercooler before increasing the boost much above the factory settings. There are several different intercooler kits available for the 911 Turbo, including kits for the early cars without intercoolers and larger, more efficient replacement intercooler kits available for the 1978 and later cars. The cooler you can get the charge air, the more power your car will produce.

Some 911 Turbo owners have been competing with their cars at track events, and they may also wish to increase their cars' performance. The following changes are only recommended for the 1978 and later intercooled 911 Turbos (930s) or earlier 911 Turbos (930s) with intercoolers added. There are several things that can be done to increase performance of the 911 Turbo Porsche for competition.

If the 911 Turbo in question is a U.S. car, the first thing to do is change the exhaust system to the R.o.W. type. (Note: 1986 and later U.S. cars already have this system and only need the catalyst and muffler changed. The 1976 to 1980 U.S. cars require a complete change of exhaust to make these other changes function properly.) For example, if the camshafts are changed to the 911SC cams, but the exhaust system is not changed, low-end performance will be greatly lacking.

Increasing the compression to 7.5:1 improves the normally aspirated performance. Increase the compression by machining the cylinder heads about 1.0 mm (0.039 inches). Machine and polish the intake ports and intake duct to increase their diameter from 32 mm to 36 mm.

Changing the camshafts to the 964, Group B, or one of the aftermarket performance cams makes a significant improvement in the 911 Turbo's performance. If you select the 964 grind you may make the change either by regrinding your own turbo cams or replacing them with a new set of 964 cams. If you use the 964 cams, set the timing to 1.16 to 1.36 mm (0.046–0.054 inches), and if you use the Group B Turbo camshafts set the timing 1.8–1.9 mm (0.071–0.075 inches). If you use a new set of the 964 cams, instead of having your original 911 Turbo cams reground, you will need to add the drive piece to the left camshaft to drive the air injector and turbocharger oil scavenge pump. If you have an early car remove the drive for the power steering pump from the right cam so that it will not interfere with engine-mounted oil cooler. The part number for the drive piece, which is a racing part, is 911.105.171.02. (Note: the left camshaft also requires machining to facilitate the mounting of this drive adapter.)

The 964 camshaft is a higher-lift camshaft than the original, whereas the Group B Turbo camshaft has essentially the same lift for both the intake and ex-

A U.S. 911 Turbo engine's exhaust system, used from 1976 to 1980. Beyond increasing the boost a little and adding a large intercooler, the exhaust system must be replaced by the European-style exhaust before any other modifications are performed. The engine in the photo has had its thermo reactors replaced with thermo reactor replacements. Many suppliers call these thermo reactor replacements "headers," but they are not really "headers." Changing to the thermo-reactor replacements helps the engine heat, but really does nothing for engine performance.

haust as the stock Turbo camshaft. If you use the 911SC or the 964 camshafts, the valve springs should be reset to the same 34.5 mm for intake and exhaust. If the 964 cams are used, set the valve springs at 34.5 mm for the intake and 33.5 for the exhaust. If you use the 964 cams and there is any possibility that the engine will ever be over-revved, you should consider replacing the valve springs and retainers. There are several good sources—Randy Asse, ANDIAL, Bob Norwood, and Jerry Woods all have good replacements.

Cooling is critical for the Turbo, and a change in the fan-drive ratio is recommended to improve engine cooling. The fan should be speeded up from the stock 1:1.68 to 1:1.8. Use the larger crankshaft pulley from the 1976 and 1977 2.7 or the 1978 and 1979 911SC fans.

Twin ignition offers the same advantages for the turbo engines that it offers for the normally aspirated engine by reducing the engine's sensitivity to a gasoline's octane. This may even be more important for the turbocharged engines than it is for the normally aspirated engines in that it safely allows higher boost pressure to be used. The problem is the availability of a good distributor for this application. It is important to use a distributor that has an advance curve designed for this purpose, so the Bosch racing distributor with its fixed advance is not really advisable. With the stock distributor the ignition timing should be set to 25 deg at 4,000 rpm with the vacuum line to the distributor disconnected.

A popular conversion for the 911 Turbo has been to change the turbocharger to one of the K27 turbocharger units. The K27 is a more modern design than the K26 turbocharger is used on the 911 Turbo; it operates more efficiently at higher levels of boost. The K27 number refers to the general type of turbocharger, or the center section of a turbocharger made by KKK. Audi's Diesel, Porsche 935s, and the Porsche 924 Turbo have all used the K27 Turbo. There is a wide selection of different size K27 turbochargers available for use on the 911 Turbo. For instance there is a K27-16 that can be used to improve the high-end performance, a K27-13 to improve midrange, and a K27-11/11 to improve low-end performance. There are also a variety of other specialized turbos available from KKK as well as other turbo manufacturers.

Both the K-27 turbocharger and the intercooler need to be modified so that the K27 turbocharger will fit in the 911 Turbo. The turbocharger should have

Turbo Cams		
Type of Camshaft	Cam Timing	Checking Height at
TDC Overlap		
1975–1987 911 Turbo	Intake open 3 deg ATDC	0.65–0.80 mm
	Intake close 37 deg ABDC	(0.026–0.032 inch)
	Exh. open 29 deg BBDC	
	Exh. close 3 deg BTDC	
1976–1977 Carrera	Intake open 7 deg BTDC	1.4–1.7 mm
1978–1983 911SC	Intake close 47 deg ABDC	(0.055–0.067 inch)
1984–1989 Carrera	Exh. open 49 deg BBDC	
	Exh. close 3 deg BTDC	
Porsche Group B	Intake open 11 deg BTDC	1.8 to 1.9 mm
Turbo camshaft	Intake close 46 deg ABDC	(0.071–0.075 inch)
	Exh. open 32 deg BBDC	
	Exh. close 8 deg ATDC	
1989–1994 964 Carrera	Intake open 4 deg BTDC	1.16 to 1.36 mm
Camshaft	Intake close 56 deg ABDC	(0.046–0.054 inch)
	Exh. open 45 deg BBDC	
	Exh. close 5 deg ATDC	

The Euro-style 911 Turbo exhaust system. Changing to this style of exhaust system will permit all of the other Turbo engine modifications. If this change is not made to one of the 1976–1980 U.S. cars, the performance below 3,000 rpm will be very poor after the modifications, particularly after changing the camshafts. There are several different mufflers that have been used with this system; all will work, but some just make more power than others. The U.S.-version 1986 and 1987 911 Turbos use this same Euro exhaust system, but with a different muffler and a catalytic converter. Both of these will also have to be changed to facilitate most of the performance modifications for the 911 Turbo.

The Turbo exhaust conversion. This 911 Turbo uses the early-style normally aspirated exhaust system to take advantage of the exhaust tuning of that system. Ideally, we would want two equal-length primary exhaust systems with short secondary pipes leading directly to the turbo. Unfortunately there is not enough room in the rear of one of these cars for the ideal exhaust system and all of the other things that need to be there. Tom Hanna

An IMSA GTO 934. This 934 has a special exhaust system with a pair of three-into-one headers leading to a large dual-inlet turbocharger. Each of the three-into-one headers was kept separate from the other and had its own wastage. The vacuum/boost control circuits for the waste gates were connected in parallel like they are on a twin-turbo 935. The performance for this engine was similar to the twin-turbo 935s. In 1983, Wayne Baker won the IMSA GTO championship with this 934, winning his class championship and Sebring outright.

10 mm milled off the mounting surface of the exhaust flange to make it fit better. The intercooler inlet tube must also be modified so that it can be connected to the K-27 turbocharger. The original mounting of this intercooler tube to the K-26 turbocharger was sealed with an O-ring. Because there is no provision on the K-27 for the O-ring," a piece of radiator type hose and hose clamps are used instead.

Intercooling, or as it is also called "charge-air cooling," has proven to be very effective in the 911 Turbo. Porsche started experimenting with intercooling with its racing cars starting with the 917 engine. The 934, 935, and 936 all relied on intercooling to assist in reliably producing high specific outputs. The racing cars have used both air-to-air and water-to-air intercooling. From 1978 on, the street 911 Turbo has also used an air-to-air intercooler (the ambient air temperature is the cooling medium). The act of compressing the air with the turbocharger heats up the intake charge air (any increase in pressure also has a corresponding increase in temperature). Some people call the intercooler an "after cooler" because it is used to cool the charge air after it has been compressed and heated up. This increase in temperature acts to cancel out some of the potential advantage of the increased boost because the increased temperature results in a less dense charge reaching the engine. The heat also raises the operating temperature of the engine making the engine more prone to detonation and damage caused by overheating the pistons, valves, and cylinder heads. An increase of charge air temperature of 10 deg will raise the exhaust temperature by 10 deg and so on. If you can reduce the charge-air temperature you can get more power at a lower level of boost.

Enter the intercooler. The intercooler is almost like perpetual motion where you get something for nothing. Where the larger more efficient intercoolers offer an advantage is that they allow you to safely run your 911 Turbo with more boost for an even larger power increase. The limit of how much boost you can actually run is detonation, which is caused by heat. By reducing the heat of the charge air you can run more boost. Just the act of compressing the intake air raises the temperature. In addition to the heat caused by compressing the charge air, the combustion heat is also influenced by the compression ratio and the ignition advance. This triangle has to be played carefully because they all increase the heat of the

158

An RCT engine kit for the 964 and the 993.

combustion process, which can cause detonation. The idea is to get the most performance from the engine without damaging it.

With more efficient intercoolers and better gasoline (higher octane) you can run more boost, compression, and ignition advance and produce more horsepower. An example of this would be the factory racing engines such as the 935, which ran very high boost and produced more than two and a half times as much power as the stock street 911 Turbos of the same period. Up to a point, the cooler the charge air the more power your car will produce and the less the risk of detonation caused by running with higher boost, and the octane requirements will also be reduced as well for a given engine output. However, this is usually compromised by increasing the boost again in search for more power output.

There are several intercooler kits available for the earlier 911 Turbos (930s) that did not have intercoolers, and there are larger more efficient replacement intercooler kits available for the newer 911 Turbos that already have an intercooler. The intercoolers must be judged by two criteria: their efficiency at cooling the charge air and the restriction that they offer to the charge air passing through them. Unfortunately

the act of running the compressed air through a cooler or heat exchanger will reduce the pressure some because of the pressure drop across the cooler.

The performance from a 911 Turbo engine with these modifications will be in the 350–400 hp range at about 5,500 rpm with 0.9 bar boost. The power can be increased by approximately 10 hp by running an open exhaust system in place of the muffler. Running more than 0.9 bar boost for track use with an otherwise stock 911 Turbo will greatly reduce the engine's longevity. As an example, a 935 that ran 24-hour races at either Le Mans or Daytona would require a complete rebuild after just one weekend of racing. The pistons and cylinders would be worn out and often the cylinder heads would require replacement as well. This is with special engines built for endurance racing and a boost limited to 1.2–1.25 bar. Similar destruction can be created in much less time with the normal racing engines and the higher boost that was used f or shorter sprint races. Consider, too, that the 935s had vastly superior oil cooling, intercooling, and air cooling to what you will be able to accomplish with a stock street-bodied 911 Turbo.

When Ruf modified the older 3.3 911 Turbos he usually increased the displacement to 3.4 liters (3,367 cc) from

A popular conversion for the 911 Turbo has been to change the turbocharger to one of the K-27 turbochargers such as this one. The K-27 is a more-modern design than the K-26 turbocharger that is used on the 911 Turbo, and it operates more efficiently at higher levels of boost. This K-27-11/11 is the most popular conversion for use on the 911 Turbos. Both the K-27 turbocharger and the intercooler need to be modified so the K-27 can be used in the 911 Turbo. The turbocharger should have 10 mm milled off of the mounting surface of the exhaust flange to make it fit better, and the intercooler inlet tube must be modified so it can be connected to the K-27 turbocharger. The original mounting of this intercooler tube to the K-26 turbocharger was sealed with an O-ring. Because there is no provision on the K-27 for the O-ring, a piece of radiator-type hose and hose clamps are used instead.

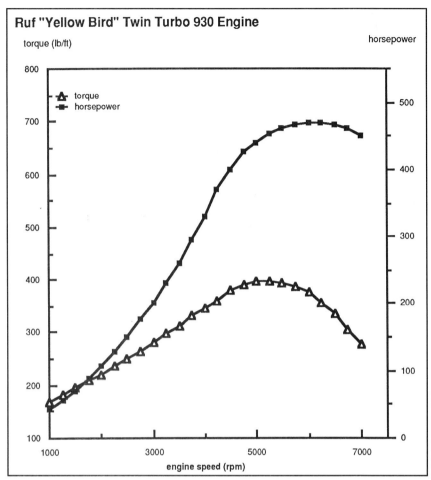

Ruf "Yellow Bird" Twin Turbo 930 Engine

Here is data on power output for the Ruf Yellow Bird *twin-turbo 930 engine.* Yellow Bird *was the car that* Road & Track *used in its "World's Fastest Cars" test.* Yellow Bird *went 211 mph, clocked 0–60 mph in 4 seconds, and turned the quarter at 133.5 mph in 11.7 seconds. The engine is a 3.4-liter conversion like Alois Ruf's other 911 Turbo conversions. However, this one uses a special digital Motronic electronic fuel and ignition system in conjunction with twin turbos to achieve the extra performance. Performance data provided by Ruf.*

the stock 3,298.8 cc by replacing stock pistons and cylinders with 98-mm pistons and cylinders. His reason for doing this was that he did not like the funny fin arrangement of the stock 3.3 Turbo cylinders, and he didn't feel that they provided adequate cooling for the high-performance Turbo engines. Though he could have gone larger than the 3.4 conversion, he would had to have bored out the crankcase bore spigots, which he did not want to do.

There were 100-mm big bore kits available for these engines which yielded 3.5-liter displacement, but they required boring the crankcase spigot bores from their stock 103 mm to 105 mm. None of these large-displacement conversions required that the top cylinder diameter be increased where it fits into the cylinder head; it remained the

same 113-mm diameter it had been since 1975 when the die-cast aluminum crankcase had been introduced for the Turbo engine.

There was also a modification for these big-bore turbocharged engines that incorporates an O-ring seal for the bottom of the cylinder where it inserts into the cylinder spigot. This seal was similar to those used by some of the Porsche 911 racing engines as well as the later 993 3.8 RS engines. Porsche called this a "profile seal ring," which is an O ring that fits into a groove cut into the crankcase spigot bore to seal the base of the cylinder to the crankcase. Whereas the standard 993 engines had an O ring groove in the bottom of the cylinder where it mates to the crankcase, this O ring seal fits a groove inside the crankcase spigot that seals

with the portion that sticks down into the spigot bore.

Ruf Turbos

There are a lot of people doing some great aftermarket turbocharger installations now, and surely one of the most famous is Alois Ruf in Germany. Ruf's most famous car is *Yellow Bird*, which was built in 1987. You may have read about it in a *Road & Track* high-performance shoot-out article; it beat all of the world's fastest super cars, including the Porsche 959S. *Yellow Bird* ran 211.5 mph in this shoot-out at the Volkswagen proving ground. At a subsequent event held on the Nardo Racetrack it turned 212.5 mph. In addition to the speed records, *Yellow Bird* clocked 0–60 mph in 4.0 sec and turned the quarter mile at 133.5 mph in 11.7 seconds.

Yellow Bird is a lightweight 911 with a 469-hp, twin turbo, 911-based 3.4-liter engine. For the CTR (Group C Turbo Ruf) Ruf uses his own intake manifold, similar in design to the Carrera manifold but larger in capacity, with a special DME fuel injection and ignition system originally developed for the Porsche 962 race cars. Instead of measuring air flow like most electronic engine management systems do, this system is a pressure sensing type that uses throttle position, rpm, engine temperature, and manifold pressure as input signals.

Yellow Bird was the first of the high-powered 911 Turbo engines that really ran right and made a lot of power. Since this car was built, many of the aftermarket tuners have been using various electronic engine management systems to greatly enhance the engine performance of the Turbo.

Ruf Automobile GmbH has been certified by the German government as an original automobile manufacturer since 1981. In 1987, Ruf Automobile GmbH also became an approved manufacturer with the U.S. authorities for safety and emissions (NHTSA and EPA).

Ruf has built 28 CTRs from new, bare chassis (no chassis numbers) purchased from Porsche, and it has also built about the same number of CTRs by converting them from existing 3.2 Carreras. The cars built from new chassis have Ruf chassis numbers and the modified cars maintain their original Porsche VIN number. A great number of the Ruf CTR owners use them primarily for track events around the world.

Ruf has worked closely with Bosch for a number of years refining its application of the Bosch Motronic system on the Ruf turbocharged engines until they have come up with today's superbly powerful and wonderful-running turbocharged engines. The challenge has been to develop a system that would work with Ruf's powerful, catalytic converter-equipped, high-flow Turbo-engines. Ruf and Bosch have achieved their goal by modifying the same Bosch Motronic system that is used on the 964 and 993 engines. In some applications they use the Porsche intake manifolds and for others they have made their own. When Porsche was still using the flapper box for air flow measurement Ruf was using a hot-film mass-flow sensor.

Ruf uses KKK turbochargers made specifically for its engine applications. It also uses Porsche's largest intercoolers to improve both reliability and engine performance. Ruf has developed its own camshafts for its engines which provide good power throughout the rev range. Ruf also backdates the 993 version of the engine to use the older style Porsche nonhydraulic rocker arms and Ruf's camshafts. Ruf also uses its own pistons to lower the compression ratio to 8.0:1 to work with turbocharging. For improved oil cooling, both the 964 and the 993 use a second oil cooler in the front left on the same side as the air conditioner condenser on the cars equipped with air conditioning. Ruf engines are rated at about 400 hp, but these are conservative ratings; Alois Ruf prefers that his cars' performance speak for themselves.

Ruf makes cars with single turbos and dual turbos and cars with both all-wheel-drive or rear-wheel-drive only. These cars perform wonderfully while managing to exceed world emissions laws. The performance and throttle response are almost comparable to normally aspirated cars—you must drive one to believe how good they are.

The Ruf engines use catalytic converters to meet or exceed all of the European emission requirements, and the BTR (Group B Turbo Ruf) engine has been approved in the United States for the strict U.S. emissions standards. Ruf plans to certify its other models in the future so that all Ruf cars, conversions, and engines will be U.S. legal.

ANDIAL Turbos

There are a number of Porsche shops or "tuners" in the United States that can do all of the same sorts of modifications for which Ruf is renowned. One of these is ANDIAL Road and Racing in Santa Ana, California. ANDIAL is not your typical U.S. tuning shop; it is also the U.S. racing department for Porsche AG. Alwin Springer, one of ANDIAL's principals, is

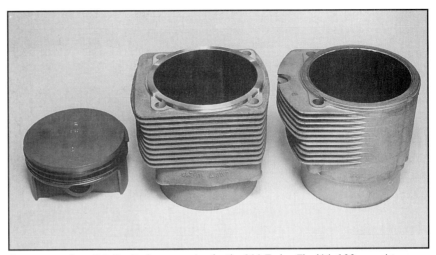

Components for a 3.5-liter Turbo conversion for the 911 Turbo. The kit's 100-mm pistons and cylinders increase the engine's displacement to 3,506 cc. The crankcase must have the cylinder spigot bores machined to accept these larger pistons and cylinders. The 3.5-liter piston and cylinder are on the left, and a stock 3.3 cylinder is on the right.

There is a downside to turbocharging. If you run turbocharged cars with too much boost, too high of a compression ratio, or not-high-enough-octane fuel, the engines will detonate, and they can seriously hurt themselves. This is a 3.3-liter 911 Turbo engine from a street car that was running very high boost with none of the other modifications necessary to allow using high boost. This engine "blew" a piston.

general manager of sports car racing for Porsche Motorsport North America, Inc. The name ANDIAL is made up of two letters from each the owner's names. The principal's names are Arnold Wagner (AN), Dieter Inzenhofer (DI), and Alwin Springer (AL). Wagner and Inzenhofer both emigrated in 1960 from Germany to Canada, where they met while they worked at the Toronto Volkswagen dealership. Inzenhofer was a line mechanic for Porsches and Wagner worked in the parts department. From Canada they both moved to Hermosa Beach,

California, where they worked for Vasek Polak Porsche.

It was at Vasek Polak's in 1969 that they met Alwin Springer, then Polak's racing technician. The three of them worked together at Polak's on various racing projects for five years before leaving to start their own business in 1975 in Costa Mesa, California. When they started they had a small facility serving 75 percent road customers and 25 percent racing customers. ANDIAL has been the major race engine builder in the United States almost since its inception.

A cylinder from the same 3.3-liter 911 Turbo street engine that was run with too much boost. Note that the melted piston also melted part of the cylinder. You can also see that the top of the cylinder had distorted and was starting to leak combustion gas. This is usually where the racing cars would fail—at the juncture between the cylinder head and the cylinder.

There are always people who want more power. Until Ruf's Yellow Bird engine, the practical limit for hot-rodding the 911 Turbo engines was about 400–410 hp because of limitations of the induction system. If you still wanted more power, the best way to achieve it was to detune a 935 engine, and this photo shows an example of this approach.

A few years ago they installed a 3.0-liter, water-cooled 962 engine in a C4. The 962 engine was tested by ANDIAL at 740 hp at 1.4 bar boost pressure. However, they decided for safety's sake that they should limit the power to 520 hp at 0.8 bar boost! When I inquired about this seemingly arbitrary choice, Inzenhofer told me that since the standard car had 250 hp and that Porsche usually employs a design safety margin of 100 percent they felt that 500 hp would be a safe limit for the Carrera 4 transmission and drivetrain. The owner still has the option, at the twist of the boost knob, of dialing in the 1.4 bar boost to make the 740 hp available.

To adapt the water-cooled engine to the 964 chassis, which was designed for an air cooled motor, ANDIAL installed a 944 radiator in the front of the car. The only obvious sign that something is unusual with this car is the air ducts exiting from the hood. The radiator has a pair of electric cooling fans mounted in the ducting from the radiator to ensure proper cooling. The plumbing to and from the engine is wonderful and totally concealed within the body.

ANDIAL also designed a clever solution to the problem of heating the occupants. It installed a pair of water heat-exchangers at the top of the engine, which they circulate the coolant through on its way back to the front-mounted radiator. When the occupants want heat, they turn on the heater fan which blows the hot air from the heat exchangers into the cabin providing

warm air for the occupants. ANDIAL has given us what may actually be the first 911 with a heater that really works.

The appearance of the car was left totally stock with the exception of the two outlets for the radiator cut into the front hood and the addition of a Turbo spoiler at the rear. At the customer's insistence the car has also been equipped with air conditioning.

The engine in the ANDIAL C4 proves very flexible because of the relatively high-compression ratio (for a turbocharged engine) of 9.13:1. Also adding to the flexibility is the fact that though ANDIAL has retained the stock 962 camshafts, it has altered the timing of the intake and exhaust cams relative to each other. When I rode in the car with race driver Dennis Aase he demonstrated its flexibility by giving the car full throttle at 1,200 rpm—it just drove off as any civilized road car would. The only real give-away that they are using an unusual engine is the racket that the straight-cut cam drive gears make.

Protomotive Turbos

The Protomotive family is several tuners that have done a lot of aftermarket Turbo conversions over the years with Todd Knighton. I had the chance to visit them at Proto Tech in Florida some time back and we went out in one of their fast turbocharged Carreras. What is interesting about Protomotive's

approach is that though it makes all of its own external components for the Turbo installation, it maintains the Bosch Motronic engine management system, albeit with modified fuel and ignition programs to make them suitable for the Turbo installation. This is the same approach that Alois Ruf has used for so long. The Protomotive cars may not be as conservatively rated as the Ruf cars, or as well tested via the autobahn, but they are very fast.

Protomotive offers a variety of Turbo engine modifications ranging from its stage one, which produces 375 hp, all the way up to its twin sequential Turbo conversion, which it claims puts out 832 hp.

All of the cars that I saw showed good workmanship, and the turbo installations were impressive. While some of the other cars discussed here started with Porsche factory racing engines that were then modified and repackaged to fit into the street 911, Protomotive starts with a production model Carrera 3.2, 964, or 993 and modifies the normally aspirated Porsche.

ProtoTech Turbos

ProtoTech, working with Protomotive Engineering in California, has spent a great deal of effort in improving the efficiencies of all of the various systems of the turbocharged engines. It has its own billet crankshaft which is stronger, has improved oiling, and is lighter than the stock crankshaft. ProtoTech developed its own large and efficient intercooler in 1984. Its intercooler is 98 percent efficient compared to the original factory intercooler, which is 17 percent efficient. (Another good aftermarket intercooler is the Fred Garretson intercooler, which is 57 percent efficient.)

ProtoTech use Carrillo connecting rods in its high-output engines. It uses the 964 oil pumps to improve the oiling along with the larger 2.0-mm piston squirters for improved piston cooling. It uses the factory 3.3-liter cylinders with pistons of its own design manufactured by JE. ProtoTech uses Child and Albert Z-gap Ductal Moly compression rings and the stock, factory oil control rings to work with the Mahle Nikasil surface on the cylinders. ProtoTech modifies its own cylinder head, installing 52-mm intake valves instead of the standard 49-mm valves. It increases the port size to 41 mm and installs phosphorus bronze valve guides.

Protomotive designed the cams to improve low-end performance without sacrificing top-end performance. To do

A 962 engine that has been converted for street use and installed in a 1989 911 Speedster. The engine has twin turbos and a Haltech engine management system that has been programmed for the street.

A 935 engine in a street-driven 911 Turbo. Detuning was limited to the use of a pair of custom-built silencers.

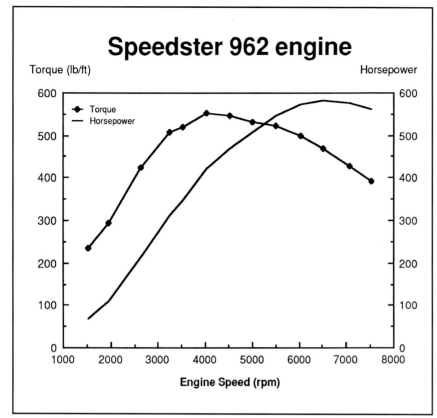

Here are the horsepower and torque curves for the air-cooled 962 engine installed in the 1989 Speedster.

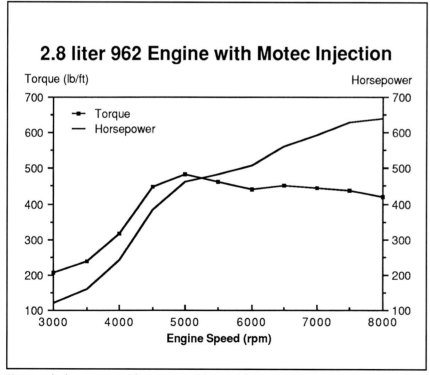

Here are the horsepower and torque curves for a 2.8-liter 962 engine with the Motec engine management system.

this they have advanced the cam timing and closed up the lobe centers. ProtoTech makes its own equal-length headers and mufflers out of stainless steel, and it has changed the size of the primaries relative to the secondaries to optimize the performance. ProtoTech uses a pair of 964 catalytic converters for the twin-turbo cars.

When ProtoTech uses the aluminum Carrera manifolds, it Extrudehones them to improve flow. For its Stage 5 engines it uses the plastic intake manifold, which is 12 percent more efficient than the aluminum manifolds. ProtoTech has made its own boost-pressure-controlled fuel-pressure regulator that increases the fuel pressure from 30 lb to 100 lb. Todd Knighton of Protomotive programs the Bosch DME chips to run with all of its high-performance turbocharged engines. Protomotive and ProtoTech offer engines in five different stages of tune with each stage increasing in power, sophistication, and expense. Their 3.8-liter 993 engine produced 751.3 hp at 6,500 rpm, and 662.0 ft-lb peak torque at 5,500 rpm with 8.5:1 compression, 1.21 bar boost using 93 octane gasoline.

Jerry Woods Turbo

One of my favorite tuners is Jerry Woods. A few years ago Woods did an interesting engine for Bruce Canepa. The car was a 1989 Speedster into which they installed an air-cooled IMSA 962 engine.

The engine was a spare from Canepa's 962. Unlike the World Endurance Championship 956 and 962 engines, which initially had water-cooled heads and later were completely water cooled, the IMSA version of the engine was an air-cooled evolution of the 935 engine. Canepa wanted to use the IMSA 962 engine with the racing flat fan to create a street car that would produce well over 500 hp. Canepa admitted that he also wanted to use the flat fan for aesthetic reasons and because he thinks they sound neat at idle.

Canepa and Woods talked about building a street motor with a lot of torque, lots of bottom-end power, and as little lag as possible. It would have to be something that you could drive around town yet take out on the freeway and go as fast as a race car. That is exactly what they ended up with—a 600 hp (actually 581.5 hp. at 1.1 bar boost) motor that you only have to turn up to 6,500 rpm. It can light the tires in first, second, and third gears. Canepa says that it can literally fry the tires in the first three gears if you aren't careful, and that's with 13-inch wide, sticky Goodyear tires. On the freeway at 2,000 rpm he says that it accelerates like a 450-cubic-inch V-8-powered car—as it should with the torque curve this engine produces. At 2,000 rpm the engine produces over 300 ft-lb torque, and from 2,500 rpm to 7,500 rpm the engine produces in excess of 400 ft-lb torque with a peak torque of 550 ft-lb at 4,000 rpm. These numbers were generated with all accessories in place including the muffler. The engine was also tested at higher boost levels where it produced in excess of 600 hp, but the 1.1-bar boost level was chosen as a practical boost level for a street-driven engine because of the pump fuels available.

With twin turbos and a modern engine-management system, the turbo lag was negligible and the car was quite driveable. Jerry Woods converted the 962 engine to 3.3 liters by using 100-mm pistons and cylinders and the 70.4-mm-stroke crankshaft. He used cams of his own design and an HKS electronic wastegate control with two preset positions and a variable position, instead of the manual valve traditionally used on modified turbocharged Porsches. Woods used a programmable twin-ignition system that he has developed and a prototype of a new engine-management system. The engine-management system takes advantage of the existing 962 intake manifolds which used twin, staged injectors. The engine runs on one set of injectors when it's in the normally aspirated mode, and the second set of injectors is phased in when the engine comes up onto the boost. This staged-injector system provides better control over the fuel mixture under all operating conditions and the car runs better for street use.

Woods has completed many interesting projects and recently converted one of the 2,857-cc 962 engines with water-cooled heads to Motec fuel injection. The reason he converted the car was that the engine-management system needed to be modified to match changes that had been made to the engine and there is really no support for the obsolete Bosch racing system. Jerry has used the Motec unit successfully in a variety of applications from street to racing, and he had no reservations about using it in this application as well. Woods has had great success with the Motec engine-management system with both normally aspirated and turbocharged racing and street engines. The advantage of the Motec system over some of the other systems is that it

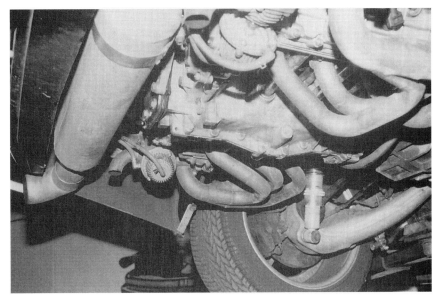

ProtoTech, working with Protomotive Engineering in California, builds its own exhaust headers for its twin-turbo installations, as well as its own combination catalytic converter mufflers. This system is on a twin sequential turbo that produces 700 hp.

uses dual processors and has more processing capacity. The Motec offers extensive programmability, and it's also able to do extensive data logging, which makes it easier to tune the system for different applications.

Supercharging Porsches

Turbocharger installations are usually preferred over superchargers for most forced-induction engines these days because they are considered to be more efficient than superchargers, but super-

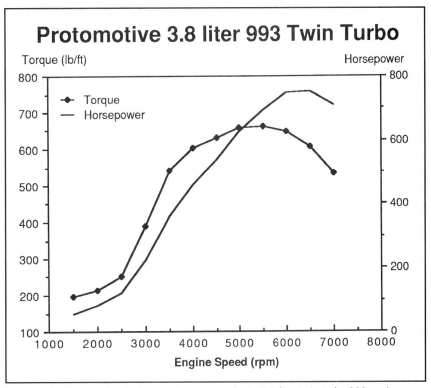

Here are the Protomotive Engineering dyno curves for its 3.8-liter twin-turbo 993 engine.

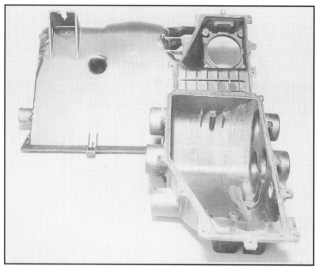

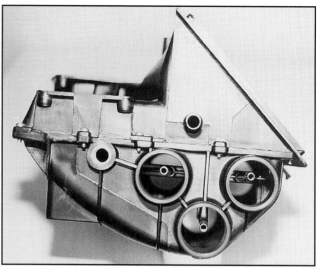

A blown CIS air box. Almost any backfire in a CIS-injected 911 will result in a blown air box. And, unfortunately, the backfires can be caused by a number of things—improper fuel mixture, bad cold start, improperly set warm-up regulator, or big swings in the climatic conditions.

Cold-start manifolding. In 1981 Porsche changed the cold-start circuit and provided manifolding for the fuel to the intake runners. This change alone seems to have eliminated about 90 percent of the blown air boxes. Unfortunately, there are still a few engines that will backfire and blow their air boxes. These backfires are usually caused by an injection problem or, again, big swings in climatic conditions.

chargers do have the advantage of instant boost with no "turbo lag."

Whipple superchargers are actually pretty efficient with efficiencies above 85 percent at the higher rpms. Whipple superchargers not only have a long drive that helps them fit in the C2 engine compartment, but they also are very compact units well suited to installation in the 911's small engine compartment. Once installed, the Whipple supercharger really looks like it belongs , a claim few other supercharger installations can make.

A couple of years ago I had the opportunity go to Tennessee and test some different technology that I really liked. Over the past 20 years or so turbocharged Porsches have become fairly commonplace—first the 911 or 930 Turbo and then the 924 and 944 turbos—but most of us have little experience with supercharged cars. Though there have been some impressive supercharged cars built, the installations often lacked that "Porsche" look. All those perceptions changed for me when I ran into a friend, Tommy Vann of Supercharging of Knoxville, who had a supercharged 964 engine on display at the Cincinnati Porsche Parade. I really liked the looks of the supercharger installation on this engine—it looked "Porsche."

Vann's project, for a customer in England, got started in fall 1992 when Steve Holgate, team manager for Exclusively Nine Racing, approached Super-

charging of Knoxville and asked if it was interested in building a supercharged 3.6 racing engine for Exclusively Nine Racing's 1992 Carrera 2 RS race car. Craig Simmis (an ex-Formula 3 pilot) had won the British Supercup championship with this same Carrera 2 RS in 1992, and now the team wanted to step up to the new BRDC National Sports GT championship. Holgate was looking for an engine configuration that would allow them to be competitive in this new Sports GT championship. The driver for the Sports GT championship in 1993 would be Nigel Barrett.

The rules for the BRDC National Sports GT racing series left the engine modifications free and allowed turbocharging or supercharging of production engines. The forced-induction engines required a 50.8 mm restrictor which limited the power to around 450 hp. Steve Holgate decided that he wanted to try to use supercharging instead of the more common turbocharging because he felt the lack of turbo lag would make the car more tractable.

Holgate called Supercharging of Knoxville to see if it would be interested in supercharging a 3.6-liter 964 engine for racing. The company was interested, and Holgate flew over and met with them in Atlanta to discuss the proposed C2 race car program. Supercharging of Knoxville took one of its supercharged 3.2 Carreras to Atlanta for Holgate to evaluate. Holgate was pleased with

what he saw, they established a game plan, and Holgate returned to England and shipped the car stateside. Supercharging of Knoxville needed the car so that it could develop the supercharger installation to fit.

Supercharging of Knoxville has been doing supercharger installations on 944s, 911SCs, and 911 3.2-liter Carreras since 1990. All installations have used the Paxton supercharger, a unit with which Supercharging of Knoxville has considerable experience. In the time that Supercharging of Knoxville has been in the supercharger business it has sold over 80 Paxton supercharger installations or kits. When it went into the supercharger business its goal was to build a high-quality bolt-on kit that would not significantly change the driving characteristics of the Porsches, just add more power. Those at Supercharging of Knoxville feel they have achieved their goals with the Paxton supercharger for the 911SC, 911 Carrera, and 944, and the next step was the 3.6-liter 964 engine.

In the BRDC National Sports GT series the Exclusively Nine Racing cars would have to have a "stock profile," meaning that the car would have to look like an original 911 C2 Carrera RS, including the rear wing in its extended position. When Supercharging of Knoxville looked into what it would have to do to fit a supercharger in a C2/C4 it found that the more conventional Paxton supercharger that it had been using with

An aftermarket pop-off valve. This little device will save the 10 percent of the CIS air intake boxes that still are going to have something go wrong and cause a backfire. This little pop-off mounts in the top of the intake plenum, and if the engine does backfire, it just vents the explosion back outside the intake tract.

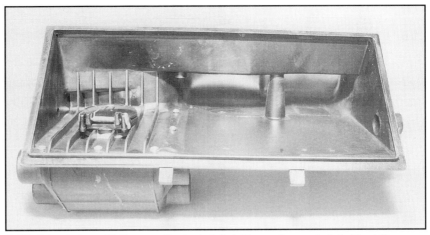

A CIS air intake box with the pop-off valve installed. These valves are installed by drilling a hole in the intake box with a hole saw and epoxying the valve in place. I recommend a little dab of epoxy on each end of the pop-off valve's hinge pin because I have seen a couple of the hinge pins work their way out, which creates an air-intake leak.

other conversions would not fit around the wing mechanism. Supercharging of Knoxville went looking for a supercharger with an extension for the drive so that it could put the supercharger back farther in the engine compartment out of the way of the rear wing mechanism. In the search for a supercharger with a longer drive, the company ran into the Whipple screw-type positive displacement superchargers.

The next problem encountered with the installation was the high, 11.3:1 compression ratio of the 964 engines. Supercharging of Knoxville has to disassemble the top end of each 964 engine it supercharges and then remachine the forged Mahle pistons to reduce the compression ratio. Two versions of this modification have been developed: one provides a 9.5:1 compression ratio for the street-car conversion and the other creates a 9.3:1 compression ratio for racing engines. The lower compression is needed for the racing version so that even higher boost levels can be used. Supercharging of Knoxville applies a 3.7 psi=1 point of compression ratio as a rule of thumb for power/calibration purposes. As an example, a 3.6-liter engine with 9.5:1 pistons and 8-lb boost makes an effective compression ratio of 11.66:1.

The standard 3.2-liter Carrera engine has a compression of 9.5:1, so Supercharging of Knoxville limits total boost to 6 lb, which, using its rule of thumb, gives an effective compression ratio of 11.1:1. A safety margin for these cars is provided by remapping the chip to provide adequate fuel and reduced ignition timing. The European Carrera has 10.3:1

compression so it is run with less boost and the ignition timing is altered to further reduce the timing for engine safety. For the 911SCs Supercharging of Knoxville uses the MSD ignition retard system which reduces the ignition advance under boost conditions to protect the engine from the combination of boost and compression that could other-

wise damage the engine. The late U.S. version of the 911SC has 9.3:1 compression while the Euro version of the 911SC has 9.8:1, so to protect the Euro version they limit the advance to even less than with the U.S. version.

Supercharging of Knoxville works with its friend Doug Wallis of EFI Systems, Inc. to establish the boost levels

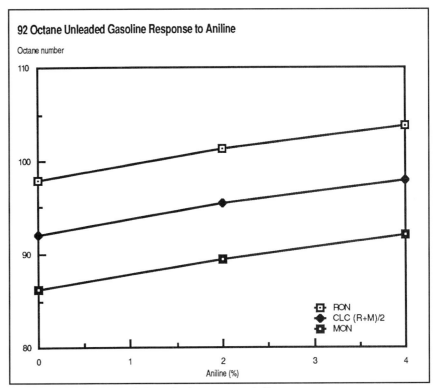

A chart of 92-octane unleaded gasoline's response to Aniline.

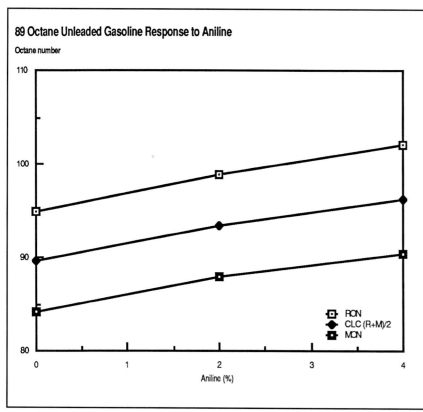

A chart of 89-octane unleaded gasoline's response to Aniline.

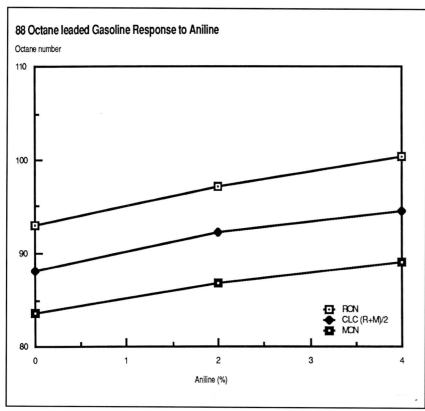

A chart of 88-octane leaded gasoline's response to Aniline.

and mapping of the Bosch Motronic systems and the limit of the ignition advance for the 911SCs. Wallis runs each of the engines first on EFI System's engine dyno to map them and establish the correct combination of boost, fuel, and timing. Next the engines are installed in the cars and test driven to assess their strengths and any weaknesses or running problems which may show up. Finally, the cars are returned to EFI Systems, Inc. where they are run on the chassis dyno and fine tuned. Wallis says that he finds the limit for each engine combination and then backs the timing or boost back to 80 percent for safety. In the case of the 3.6 964 engines we tested, its 10 lb of boost were dialed back to 8 lb for safety. The pulley drive ratio to the supercharger is set up to provide 10 lb of boost, and then the pop-off valve is used to limit total boost to 8 lb.

Keller Wallace does all of the fabrication for Supercharging of Knoxville. He makes all of the manifolding and brackets for its supercharger installations from stainless steel. The workmanship and quality is superb, and the new parts that he made up to install the Whipple on the 3.6-liter 964 engines are no exception. The 911SC and Carrera 3.2-liter engines use the stock intake manifolds, but new manifolding is required when the Whipple is used. The 964 and the 3.2 engines need completely new intake manifolds to fit the Whipple supercharger down low on the engine. Supercharging of Knoxville's 964 intake manifold looks sort of like a replica of the 911 turbo intake manifold only all fabricated from stainless steel tubing.

Most of the 3.6 964 engines that Supercharging of Knoxville has done to date have been the early version with no head gaskets, so the company has used the interlocking sealing rings that the 935s used for a head gasket. These head gaskets require machining a groove in both the cylinder and the cylinder head to accept the stainless steel ring. Later engines just use the factory head gasket.

Both the supercharger and air conditioner are driven with a polyrib, serpentine belt, and use a Ford belt tensioner. In 1981, when Porsche speeded up the flat fan on the 935 race cars it changed to one of these belts to drive the fan because it felt that the increased loads were potentially too much for conventional "V" belts.

The Exclusively Nine race car was a great success, and they finished the season second overall and class B champion in the BRDC National Sports GT championship for 1993 and ran the supercharged engine in 3,500 miles of racing.

Supercharging the 3.6-liter 964 engine is, effectively, like increasing the displacement by a factor of 1.5. If we use this handy rule of thumb we end up with a 911 of roughly 5.4 liters, and in both the C2 and C4 this really feels like that is the case. When I road tested the cars they were both using racing gas and 10 lb of boost, and both produced in excess of 430 hp. Before the cars were returned to street use, boost was reduced to 8 lb for safety, thus cutting the power to around 400 on pump gas. The engine has really pleasant with even throttle response all across the board; it's not peaky or fussy like a race engine or a turbocharged engine with similar power outputs.

For the racing engine Supercharging of Knoxville used a large intercooler that holds the charge-air temperature to nearly ambient air temperature under all conditions. A small intercooler on the right side of the engine behind the air conditioner compressor is used for street installations. Although the intercooler on the street car is small and no special air ducting is provided, it is very effective dropping the 175 deg F inlet temperature to 125 deg F at the intercooler's outlet.

Another interesting supercharger installation is the TechArt CT3, which is based on the 993. TechArt is a respected supplier of trim, body parts, and wheels in Germany, and many of the TechArt components are sold by Porsche itself. The CT3 uses a planetary supercharger made by Cetoni, an offshoot of the ZF Corporation, the transmission manufacturer. This supercharger was originally called the "ZF Turmat" and is now called the "Cetoni Turmat."

This supercharger uses a planetary gear system that multiplies the speed of the crankshaft-driven input shaft by a factor of 15. This results in a final speed as high as 110,000 rpm. The efficiency of this type of supercharger is supposed be higher than of most other supercharger types, and like other superchargers, there is no lag because it is positively driven. The disadvantage is that there is a loss of about 45 hp to drive this supercharger. Like the Supercharging of Knoxville unit, the CT3 supercharger is also spun by a polyrib belt driven off the front of the engine's crankshaft. A fairly modest boost of 0.8 bar produces 462 hp at 6,000 rpm with a peak torque of 406 ft-lb at 5,500 rpm.

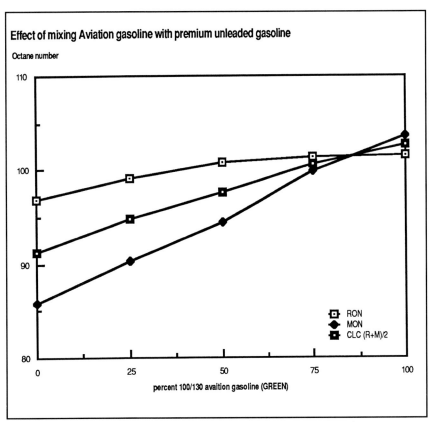

A chart of the effect of mixing aviation gasoline with unleaded premium gasoline.

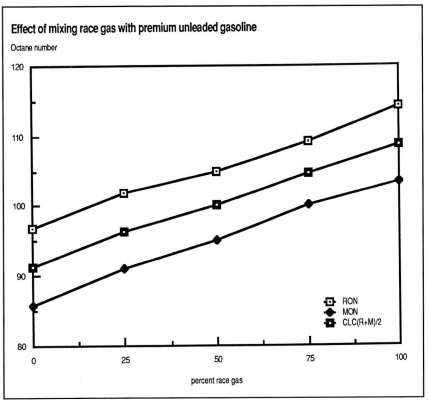

A chart of the effect of mixing racing gasoline with unleaded premium gasoline.

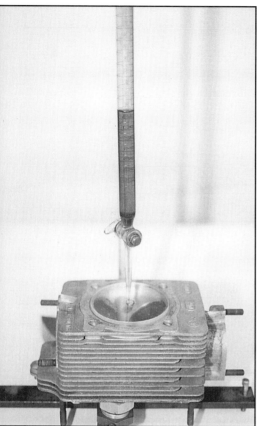

"CC-ing" a cylinder head. For the cc-ing process, the cylinder head should be assembled, and the spark plug should be installed. The edge of the plexiglass plate should be coated with grease so that it will seal to the cylinder head. When the burette is full, it will read zero cc. As the solvent is drained into the combustion chamber, the level in the burette will fall. When the chamber is completely full, the burette reading will be equal to the combustion chamber volume in cc.

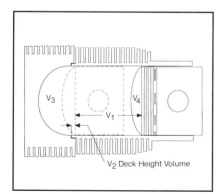

Determining the beginning of the dome. Visualize the piston as a flat-top piston and pick that edge as where the dome starts.

Mahle Pistons and Cylinders for 911 Engines

Bore Size	For Stroke	Resulting Displacement
80 mm	66 mm	2.0 liters, (1991 cc)
81 mm	66 mm	2.1 liters, (2041 cc)
85 mm	66 mm	2.3 liters, (2247 cc)
86.7 mm	70.4 mm	2.5 liters, (2494 cc) long-stroke 2.5 liter
87.5 mm	66 mm	2.4 liters, (2381 cc)
89 mm	66 mm	2.5 liters, (2464 cc) short-stroke 2.5 liter
90 mm	70.4 mm	2.7 liters, (2687 cc) Carrera RS, 8.5:1 compression
90 mm	70.4 mm	2.7 liters (2687 cc) 10.3:1 compression for racing
91 mm	70.4 mm	2.75 liters (2747 cc)
92 mm	70.4 mm	2.8 liters (2808 cc)
92.8 mm	70.4 mm	2.8 liters (2857 cc) 935 Turbo
93 mm	70.4 mm	2.9 liters (2869 cc) 9.8:1 compression for CIS
93 mm	70.4 mm	2.9 liters (2869 cc) 10.5:1 compression for racing
95 mm	70.4 mm	3.0 liters (2994 cc) 10.3:1 compression for racing
95 mm	70.4 mm	3.0 liters (2994 cc) 10.5:1 compression for racing
95 mm	70.4 mm	3.0 liters (2994 cc) CIS, 8.5:1 compression
95 mm	70.4 mm	3.0 liters (2994 cc) CIS, 9.8:1 compression
95 mm	70.4 mm	3.0 liters (2994 cc) 935 Turbo, 6.5:1 compression
95 mm	74.4 mm	3.2 liters (3164 cc) 935 Turbo, 7.2:1 compression
97 mm	70.4 mm	3.12 liters (3122 cc) 935 Turbo, 6.5:1 compression
98 mm	70.4 mm	3.2 liters (3186 cc) 10.3:1 compression for RSR
98 mm	70.4 mm	3.2-liter turbo from 3.0-liter, 7.1:1 compression
98 mm	70.4 mm	3.2 liters (3186 cc) 9.3:1 compression for 911SC
98 mm	70.4 mm	3.2 liters (3186 cc) Max Moritz wedge-shape dome originally for CIS, 9.3 1 compression.
98 mm	74.4 mm	3.4 liters (3367 cc) racing pistons, 23-mm wrist pin
98 mm	74.4 mm	3.4 liters (3367 cc) Ruf 3.4 Carrera conversion 23-mm wrist pin
98 mm	74.4 mm	3.4 liters (3367 cc) Turbo, 23-mm wrist pin
98 mm	74.4 mm	3.4 liters from 3.2 Carrera, (Motronic) 23-mm wrist pin, 9.8:1 compression
98 mm	74.4 mm	3.4 liters from 3.2 with mechanical injection, 23-mm wrist pin, 10.4:1 compression
98 mm	74.4 mm	3.2 to 3.4-liter conversion for Turbo, 23-mm wrist pin 7.1:1 compression
100 mm	70.4 mm	3.3 from 3.0-liter 10.5:1 compression, mechanical injection, 22-mm wrist pin.
100 mm	74.4 mm wrist pin	3.5 from 3.2-liter 9.8:1 compression, Motronic, 23-mm
100 mm	74.4 mm	3.5 liters (3506 cc) 22 mm wrist pin, normally aspirated racing special, 935 crankshaft
100 mm	74.4 mm	3.2 to 3.5 liters (3506 cc) 23 mm wrist pin, normally aspirated racing, 10.5:1 compression
100 mm	74.4 mm	3.3 to 3.5 liters (3506 cc) 23-mm wrist pin, Turbo, 7.1:1 compression
100 mm	74.4 mm	3.3 to 3.5 liters (3506 cc) 23-mm wrist pin, Turbo, 7.5:1 compression
100 mm	76.4 mm	3.6 from 3.0/3.2-liter CIS/Motronic, 9.8:1 compression 23-mm wrist pin
100 mm	76.4 mm	3.6 from 3.0/3.2-liter CIS/Motronic, 10.5:1 compression 23-mm wrist pin
102 mm	76.4 mm	3.8-liter racing, 964, 11.3:1 compression, 23-mm pin
102 mm	76.4 mm	3.8-liter racing, 993, 12.0:1 compression, 23-mm wrist pin
102 mm	76.4 mm	3.8-liter 964 Turbo, 8.0:1, 23-mm wrist pin
102 mm	76.4 mm	3.8-liter 993 Turbo, 9.0:1, 23-mm wrist pin
102 mm	76.4 mm	3.8-liter from 3.0/3.2, 9.8:1 compression, Motronic, 23-mm wrist pin
102 mm	76.4 mm	3.8-liter racing with special reinforced cylinder, 109-mm bore in crankcase, 11.3:1 compression, 23-mm wrist pin

Note: Most racing pistons for the 911 engine were made with a 10.3:1 compression ratio. However, they must be checked because they will vary depending upon their original intended application. All wrist pins 22 mm unless otherwise stated. Some of these piston/cylinder combinations will still be available through Mahle or ANDIAL in the United States, though some will not.

The TechArt CT3 also uses modified pistons, titanium valves, TechArt sport exhaust, modified Motronic, a large intercooler, and a special Techart crankshaft.

Pistons and Cylinders

Mahle pistons and cylinders have become so expensive in the United States over the past decade due to devaluation of the dollar and price increases that a number of engine builders are using other piston makers such as JE, Cosworth, and Wiseco. The one remaining problem is that there is no aftermarket source for cylinders of the same quality as the Mahle Nikasil cylinders. Some engine builders have had their pistons made to fit existing Mahle cylinders, and others have sleeved both Mahle and Schmidt cylinders for use with their aftermarket pistons.

One of the advantages of the Mahle pistons and cylinders with the Nikasil-coated aluminum cylinders is that Porsche has been able to use very tight running clearance between the pistons and cylinders (from a little less than 0.001 inch to about 0.0025 inch). If the piston-to-cylinder running clearance is more than 0.004 inch, then Porsche says the bore is excessive and the piston and cylinder set should be replaced. One of the problems that engine builders have had in the past with some of the aftermarket pistons is that because of design problems, the expansion rate of the pistons were such that excessive piston-to-cylinder clearance had to be used. If the running clearances are in excess of 0.004—as they were with some of the aftermarket piston designs—you are actually buying wornout pistons and cylinders, or if you prefer, brand new replicas of wornout pistons and cylinders. If you use pistons and cylinders with excessive running clearances the pistons rock back and forth in their bores and the rings cannot work properly. In fact, the rings themselves can be worn out before the engine is broken in.

On the facing page are some of the racing or specialized Mahle pistons and cylinders that have been available or are available for 911 engines.

Connecting Rod Dimensions

The table at right shows all of the important dimensions of the different connecting rods used in the 911 and 930 engines.

CIS Fuel Injection and Blown Air Boxes

The CIS (Bosch K-Jetronic) fuel-injection system was introduced on the 911T

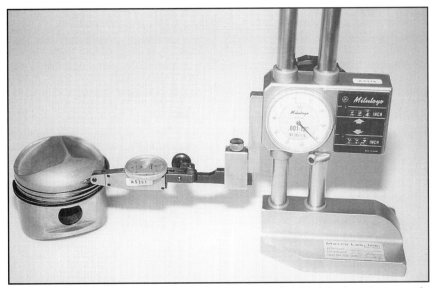

Shown here is the measuring of the height of the dome. The height of the dome is measured from the point determined to be the beginning of the dome to the top of the dome.

in January 1973 and was used by all 911s from 1974 until the introduction of the 911 Carrera in 1984. The CIS fuel-injection system is a relatively simple mechanical unit for gasoline engines. The air that is sucked into the engine is controlled by the throttle valve, then the volume of that air is measured by an air-flow sensor that in turn controls the position of a fuel metering piston in the fuel distributor. From the fuel distributor the fuel goes out the various fuel lines to the injectors. CIS is based on a fairly simple demand-type system which controls the engine's mixture by measuring air flow. Its simplicity is deceptive, however, as there are a number of compensating devices hung around the system to help it run properly.

The CIS system was a reasonable solution at the time it was introduced in that it provided reasonable performance and fuel consumption while making it easier and cheaper to meet emissions laws, which at that time were getting stricter every year.

The CIS system does have a few shortcomings, however, some easier to live with than others. Because of the air-flow measurement method, an engine with CIS injection is limited to the use of relatively mild camshafts, thus limiting the engine's performance potential. A bigger problem is the fact that most of the components in the system handle fuel, so that the CIS system has a much greater exposure to possible fuel contamination.

It is important to supply the CIS with good-quality, clean fuel. Be careful of gasohol and the new premium fuels which use alcohol and as an octane booster. Alcohol will put any water in the system in suspension so that it can enter the injection system and cause contamination and corrosion.

CIS-injected 911s also have a problem with out-of-adjustment or nonfunctioning warm-up regulators. Without the proper mixture during the warm-up cycle you may be playing Russian

911 Connecting Rod Sizes

Engine Size Prod Cars	Length (measured center to center)	Big End Diameter	Big End Width (@ crankpin)	Wrist Pin
2.0–2.2	130 mm	61.0 mm	21.8 mm[1]	22 mm
2.4, 2.7, 3.0	127.8 mm	56 mm	23.8 mm[1]	22 mm
3.0 SC	127.8	56 mm	21.8 mm[1]	22 mm
3.3–3.8	127.0 mm*	58 mm	21.8 mm[1]	23 mm

*Note: 0.8 mm (0.031 inch) shorter than 911SC connecting rod
[1] Bearing width of 22 mm

Roulette with the air box. If your 911 starts with difficulty when cold and runs rough for the first minute or so, it is trying to tell you something which you should heed. Have the warm-up regulator adjusted or replaced before you need a new air box as well.

The warm-up regulator is not the only thing that can cause an air box to blow. Actually, any poor running condition should be looked into as it is possible for any number of rough-running conditions to cause a backfire capable of blowing the air box. I've even seen a few 911s that have been running fine, then backfire unexpectedly, and blow their air boxes when it first gets cold in the winter and again when it first warms in the spring.

The cold-start circuit has also contributed to these random explosions in that the fuel was sprayed into the intake plenum in a fairly uncontrolled manner. If the engine is cold when you try to start it, the voltage will be applied to both the starter and the cold-start valve.

This cold-start valve is a solenoid-operated injection valve—the "seventh injector." A thermo/time switch determines if it is cold enough to operate the seventh injector and if so for how long. The original cold-start system relied on the high primary circuit pressure to sufficiently atomize the fuel by the swirl of the nozzle. However, this spraying of raw gasoline into the intake plenum actually proved to be one of the causes of blown air boxes. The problem is that the mixture is too lean to some of the cylinders, and an excessively lean mixture burns slowly. The slow mixture can still be burning the next time the intake valve opens and may ignite the fuel in the intake runner, resulting in a backfire and a blown air box.

In 1981, a change was made to the cold-start circuit—a cold-start mixture distributor was added to the air box plenum—in order to provide a more uniform distribution of the cold start mixture to all of the engine's cylinders. This distributor injected the cold-start fuel into the plenum's central tube where it was mixed with the auxiliary air from the auxiliary air regulator and then injected into each of the six manifold runners. This ensured that a proper mixture reached the cylinders to help with the starting process, and it also prevented raw gas from being dumped into the intake plenum just in case there was a backfire.

A number of 911 owners have protected their air boxes by installing a Backfire Pressure Relief Valve (BPRV). This valve looks very much like the little plastic valve in the bottom of the float chamber of a modern toilet. The BPRV allows any explosions or backfires in the induction system a free path of escape, the theory being that if the excess pressure from the backfire is allowed to escape through the valve it will not seek its own path out by either blowing off the boot or exploding the air box.

Motronic

Motronic-Bosch Digital-Motor-Electronics (DME) system-injection and ignition control was first used in 1984 for the 911 engines. This has been a reliable system, and it is uncommon for the DME box itself to fail. Most of the failures are with the sensors providing information to the control unit.

The advantage of the Motronic engine management system is its ability to accurately control the fuel mixture and to quickly respond to changing engine requirements with quick adjustments to the fuel mixture and ignition timing. The Motronic system allows engine designers

Measure the dome height above the cylinder, Depth #1. Install one of the pistons and cylinders on the engine and bring the piston to TDC. Use a pair of accurate measuring spacers (Jo blocks) to space the depth micrometer up so that Depth #1 can be measured. Measure the dome height above the cylinder. With the piston at TDC measure down to the top of the piston to get Depth #1. Knowing Depth #1 will permit the calculation of the deck height. For deck height, add dome height and Depth #1 and then subtract the Jo block height.

to map these systems to optimize both fuel supply and ignition curves for the best overall performance for all operating conditions while taking into consideration such things as emissions, fuel economy, performance, and driveability.

The Motronic system has some of the same limitations as the CIS system. For example, because it uses an air-flow measuring system to determine engine fuel needs, it is somewhat sensitive to pulses in the intake air and must use relatively mild cam timing. Engine designers have had to work around this limitation to get back to the same high engine outputs that we had with production car engines in the 1960s and early 1970s. Porsche designers have done just this with the latest version of the 993 engine with its tuned exhaust and Varioram induction system.

Gasoline

Octane is a widely used, often misunderstood term used to describe gasoline's ability to deal with the high pressures and temperatures in the engine's combustion chamber without knocking. In 1926, researchers developed a special variable-compression-ratio engine capable of operating at compression ratios of up to 15:1. Their work in 1927 with a series of pure hydrocarbons of the paraffin, olefin, naphthene, and aromatic families led to the use of n-heptane and iso-octane as the standards for measuring the antiknock quality of gasoline.

The higher the octane, the higher the combustion temperature before engine knock occurs. What this means to the end users is that higher-octane gasoline can be heat-compressed more by the pistons before the engine will knock or ping. And generally speaking, higher compression means higher power and better fuel economy. For a high-performance engine, the idea is to burn the gasoline at the highest compression possible without any knock. The compression ratio versus required octane is not a linear relationship. Thermal efficiency will vary for different engine configurations.

Octane ratings help an owner to buy the correct gas to meet his engine's needs. For Porsche owners this should not be much of a problem because the unleaded fuels that are available today will meet most of their cars' octane needs. It does no good to run a higher-octane gasoline than your Porsche engine requires—you will not get better performance, you will just spend more money, and in some cases you may reduce performance.

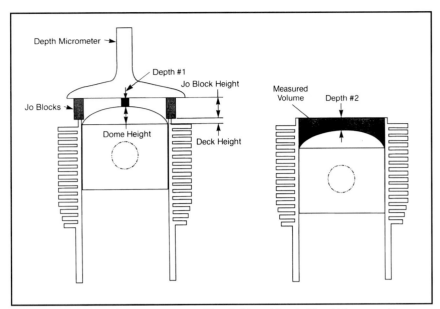

These drawings show the measurements of Depth #1 and Depth #2, which are used to calculate dome volume. Install another one of the pistons into one of the cylinders. Lightly grease the cylinder so that the rings will form a seal to the cylinder. Push the piston up toward the top of the cylinder, but stop before reaching the top. From where the piston stops, measure down to the top of the piston from the top of the cylinder; this measurement is Depth #2. With Depth #2 in hand, the theoretical volume can be calculated.

The United States uses a different octane rating method than is used in Europe. Stateside we use the "average method" or what is called the "CLC RON+MON/2 method" (U.S. Cost of Living Council octane rating). Regular fuels in Europe have octane ratings ranging from 91 to 98 RON (Research Octane Number), which corresponds to 87 to 93 CLC (average method). As an example the 1977 911S/Turbo Carrera owner's manual states that the 911S engine requires 91 RON octane or 87 CLC octane, thus it can readily run on unleaded regular. The same manual says that the Turbo Carrera for racing or sustained high-speed driving requires 96 RON octane or 92 CLC octane.

The testing method that the RON is averaged with to derive our CLC numbers is the Motor Octane Number (MON), which is a much more severe testing method. The motor method tests the engine at a higher speed than the research method. Both of these tests relate the knocking characteristics of gasoline against standards to establish the octane numbers. RON is considered a better test of antiknock characteristics for engines operating at full throttle and low engine speeds. The MON test is considered to be a better indicator of antiknock characteristics at full throttle and high engine speed and part throttle

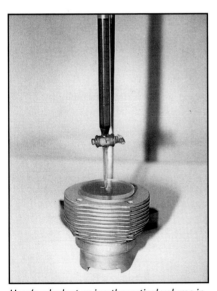

Here's a look at cc-ing theoretical volume in the cylinder for calculation of dome volume. The edge of the plexiglass plate should be coated with grease so that it will seal to the sealing surface of the cylinder. When the burette is full, it will read 0 cc. As the solvent is drained into the theoretical cylinder through the plate filling the cylinder, the level in the burette will fall. When the cylinder is completely full, the burette reading will be the measured volume in cc. The volume of the piston dome is calculated by subtracting the measured volume from the calculated theoretical volume.

An improperly repaired intake manifold stud. While this particular poor repair job is probably not causing any harm, I have seen a similar poor repair job on an intake-manifold stud for a 928 necessitate an engine overhaul.

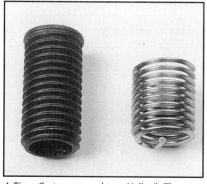

A Time-Cert compared to a Helicoil. The Time-Cert is a one-piece threaded insert, while the Helicoil is, as its name would imply, a wound-up coil of wire. The illustration shows the strength of the Time-Cert.

at low and high engine speeds. The CLC method attempts to create a more meaningful rating by averaging the two.

The CLC octane rating will usually be four to five points lower than the RON rating. For example, the current production European Carrera has a compression ratio of 10.3:1 and requires a fuel quality of 98/88 RON/MON leaded, or unleaded with an identical octane number. Using our CLC average system this works out to be 93 octane. This is contrasted with the U.S. version which has a compression ratio of 9.5:1 and requires fuel quality of 87 CLC octane unleaded. The U.S. version is rated at 217 hp with 195 ft-lb of peak torque versus

the Euro version at 231 hp with 209 ft-lb peak torque.

Fuel Additives

Can we use U.S. pump gasolines in today's hot-rod 911s? For the most part the answer is yes.

Premium unleaded fuel is adequate for any of our Porsches that require unleaded fuel, and most of them only require unleaded regular. Although fuel additives will not harm the catalytic converters or oxygen sensors, they are very expensive to use.

Most 911s will do fine on U.S. pump gasoline. However, there are a few of the early 911s and some of the European 911s that are marginal, and there are some performance combinations the owners have created that overstep the bounds of reason. An example of this would be using the 2.8 RSR cylinders and pistons on the 2.7 engine where the compression ratio ends up in the 11:1 range. In general, any of the 911s with less than 10:1 compression will do fine with 92 or higher unleaded premium.

The biggest need for higher octane fuels is at the track events that are becoming so popular across the country. The octane ratings that you might be able to get away with in a 911 for street use are just not adequate for the sustained hard running that occurs at these track events. Under these circumstances, you must increase the octane to protect your engine from detonation damage.

Probably the best solution for these track events is to buy some racing or aviation gasoline or a fuel additive that contains aniline—the most effective ingredient in octane boosters—to mix with your pump gas and raise the octane to an acceptable level to prevent detonation. Though aniline is the most effective octane-boosting additive, it is toxic, like lead, so it is being phased out.

The biggest shortcoming of octane-boosting additives is the expense. It would take three pint cans of 100-percent aniline (about $12 per can) to raise the octane rating of 20 gal of gas about three octane points—a rather pricey fill up.

Before the removal of lead from gasoline we were able to mix unleaded premium gasoline and leaded regular gasoline and boost the octane above that of the unleaded premium. The reason that this worked was that gasoline producers were mixing more lead than was necessary in the leaded gasolines.

Where the principle of mixing leaded and unleaded gasolines together to boost the octane of the unleaded fuel can still be applied is at track events. You can use either racing or aviation gasoline, both of which still use tetraethyl lead as their octane-boosting agent. As you can see in the accompanying chart, either of these leaded gasolines will provide a significant boost in octane to the unleaded premium used as the base stock. The aviation gasoline has a lower specific gravity so the induction system will have to be richened up to compensate for this.

The Elusive Search for Perfect Combustion

Well known to all automotive enthusiasts are the four-strokes of a four-cycle engine. For review, they are (1) induction: the down stroke on the first revolution where the cylinder draws in the fresh air/fuel mixture; (2) compression: the upstroke where the air/fuel mixture is compressed; (3) power: ignition starts the combustion, or power, stroke on the downstroke of the second revolution; and (4) exhaust: the upstroke where exhaust gases are expelled.

The power, or combustion and expansion, stroke is the one we are most concerned with when we are dealing with detonation. Snap your fingers. Sorry, not fast enough! The interval required from the time the spark plug first ignites a properly mixed air/fuel mixture in the combustion chamber until combustion is complete takes less time than the snapping of your fingers. During this process your engine is converting

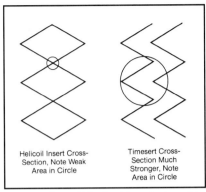

Helicoil Insert Cross-Section, Note Weak Area in Circle

Timesert Cross-Section Much Stronger, Note Area in Circle

Compared to a Helicoil, a Time-Cert provides considerably greater strength, as shown in this illustration.

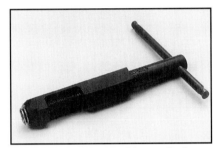

This is the installation tool for a Helicoil.

Gasoline's Octane Response to Aniline

Gasoline and percent aniline used	RON	MON	R+M/2	R+M/2 Increase	R+M/2 Increase for 1% Aniline
92 octane unleaded	97.9	86.3	92.1	—	—
92 octane unleaded + 2 percent aniline	101.4	89.5	95.4	3.3	1.6
92 octane unleaded + 2 percent aniline	103.8	92.1	98.0	5.9	1.5
89 octane unleaded	94.9	84.2	89.6	—	—
89 octane unleaded + 2 percent aniline	98.9	87.9	93.4	3.8	1.9
89 octane unleaded + 4 percent	102.0	90.3	96.2	6.6	1.6
88 octane leaded	93.0	83.5	88.2	—	—
88 octane leaded + 2 percent aniline	97.2	86.8	92	3.8	1.9
88 octane leaded + 4 percent aniline	100.3	89.0	94.6	6.4	1.6

Effect of Mixing Aviation or Race Gasoline with Premium Unleaded Gasoline

Gas Used as Additive	Mixture	RON	MON	R+M/2	Specific Gravity	Approx. Lead Content (g./gal.)
	unleaded premium	96.8	85.8	91.3	0.7579	0
100/130	75 % UP/25 % Av gas	99.2	90.3	94.8	0.7416	1
aviation-gas	50 % UP/50 % Av gas	100.9	94.4	97.6	0.7256	2
(green)	25 % UP/75 % Av gas	101.3	99.8	100.6	0.7093	3
	100 % Av gas	101.5	103.7	102.6	0.6926	4
	unleaded premium	96.8	85.8	91.3	0.7579	0
RACE GAS	75 % UP/25 % race gas	101.8	91.1	96.4	0.7547	1
	50 % UP/50 % race gas	104.9	95.1	100.0	0.7491	2
	25 % UP/75 % race gas	109.2	100.1	104.6	0.7440	3
	100 % race gas	114.2	103.5	108.8	0.7408	4

chemical energy (burning gasoline) to mechanical energy via the pistons turning the crankshaft and ultimately the car's wheels.

The air/fuel mixture ignited in your engine will produce about the same amount of energy when it burns whether it is contained in your engine or ignited in the open. Your engine can be optimized to produce more work for the released energy by igniting the mixture at just the right instant and controlling the burn. One important factor in this process is the engine's compression ratio. After the piston has moved down to suck in the air and gasoline mixture, it returns upwards to compress the mixture before the spark plug ignites it. If the piston allows room for nine units of space in the cylinder at the bottom of its stroke, but only enough room for one unit when at the top, the engine has a compression ratio of 9:1. A higher compression ratio makes the engine more thermodynamically efficient so that it can get more work out of the fuel.

If everything goes right, in less time than it takes you to snap your fingers, you have perfect combustion and extract the maximum power from the gasoline used. The proper air/fuel ratio for perfect combustion is a mixture of 14 parts air to 1 part gasoline. In a carbureted engine most of the air/fuel mixing is done in the carburetor. In a fuel-injected engine fuel is injected into the intake air stream. In both cases, the air/fuel mixture is drawn into the cylinder and swirled around, further mixing it on its the way into the cylinder. Once the compression stroke begins, the mixing process is accelerated as the air and fuel is forced into a smaller and smaller volume. By the time ignition occurs, the fuel and air have attained a near perfect mixing. The problem is that "perfect combustion" is not always obtainable, and there are a number of reasons for that.

Combustion, as we said, is started by the spark plug; the combustion spreads through the combustion chamber behind what is called the flame front. As the gas temperature rises they expand and continue to compress the unburned gasses even more. If the temperature of the explosive mixture is raised sufficiently, the mixture will eventually explode spontaneously. This spontaneous combustion gives rise to the characteristic metallic sound that we call knocking or pinging. Knocking can vary in magnitude between a mild form oc-curring only at relatively low speeds and wide throttle openings, to such violent reactions that the engine will actually misfire. In addition to being annoying, in severe cases knocking may lead to uncontrolled pre-ignition, which can burn piston crowns or cause other damage. The point at which this spontaneous combustion occurs is affected by a number of things including compression ratio, combustion chamber design, ignition timing, atmospheric conditions, and gasoline octane.

In some engines, a higher compression ratio can improve the flame propa-

This is the installation tool for a Time-Cert. The tool is a forming tap.

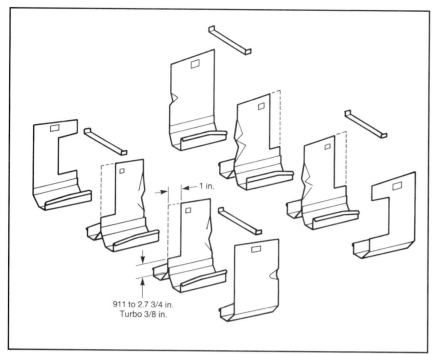

In 1977, Porsche made a modification to the middle air deflectors under the cylinders. They were made an inch narrower than on earlier engines. This change to the middle deflectors made the cooling-air distribution more even over the cylinders and cylinder heads. The old air deflectors can be modified with a good pair of tin snips. This drawing shows which areas of the old air deflectors should be modified. The air deflectors were updated in March 1977 for all 911s and 930s, and modification should be made to any of the earlier 911 engines any time that they are apart. This modification has been said to drop the operating temperature by 10 to 15 deg F, which can't help but reduce the stud-pulling problem on the 2.7-liter engines.

gation and combustion and reduce the engine's sensitivity to knocking by reducing combustion chamber size. This is not always the case, and the 2.0-liter 911 engine is one of the exceptions. The 2.0 911 engine has a small, steep, hemispherical combustion chamber in a cylinder head with two large valves. The large valves place the spark plug off to one side, away from the ideal position. When the compression is raised on these engines, the piston dome protrudes into the combustion chamber so that the flame front has to travel over and around the piston to get complete combustion. The higher the compression the worse the problem. This is one of the reasons that Porsche chose to use twin spark plugs for the 906 engine, which used this combustion chamber shape.

In the later-model 911 engines, the flame travel problem was virtually eliminated by two changes. First, all 911 engines from 1970-on have had a more shallow, open combustion chamber design. Second, each displacement increase reduced the need to crowd the combustion chamber in order to maintain high compression ratios. Remem-

ber, the compression ratio is the volume of the cylinder with the piston at bottom of its travel compared to the volume with the piston at the top of its travel. As the bore and stroke have gotten larger, the volume of the cylinder has gotten proportionally larger, while the volume of the head has increased in size to a lesser extent. A smaller dome would maintain the same compression ratio. You can see this difference in the size of the domes when you compare Porsche's pistons from their various racing 911 engines. Effectively, Porsche has maintained a nominal compression ratio of 10.3:1 for all of its normally aspirated racing engines. Whereas the larger displacement engines just have a nice smooth bump on the top to maintain the same compression ratio, the 2.0-liter piston has a very steep dome. The larger pistons with their relatively smaller domes do not obstruct the combustion chamber, hence the flame travel is less impaired and the engine is much less prone to knocking or pinging.

Obviously the choice of gasoline has a great influence on detonation in your Porsche. There are gasolines available

now that are safe for all Porsches in almost all applications. Modern, high-grade unleaded gasoline allows high compression ratios to be used with the combustion and expansion process under complete control. Special racing gas is available for competition purposes that will allow 10.3:1 compression ratios and turbocharged engines to run without detonation.

With high-compression engines it is possible to have slight detonation but none of the indications we normally expect with pre-ignition. For example, the pre-ignition can occur at higher rpms when it might not be heard over car and engine noises. This was a problem with some of the early 2.0-liter 911 and 911S engines with their tight combustion chambers. If you own one of these early cars, always use the highest octane fuel available. If you still have a detonation problem you might consider lowering your engine's compression ratio by changing the pistons.

Compression Ratio

An engine's compression ratio is the ratio of the total swept volume (the volume of the cylinder when the piston is at BDC, including the volume of the cylinder head, and so on) to the unswept volume (the volume of the cylinder when the piston is at TDC).

The formula for compression is:

$$\frac{V1+V2+V3-V4}{V2+V3-V4}$$

Where:
V1 equals swept volume
V2 equals deck height volume
V3 equals cylinder head volume
V4 equals piston dome volume

To show how this formula works, let's go through the process of figuring the compression ratio for a 2.0-liter racing engine with 1-mm overbore pistons. The bore is 81 mm and the stroke is 66 mm for a displacement of 2,040.6 cc.

Calculating V1 (Swept Volume)

To determine the compression ratio you don't need to measure V1, the swept volume of one cylinder. In fact, it is easier to compute it from the bore and stroke.

Swept Volume (V1) =
Bore^2 x Stroke x 0.7854
(bore and stroke expressed in centimeters)

Since the formula uses bore and stroke in centimeters, we will have to convert those numbers from millimeters by moving the decimal point one place to the left. Now plug the numbers into the formula:

$$Swept\ Volume\ (V1) =$$
$$8.1^2 \times 6.6 \times 0.7854 = 340.09\ cc$$

Calculating V2 (Deck Height Volume)

First the dome and deck heights must be measured. This involves two steps, the first of which is done with a piston and cylinder set that is not installed on the engine. The bottom of the dome must be determined and then the distance is measured from that point to the top of the dome with a height measuring gauge. For our example, that measurement will be 0.675 inches. Next, the dome height must be measured with a depth micrometer with the piston and cylinder installed on the engine and set to TDC. Since the dome sticks out of the cylinder, the depth micrometer must be spaced up to facilitate the measurement. In our example we have used Jo blocks to space up the depth micrometer 0.700 inch. With piston at top dead center, measure down to the top of the piston. This measurement will be Depth #1, and in our example Depth #1 will be 0.046 inch. Knowing Depth #1, the height of the dome, and the height of the Jo blocks will permit the calculation of the deck height.

$$Deck\ height =$$
dome height + Depth #1 - Jo-block height
$$0.675 + 0.046 - 0.700 =$$
0.021 inch deck height

Deck height volume can now be calculated using the same formula as used to calculate swept volume, but substituting deck height (after converting it to centimeters) for stroke in the formula.

Convert inches to centimeters by multiplying by 2.54 (0.021 x 2.54 = 0.053) before plugging into the swept volume formula.

$$Swept\ volume =$$
$$Bore^2 \times stroke \times 0.7854$$
$$8.1^2 \times 0.053 \times 0.7854 =$$
2.73 cc V2 deck height volume

Calculating V3 (Combustion Chamber Volume)

Because of the irregular shape of the combustion chamber, measuring its volume involves physically filling it with liquid and then seeing how much liquid it took to do the job. The most convenient method for doing this is

As you approach crankcase modifications, here is what the stock crankcase looks like to a piston on its way down to BDC.

with a graduated chemist burette and a Plexiglas disc to seal the combustion chamber.

Even if you are not going to calculate your compression ratio, you may want to "cc" your heads to ensure that all of the combustion chambers are within one cc of each other. Porsche heads are generally pretty accurate, and whatever differences you find can usually be adjusted for by sinking the valves a little deeper in the heads with the smaller combustion chambers. This, of course, requires redoing the valve job.

Before "cc'ing" the head, install the valves and springs and the spark plug. You can get away without installing the valve springs if you smear a light coat of grease on the valve faces. Place the head on a level surface so the combustion chamber faces upward. It is helpful to have a jig to hold the head so that it can be accurately leveled.

Cut a piece of clear Plexiglas so that it will just fit into the cylinder head and seal against the cylinder head sealing surface. The Plexiglas must be thick enough so that it will not deflect and throw off the reading. Drill a small hole in the center of your Plexiglas plate just large enough for the tip of your burette. Spread the sealing surface of the cylinder head with a thin coat of grease and press the Plexiglas disc down tight against the head.

Mix some automatic transmission fluid into some clean solvent and fill the

burette. The coloration of the ATF makes it easier to see what you are doing. Fill the burette to "0" and the graduations on the side of the burette will be direct reading. Position the tip of the burette over the hole in the Plexiglas and fill the combustion chamber until there are no bubbles. The reading on the burette will be the cylinder head's combustion chamber volume in cc's. In the case of the 2.0-liter heads, the volume will be between 70 and 75 cc, partially depending on the wide range of valve sizes. For our example, V3, the combustion chamber volume, will be 71 cc.

Measuring V4 (Dome Volume)

The final step before using the formula to calculate the compression ratio is measuring the volume of the piston dome. Again, with the piston and cylinder off the engine, insert the piston into its cylinder. Spread a light coat of grease a little below the top of the cylinder. Push the piston up in the cylinder until the top ring is sealed by the grease and the piston dome is still below the top edge of the cylinder. Measure the distance from the top of the cylinder to the top of the piston dome with a depth micrometer; this measurement will be Depth #2. Using Depth #2, the theoretical volume can be calculated using the swept volume formula—just substitute Depth #2 plus the dome height (after converting it to centimeters) for stroke in the formula.

The crankcase after modifications. These modifications make it easier for the air to flow around in the crankcase, reducing wasted horsepower. There is always a piston going up when another is going down, so the air being pushed by the piston going down will have to find its way to the bottom of the piston that is going up. The factory recommended this modification for 2.0-liter racing engines, saying it would increase the output by about 10 hp.

A Turbatrol fender-mounted auxiliary oil cooler. These Turbatrol oil coolers are more efficient than any other cooler in this application. Lemke Design

Deck height	= 0.021 inches (0.533 mm)
V1 Swept volume	= 340.0 cc
V2 Deck height volume	= 2.73 cc
V3 Cylinder head volume	= 71 cc
V4 Piston dome volume	= 37 cc

Plugging the numbers into the compression ratio formula

$$\frac{V1+V2+V3-V4}{V2+V3-V4} = compression$$

$$\frac{340.0+2.73+70.6-36.6}{2.73+70.6-36.6} = 10.26$$

The compression ratio for this engine is 10.26:1, which is just about right for a 911 racing engine, Porsche always aims for 10.3:1 as a nominal value for its racing engines.

Remember that the engines bore, stroke, combustion chamber size, deck height, and piston-dome size determine the compression. If any of these are changed the compression ratio will also be changed. Bigger bore and longer stroke will increase the compression ratio if the dome on the pistons are not changed to compensate. Porsche designs its engines with this fact in mind so you will have to exercise caution when mixing pistons and cylinders for one engine displacement size to another. For example, if you were to use 84-mm pistons and cylinders from a 2.2-liter engine in place of the 84-mm pistons and cylinders made for the 2.4-liter engine when building a 2.4-liter engine, the compression will be increased by the effect of the longer stroke. To compensate for this change the dome was made smaller on the pistons for the larger displacement 2.4-liter engine.

A few Porsche engines use flat-top pistons. It is easier to solve the equation

Height of calculated theoretical volume = Depth #2 + Dome height

0.144 + 0.675 = 0.819 inches

Convert this to centimeters by multiplying by 2.54 (0.819 x 2.54 = 2.080) before plugging into the swept volume formula.

Swept volume = Bore^2 x stroke x 0.7854
8.1^2 x 2.080 x 0.7854 = 107.18 cc

107.18 cc is the calculated theoretical cylinder volume. This is the calculated volume of the cylinder, not taking into account the presence of the piston dome.

Next is "cc'ing" the "theoretical cylinder volume" in the cylinder for the piston-dome volume calculation. Coat the edge of the Plexiglas plate with grease and place it on top of the cylinder and press down so it will seal to the sealing surface of the cylinder. Fill the burette with the solvent and automatic transmission fluid to "0" and fill the "theoretical cylinder volume" with the fluid. When the theoretical volume is completely filled the burette reading indicates the measured "theoretical cylinder volume" in cc's. In our example the measured volume will be 70.6 cc. The volume of the piston dome can now be calculated by subtracting the measured volume from the calculated "theoretical cylinder volume."

Dome volume = calculated "theoretical volume" - measured volume

107.18 - 70.6 = 36.58 cc dome volume

We now have all the numbers (following) to calculate the compression ratio.

Number cylinders	= 6
Bore	= 81 mm
Stroke	= 66 mm

The cylinders also have to be modified to let the air move around more freely in the crankcase. The cylinder on the left is stock, and the one on the right has been modified to improve crankcase breathing.

for compression ratio for these engines, as you just leave out V4 (dome volume) in the equation. The deck height is also easier to measure with a flat-top piston; you just measure down to the top of the piston from the top of the cylinder with a depth micrometer.

Checking Valve-to-Piston and Piston-to-Head Clearance

When assembling an engine, it is always a good idea to measure the deck height (whether or not you are calculating compression ratio). For the 911 engine the minimum piston-to-cylinder head clearance should be around 0.035 inches (0.090 mm). Because the shapes of the piston dome, the combustion chamber deck height, and the piston-to-head clearance are not the same, the minimum piston-to-head clearance must be measured to prevent engine damage. If you are using pistons made by any manufacturer other than Mahle or Karl Schmidt, or if you have done anything to alter the compression or the valve sizes, you should plan to check both the piston-to-head clearance and the valve-to-piston clearances.

Check the clearances by placing a strip of modeling clay, at least 3/16-inch thick, in the partially assembled engine, on top of the piston in the area of both the intake and exhaust valve pockets and over at the edge of the piston where it will first hit the combustion chamber. Install the head and torque it to 25 ft-lb. You can check the piston-to-head clearance without assembling the engine any further by just turning it over for two complete revolutions. However, if you are interested in the valve-to-piston clearance as well, it will be necessary to assemble the engine up through timing the camshaft and adjust the valves on the cylinder under test and then rotate the crankshaft through two complete revolutions. This will allow both intake and exhaust valves to open and close. After rotating the crank, carefully disassemble the head. If the valves make an impression, cut the clay in half with a sharp knife and measure its thickness at the thinnest point with a vernier caliper.

Another measuring media preferred by many mechanics is solder in place of the modeling clay. If you use this method, use solder with an uncrushed diameter of 0.100 inch. Minimum clearance should be 0.060 inches (1.5 mm) for the valves. If there is not adequate clearance between the piston and the cylinder head, it will be necessary to use

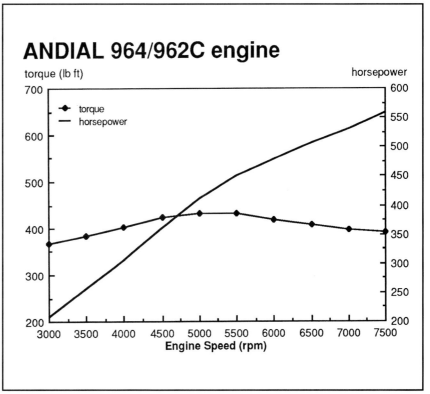

Performance data for an ANDIAL 962 engine for the C4, as run on a dyno. The power was restricted because of concern for the transmission and drivetrain of the C4.

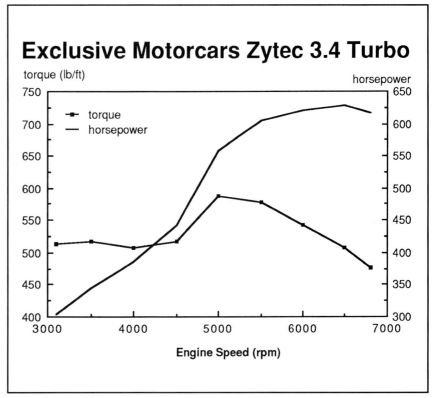

Performance data for an Exclusive Motorcars 3.4-liter turbocharged engine using Zytec engine management.

more cylinder base gaskets to increase clearance. If there is adequate piston-to-head clearance but not enough valve clearance, it will be necessary to deepen the valve pockets. This all gets very tricky and you should not really deepen the pockets unless you are sure that doing so will not reduce the thickness of the piston material to less than 0.200 inch (5 mm) because doing so will weaken the dome structure and may lead to piston failure.

Studs and Inserts

In 1968, Porsche changed its method for manufacturing the 911 crankcase. Prior to that model year, the crankcase had been die-cast aluminum, but beginning in 1968 it was changed to high-pressure cast magnesium. At the time, there were several advantages to this change: the pressure-cast crankcase was a more precise piece requiring less machining; magnesium machines more easily, saving machining time; and the

finished crankcase weighed 22 lb less than its aluminum predecessor. When Porsche had Mahle make these castings, they were the largest magnesium pressure die castings ever made, and Mahle won a design award from the Magnesium Association for its work.

All would probably have been fine at this point if Porsche had left the 911 engine at its 2.0-liter displacement. But because of displacement increases, several weaknesses have showed up in the magnesium crankcase. The crankcase itself was redesigned several times to compensate for the displacement changes and was finally replaced with a much stronger high-pressure cast-aluminum crankcase.

By 1978, all of the 911-derived engines were using the new pressure-cast-aluminum crankcase developed for the 911 Turbo and introduced with the 1975 model Turbo; all of these crankcases have a 911 Turbo part number. During this evolution of the crankcase, the cylinder head retaining studs were overlooked.

In their racing engines, Porsche had recognized the head stud problem in the early 1970s and had taken steps to rectify it. Porsche had found that the difference in rate of thermal expansion for the aluminum and magnesium (which are about the same) used for the crankcase, cylinders, and cylinder heads was about double that of the steel cylinder head retaining studs.

The result is that the cold, or room temperature, stress is increased by the different thermal expansion rates resulting in the heads being overly torqued at operating temperatures. The result is that with time, many of the head studs would pull and deform the crankcase where the head studs screw in. Also in some instances, the head retaining studs themselves break under this stress.

In the race cars, the solution for this problem was the use of head retaining studs made of a Dilavar steel alloy that has a thermal expansion rate that is about the same as aluminum and magnesium. The use of Dilavar head retaining studs in the racing engines greatly reduced the stress changes due to temperature changes and solved the problem for the racing engines.

This same technology was also applied to the production 911 engines. 911 Turbo engines, all 911SC engines, all 911 Carrera engines, and some of the late-1977 2.7 911 engines use Dilavar head studs. The 911 Turbo engines use all 24 Dilavar head studs, while the nor-

This shows the supercharging of a Knoxville 3.2-liter Carrera with a Paxton supercharger. The supercharger increases the output to 345 hp at 6,200 rpm.

This shows the supercharging of a Knoxville 3.2-liter Carrera with a Whipple charger. The Whipple charger increased the power output of the 3.2 to 435 hp at 5,000 rpm.

mally aspirated 911 engines use 12 Dilavar studs just for the bottom row of head retaining studs.

Unfortunately, this was not the end of head retaining stud problems. Engines built prior to the 1980 production run used a Dilavar stud that was shiny silver and quite a number of engines built with these studs had one or more breaks. Because of a corrosion problem, the Dilavar head studs were changed twice after the original shiny-silver version. The Dilavar studs manufactured after 1980 had a gold, textured finish, and the studs manufactured after 1984 had a black epoxy coating over the center portion of the stud. Unfortunately, examples of all of these studs have broken. Most of the failures seem to be due to corrosion, and broken studs in older cars are caused by corrosion on the Dilavar head studs. The early studs did not have the epoxy coating and were prone to this problem. Some of the later engines with epoxy-coated head studs also show signs of this problem if the epoxy coating is somehow damaged or scraped off while the engine is being disassembled, assembled, and reassembled.

Another problem that has occurred with the Dilavar head studs and over the past few years is their failure right after an engine is assembled. One mechanic told me that he had just torqued up the heads and was walking out of the room when he heard a loud "Ka-ping" noise and something bounced off of the wall. He said he wasn't sure what is was and went about his business. The next morning when he resumed work on the engine he was rebuilding he discovered that three of the head studs had broken.

I started getting regular reports on these missiles flying through peoples' workshops. Porsche says that nothing has been changed in the manufacturing process and it is at a loss as to the cause of the failures.

For a long time I had recommended using Dilavar head studs, but now that I have seen so much trouble I am cautious about recommending their use. I suggest that you use the RaceWare head studs along with Time-Cert threaded inserts or some other suitable insert.

Even though the Dilavar stud failure rate has never approached the high failure rate of the pulled 2.7 cylinder-head studs, there have been a number of instances of these studs failing. Porsche has gone away from the Dilavar head studs on the later 964 and 993 engines and are again using a steel stud.

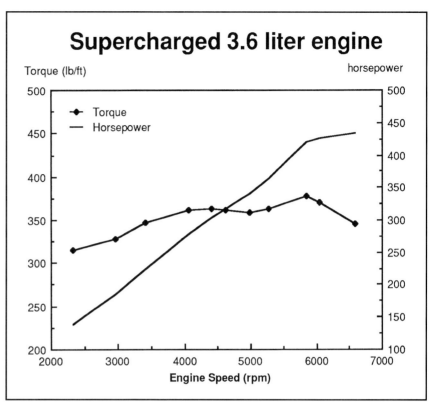

Here is the power curve for supercharging of a Knoxville 3.6-liter Carrera with a Whipple supercharger.

Techart also has a supercharger installation on a 993 engine that it calls the 911 CT3. The CT3 supercharger drive is also by a polyrib belt driven off the front of the engine's crankshaft. They use a fairly modest boost of 0.8 bar and produce 462 hp at 6,000 rpm with a peak torque of 406 lb-ft at 5,500 rpm.

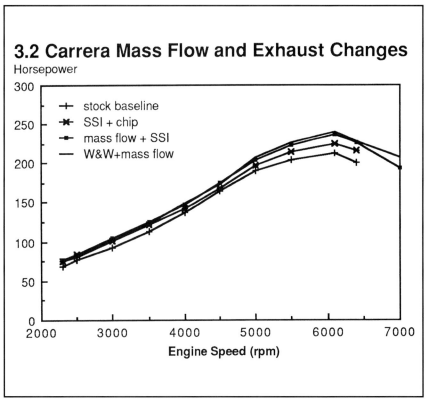

Chip and Exhaust Comparison

Horsepower

- ✱ stock
- ◆ best of chips
- — exhaust

This data compares the use of varied aftermarket chips to exhaust system changes.

3.2 Carrera Mass Flow and Exhaust Changes

Horsepower

- ┼ stock baseline
- ✱ SSI + chip
- ■ mass flow + SSI
- — W&W+mass flow

This data shows the results from when Exclusive Motorcars compared various mass flow air meter and exhaust changes on a 3.2 Carrera.

Removal and Repair of Pulled or Broken Studs

Broken and stripped fasteners are problems you will have to learn to deal with. If you have a thermal reactor car, you will find that thermal reactor studs usually break in the middle because that's where Porsche has tapered them. This is done to allow some thermal expansion and to shift the highest concentration of stress away from the threads. You can try a pair of vice grips on these studs when they break, but I have found that the best approach is to weld a nut onto the end of the broken stud, heat the head with a torch, and then remove the broken stud as you would a bolt. It also helps to heat any frozen nut that holds any exhaust component until it is cherry red before trying to remove it. This heating process does two things to help you: one, loosens any corrosion or rust; and two, expands the nut making it easier to get off. When you assemble any exhaust system components always assemble them with "Never-Seez" antiseize lubricating compound. This will make it much easier to disassemble next time.

Conventional studs will usually break flush with the surface of the work piece or slightly below the surface because this is where the highest stress is—the root of the threads. A common error is try to use an "easy-out" to remove these broken studs. (An easy-out is a device intended to remove a broken stud by drilling a hole into the broken stud, inserting the easy out, and backing out the broken stud.) If you broke a frozen fastener, you will not be able to remove it with an easy-out. In fact, you will probably break the easy-out and then you will really be in a world of hurt. It should be noted that normally, an easy-out is only used on fasteners that have been broken off in shear. I recommend that under any other conditions, the broken off stud be drilled out. Now this does not mean that you just drill out the offending fastener. The reason for this is that there is hardly any chance that the drill is going to go exactly central with the existing threads, hence the original threads will be damaged. The work should be done on a drill press, or better yet a milling machine. If the work must be performed freehand, I recommend the use of a steel guide block or fixture to ensure drilling on center.

Another trick that you can use is a left-handed drill. The beauty of this is that the left-hand drill will be exerting every bit of force trying to get the stud to back out from the very start. Drilling under these circumstances tends to loosen the broken bolt or stud. Often you will find that this technique will back the broken stud right out as soon as you start to drill it. If it doesn't, you are no worse off than if you had planned to drill out the offending fastener and retap the hole for a Helicoil insert or a "Time-Cert." Left-handed drills are available from Snap-On tools in a set of five: 1/8, 3/16, 1/4, 5/16, and 11/32 inch.

A Helicoil insert is a wound piece of wire that in its cross-section is the shape of a diamond. The inside is the same thread as the thread to be repaired, and the outside is some larger size, but the same thread pitch. Good as they are, they do have limits. One of these is the fact that the fix is only a piece of wire and it does not take much of a burr, cross-threading, and so on, to pull some of the wire out and ruin the fix. Furthermore, they depend on the "spring" effect of the coil to secure the wire in the hole. Once damaged, they can be difficult to remove. They can also present problems on insertion because, due to the "spring" effect, they have to be prewound with a special tool. The problem comes when there is a lip or other intrusion near the hole and the inserting tool has to be held away from the workpiece. The insert sometimes leaves the inserting tool before the threads are engaged. So much for helicoil inserts.

Enter "Time-Certs." These are a more modern fix. A Time-Cert is a solid piece of steel in which the threads are "timed" to one another, inside diameter to outside diameter. The advantage of the timing is that it makes this a very small insert that requires little space. The Time-Cert is stronger than the helicoil type due to the increased cross section and it is locked in place by installing with a roll tap. (A roll tap is one that does no cutting, but forms the threads. This is done by "pushing" the material from the valleys to form the ridges of the thread—a strong method.) On the Time-Cert the bottom few threads are incomplete (that is, left at pitch diameter) and the roll tap forms them all the while wedging the bottom on the insert, locking it into place. The Time-Cert takes more time to install, but it is a superior fix to the helicoil inserts for most applications. The Time-Cert or some other one-piece insert is the only proper fix for pulled cylinder-head studs on the magnesium crankcases.

There are critics of Time-Certs who say that they have seen them fail and have other inserts that they prefer. However, I started using Time-Certs about

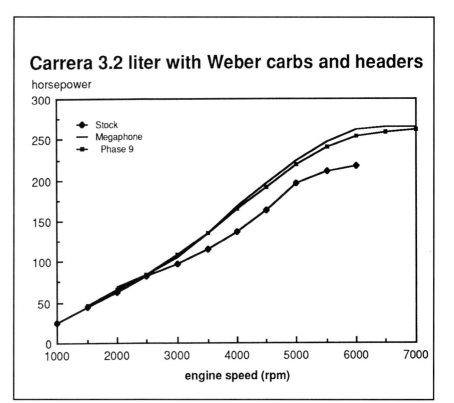

Carrera 3.2 liter with Weber carbs and headers

This data shows the effects of when Jerry Woods Enterprises modified a 3.2 Carrera engine by changing exhaust and induction systems, using a set of racing headers, and using a pair of 46 IDA Weber carburetors.

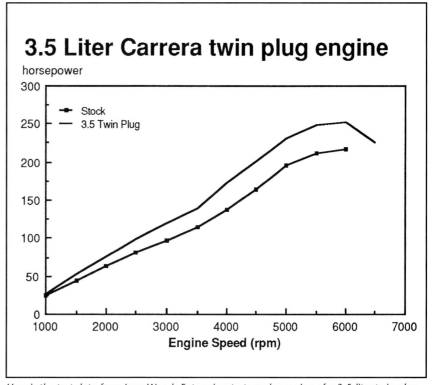

3.5 Liter Carrera twin plug engine

Here is the test data from Jerry Woods Enterprises tests and mapping of a 3.5-liter twin-plug Carrera.

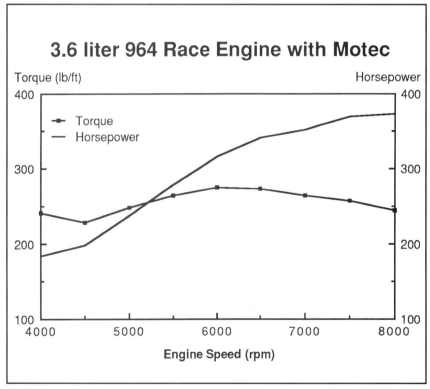

Modified 3.6 liter 964 Engine with Webers

Torque (lb/ft)   **Horsepower**

- ■ Torque
- Horsepower

Engine Speed (rpm)

Jerry Woods Enterprises builds a simple race motor from a Carrera 3.6. The engine retains stock pistons and cylinders and uses a set of special cams designed to improve performance without requiring additional valve clearance, a set of 46 IDA Weber carburetors, and one of the Woods and Weber exhaust systems.

3.6 liter 964 Race Engine with Motec

Torque (lb/ft)   **Horsepower**

- ■ Torque
- Horsepower

Engine Speed (rpm)

This is the test data from a 3.6-liter racing engine with GE 100 cams, racing exhaust, and Motec engine management.

15 years ago and I still feel that they are a reliable fix when properly installed.

Not much can be done to repair damaged male threads. They can be chased with a rethreading die and made serviceable in an emergency, but replacement is the only appropriate repair.

Cylinder Cooling Air Deflectors

Porsche modified the cooling air deflectors to improve the engine cooling in March 1977. The middle two cooling deflectors on each side of the engine were made narrower by 25 mm (1 inch) out by the cylinder head. The cooling fins were modified to lower the critical cylinder temperature and to even the cooling temperature on the cylinders, cylinder heads, and crankcase. When any of the older engines are rebuilt, the cooling deflectors should either be replaced with the later, narrower cooling deflectors or modified with a pair of tin snips. The modification is good for a 10–15 deg F temperature drop, and because it provides more even cooling to the cylinders and cylinder heads, it reduces the likelihood of cylinder-head stud pulling. This is one of the changes you can perform that will help make the 2.7 engine even more reliable.

Crankshafts

I strongly recommend against using damaged crankshafts in high-performance applications. I have tried to have a couple of 911 crankshafts repaired over the years, and in neither case were they suitable, long-term repairs. If your crankshaft "fix" doesn't work you will have to take the engine apart again to repair the crankshaft correctly.

Send your crankshaft out to someone you are sure you can trust to have it magnaflux-inspected for cracks. If the crankshaft passes the magnaflux crack test you should have it micropolished. I am not fond of regrinding Porsche crankshafts. However, if your crankshaft must be ground, make sure that whoever does the work removes the oil galley plugs before rehardening the crankshaft. If the plugs are not removed so that the crank can be properly cleaned after the atmospheric gas nitriding hardening process, the residue from the process will erode the plugs and loosen them. After the crank is ground hardened and cleaned, new plugs must be made to plug the galleys. If you have a crank that must be reground, it is important to find someone who knows precisely what they are doing.

If your crankshaft passed the magnaflux test and you had the journal surfaces micropolished, you must now thoroughly clean the crankshaft to remove any trapped dirt and grit. I don't recommend removing the plugs in the crankshaft to do this cleaning. I have seen more damage done by the improper replacement of these crankshaft oil passage plugs than I have seen caused by dirty crankshafts. However, I have also seen engines ruined within the first few hundred miles because they were put back together with dirt or polishing grit still in the crankshaft, so it is very important to get the crank clean. The best method of cleaning the oil passages is to use an aerosol carburetor cleaner with a long plastic nozzle. Thoroughly spray in each passage and then blow out with compressed air. Remember that the drillings in the crankshaft start from each end (number one and number eight main journal) and work their way toward the center, providing oil drilling for each connecting rod throw.

For racing applications, the 66-mm stroke 2.0/2.2-liter crankshafts are almost indestructible. When Porsche stroked the crankshaft for higher-displacement engines they had some problems with crankshaft breakage at high rpms, caused by the fact that there is more of an overhang due to the increased stroke.

Porsche made special versions of both the 70.4-mm and the 74.4-mm crankshafts for racing. These crankshafts had a large fillet which is round and makes a smooth, gentle transition from the rod journal to the crankshaft counterweight. Because of these special large fillets these crankshafts require special bearings with a relief provided for the fillet.

Porsche recommends using its special racing crankshafts for constant high-speed use above 7,000 rpm. We have found that if you shuffle-pin the magnesium crankcases (install interlocking dowel pins in the mating surfaces of the two crankcase halves so that they can't "shuffle" in relation to one another) and restrict your rpm to the 7,500–7,800 rpm range, the 2.4- to 3.0-liter 70.4 mm crankshafts are quite reliable.

Connecting Rods

When you have your 911 engine apart, the connecting rods should be measured and compared against the factory specifications. If they are out of spec either recondition them or replace them with new parts. Reconditioning consists of resizing the big-end bores, installing new wrist pin bushings, boring the wrist pin bushing to reestablish the end-to-end length, and honing the pin bushing

Woods and Weber racing exhaust with silencers.

to size. All of the dimensions are critical, so this operation must be performed by a competent automotive machine shop. Specifications are given in the workshop manual and spec books.

Most of the Porsche's connecting rods are the best that you can get for use in the 911 engine. There are exceptions: the 2.2 connecting rods did not seem to hold up well in racing and the 3.2, 3.3, and 3.6 connecting rods have connecting rod bolts that are marginal in strength. When the displacement of these engines was increased, Porsche reduced the size of the rod bolts by 1 mm in diameter to 9 mm. The rod bolts had always been 10 mm, providing the safety margin one expects from Porsche. If you are going to use these connecting rods in a racing application you should replace the rod bolts with special rod bolts such as those from Raceware or Automotive Racing Products (ARP).

On the 2.0- to 3.0-liter engines, the stock 911 connecting rods are suitable for racing applications for engine rpms up to about 7,800; beyond that you should plan to use a set of titanium connecting rods. I also recommend the use of Raceware bolts in this application.

Carrillo racing connecting rods have proven popular for the large racing engines. A side benefit to using Carrillo connecting rods is that you can have them made in any length you want for special applications. They can be made with either 22-mm or 23-mm wrist pin bushings. Do not use billet aluminum connecting rods; they will break. Alu-

A Motec engine-management box.

minum is not a suitable material for connecting rods.

Balancing

Because the 911 engine is a flat, opposed, six-cylinder engine with 120-deg crankshaft throws, balancing is not nearly as critical as it is for an inline engine or V-8. Still, balancing all of the reciprocating components of the engine will make an improvement, the change just will not be as obvious as it would with other engine types.

The first step is to balance all of the components for static weight. The pistons, wrist pins, and connecting rods are made to weigh the same by removing metal from the heavy components. The rods must be balanced end-to-end as well. Have this work performed by someone who has a reputation for quality work, because balancing is an exacting and precise procedure.

If any of the connecting rods require replacement, be sure to replace the dam-

Jerry Woods' solution to nozzle location for a Motec installation. He has proven this location will improve atomization and performance.

aged connecting rod with one from the correct weight group. Porsche recommends no deviation greater than 6 grams among the rod weights in an engine.

Because the 911 engine is inherently well balanced, you can get away with doing things with it as far as balancing the engine components that you could not with other types of engines. For instance, you can usually match the rods up fairly well into three pairs weight-wise and install the heaviest pair on cylinders number three and six—across from each other at the rear of the engine—then the next pair on cylinders two and five, and the final pair on cylinders one and four. If the whole rod set was originally balanced within factory specs, this subbalancing will give the engine a nearly perfect balance.

Shot Peening

Shot peening is a process wherein the surface of a part is bombarded with round, steel shot to produce a compressively stressed surface layer. The idea is that a crack will not propagate into a compressed layer of metal. A rough surface in compression will resist failures more than a smooth surface in tension. Over the years Porsche has used localized polishing, soft nitrating, and shot peening to prevent failure caused by crack propagation. Shot peening has proven to offer superior durability when properly applied.

Dowel Pinning the Crankcase Halves

In racing applications where more than 250 hp is anticipated, I recommend that you have the magnesium crankcase shuffle pinned to reduce case movement. This modification will extend the life of the crankcase and the crankshaft by reducing flexing and movement. The modification consists of installing 10 dowel pins, one on each side of the main bearing, to prevent the case from shuffling around the main bearing. If you limit your engine revs to 7,500–7,800 rpm with only occasional excursions above 8,000 rpm, this modification will allow you to run a stock

Left
A full-flow oil filter for racing applications. The C2 Turbo was the first production Porsche 911 to have a full-flow filter in the pressure circuit. This was possible because there is no oil cooler mounted on the C2 Turbo's engine. This will also work on racing engines where an engine-mounted cooler is not used.

crankshaft and give you a bulletproof engine. This process is not necessary for the aluminum crankcases, nor does it seem to work properly if applied.

Boat-tailing the Crankcase Main-Bearing Webs

Boat-tailing of the crankcase is done to improve airflow through the inside of the crankcase. The principle is based on the fact that every time a piston goes down there is another one on the other side that will be going up, and you want to make it as easy as possible for the air to pass through the crankcase to that piston going up. The idea is to make the back side of the main bearing webs smoother and more streamlined so that the air can flow past them. I prefer to do this process by hand and remove minimal material. I have seen crankcase webs modified to a point where I felt that too much material had been removed from the webs, and I have seen some of these break. The cylinders have to be modified as well with an eyebrow cut at each side to help the air pass out from under the piston that is going down.

Cylinder Heads

High-performance heads are the secret to horsepower in all engines. Most production car heads leave a great deal of room for improvement, and as a result there are some people in the head development business that have made quite a reputation for themselves. Porters and polishers are equipped to weld up and recontour ports, install seats and larger valves, reshape combustion chambers, grind valves and seats, and flow test the finished product.

The 911 engine has a much better port design than the average production car. Unless you are going to race your 911, it is difficult to justify having a set of heads ported. Modifying heads is a time-consuming, expensive process. If you are modifying an engine for street use be careful that your ports do not end up too large and cost you your broad, flexible power curve.

A few people have gained a reputation for their exceptional skill at achieving more power. One of those people is C. R. Axtell in Sun Valley, California, and another is Michael Stimson of Pacific Performance in Redwood City, California. Surely there are others, but it is important to check their credentials before you give them your heads and your money; you need to be sure you will get what you are paying for. If you want to have a set of heads ported and flow tested, I recommend that you contact the

A racing filter mounted on the Porsche Turbo full-filter mount. These oil filter mounts were used on the C2 3.3 and 3.6 Turbos, and the 993 Turbo and normally aspirated engines.

engine builder that is currently having the most success with the type, size, and class of engine that you are planning to build. Ask them if they do their own heads, and if they don't, find out who does their work.

I have a Superflow flow bench and I have ported and flow tested many heads over the years. I learned enough to know that there are people who are much more skilled than I. There are no "cookbook" answers to port development, just a lot of hard work. Consequently, there are many different approaches to port development. The only way to tell if the port development works is by first testing the heads on the flow bench, then on a dynamometer, and finally at the track. Practically speaking, unless the shop that does your

187

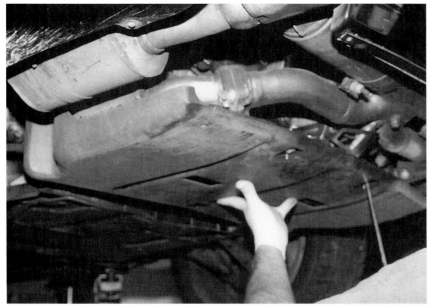

For the 993, I recommend removing the engine sound trays. Even though they are not as restrictive as those on the 964, I feel that they will be responsible for the 993 running too hot. We have seen indications that the 964s run too hot with these sound trays because all of the engines that we have seen apart have had excessively worn exhaust guides.

Here is an example of Jerry Woods Enterprises valve springs and retainers. If you use the 964 cams and there is any possibility that the engine will ever be overrevved, you should also consider replacing the valve springs and retainers. There are several good sources, including Randy Aase, ANDIAL, Bob Norwood, and Jerry Woods.

heads makes the ports too large for your application, they are not likely to do you any harm beyond wasting your money.

Camshafts

Be careful when selecting the camshaft grind you will run in your engine. For a street engine you will want to make sure that you don't run a camshaft that is too wild. You will find that in day-to-day driving a nice, broad power curve with a lot of area under the curve makes for a much more fun-to-drive car than one with a peaky power curve. It is equally important to select the proper camshaft for a racing engine because you will want the engine to produce all the power it can.

My experiences with carbureted, street, hot-rod engines and tuned-exhaust-type heat exchangers is that using either the 1966 911 cam (Solex cam) or the 911 E camshafts makes for nice street cars offering a nice broad range without sacrificing peak power. The 911 E cam has a little broader power curve than the 1966 911 cam, where the latter produces a little more peak power. These cams are great for all street cars from 2.0 to 2.7 liters.

For the larger displacement 3.0–3.5-liter carbureted street engines with tuned exhaust you will need a slightly more aggressive camshaft to provide performance with the same character that the smaller engines had with their 1966 911 and 911 E grinds. For the 3.0- and 3.2-liter engines I recommend either the 911 S camshaft or the Jerry Woods Enterprises GE-40 cam. For the 3.4- and 3.5-liter engines, I'd use the old 906 racing cam or a Jerry Woods GE-70 cam that has been used on an experimental basis in engines this size.

For the smaller displacement 2.0–2.5-liter racing engines I recommend either the 906 cam or the Jerry Woods Enterprises GE-80 cams. For the 2.7–3.0-liter racing engines I recommend the RSR Sprint cam or the Jerry Woods Enterprises GE-80. For the really big 3.2 liter to 3.8 liter 911 race engines I recommend the Jerry Woods Enterprises GE-100.

Production 911 engines through 1977 (2.0–2.7 liter) have small diameter 47-mm rod journals. Later 3.0–3.3 turbos have the larger 49-mm journals. Racing or specially modified engines may vary.

On the opposite page is a table providing a comparison of the duration, lift and center lobe spacing of a number of the camshafts available for the normally aspirated and turbocharged 911 engines.

Porsche Oil Circulation

There are mixed opinions on whether the oil cooling in an engine with a dry sump system should be done on the scavenge side or the pressure side of the oil system. Porsche actually cools on both sides of the system for the 911 production car engines. The engine-mounted oil coolers cool the oil in the pressure side of the system and the front-mounted, external oil coolers cool the oil in the scavenge side of the system. However, in both of these cooling schemes the oil is pumped through the oil cooler by one of the two oil pumps.

The Porsche dry sump system uses a tandem oil pump; one pump to scavenge the oil from the engine back to the oil tank and another pump to take the oil from the tank and provide the system with pressurized oil to lubricate the engine. All Porsche racing cars with 911-derived engines use the oil scavenging system for the engine oil cooling.

Porsche uses the scavenge system for the external oil cooler because the lines are so long that you would risk starving the engine for oil if you did this cooling in the pressure circuit. However, I have some friends who have experimented with using a small, external oil cooler in place of the engine-mounted oil cooler on their race car and said that it is amazing how much more effective the cooler is in the pressure circuit. The car originally had a large, front-mounted oil cooler in the scavenge circuit, and now there is a small helicopter cooler mounted at the rear of the car with the air ducted through the car. This much smaller cooler keeps the engine cooler than the original large, front-mounted cooler

Porsche engines are both air and oil cooled, and with their oil squirters for piston cooling and other oil cooling techniques, they are becoming more and more cooled by oil. Using engine oil for cooling has the advantage of using an internal fluid that is in intimate contact with the heat-producing surfaces in the engine so that the engine's heat is transferred directly into the oil. Using oil as a cooling media also has its negative side in that oil is a poor conductor of heat compared to conventional liquid coolants. Also, as the oil starts to cool in the oil heat exchanger, it becomes thicker and its flow is reduced. This reduction of flow at the surface has the effect of being an insulating barrier between the hotter flowing oil and the heat exchanger.

With any of the larger displacement, high-power output, normally aspirated engines or turbocharged engines, the cooling capacity of any of the production car oil coolers or their derivatives will be taxed beyond their limits when the cars are used for track events. For track applications you should consider using one of the larger radiator-type oil coolers to ensure adequate cooling. You can use the type used by Porsche for its racing cars or any other radiator-type coolers as long as they don't restrict the oil flow. The connecting hoses and fittings used for this application should be –12 or larger to prevent restricting the oil flow to and from the cooler back to the oil tank.

Oil Coolers

In 1969, Porsche first added an external oil cooler to the production 911S. The 911 S produced 170 hp, so I guess we can assume that once a 911 engine reaches 170 hp we should consider adding an external oil cooler. The engine's operating oil temperature should be around 200 deg F (93 deg C). The proper operating temperature range for the 911 engine is from 180 deg F (82 deg C) to 220 deg F (104 deg C). An oil temperature of 230 deg F (110 deg C) is warm, 240 deg F (115.5 deg C) is hot, and 250 deg F (121 deg C) is too damn hot. I wouldn't worry too much about seeing either hot or too damn hot on a trip, it would be on an everyday driving basis or with a dedicated track car that these temperatures would concern me.

The thermostat unit for both the engine-mounted oil cooler and the front-mounted external oil coolers have the same control unit. It is a paraffin vile and it melts at a little above 180 deg F. Over the years the different thermostats' opening temperatures have varied from 83 to 87 deg C (182 to 189 deg F).

If you have an engine and car that did not come with an external oil cooler, and if you ever modify your 911 so that it will produce more than 170 hp, then you should probably add one. If you lack an external oil cooler at horsepower levels above 170, the engine oil temperature will increase approximately 20 deg F (11.2 deg C) for every 10 deg F (5.6 deg C) increase in ambient temperature.

As the power output of the 911 engine in the older cars (1965–1989) increases, we must find ways to increase the oil cooling capacity. For track cars with larger displacement engines, you will need a front-mounted, radiator-type oil cooler with a hole in the front spoiler to allow air flow through the cooler. A cooler and lines kit made by Fred Garretson works well. B&B Fabrication also has a nice cooler, as does Ruf GmbH. The Ruf spoiler works particularly well. It is made of the same type of plastic material as the 928, 944, 968, and Carrera 4 and 993 bumpers and is a real quality part.

Some of the aftermarket oil cooler conversion kits are too restrictive. If you run a cooler that does not have large enough tubes, lines, or fittings it will restrict the oil flow. This is important be-

Camshaft	Intake			Exhaust		
	Duration (deg)	Lift (inches)		Duration (deg)	Lift (inches)	Lobe Center (deg)
Factory Camshafts						
Turbo 930/53	209 deg	.378		200 deg	.343	108 deg
911 T	216 deg	.387		207 deg	.345	105 deg
911SC	229 deg	.455		220 deg	.402	113 deg
911 E	229 deg	.408		223 deg	.393	102 deg
964	240 deg	.464		230 deg	.425	not available
Turbo Group B	237 deg	.374		220 deg	.339	not available
BTR	230 deg	.367		220 deg	.341	107/104 deg
CTR	245 deg	.449		255 deg	.449	107.5/105 deg
911 L	244 deg	.439		234 deg	.406	97 deg
66 911	244 deg	.439		234 deg	.406	97 deg
934	250 deg	.408		251deg	.406	102.5 deg
935	261 deg	.446		274 deg	.446	104 deg
911 S	267 deg	.459		235 deg	.396	97 deg
3.0 RSR	278 deg	.464		267 deg	.450	101 deg
906	281 deg	.462		251 deg	.403	95 deg
Aftermarket Camshafts						
GE 20	248 deg	.455		230 deg	.425	98 deg
GE 40	256 deg	.470		238 deg	.440	102 deg
GE 60	266 deg	.490		248 deg	.455	102 deg
GE 80	274 deg	.500		256 deg	.470	100 deg
GE 100	284 deg	.520		266 deg	.490	100 deg
Comparison of Some Street Cams and Aftermarket Cams						
911SC	229 deg	.455		220 deg	.402	113 deg
911 T	216 deg	.387		207 deg	.345	105 deg
911 E	229 deg	.408		223 deg	.393	102 deg
911 S	267 deg	.459		235 deg	.396	97 deg
GE 20	248 deg	.455		230 deg	.425	98 deg
GE 40	256 deg	.470		238 deg	.440	102 deg
Timing Specification for Some Common Racing Cams						
GE 20	4.0 to 4.3 mm					
GE 40	4.2 to 4.5 mm					
GE 60	4.8 to 5.2 mm					
GE 80	6.0 to 6.3 mm					
GE 100	6.5 to 6.8 mm					
Carrera 6 engine	6.8 ± 0.1mm					
RSR sprint cams	6.1 to 6.3 mm					
BTR*	1.90 mm					
CTR*	3.0 mm					
*CTR valve springs	34.5 mm					
*BTR valve springs	33.5 mm					

A chain tensioner update for engines that don't lend themselves to being updated. This is a 1968 911 with the smog pump drive on the left chain-housing cover. The only way to update the tensioners is to make your own boss for the fitting. This is done by welding up a section of the cover where the boss has to be and then machining the cover to accept the fitting.

cause the oil cooling in the 911 engine is done in the scavenge circuit. If your oil cooler restricts the flow from the scavenge portion of the oil pump it can cause excessive wear and possible failure of your engine's oil pump. I have seen two engine failures that were traced to either an overly restrictive oil cooler or the use of oil lines which were too small. The restriction on the oil pump caused the bearing surfaces in the pump to wear, allowing the pump gears to bind up and snap the interconnecting shaft between the layshaft and the oil pump.

Oils

Porsche started using synthetic oil in August 1992, shipping all cars with SAE 5W-40 synthetic oil. The owner's manual has an elaborate chart of all of the different oils that you can use for various operating conditions with both mineral-based and synthetic-based engine oils shown on the chart. For most climates in the United States use either an SAE 14W-40 or an SAE 20W-50 mineral-based oil or SAE 10W-40, SAE 15W-40, or SAE 15W-50 synthetic-based oil. I recommend Mobil 1. It is safe because it has been around for over 20 years now, and it is the oil the auto manufacturers usually suggest when they recommend a synthetic.

On January 4, 1996, Porsche announced that it was long-term partners with Mobil 1 both in research and development and in racing. All new Porsches will be lubricated with Mobil 1 oils and Porsche will exclusively recommend Mobil 1 to its dealer network.

I recommend Kendall, Quaker State, Valvoline, and Pennzoil petroleum oils or Mobil 1 Synthetic engine oils. I suggest that you use either the SAE 15W-40 or SAE 20W-50, or if you choose to use a synthetic, SAE 15W-50.

Porsche has revised its oil viscosity recommendations for ambient temperatures to include separate recommendations for synthetic-oil-based engine oils. On the opposite page are its recommendations by temperature.

Oil pressure should be checked with the engine warm (oil temperature 80 deg C/176 deg F) and running at 5,000 rpm. (For the Carrera 3.2 the oil pressure should be above 4.0 atmosphere (59 psi.), but should not exceed 7.0–9.0 bar (101–130 psi.) The earlier cars had a lower safety bypass pressure than the later cars. Some of the earlier cars recommended 4.0 bar pressure at 5,000 rpm, and the 993 is 6.5 bar, so somewhere between 4.0 and 6.5 bar would be the expected 911 oil pressure using this test. Our rule of thumb check for a 911 warmed to operating temperature is 10 lb to 1.0 bar of oil pressure for every 1,000 rpm engine speed.

The oil level gauge in your car indicates the amount of oil in the car's oil tank. This gauge should be regarded as just a general indication of the oil level. In some of the earlier cars the gauge was calibrated in liters/quarts, but in the mid-1970s Porsche changed them to a less precise scale. When using the dipstick to check the oil, make sure that the oil level is half-way between the two marks on the dip-

The engine management is the easy part; the manifolds and the wiring harness are the hard part. You can use slide-valve manifolds and all sorts of other manifolds as well. Here is a set of slide valves with Jerry Woods air cleaners.

stick. The dipstick reading should always be believed before the guage.

Check the oil gauge when the car is at idle and parked on level ground. The engine needs to run long enough to get it up to operating temperature (176 deg F/80 deg C). The reading should not drop into the red range when the engine is warm. It is normal for the gauge needle to drop as engine speed rises and oil circulates through the engine.

Porsche Recommended Oil Viscosity

Ambient Temperatures (Seasonal)	SAE Viscosity Range Mineral oil-based engine oils	SAE Viscosity Range synthetic oil-based engine oils
Mostly Greater Than 50 deg F/10 deg C	15W-40 20W-50 40W	10 W-40 15 W-40 15 W-50
Mostly Lower Than 50 deg F/10 deg C	15 W-40 10 W-40 10 W-30	
Mostly Lower Than 14 deg F/-10 deg C	10 W-30 5 W-30	10 W-40 10 W-30 5W-30

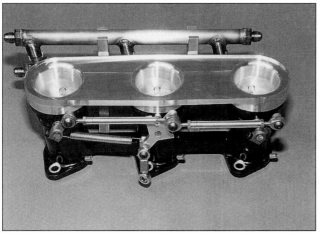

These are the Motorsport Designs throttle valve manifolds, suitable for normally aspirated and turbo installations.

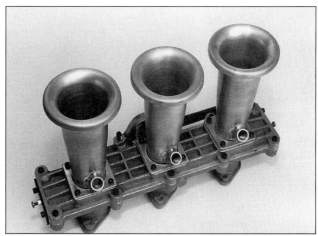

Here is a set of slide valves, which Jerry Woods imports from England.

This is the Jerry Woods Enterprises Madonna setup for installing injector nozzles in the air-cleaner housing.

Len Cummings, Autosport Engineering, Inc., makes his own adapters for the mechanical injector throttle bodies to fit them to the 964 and 993 engines.

TWM Induction has a couple of different manifold solutions. One bolts onto a set of Weber manifolds that has a location for the nozzle and throttle-position switches.

TWM Induction also has a stand-alone set of manifolds that bolt right onto the 964 and 993 cylinder heads. These manifolds have the fuel rails and the twin-injector fitting built right in.

Do you need a funny displacement engine? Don't worry, Jerry Woods Enterprises has been sleeving cylinders and making up its own pistons to fit all sorts of strange combinations.

So you built an engine and it turned out to be too wide and you had to deal with the chains being too short, eh Bunky? Well don't worry. German Precision has come up with a solution that has some tiny idler wheels. I'm sure that if you end up going the other way, German Precision probably has some larger chain wheels as well.

A set of Advantec four-valve heads for the 911 engine.

A Motorsport Design engine with the company's headers and intake manifolds.

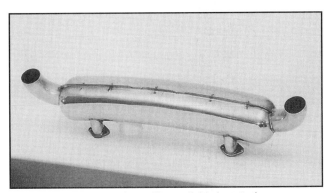

An original-style twin-outlet muffler available from Performance Products. There were a number of people modifying standard mufflers by adding the second tail pipe on the right side, and now Performance Products is having them made. Performance Products

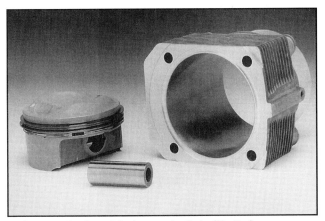

Performance Products 3.8 piston and cylinder kits. Performance Products

Chapter 6

Suspension, Brakes, Wheels, and Tires

Suspension design and settings are a compromise for any car, but this is particularly true when it comes to sports or grand touring cars such as the Porsche. Porsche has established a compromise that the company feels is the most reasonable for ride versus handling. If we want the car to handle really well, it won't ride that great—it is bound to be rough over bumps. If we really want the car to ride well we would use high-profile tires; narrow, smaller diameter rims; no sway bars; soft spring rates; and light-acting shock absorbers. This is just what Porsche did when it created the comfort group that was standard equipment for the 911E and optional for the other 911 models back in the late 1960s and early 1970s. All these things are just the opposite of what would be done if we wanted to make a 911 handle better. We have grown to expect that better-handling cars have short tires on larger diameter wheels and springs and shocks that are as stiff

as we can get by with, all at the expense of ride quality, of course. These latter steps are exactly what Porsche does when it modifies its production cars for racing. For most of us the compromise that Porsche has made with its production suspension is just fine.

Shock Absorbers

Most other car makes can have their suspension performance greatly improved just by installing a better-quality shock absorber. This is because most car manufacturers use the cheapest, softest shock absorbers available. Porsche has denied us this quick fix by using quality components throughout its car. Because of Porsche's commitment to quality, it is important that when you consider modifying your 911 that you take care not to install parts that are of a lesser quality than those you are taking off.

Actually "shock absorber" is a misnomer—they are, in fact, suspension dampers in that they damp out suspen-

sion oscillations. The tires and the springs absorb the shock and store it as energy. The shock absorbers work in concert with the suspension's springs (or in the case of the 911 through 1989, torsion bars) to damp the suspension movement. The more damping force they provide, the sooner they will damp out the oscillations. When you hit a bump, the suspension deflects, the spring compresses, and a large amount of energy is stored in the spring. After the bump the spring releases the energy by pushing down on the wheel, and up on the car's body. If this action is left undamped, the suspension will go into wild oscillations and the car body will oscillate up and down until it damps out in its own good time. The ride would be horrid because the car would be bouncing up and down all the time. Handling wouldn't be much better, because the wheel and tire would be doing the same thing—distressingly, the weight of the car would not be on the tires' contact patches much of the time.

Shock absorbers must be matched to the spring rate in order to function properly—much like a tuned circuit in electronics. Most racing cars use double-tube, hydraulic, adjustable shock absorbers because of the need to be properly tuned. Adjustable shocks can be

The body had to be modified to provide access to the torsion bars after the change to the new, longer G-50 transmission. The rear torsion-bar tube has a bent center section to provide additional clearance for the transmission. The additional clearance is required for the new clutch disc with larger rubber damper center section. Because the torsion-bar tube is bent in the center, the torsion bars can no longer butt up against each other in the center. Because of this change, it was necessary to modify the body so that the torsion bars could be removed. Note that they have also added lift points for repair shops to pick up the 911 with a hoist.

A front sway bar mounting torn from an improperly mounted aftermarket sway bar. A larger-than-stock sway bar had been mounted in this car using a pair of U-bolts.

A 935 cockpit-adjustable front sway bar. The bar was adjustable by twisting the blades on each end of it. In the photograph, the adjustable blade is in the horizontal or soft position. The blades were made of titanium and could be rotated through their 90 deg of rotation with a pair of Bowden cables, which were controlled by a lever behind and to the right side of the gearshift lever. When these blades were twisted vertically, they were very stiff, and when they were twisted horizontally, they were less stiff. The range of adjustment from soft to hard is 1:8. This adjustment range was provided to allow compensation for the change in weight as the fuel was used from the 120-liter fuel cell. The change in weight from full to empty was almost 200 pounds, which would have a significant effect on the car's handling.

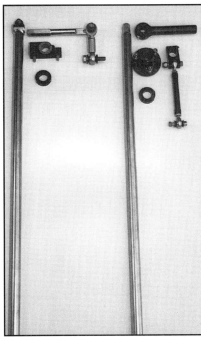

The Charlie Bar through-the-body-style adjustable front sway bar and adjustable rear sway bar kits. This type of sway bar is a must for competition because it offers better control. A wider selection of bars and related components are available for this sway bar. The Charlie Bar adjustable sway bar kits allow you to adjust the stiffness of the bar by sliding the pickup for drop link in and out the length of the arm. Adjusting the link so it is further out on the arm softens the effect of the sway bar, while moving the link in on the arm acts to stiffen the effect of the sway bar. The difference between the various sway-bar kits on the market is the quality of the mounting hardware.

tweaked until the circuit is properly tuned to match the spring rates, weights of both the car and the suspension, and the road's surface. Single-tube, high-pressure gas shock absorbers will work better over a wider range of conditions, and they do ride better over small jounce bumps than the double-tube, hydraulic shock absorbers. The disadvantage of some high-pressure gas shock absorbers is that they are not adjustable, hence they cannot be matched to different spring rates. Racing teams that use these nonadjustable, single-tube gas shocks are forced to carry a steamer trunk full of shock absorbers so that they will have the proper shock absorbers with the correct damping factor for each different set of spring rates that they might use.

A good rule of thumb is that the same type and brand of shock absorber should be used front and rear because their characteristics will be matched. There can be and are exceptions to this rule where one manufacturer makes both types of shocks and has gone to the trouble of matching the characteristics of hydraulic and gas pressure shocks so that they can be used as a set. There are other exceptions where the car manufacturer has matched shock absorbers from two different manufacturers (as an example, Porsche did this with its 944 where it used Volkswagen-made shocks on the front and Fichtel and Sachs shocks on the rear).

In the past, 911 owners have been forced to choose between ride and handling by choosing between the double-tube hydraulic shocks and the single-tube gas pressure shocks, but now Boge has new, low-pressure gas, double-tube shock absorbers for the 911. Porsche started to offer the Boge double-tube gas pressure shock absorbers as a sport option in 1985. They worked so well that for 1986 and 1987 Porsche made the Boge double-tube gas pressure shock absorbers standard equipment for the 911 Carrera and 911 Carrera Turbo-look. Koni also offers a new line of adjustable, low-pressure, double-tube front shock absorbers matched to work with its new, adjustable, high-pressure, single-tube rear gas shock absorbers for the 911 Porsches. These low-pressure gas shocks should prove to be the best of both worlds, particularly the Koni shocks because of their adjustability. Bilstein high-pressure, single-tube shock absorbers were still standard equipment for the 911 Turbo and were offered as an option for the other 911s for 1987.

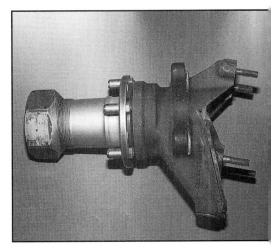

A 935 cast-magnesium front hub carrier with a ball joint mount at the bottom. These hub carriers clamp around the shock absorber.

Camber adjustment on the front of a U.S.-made 935.

Weld-in adjustment camber/caster plates from the Racers Group.

The 935 adjustable rear sway bar. Notice that the suspension pivots from a heim joint where the torsion bar mounts on the production 911.

The Koni adjustable shocks usually have the edge for high-performance applications because of their extra control and their tunability, but now that you can get adjustable Bilsteins as well, this should level out the playing field. The current 911 GT 2 cars have remote-reservoir, adjustable, Bilstein shock absorbers.

The 911s were available, over the years, with a number of different shock absorber options, and some of the earlier 911s were equipped with Koni shocks. If your 911 has Koni shocks, it is a simple matter to install new inserts. If your 911 was originally equipped with Boge or Woodhead struts, Koni also makes inserts that will fit these (Boge and Woodhead both accept the same insert). The Woodhead shocks are a shock absorber made to the Boge license in England, so inserts for the Boge struts will work fine. For a number of years Koni made inserts for Bilstein front struts, but they have recently discontinued manufacturing this insert. These inserts, part number 282R1863, only worked in the older Bilstein front struts. If your 911 was newer than 1980 and had Bilstein shocks, these Koni inserts wouldn't work because Bilstein changed the construction of their struts in 1980. It looks like if you want to try Koni shocks and your 911 has Bilstein shock absorbers you will have to replace the complete front strut. There are Koni inserts available for the 1985–1987 911s with Boge gas struts; however, they require an adapter to make them work.

Springs

There are some things you need to know about springs and torsion bars. Assume you have a coil spring that is 20 inches long and it is a 100-lb-per-inch spring. If you cut this spring in half you will not only have two 10-inch-tall springs, but they will now be 200-lb-per-inch springs. Now we know you're not likely to cut springs in half, but why this

Adjustable Unibal front shock mounts from the Racers Group. Note the extra holes, which allow extra camber adjustment without having to modify the body.

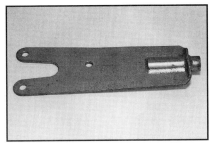

A 935 rear spring plate.

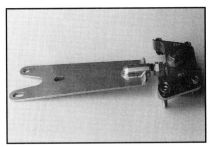

An aftermarket rear spring plate made by ERP (Eisenlohr Racing).

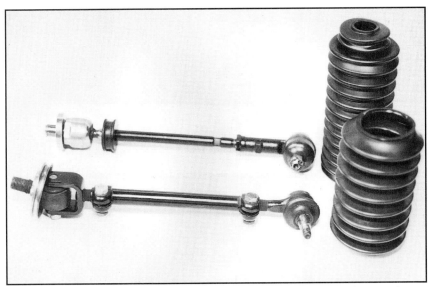

Production 911 and 911 Turbo steering tie rods. The tie rod in the foreground is a regular 911 tie rod and steering boot, and behind it is the 911 Turbo tie rod and steering boot. Note that the 911 tie rod uses a rubber isolation joint at the end that mounts to the steering rack. The 911 Turbo tie rod has a uniball joint in place of the rubber joint of the production 911 tie rod. The Turbo tie rod is a popular conversion for the performance-minded 911 owner.

might be important to you is that you might cut some coils off of a spring to lower the car. If you do this, what you should realize is that the resulting spring will also be stiffer. For instance, if you have a 10-coil spring and cut one coil off to lower the car, the resulting spring will be about 10 percent stiffer than the original. Another thing you need to know about springs is that whether they are torsion bars, coil springs, or leaf springs they are all springs. Porsche uses coil springs or torsion bars on their various models depending on which fits best in a given application.

The MacPherson strut suspension used in front of all torsion-bar 911s was selected because it allowed room for a much larger trunk than would have been possible with any other arrangement. In most racing applications Porsche will use either a combination of torsion bars and coil-over springs or just the coil-overs to get the control that it needs. With either coil springs or torsion bars, increasing the wire or torsion bar diameter will increase the stiffness by the fourth power. What this means is that if you double the diameter of the torsion bar you would multiply the stiffness by a factor of 16—a small change in wire or bar diameter has a significant effect in the spring rate.

For high-performance applications for later 911s (1978–1989), use 22-mm front torsion bars and 28-mm rear torsion bars. In the earlier, lighter 911s (1969 through 1977) use 21-mm front and 26- or 27-mm rear torsion bars. Larger torsion bars will make the 911 much more predictable and fun to drive but without as much degradation of ride quality as would be experienced with stiffer sway bars. Stiffer sway bars tend to make for a choppy ride over

potholes and the like; whereas stiffer torsion bars just firm up the overall ride, but not to an objectionable degree.

The source for good-quality torsion bars is Glen Sander Engineering. The available torsion bars are in both solid and tubular configurations. Their bars are higher quality than other bars on the market and have splines that fit well with the existing Porsche parts.

If your are really serious about good handling, the next step is 22 mm sway bars front and rear for the 911. The adjustable bars are particularly handy because they let you balance the car's handling to suit your needs or desires. I recommend "Charlie Bars." These are more expensive than the more common aftermarket sway bars, but they are of Porsche quality. "Charlie Bars" are made by Charlie Spira of Wrightwood Racing, and they are much better quality than others that are on the market. Charlie

Bars are sold by a number of Wrightwood Racing's dealers.

Another good source for both sway bars and torsion bars is AJ-U.S., Inc. (Alan Johnson Racing, Inc.). AJ-U.S., Inc. has its own line of quality sway bars and torsion bars. Automotion also has an extensive line of suspension products under the trade name Weltmeister.

The torsion bar sizes in the 911 model have changed several times over the lifetime of the 911, but for years the fronts were 18.8 mm and the rears have been 24.1 mm. In 1986, the rear torsion bars were increased in diameter to 25 mm to compensate for the car's gradually increasing weight. Because the rear of the 930/911 Turbo is so much heavier than the normally aspirated 911, they have had a stiffer 26 mm bar all along.

With the introduction of the C4 (Carrera 4) in 1989 Porsche went from torsion bars to all-coil suspension. The

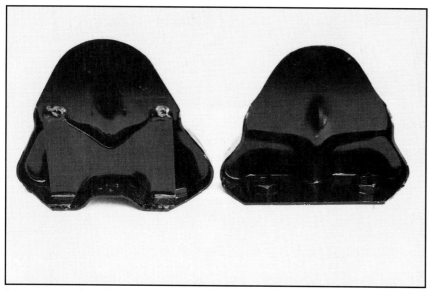

It is common to have the rear sway-bar mounts break. As far back as I can remember it has been so, and I am not sure why it took so long for someone to do something about them. Because many people use larger-than-stock sway bars (which just makes the problem worse), a lot of people welded small braces to the existing sway-bar mounts. I noticed that Automotion advertised an improved 911 sway-bar mount in their catalog, so I checked with them to see how improved its mount was. The new piece is actually an improved part from Porsche that is a bit larger than the original and has a butterfly-shaped brace welded on one side (see the photograph of the new and old sway bar mounts). This new part looks like a big improvement and can be used to repair all 911s, as long as you replace both mounts. Your best bet is to grind all of the original mounts off and weld the new ones on. This is best done by a professional.

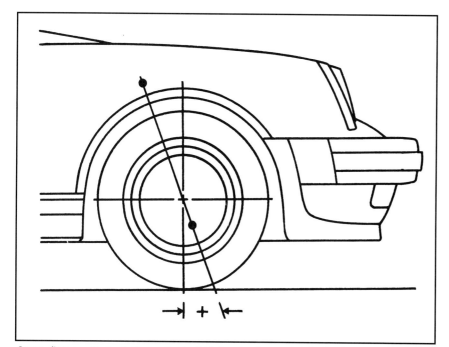

Caster diagram. Caster is the angle at which the steering angle is inclined. Positive caster helps with straight-ahead stability. Think of it as being like the front fork on a bicycle. Caster determines how much the tires lean when you steer into a turn. The 911s have positive caster, meaning that the tires lean into the turn when steered. The positive caster creates the self-centering effect that returns the steering to the straight-ahead position. Uniroyal Goodrich Tire Company

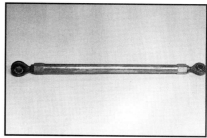

A 935 tie rod. Porsche used these tie rods because of their lightweight, very positive joints and because they could adjust the bump steer. The steering arm was set up on the strut so that they could use spacers between the steering arm and the tie rod to adjust the bump steer.

suspension of the 964 C4 was all new, with MacPherson-strut independent suspension in front with aluminum lower control arms. The rear suspension was also revised with aluminum, rear semi-trailing arms. There is a coil-spring shock assembly at each of the four corners now instead of the familiar torsion bars.

The C2 (Carrera 2) replaced the original 911 in 1990 as the two-wheel drive 911 model. The C2 had suspension identical to the C4. In 1994, when the 993 was introduced, the front suspension was revised with different front geometry for improved stability. The rear suspension was the all-new multi-link rear suspension, with five links per side controlling the rear suspension geometry. Porsche called this the LSA system (Light Strut Axle or the Light Stable Agile) system. The fifth link in this system controls toe in and makes the car more stable when cornering. This whole assembly is mounted on a sub-frame that mounts to the body with rubber mounts. The toe correction is supposed to act similar to the way the Weissach axle did on the 928s.

Sway Bars

The function of the sway bar is to reduce a car's body roll while cornering. Sway bar is probably another misnomer because it doesn't really describe what the device does at all. Actually these bars should be called antiroll bars because that is what they do—resist body roll and control the weight transfer distribution. Sway bars are used in conjunction with the springs or torsion bars to keep the stiffness relationship between the front and the rear of the car reasonably constant and adjusted for neutral handling. Too much stiffness in the front will cause understeer, plow, or push, and too much stiffness in the rear will cause oversteer or rear-end looseness. The difference between the two extremes—assuming you are going to lose control of your car, leave the road, and hit a tree—is that if the car understeers you will hit the tree head on, and if the car oversteers you will spin and hit the tree tail first. Generally speaking people feel that a car that has a little understeer or "push" is easier to drive fast in very fast corners because it is less likely to spin out, but a car that has a little oversteer or is "loose" might be faster around slower corners because it will "turn in" better. Translated, this means that you wouldn't want a car that oversteered at Indy and you wouldn't want a car that understeered at a low-speed autocross, but anything in between is probably up for grabs.

Bump Steer

Bump steer is the change in toe setting at the wheels as the car is moved up and down on its suspension. Bump steer can happen in either the front or rear suspension. Ideally, there would be no change of the toe at all as the suspension is raised and lowered, because the resulting bump steer is the cause of many of the elusive wiggles and twitches that make the difference between an average and an excellent handling car.

The way the Porsche is designed, there isn't much that can be done about the rear bump steer except to establish a rear toe setting that minimizes the effect for the tires in use and the rest of the suspension settings. There are steering rack spacer kits available for lowered 911s and 914s that allow the steering rack to be spaced back up so that the tie rods are nearly horizontal again, greatly reducing problems with bump steer in the front end. Actually you will still want to measure the effect of bump changes on the toe then adjust it so that it has little or no effect on the toe in or around the static ride height. On most cars it will be necessary to heat and bend the steering arms in order to adjust the bump steer properly once the ride height has been altered. This is an extensive procedure when done properly, but it is a must to get the most out of your modified Porsche.

Weight Checking

The purpose of weight checking is to ensure that the weight is distributed evenly on the four tires. Assuming the 911 has a weight distribution of 40/60 front to rear, then 40 percent of the left-side weight should be on the left front

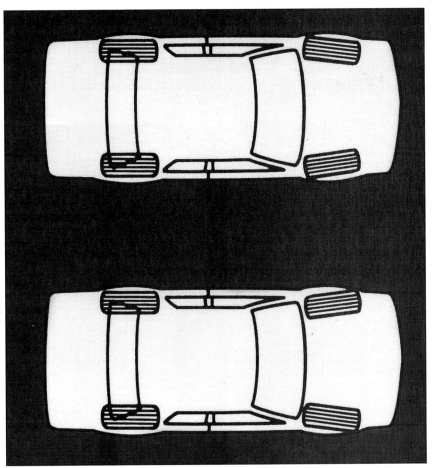

Toe diagram. The top diagram shows a car with toe in, and the bottom diagram shows a car with toe out. Uniroyal Goodrich Tire Company

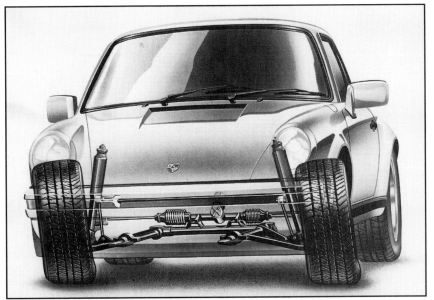

A drawing of a 911 showing the effect of body roll on the wheels' camber. If the 911 has stiffer torsion bars, is lowered, and has a stiffer sway bar, the body roll and hence the camber changes caused by cornering will be reduced, and the car will handle better. Uniroyal Goodrich Tire Company

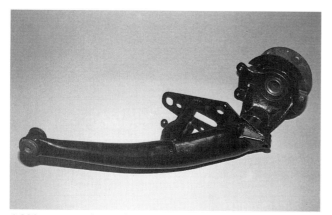

A 911 rear control arm. Shown is the standard fabricated rear control arms used from 1969, when the wheelbase was lengthened, until the arm was replaced with a cast-aluminum arm in 1974.

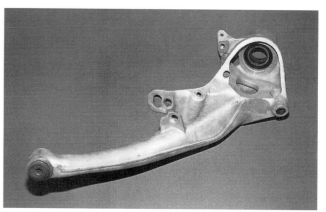

The 1974 cast-aluminum rear control arm for production 911s. The cast control arm replaced its fabricated predecessor while retaining the original suspension geometry, and it was stronger, lighter, and cheaper than the fabricated steel arms.

wheel, and so on. Weight checking is particularly important if your Porsche has been wrecked. If the car does not carry its weight evenly, it is said to have weight "jacked into" the chassis.

People who race cars on circle tracks have made a science out of weight jacking in order to find the fastest way around a race track. For most Porsche owners, weight jacking is not a goal, but something to be avoided. If a car has been wrecked then improperly repaired, it can end up with the weight jacked di-agonally across the car. This can cause strange handling characteristics and tire wear even if the repaired car appears to sit evenly on its four wheels and has been aligned properly. Ideally the weight differences should be less than 20–30 lb, but if the weights differ by more than 50 lb per wheel, the suspension must be readjusted or you will feel the effect on the handling and driveability. Porsche says that the weight difference from left to right may not exceed 20 kg (44.1 lb) for the 911 or 10 kg (22.5 lb) for the 911 Turbo. It also states that the difference in height from the left to the right may not exceed 8 mm (0.3 inches) on the rear axle or 5 mm (0.2 mm) on the front axle. If the car is "bent," however, you may want to exceed these height differences to get the weights correct.

Changing the ride height on one side will cause a simultaneous change in the wheel loading. When the wheel loading is changed for one wheel it will also change the loading of the other wheels. Increasing the initial setting, or spring tension, on one side will raise the car, increasing the load on that wheel. Decreasing the initial setting or spring tension on one side will lower the car, decreasing the load on that wheel. A change in load on one wheel will always affect the wheel diagonally across the car from that wheel. If the wheel load is increased or decreased on one wheel, the same will happen on the wheel diagonal from it.

Alignment

First let's define all those alignment terms—camber, caster, toe-in. Camber is the angle of the wheel and tire from vertical. Zero camber means that the tire's tread surface is flat on the ground. If the tire tilts outward at the top it is called positive camber. If the tires tilt inward at the top it is called negative camber. Toe-in is the difference in measurement between the fronts and the rears of a pair of tires on the same axle. This can be either the front or the rear axle. Zero toe is when the tires are parallel. Toe-in is when the front of the tires are closer together than the rear of the tires. Toe-out is when the fronts of the

The rear suspension pickup points for the Carrera RSR were revised to improve the handling. The change itself consisted of using a shorter rear control arm and then moving the pickup points away from the center by 22 to 25 mm (0.87–0.98 inch) and rearward 47.5 mm (1.9 inches) to compensate for the shorter arms. This change actually increased the camber changes due to suspension travel and more nearly matched the camber change to body roll. This works in racing cars because of the stiff spring rates, but tends to make street cars feel unstable.

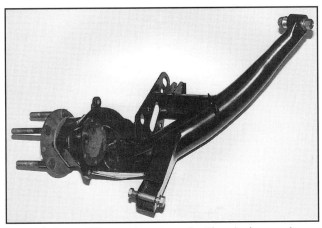

A special, shorter RSR control arm to work with revised suspension pickup points.

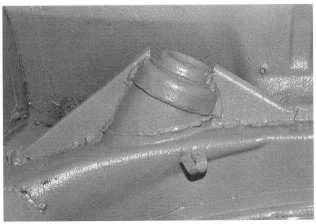

The rear shock mount area of the RSR. Note the reinforcement to the shock mount and to the corner of the engine compartment.

tires are farther apart than the rears. Caster is the angle at which the steering angle is inclined, and it helps with straight-line stability. Think of caster as being like the front fork on a bike. Caster determines how much the tires lean when you steer into a turn. The 911 has positive caster, meaning the tire leans into the turn when steered. Positive caster creates the self-centering effect that returns the steering to the straight-ahead position. Alignment specifications are given in degrees (deg) and minutes (min). There are 360 degrees in a circle and 60 minutes to a degree.

There is an excellent procedure for aligning the 911 in the factory workshop manual that details all aspects of setting up the 911 suspension, including setting ride height and weight checking the chassis using digital scales.

Suspension alignment is always a compromise. In the case of the 911, it is aimed at providing a decent ride, good handling, and reasonable tire wear.

Ride Height

In 1975, and for the rest of the late 1970s and early 1980s, the 911s were raised up on their suspensions for the U.S. market to comply with the U.S. 5-mph bumper laws. This change threw a kink into the compromise, and these raised cars just didn't handle as well. When set at these higher ride heights, the 911 had some rather unusual alignment specifications. The cars were set 9–15 mm higher (0.35-0.6 inches) in front and 21–25 mm (0.82–0.98 inches) in the rear. These raised cars had positive camber in the front and zero in the rear.

What most people consider to be "Euro Spec" is actually lower than the

true European specifications. The correct ride height will result in a measurement of about 25 inches when measured from the ground to the rear fender lip. The 911 should have a slight nose-down attitude (approximately 1 deg slope), which will result in a measurement about 1/2 inch higher at the front fender lip (about 25 1/2 inches) than at the rear. There is a more sophisticated procedure for measuring the car's ride height outlined in the workshop manual, which relates the center line of the torsion bars front and the rear to the center line of their respective axle.

Measuring up from ground to center line of axle and from ground to center line of torsion bar, front and rear, the difference should be
- Front = 108 mm ±5 mm (center line of wheel above torsion bar center line) (maximum difference between left and right 5 mm).
- Rear = 12 mm ±5 mm (center line of torsion bar above center line of wheel) (maximum difference between left and right 8 mm). We have found that for lowered cars the center line of the torsion bar can go as far as 1 1/2 inches below the center line of the axle and that 1 1/4 inches works very well. Anything below 1 1/2 inches is probably too much and the suspension geometry will not be correct.

A final note on lowering 911s. If your 911 was one of those raised to comply with the 5-mph U.S. bumper laws, Porsche installed a large washer on top of the shock absorber to space the shock absorber back down to its operating range. This washer is big—60-mm outside diameter, 18-mm inside diameter, and 10-mm thick—it makes a great

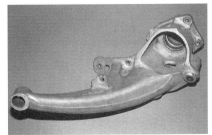

The Turbo control arm. When the 911 Turbo (930) was introduced in 1975, similar suspension changes were incorporated in the rear with the new cast-aluminum trailing arms. The Turbo trailing arms were shorter, and the pickup points were moved to relocate the suspension's fulcrum points, similar to what had been done to the RSR. In addition to being moved away from the center by 22 to 25 mm (0.87–0.98 inch) and rearward 47.5 mm (1.9 inches) to compensate for the shorter arm, they were also moved up 10 mm (0.4 inch) to give the rear suspension anti-squat characteristics. To facilitate this change for the 930, Porsche used a new rear torsion-bar tube (rear-axle transverse tube) with different suspension pickup points made as part of the tube.

paperweight once removed. When you lower your 911 you must take this spacer out, otherwise you will have the front shock absorber out of its range at the other extreme, where it is vulnerable to bottoming out.

Alignment Specs for Torsion Bar 911S Front Suspension
- Camber: 0 deg negative ±10 min (maximum difference between left and right 10 min)
- Caster: 6 deg 5 min ±15 minutes left and right (maximum caster difference

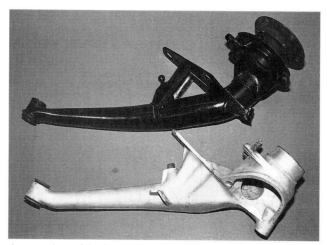

A comparison of the fabricated control arm and the cast-aluminum replacement arm.

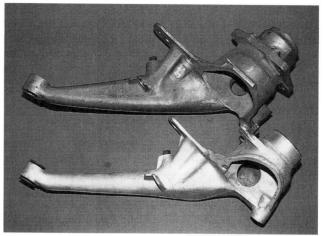

A comparison of the cast-aluminum Turbo arm (top) and the cast-aluminum arm used on the 911. Note that on the Turbo arm the brake-caliper mounting was moved to the rear, while the caliper mounted in front on the 911. You can also see that the wheel-bearing mounting has been moved further out for the wider track of the Turbo.

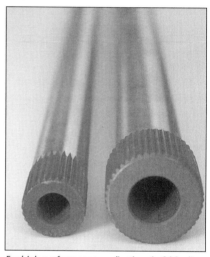

For high-performance applications in 911s, it has become common to use 22-mm front torsion bars and 28-mm rear torsion bars in the heavier, late-model 911s (1978–1989), and 21-mm front and 26- or 27-mm rear torsion bars in the earlier, lighter 911s (1969–1977). These larger torsion bars will make the 911s much more predictable and fun to drive, but at the expense of ride characteristics. I recommend Glen Sander Engineering for quality torsion bars that are available in both solid and tubular configurations. These bars are higher quality than other bars on the market and have splines that fit well with the existing Porsche parts. Some people run much stiffer spring rates on the rear of their cars than what I recommend for track events, and they swear by it, but I have no personal experience with this setup. They are running with the 22-mm front and 31-mm rear torsion bars. These same people also are using a much stiffer rear sway bar.

between left and right 30 min)
- Toe-in: +15 min ±5 min (not pressed)
- Toe-in: 0 deg (wheels pressed with press bar at front of tires)

Rear Suspension
- Camber: 1 deg negative ±10 min (maximum difference between left and right 20 min)
- Toe-in: +10 min ±10 min (maximum difference between left and right 20 minutes)

For a compromise street and competition setting increase the negative camber setting front and rear by 1 to 1 1/2 deg. Increased camber will improve the cornering potential, but at the expense of greater tire wear. You will want more front camber if you are autocrossing the car to get more bite in the front. The desired camber will change depending on the tire construction.

The 911 Turbo (930) uses the same alignment specifications as the 911, with the exception of the rear camber setting. The rear camber for the 911 Turbo is -30 minutes ± 10 minutes. The reduced camber setting is used because of the revised rear suspension geometry. If you use wider rear wheels on the 911 Turbo than the 8- or 9-inch rims that the cars come with, the rear alignment becomes even more critical. With 10- or 11-inch rear wheels, I recommend that you reduce the rear camber to 0 for increased stability.

A 1 deg change in spring strut inclination = approximately 7 to 9 mm change in car height.

Adjusting Rear Torsion Bars
Old Version 44/40 teeth
- Adjusting the torsion bar one inside tooth up and the swingarm one tooth down produces a swingarm change of approximately 50 min and a vehicle height change of approximately 6.5 mm.
- If the torsion bar is turned one tooth on the inside, the adjustment is equal to 9 deg.
- If the spring strut is turned one tooth the adjustment is equal to 8 deg 10 min.

New Version 47/46 teeth (1987–89 and 1989 Turbo)
- Adjusting the torsion bar one inside tooth up and the swingarm one tooth down produces a swingarm change of approximately 10 min and a vehicle height change of approximately 1.4 mm.
- If the torsion bar is turned one tooth on the inside, the adjustment is equal to 7 deg 50 min.
- If the spring strut is turned one tooth, the adjustment is equal to 7 deg 14 min.

If you use stiffer-than-stock torsion bars, you will be able to lower the 911 about 1 inch without suspension travel problems, but you may have to modify the alignment slots to facilitate a proper alignment and you will have to be very careful going in and out of driveways. A lower ride height will reduce roll and lower the center of gravity, which will improve the 911's cornering power and make it smoother in the corners.

Special Cases

If you are planning to run your 911 in speed events you may wish to alter the alignment specifications by adding more negative camber. How much negative camber will depend upon a number of things. If your 911 is a daily driver as well, don't get too carried away with negative camber. Too much negative camber will make the 911 a little darty and cause premature tire wear.

On the other hand, if your primary use for your 911 is autocrosses, driver education, or time trial events at race tracks you will want to run more negative camber, how much will depend upon your car's ride height, how stiff your torsion and sway bars are, and what type of tires you are using.

On a track-type car, additional negative camber is used to help compensate for the car's body roll. Ideally your tires would have zero camber and the car wouldn't lean so the camber would stay at 0. A well set-up suspension will minimize the camber change so you will not need as much negative camber to keep the tire flat on the ground. You will want keep the outside (loaded) tire flat on the ground in a corner, and too much negative camber can be almost as bad as too little camber, so you will have to be careful not to overdo a good thing.

Suspension Revisions

Porsche revised the rear suspension pickup points in 1973 on the second series of 2.7 RS Carreras and on the 3.0 RS Carrera. The change was made in an effort to better match the camber changes to the body roll so that when the suspension was properly set up, the outside, or loaded, wheel in a corner would stay more nearly vertical, or more near to the proper suspension setting. This change was only used for the RS Carreras and the RSRs and not carried over into the rest of the production 911s. The change was made on the RS Carrera so that it could be homologated and available for use by the RSR race cars. This rear suspension change was not necessary for production 911s, and it did have some negative effects on straight-line stability. The change itself consisted of using a shorter rear trailing arm and then moving the pickup points away from the center by 22 to 25mm (0.87–0.98 inches) and back 47.5 mm (1.9 inches). This change actually increased the camber changes due to suspension travel.

There was also an optional raised

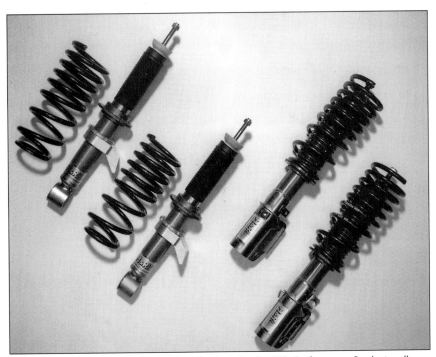

Here is the H&R performance spring and shock set for the 993. Performance Products sells three grades of springs made by H&R—street, competition, and a go-crazy race setup. The street setup, which is just springs that will lower the 993 by 1 to 1.5 inches, costs less than $400 for the four springs. These are progressive springs that will improve the handling without seriously degrading the ride. The Super Street Performance setup, which has H&R threaded-body shocks and variable-rate springs, gives improved handling without the harsh ride of a race car and costs about $3,300. The height is adjustable from 1 to 2 inches lower than stock. The go-crazy race setup for the 993 replaces the shocks with stiffer ones with mono-ball aluminum upper strut bearings and stacked double springs. This is the ultimate H&R setup for club racing and costs less than $5,500. The height is adjustable from about 1 to 2.75 inches lower than stock. All of the European teams are using similar dual springs on adjustable shocks; most of these teams use Eibach springs on Bilstein shocks and struts, which are also available from Performance Products with a variety of spring rates. They also have similar kits available for the 964. Performance Products

A European Tuners double-spring kit with Bilstein shocks installed on an RS America. Warren Gardner

spindle offered for the RS Carrera series so that it would be available for the RSR race cars. The spindle was raised on the front struts by 18 mm (0.71 inches), which was 126 mm (4.96 inches) above the standard ball-joint center instead of the standard 108 mm (4.25 inches). This change was made so that the front of the car could be lowered by the 18 mm (0.71 inches) without excessively lowering the roll center. The modification also leaves the remainder of the suspension geometry unaltered and gives full suspension travel before bottoming out on the bump stop with 15-inch wheels. If the spindle had been moved more than 18 mm, the ball joint would have interfered with the rim. Of course, with larger diameter wheels (the RSR used 15-inch wheels) you would be able to make a larger change in the spindle position before running into the ball joint and wheel interference problem.

When the 911 Turbo (930) was introduced in 1975, similar suspension changes were incorporated in the rear with the new cast-aluminum trailing arms.

The Turbo trailing arms were shorter and the pickup points were moved to relocate the suspensions fulcrum points

Porsche steel wheels. When the 901 was introduced in 1963, it used steel wheels that were 15 inches in diameter and 4.5 inches wide. In 1968, their width was increased to 5.5 inches for the 911T and 6 inches for the 911E in 1969. Nineteen seventy-four was the last year that steel wheels were standard equipment on the 911. Having the steel wheels as standard equipment created a misleading base price for the cars since no one bought the 911 with steel wheels.

The forged Fuchs aluminum-alloy wheels were introduced on the 911S in 1967. When it was introduced, it was a 15-inch wheel that was 4.5 inches wide. In 1968, the width was increased to 5.5 inches. In 1969, the Fuchs alloy wheels were increased to 6 inches wide. The 1973 Carrera RS introduced the use of different-sized wheels front and rear, with sevens in the rear and sixes in the front. Porsche used forged wheels as racing wheels for a while and mounted nines on the front and elevens on the rear of the IROC RSRs.

Fuchs alloy wheels were 14 inches in diameter and 5.5 inches wide for the Comfort Group from 1969 to 1971. For 1969, the 14-inch wheels were a mandatory part of the Comfort Group when it was sold with the Sportomatic transmission. For 1970 and 1971, they were sold as an option. The 14-inch wheels were offered again in 1977 as part of another comfort group.

The 1969 Mahle cast-magnesium wheel was the lightest wheel that was ever used on the 911, at 4.5 kg (9.9 lb). Unfortunately, the Mahle magnesium wheel was only made in the 5.5-inch width, so there weren't many applications for it. The forged alloy wheels were already 6 inches wide for the 911E and 911S, so the only application for the 5.5-inch cast-magnesium wheels were on the 911T and the 914/6.

similar to what had been done with the RSR. In addition to being moved away from the center by 22 to 25mm (0.87–0.98 inches) and rearward 47.5 mm (1.9 inches) to compensate for the shorter arm, they were also moved up 10 mm (0.4 inch) to give the rear suspension some anti-squat. To facilitate this change for the 930, Porsche used a new rear torsion bar tube (rear axle transverse tube) with different suspension pickup points made as part of the tube.

The Turbo-look cars also used this geometry change, and when the G 50 transmission was introduced in 1987 there had to be a special Turbo-look torsion bar tube that would both retain these revised suspension pickup points and provide room for the larger transmission. The rear torsion bar tube has a bent center section to provide additional clearance for the transmission. The additional clearance is required for the new clutch disc. This new center section for both the normal Carrera and the Turbo-look Carrera was cast iron to make it easier to produce and to provide more accurate location of the suspension pick-up points and transmission mounts.

In 1974, the regular 911s had the trailing arms changed to cast aluminum. However, unlike the Turbo arms, the 911 arms were made as direct replacements for the fabricated steel arms and the original suspension geometry was retained.

The front suspension geometry on the 930 was also modified to provide some antidive. Modifications were made to the floor pan at the rear of the front suspension to allow raising the front cross-member by 13 mm (0.5 inches). This change raises the whole rear portion of the suspension by about 0.5 inch. The front mounting was also spaced down with 6-mm-thick steel spacers, which had the effect of lowering the front mounting point by 6 mm. The net effect of raising the rear of the suspension by about 0.5 inch and lowering the front by over 0.2 inches is a change of about 0.75 inch. This change provided antidive geometry in the front.

Both the front and rear suspension changes were made on the 911 Turbo (930) to provide a better basis for the racing 934, which could not have its suspension pick-up points changed from the homologated 930.

C2/C4 Lower and Align

There are a lot of options for lowering these cars and many different spring kits available. I like them lowered to about the same height as the Euro Carrera RS and aligned the same. The ride

Fuchs alloy wheels and a space-saver folding spare tire. The mixture of sizes for the front and rear wheels, along with the wheels and the gas tank getting larger, necessitated a new solution for a spare tire and wheel, so the folding space-saver spare was a graceful solution to several problems. Porsche AG

height of the Carrera RS is 23 mm lower than the R.o.W. Carrera 2/4, and the U.S. cars are about 10 mm higher than the R.o.W. cars; hence, the ride height of the RS is about 1.3 inches lower than the U.S. cars. If you use the H&R springs they will lower the car 1.5 inches, a little lower than the RS.

Lowering can be done a number of different ways:
• Factory (Euro) lowering springs (sport, regular, turbo, and so on)
• European RS springs and shocks
• Third-party lowering springs
• Double-spring suspension (new shocks plus spring pairs and retainers)

For most people, the easiest way to lower the 964 is to install the correct lowering springs for the given car and keep everything else, including the shocks, the same. A set of these lowering springs cost $200–$400, and the labor will run even more. Labor includes changing all of the springs and realigning the car.

The ATS cast aluminum "cookie cutter" wheel was introduced in 1973 as a 6-inch wheel. The "cookie cutter" wheel was standard equipment for the 911E in 1973 and an option for the other models. In 1975, the ATS replaced the steel wheel as standard equipment. In 1978, ATS also made a 7-inch version of the wheel, and the wheel continued to be standard on the 911SC.

In 1984, with the introduction of the 3.2 Carrera, the "telephone dial" wheel replaced the ATS "cookie cutter" wheel as standard equipment.

A BBS three-piece modular center-lock racing wheel.

A BBS 16-inch modular center-lock racing wheel with a BBS wheel fan.

A BBS 19-inch modular center-lock racing wheel with a BBS wheel fan.

In contrast, the double-spring suspension with everything replaced can cost $4,000–$5,000 in parts alone.

I recommend the European RS alignment specifications for a combination of street and track use.

Specs for Carrera RS
The alignment specifications for the Carrera RS are:

Front
Toe: +25 min +5 min (total)
Camber: -1 deg ±10 min (maximum difference left to right 10 min)
Caster: 4 deg 25 min ±15 min (maximum difference left to right 15 min)
Toe difference angle at 20 deg steering lock: 1 deg 50 min ±30 min
Rear
Toe: +15 min +5 min (each wheel)
Camber: -1 deg 15 min ±10 min
These alignment specs will improve the

handling without severely affecting tire wear.

Stick with street shocks for a car that will be primarily a road car. Either Koni or Bilstein are good.

993 Lower and Align
The standard European 993 is 20 mm (0.78 inches) lower than the standard U.S. car. The Euro car with sport suspension is 30 mm (1.18 inches) lower than either the standard U.S. car or the U.S. car with sport suspension (both set at the same height). The Carrera RS is 50 mm (1.968 inches) lower than the U.S. cars.

You have essentially the same options with the 993 as you do with the 964 as far as lowering.
• Factory (Euro) lowering springs (sport, regular, turbo, and so on)
• European RS springs and shocks
• Third-party lowering springs

• Double-spring suspension (new shocks + spring pairs and retainers)
Again, for most people the easiest thing to do with the 993 will be to just change the springs. The H&R springs are supposed to simulate the RS spec, which is about 40 mm (1.57 inches) lower than U.S. stock.

The front shocks have adjustable spring perches, but the typical amount of adjustment for lowering the car is only about 0.5 inch or less. The rear shocks have no adjustment at all in the spring perch; however, to compensate for the tolerance in spring heights there are three different spacer thicknesses available. The adjustment that Porsche has provided for the front and rear is just for fine tuning the ride heights to get the weight correct on the four wheels. If you want to change the height of the 993 you must change the springs.

BBS modular wheels with BBS wheel fans on a street racer 930 slope-nose.

The Ruf 17-inch aluminum-alloy wheels. Ruf has these wheels made by Speedline of Italy. Speedline makes several of the Formula 1 teams' wheels and the wheels for Porsche's 962Cs. Exclusive Motorcars, Inc.

The springs come in a variety of heights and spring rates for the different 993 models (C4, Turbo, and so on), so you need to be specific about the springs you want. Specify the springs' desired heights and rates, sport or non-sport use, and weight class. Even the Turbo and the Carrera 4S use different rear spring rates because of the difference in weight over the rear axles.

If you change the spring rates it is important that the rate and shock absorbers be matched with each other; some of the spring kits come with springs that are too stiff. With the stiff springs, the stock shocks do not match the spring rates, and the cars will hop around a lot. If you want to go with the stiffer springs, you should change the shocks as well.

Most of the high-performance shock absorbers for the 993 have threaded shock absorber bodies and adjustable spring perches. This means that if you change both the springs and the shock absorbers, the ride height will be adjustable and you will be able to tune your ride heights pretty much to your needs. When fitting these high-performance shock absorbers make sure that the shock mounts and washers are all correct and that they are properly installed. Different manufacturers use different hardware, so make sure what you have is correct. You should also corner balance your car if you use these shocks because you can easily end up with weight jacked across the car.

European RS Alignment Specs

I have been recommending the European RS alignment specifications, for a combination of street and track use:

Front
Toe: +5 min ±5 min (total)
Camber: -1 deg ±10 min
Caster: 5 deg 20 min +15 min -30 min
Rear
Toe: +15 min +5 min - 0 (per wheel)

Ruf 18-inch wheels.

Camber: -1 deg 20 min ±10 min
Everything else is the standard settings.

These alignment specs will improve the handling without affecting tire wear severely.

Different tires may require more or less negative camber, so you may have to alter the camber settings some to optimize the handling for a car intended primarily for track use. Everything else is the standard settings.

Olaf Lang, Porsche customer service advisor, recommends the following 993 alignment specifications for the 993s intended for race track use. These specs are based on his testing experience at Hockenheim in Germany.

Front:
Toe: +5 min (total)
Camber: -2 deg 10 min
Caster: 5 deg 20 min +15 min/-0
Rear:
Toe: +10 inches +5 min/-0 (per wheel)
Camber: -2 deg 10 min

Everything else is the standard settings. *Note:* tire wear will increase with these settings over the standard settings.

Lang says that his fastest time at Hockenheim was with this alignment, 18-inch wheels, and Pirelli P-Zero tires. On 17-inch wheels with Michelin MXX3 tires and Bridgestone Expedia S-01 tires, the times were identical.

Porsche tested the Pirelli P-Zero, the Yokomhama A-008 P, and the Bridgestone Expedia S-01 tires on 18-inch wheels, and the tires finished in that

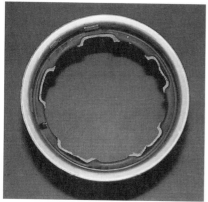

There is a very nice selection of both Porsche wheels and aftermarket wheels available to the discriminating Porsche owner, so be careful that you don't buy one of the inferior makes. This example of an inferior wheel is one of the cast replicas of the Fuchs forged alloy wheel. The problem with this wheel was that there was no added reinforcement to make up for the weaker casting procedure; the resulting wheel is not nearly as strong as the wheel it copied, and as you can see, the wheel broke. The real Fuchs forged wheels will not break, even in an accident; they will only bend. Unfortunately, there is no organization that makes sure that we cannot buy inferior wheels like these. In Germany, the TUV, which is like our Department of Transportation (DOT) only much stricter, looks after the German citizens. Everything that the German people use or consume must be approved by the TUV. Wheels are tested by the TUV's automotive division. There is no required U.S. equivalent to the German TUV's wheel testing. In fact, the only U.S. test for wheels is a voluntary test by the SFI Foundation, is a nonprofit organization made up of the member wheel companies who voluntarily agree to meet the SFI's specifications for manufacturing wheels and have their wheels tested to those specifications. If you can find a wheel that is approved by either the German TUV or the SFI, it should be safe. Do yourself a favor and check out any wheel that you plan to purchase carefully; if one fails, the results can be tragic.

order. Five different tires were tested on 17-inch wheels with the Bridgestone Expedia S-01 and Michelin MXX3 tires tied for first, Yokohama A-008 P third, Pirelli P 700-Z fourth, and Continental CZ 91 fifth.

All of the 964 and 993-based factory race cars use double springs, one soft one and one stiff. I first noticed this arrangement on Porsches when Porsche built the 911 Turbo Le Mans that Brumos raced at Daytona and Sebring in 1993. Corner balancing is nice but by no means a necessity when you put in the fixed-length lowering springs. But for the double-spring suspension it is necessary as you can end up with weight jacked across the car very easily. Since you have infinite adjustability of the ride height at each corner, you have no easy reference point for setting the height of the spring perches. It can only be done by careful measurement, counting the number of exposed threads on the shock bodies and comparing the left side to the right side. Ultimately, this should be checked by measuring the corner weights and fine tuning it right

on the scales. Some like to set the ride height (and therefore corner weights) with the driver or equivalent weight in the driver's seat, and typically with the fuel tank full or at least half-full, depending on the car's intended use. Others will set their cars straight up with no compensation for the driver's weight, as Porsche does with its street cars.

We have found that the measurements up from the ground to the fender lips for a Carrera RS is about 24.5–24.625 inches at all four fender lips. The same fender lip measurements for the lowering spring solution is about 25 inches all the way around.

Wheels

Wheels are an important and often overlooked aspect of performance tuning. When Porsches were slower and competition consisted of parking lot events, wheels were not nearly as important as they are in this era of high-speed track events and high-performance Porsches.

Porsche long made one of the best wheels in the world in the form of the

The tire inflation pressure chalk test, showing proper inflation. Uniroyal Goodrich Tire Company

Fuchs spoked forged alloy wheels—they are probably the best all-around wheel you can buy for your older Porsche. When the 911 was introduced in 1963 the commonly used wheels of the day were steel—4 1/2x15 inch in the case of the new 911. The forged alloy wheels were introduced for 1967, and still measured 4 1/2x15. Steel wheels were still offered as standard equipment on the base 911, and in fact, were standard through 1974. Starting with 1975 first the ATS "cookie cutters" were offered, then in 1984 the "telephone dial" wheels became standard equipment. In 1987, forged 15-inch alloy wheels became standard equipment in the United States, 7-inch in front and 8-inch in the rear (these were available through 1989, after which Fuchs were no longer offered).

Aftermarket road wheels have become a big item in the past few years. The majority of the aftermarket road wheels are made of cast aluminum by several different methods and many different manufacturers. There are even a few that are made by the forging process like the factory Fuchs alloys. A forged wheel is made by forming a piece of aluminum under high pressure, like the process for making racing pistons. Forgings are denser and have more structural integrity than do castings, which usually vary in density and

Bob Strange, test engineer consultant to BF Goodrich, demonstrating use of a tire pyrometer. Uniroyal Goodrich Tire Company

The tire inflation pressure chalk test, showing overinflation. Uniroyal Goodrich Tire Company

The tire inflation pressure chalk test, showing underinflation. Uniroyal Goodrich Tire Company

The aluminum S-type brake caliper on 1973 Carrera RS. These brake calipers were originally introduced on the 1969 911S. The aluminum S brake calipers were used on the top-of-the-line production cars from 1969 to 1977. James D. Newton

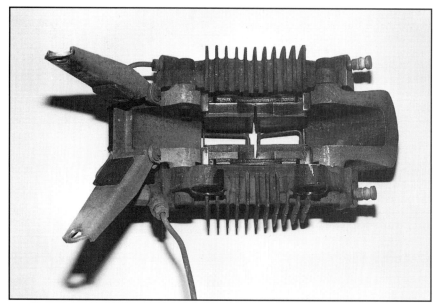

Porsche 917-style brakes, as used on the RSR. Note the mechanical hand brake arrangement.

Porsche 917-style brakes used on the front of a 935/78. Note the clamshell air ducting for brake cooling and the cockpit adjustable-front sway bar.

exhibit some porosity. A quality forged wheel has both the strength and durability required of a wheel for street use and the light weight required of a competition wheel.

For most Porsche owners, BBS and Speedline wheels are perhaps the best known of the aftermarket wheels, both because they have been in the business for a number of years and because Porsche has used them on several of its racing cars. Porsche also offers them for sale as an option at Werk I as part of their *Sonderwunsch* (special wishes) program.

There are a number of quality, one-piece, cast-aluminum wheels made for the aftermarket by several reputable manufacturers. There are any number of wheels made that look like the original modular BBS wheels with a cast center and formed sheet-aluminum outers. The strength of some of these wheels is questionable so check any you are considering very carefully. If you use cast wheels for competition, you should plan on having them crack checked by a nondestructive test lab at least once a year for safety and each time you hit something—they can and will break.

There is a nice selection of wheels available to the discriminating Porsche

owner. Fuchs, BBS, Ruf, Speedline, Oz, the new Etoile wheels, and many other quality wheels are approved by the West German *Technischer Uberprufungs Verband* (TUV). The German TUV is like our Department of Transportation (DOT), but much stricter. Everything that the West German people use or consume must be approved by the TUV. Wheels are tested by the TUV's automotive division.

There is no required U.S. equivalent to the German TUV's wheel testing. DOT doesn't require any testing, and, in fact, the only U.S. test for wheels is a voluntary test by the SFI Foundation. The SFI Foundation is a nonprofit organization made up of the member wheel companies who voluntarily agree to meet SFI's specifications for manufacturing wheels and have their wheels tested to those specifications.

A final word on wheels. All modern "mag wheels" represent a considerable investment and deserve good care. You should schedule a maintenance program for whatever make of alloy wheel you have. The factory Fuchs alloy wheels require special care. Their maintenance program should start with a frequent (every week or two) good wheel cleaning using pH-balanced cleaner. Porsche recommends acid-free cleaning products with a maximum pH value of 10 (7 is neutral, lower values are more acidic while higher values are more alkaline). Anything that gets on Fuchs alloy wheels that is either too strongly alkaline or too acidic will stain or damage them. P21S wheel cleaner and the Porsche light-alloy rim cleaner available from Porsche dealers are two pH-balanced cleaners that are great for cleaning the Fuchs wheels, or for that matter any alloy wheel. These pH-balanced wheel cleaners are somewhat like your shampoo.

The reason that the Fuchs alloy wheels are so special is that instead of having a painted surface like almost all other types of wheels, they have an aluminum finish that is clear anodized. This is one of a number of anodic coatings where the surface of the metal is protected by an oxide coating or film that is produced by electrolysis. This oxide coating is porous, and it is susceptible to staining.

Porsche also recommends that every three months after a regular cleaning, the anodized Fuchs wheels be coated with petroleum jelly. They say to rub this in well with a clean cloth. This will actually help with wheels that are stained if they aren't too badly stained. Porsche further admonishes you not to ever use an abrasive or metal polishing cleaning agent on your wheels.

The only way to restore the finish would be to send them to someone who can strip off the old anodized coating, recondition the surface, and then re-anodize the surface. Even shops that can do an excellent job of reconditioning your wheels will never be able to match the finish of your old wheels. If you need to have one or more wheels refinished, send them all to whoever will do the refinish work.

All other Porsche wheels are painted or have a clear protective coating over them. The finish on these wheels, as with the Fuchs forged wheels, is as fragile as the car's painted surfaces and should always be treated with care.

Tires

Tire technology is changing constantly. In the early 1990s, the hot tires

Porsche 917-style brakes used on the rear of a 935/78. Note the rear spring plate with a heim joint pivot and an adjustable rear sway bar.

Porsche 935 big brakes used on front of a 935/79. Note the cockpit-adjustable front sway bar and the clamshell air ducting for brake cooling.

were the A008R, the RE71R, the BFG R1, and others. Yokohama revised it as the A008-RS, then quickly moved on to the A008RS-II. The Bridgestone RE71-R has faded from view for the most part, though with its Firestone deal we can expect some new development at some point. The BFG R1 was completely redesigned a few years ago to have a new compound and an asymmetric sidewall construction that builds in something like 1 degree of negative camber for free.

The "autocross" versions of most of these tires have disappeared. For a short time it was a trend to have a "track" and an "autocross" version, but the autocross products were short-lived for a variety of reasons.

The Hoosier R3S02 (and A3S02 au-

tocross) along with the Goodyear GS-CS seem to have added something new to the track-tire war. It was probably Goodyear that first found and exploited a technical angle in the DOT requirements. Their GS-CS tire has a couple of narrow rain grooves toward the inside edge of the tire, giving it a "tread pattern" of legal "tread depth." Of course, there isn't really any tread per se which actually extends to this depth—it's basically a racing slick with a "tread imprint." Apparently it's all crafted together in a package that meets federal requirements. Once you have scuffed them in, you have a set of DOT-legal racing slicks with a basic provision for light rain, and one of the best track tires you can buy and still hope to drive home on (if it isn't very slippery). The Hoosier R3S02 is basically designed to the same recipe, and it has fiberglass belts to make it as light as possible.

The Pirelli P-Zero-C is currently a popular tire among a small audience, as the tire has been unavailable in the United States in 1996, and only available in limited numbers in Canada. It is much sought-after in Europe. This is basically the 1995–96 SuperCup tire—a competition version of the famous P-Zero tire, which is a Porsche OEM tire. According to rumor, this is the first DOT-legal 18-inch track tire, and since it's a much softer compound than the regular P-Zero street tire, it overcomes the P-Zero's only serious limitation. Reportedly this is an excellent tire that wears better than many of its competitors, especially on abrasive tracks.

Yokohama introduced the A032R during 1996, but since it did not meet the SCCA's deadline for availability, the A032R was not legal for SCCA Solo II in 1996. The A032R is basically a slick tread pattern with a curved set of "V" grooves for channeling rain away. It seems to be a very aggressive compromise between a slick and a rain tire, somewhat like a hand-grooved slick of intermediate style. These tires come with an 8/32-inch tread depth, which is somewhat deeper than the BFG R1 and others at 6/32 inch.

Tread wear rating is one way of evaluating tires. For years people buying family car tires have used the higher tread-wear rating to guide them in which tires to buy. The higher the tread wear rating, the longer the tire lasts. They also don't grip as well, but that's less of a concern for normal use. For track tires, grip is good, and so a lower, "poorer," treadwear rating is the first sign of a really sticky tire. To an extent this is countered somewhat by the new silicate compounding used in tires like the P-zero and the Bridgestone S-02, but for now it is still the easiest way short of a durometer (hardness gauge) or an actual track test.

A typical street tire will be in the 180, 200, or higher range to make it last acceptably long. An "ultra high-performance" street tire like Porsche uses for OEM equipment is currently in the 140 range. And a good track tire is typically below 100. The R1 and the A032R are rated in the 60 to 80 range. And the Hoosier is rated 0; that's right, 0!

The easiest way to get the current state of the tire wars is to go to the track and talk to owners of similar vehicles or at least cars with wheels similar to yours. You can also get on the Internet and start browsing all of the Web sites. Many of the tire manufacturers have resorted to posting Web pages to keep the information flowing on their current weaponry in the tire wars, and for those that don't, leading wheel and tire dealers such as the Tire Rack (www.tirerack.com) are also on-line. Tire sellers typically have their own compilation of tire choices, and this is probably the easiest way to collect and sift through all the information.

Porsche 935 big brakes on the rear of a 935/79. Note the adjustable rear sway bar and the uniball pivot for the spring plate.

A rear fiberglass cooling scoop for 935 rear brakes. The scoop mounts to the rear trailing arm and the leading edge hangs down into the air stream, scooping up cooling air.

Rim and Tire Size Considerations

For good, high-performance street tires I suggest you read all of the tire tests, pay your money, and take your chances. We are into the 17- and 18-inch wheels now, and soon we will be on to even bigger. The decision of 17 or 18 depends on if you can get the tires that you want in these sizes.

For wheel and tire fitting, the 964 stock was 6x6x16, then 7x8x17, but you can run 7.5-, 8.0-, or even 8.5-inch rims in the front, and 8.5-, 9.0-, 9.5-, and even 10.0-inch in the rear—if you can control your offsets carefully, lower and stiffen the car, get some negative camber, and take responsibility for your actions.

For the 993, Porsche started with 7- and 9-inch 16s (front and rear respectively), then 7- and 9-inch 17s; but again you can go right up to 8.5 and 10, and it's a little easier than it is on the 964, implying that even wider might be possible. You have to be really good to make an 8.5-inch wheel fit up front. Perhaps 7.5 and 9.0 on a 964, and 8.0 and 10.0 on a 993. Porsche's street RS cars follow this formula.

In terms of tires, the hot setup for both the 964 and the 993 is 235 front and 275 rear, at least in the BF Goodrich R1 track tire. Its 245 front won't fit because the diameter is too big. BFG's 275 rear just barely fits and offsets have to be just right or the tires will hit on either the inside or the outside but not both.

The older cars, 1978–1989, will have front tire clearance problems. We have been putting the 911 7x16-inch wheels on the front with the standard 205/55VR16 tires for some time now. They will usually hit on a lowered car, and it can go either way on a car that is not lowered. It is usually the left side that rubs, but not always. The bodies just are not built that accurately. Porsches have had this problem since the 356 days—except it was the right rear fender that rubbed on those cars. The problem only shows up when you are crowding the tire sizes. One of the solutions I have seen to eliminate the problem is to run excessive negative camber, which pulls the top of the tire away from the fender lip. This is fine for a car that is used exclusively for autocrosses and track events, but it will result in excessive wear on a car used for street use. Another way to gain some clearance and help save your tires is to roll the front fender lips up.

The problem is that the Fuchs wheels for the 911, with 10.6 mm of offset, place the wheel and tire too close to the fender. The only Fuchs wheels that really work well in the front are the 7x15-inch wheels that were made for the 911R. Ac-

One of the first things that you should try with a 911 you are using for racing or track use is to duct air into the brakes. You should start with the front brakes because the weight transfer of the car will cause the front brakes to do most of the braking. You can either fabricate your own brake scoop and ducting or purchase a kit. One good-looking kit for the 911 that doesn't require cutting holes in the front air dam is offered by AJ–USA, Inc. The fiberglass scoop mounts on the bottom of the front A-arm, where there is always plenty of cool air. From the scoop, the cool air is ducted via hose and funnel to the eye of the rotor.

tually with 49 mm offset, these had excess offset as well. One of the wheels that people have found they can stuff under the front of these cars is the 8x16 Fuchs wheel that was made for the rear of the 944 Turbo. These wheels have a 23.3 mm offset, which moves the wheel and tire in a little from the fender lip. They can be identified by the fact that the wheel lugs were countersunk whereas the 911 8-inch rear wheels were not. Because these wheels were fitted to the 944 Turbo they also have extra clearance for large brake calipers. The 944 wheels are usually used with 225/50x16 or 225/45x16 tires.

Most people use the 8-inch wheels in front with the 9x16-inch 911 Turbo wheels in the rear with either 245/50x16 or 245/45x16 tires. These were the wheels introduced on the Turbo in 1986. This wheel looks like the 944 Turbo wheel and has counter-sunk lug nuts and extra brake caliper clearance. There was also a 7x16-inch wheel used on the 944 Turbo that may be useful in some applications. Even though the offset is the same 23 mm as the 911 7x16-inch wheels, these 944 wheels have the additional brake clearance and the countersunk lug nuts of the 944 Turbo wheels.

The wheel offset will be critical with some of the larger wheel recommendations, so be sure to check with the wheel manufacturer for precise fitting information. You may also want to check for yourself that the tires and wheels you have selected actually fit. This is particularly true in the rear of the 1969–1977 cars with their smaller rear fender flares. Some of these cars will not tolerate the 7-inch wheels with the 205/60x15-inch tires—the wheels offset must be correct.

I recommend that you carefully check the clearance before you put the wheels and tires on and drive away. Get two big strong friends to help you with this. Have them bounce the rear of the car up and down while you watch the tire and fender clearance. You will be able to determine by this method of watching the arc of the tire if you will have a problem with tire clearance. You will have to judge for yourself; the penalty for a mistake is blistered paint on the rear fenders. The problem occurs about 1 1/2 inches up from the fender lip, so focus your attention there while your friends bounce the car. To be safe, you should be able to fit a finger between the tire and fender when you are all done. Don't try this while your

Wheel and Tire Combinations

Years	Standard wheels & tires	Recommended wheels & tires
1965-67	4.5x15—165-15	5.5x15—185/70-15 or 5.5x15—195/6515
1968	5.5x15—165-15	5.5x15—185/70-15 or 5.5x15—195/6515
1969–74	5.5x15—165-15	7x15—205/60-15
1969–72	5.5x14—185-14	5.5x14—205/60-14
1969–77	6.0x15—185/70-15	7x15—205/60-15
1974–75 Carrera	front 6x15—185/70-15 rear 7x15—215/60-15	7x15—205/60-15 8x15—215/60-15 or front 7x16—205/55-16 or rear 8x16—225/50-16
1976–77 Carrera	front 6x15—185/70-15 rear 7x15—215/60-15 or front 7x15—205/50-15 or rear 8x15—225/50-15 or front 5.5x14—185 14 or rear 5.5x14—185 14	7x15—205/60-15 8x15—215/60-15 or front 7x16—205/55-16 or rear 8x16—225/50-16 or front 5.5x14—205/60-14 or rear 5.5x14—205/60-14
1975–77 911 Turbo (930)	front 6x15—185/70-15 rear 7x15—215/60-15 or front 7x15—205/50-15 or rear 8x15—225/50-15	9x15—225/50-15 11x15—285/40-15 or front 7x16—205/50-16 or rear 9x16—245/45-16 or front 9x17—235/40-17 or rear 10x17—255/40-17
1978–85 911 Turbo (930)	front 7x16—205/55-16 rear 8x16—225/50-16	9x15—225/50-15 11x15—285/40-15 or front 9x16—225/50-16 or rear 10x16—245/45-16 or front 9x17—235/40-17 or rear 10x17—255/40-17
1986–89 911 Turbo (930)	front 7x16—205/55-16 rear 9x16—245/45-16	9x15—225/50-15 11x15—285/40-15 or front 7x16—205/50-16 or rear 9x16—245/45-16 or front 9x17—235/40-17 or rear 10x17—255/40-17
1978–83 911SC	front 6x15—185/70-15 rear 7x15—215/60-15 or front 6x16—205/55-16 or rear 7x16—225/55-16 or front 7x15—185/70-15 or rear 8x15—215/60-15 or front 8x16—225/50-16	front 7x15—205/60-15 rear 8x15—215/60-15 or front 7x16—205/55-15 or rear 8x16—225/50-15 or front 7.5x16—205/55-16 or rear 8.5x16—225/50-16 or rear 9x16—245/45-16 or front 8x17—215/40
1984–89 3.2 911 Carrera	front 6x15—185/70-15 rear 7x15—215/60-15 or front 6x16—205/55-16 or rear 7x16—225/50-16 or front 7x15—185/70-15 or rear 8x15—215/60-15 or rear 8x16—225/50-16	front 7x15—205/60-15 rear 8x15—215/60-15 or front 7x16—205/55-16 or rear 8x16—225/50-16 or front 7.5x16—205/55-16 or rear 8.5x16—225/50-16 or rear 9x16—245/45-16
1989–94 C2/4	front 6x16—205/55-16 rear 8x16—225/50-16 or rear 8x16—225/50-16 or front 7.5x17—205/50-17 or front 7x17—205/50- 17 or rear 8x17—255/40- 17	front 8x16—225/50-16 or front 8.5x17—235/45-17 or front 8.5x18—225/40-18 rear 8.5x16—255/50-16 or rear 9.5x17—275/40-17 or rear 9.5x18—265/35-18
C2 Turbo	front 7x17—205/55-17 rear 9x17—255/40-17	front 8x18—225/40-18 rear 10x18—265/35-18
3.6 Turbo	front 8x18—225/40-18 rear 10x18 265/35-18	front 8.5x18—225/40-18 10x18—285/30-18
1994–96 993	front 7x16—205/55-16 rear 9x16—245/45-16 or front 7x17—205/50-17 or rear 9x17—255/40-17 or front 8x18—225/40-18	front 8x 16—225/50-16 rear 8.5x 16—225/50-16 or front 8.5x 17—235/45-17 or front 8.5x18—245/40-18 or rear 9.5x17—275/40-17 front 8.5x17—245/45-17 rear 10x17—275/40-17
	or rear 10x18—265/35-18	or rear 9.5x18—265/35-18 or rear 10x18—275/35-18 or rear 10x18—285/35-18
96 Turbo	front 8x18—225/40-18 rear 10x18—285/30-18	

friends are bouncing your car, however. Also remember, during this test, that as the car goes down, the camber becomes more negative, pulling the top of the tire away from the fender. You can gain extra clearance by running excessive negative camber, but at the expense of excessive tire wear.

Of course, there are various versions of some of these wheels with different finish treatments, some with silver spokes, some with black spokes, and so on, but these are the basic Fuchs forged-alloy wheels for the 911s. There were also 5.5x15-inch Mahle cast-magnesium wheels available, Cookie Cutter ATS wheels in 6x15 inch, and the newer telephone-dial 928-style wheels available in a number of sizes.

For racing tires, talk to tire engineers from any of the companies that sell racing tires and ask their advice. This used to be simple: one just went through the Goodyear catalog and picked out what you thought would best suit your car and driving conditions. But now everyone has gotten into the act and recently we have seen Yokohama, Goodrich, Bridgestone, Michelin, and Hoosier tires all winning races.

Tire Pressures

Porsche recommends tire pressures that work as a compromise between handling and tire wear, but because of the wide range of potential driving conditions worldwide this is a challenge.

When modern, low-profile tires are run underinflated at high speeds they will probably show excessive wear in the center. This may run counter to your experience with older, conventional, cross-bias tires, which wore on the outside when they were underinflated. Wide, underinflated, low-profile tires will wear in the center due to carcass flex caused by incredible centrifugal force. At 65 mph the centrifugal force is approximately 250 g, and at 125 mph the centrifugal force is about 1,025 g. A German driving a 911 on the Autobahn at 125 mph is more likely to have this centrifugal-force-induced wear problem than we are here in the top-speed-restricted United States.

Check your owner's manual for Porsche's recommendations for tire pressures for different tire and wheel combinations. I suggest that you start with these inflations, watch your tire wear, then customize the pressures for your 911 based on your observations and experiences. You might actually want to buy a tire depth gauge and check your tire wear across each tire's road surface every 1,000 miles or so.

If you have a newer 911 with the 16-, 17-, or 18-inch wheels and experience wear in the center with the Porsche's recommended pressures, but you never drive more than 70–75 mph, you might want to try reducing the pressure by a few pounds. At the reduced speeds here in the United States you probably will not need such high pressures to compensate for centrifugal forces. In fact, some of the tire manufacturers do recommend 36 psi inflation for the 265/35ZR18 rear tires on the Carrera 4S instead of the 44 psi inflation recommended by Porsche.

Competition Tire Pressures

Bob Strange, BF Goodrich test engineer and race driver, has a great deal of experience with radial tires on Porsches and was willing to share some information that he put together for one of BF Goodrich's ads ("BF Goodrich Update #29, Tire Inflation Pressure"). In the ad

Factory Fuchs Five-spoke Alloy Wheels

Size	Offset	Part Number
6x16 inch	36 mm offset	911 632 113 00
7x16 inch	23.3 mm offset	911 362 115 00
7x16 inch	23.3 mm (more brake caliper room)	951 362 115 00
8x16 inch	10.6 mm 911 offset	911 362 117 00
8x16 inch	23.3 mm 944 offset	951 362 117 00
9x16 inch	15 mm offset	911 362 119 00
4.5x15 inch	42 mm offset	901 361 012 01
5.5x15 inch	42 mm offset	901 361 012 04
6x15 inch	36 mm offset (early)	901 361 012 06
6x15 inch	36 mm offset (late)	911 361 020 10
7x15 inch	911R offset 49 mm	901 361 012 05
7x15 inch	23.3 mm offset	911 361 020 41
8x15 inch	10.6 mm offset	911 361 020 42
9x15 inch	3.0 mm offset	911 361 020 03
11x15 inch		911 361 020 05
5.5x14 inch	46 mm offset	911 361 016 10

An alternative cooling scheme used in conjunction with 935 big brakes. Instead of being forced into the eye of the rotor, the cool air is forced on the inside of the rotor.

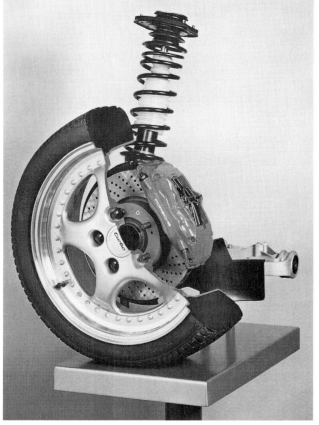

Porsche big red brakes. First introduced on the 3.6 Turbo in 1993, they are now used on the Bi-Turbo and the Carrera 4S and are called their 2,000-hp brakes. Porsche AG

Bob explains:

The question most people ask me about their tires is how much air they should put in them. Of all the factors that can directly affect your tires' performance, inflation pressure is one of the most important, and sadly, one of the most neglected.

The fact about inflation pressure is that the amount of air in your tires affects the way in which the tread comes in contact with the road. By varying the pressure, you vary your car's performance.

Over and Under

Overinflation and underinflation each have their own problems. When tires are overinflated, they absorb less of the shock of driving and that puts an extra strain on suspension systems. Also, because the extra pressure lifts the shoulders off the road, traction can be substantially decreased. On the other hand, underinflation can make tires sluggish and unresponsive.

Our tires are designed to have the proper balance of rolling resistance, cornering, and resistance to hydroplaning when correctly inflated.

What is the right pressure for your vehicle? For the everyday driver, the proper inflation numbers are specified on your vehicle and in your owner's manual. For all cases, the pressure should never be below the vehicle manufacturer's recommendation or above the maximum branded on the tire sidewall. For light truck tires, pressures are generally higher because they have reinforced sidewalls to carry additional loads.

The Pressure of Competition

When racing, all the rules of inflation pressures change. In autocross, pressures can run much higher than for everyday driving. The higher pressure quickens steering response and can increase cornering and traction. Off-road racers run with lower pressures to provide a smoother ride, more bruise resistance, and increased traction thanks to the tires' larger footprints. In competitive situations, inflation pressures are often used to compensate for oversteer or understeer. Lower front tire pressures and higher rear tire pressures generally increase understeer, while higher front tire pressures and lower rear tire pressures increase oversteer.

Check the Chalk

The most common method of finding the right inflation pressure for a competitive vehicle/tire/track combination is the chalk test. Chalk the outside shoulder sidewall area in two or three places around the circumference of the tire, and, after a race or practice session, check how much chalk has been worn away. Ideally, the chalk should be worn away within 1/4 inch of the point where shoulder rib and the sidewall meet. If the chalk remains on the tread/shoulder rib, the tire is overinflated or has too much negative camber. If the chalk is all worn away, the tire is running on the sidewalls and is underinflated or has too much positive camber. When either situation

occurs, add or subtract air in 2 psi increments or modify the camber. Rechalk the tire and try again until the chalk shows your tires are properly inflated.

The chalk method is good for rough estimates, but the method most professionals use to precisely set the right inflation pressure uses a pyrometer—a thermometer for your tires. After a practice session or a race, a needle-like device is inserted in the center of the tread and in each shoulder, and the temperature is read. An overinflated tire runs heavier on the center of the tire than on the shoulder, so the center will be hotter. An underinflated tire runs heavier on the shoulder, so the shoulder will be hotter than the center.

Brakes

Ever faster 911s and 911 derivatives have continued to push improvement in brakes. The first change was 1967 when vented rotors were introduced on all four corners of the new 911S model. The next significant change was for 1968 when all models received dual master cylinders. For 1969 the front calipers were increased in size and made of aluminum for the 911S model. Also in 1969 the rear calipers for all models were replaced with the larger "M" caliper, which had been used as the front caliper on all 911s. M calipers fitted to the rear used smaller, 38-mm pistons. Now that the M calipers were used both front and rear, the same size pads were also used

A Ruf brake kit to adapt 928 S4 brakes to the 930 Turbo. These kits are available with both 12- and 13-mm rotors. Exclusive Motorcars

The GT 2 front brakes. These calipers are even larger than the red calipers, with 380-mm (14.96-inch) front rotors and 322-mm (12.68-inch) rear rotors. The front calipers have two 42-mm pistons and two 34-mm pistons, and the rear calipers have four 28-mm pistons.

on both ends for the 911 T and E models. The 911 Ts had solid rotors, while the 911 E and S had the vented rotors. S models used larger front pads because they were fitted with aluminum front calipers. In 1970, the 2.2 911 Ts also received the vented rotors.

When the 1973 2.7 Carrera RS was introduced it received the 911S brakes. The limited-production 3.0 Carrera RS for 1974 had the brakes from the 917 race car, the first four-piston calipers installed on a production 911.

In 1975, the 911 Turbo (930) had the same combination of brakes that had been used first on the 2.0-liter 911 S in 1969. In 1976, the new A-series caliper was introduced on the 911s and Carreras, while the 911 Turbo continued to use the S aluminum calipers. The new

A caliper was an existing model that ATE made for Alfa-Romeo; they were the same size as the aluminum S caliper and used brake pads of the same area. The A caliper is a little narrower, however, so instead of using brake pads that are 13 mm thick, like the S caliper used, it used a 10 mm brake pad. For 1977, the 911 and the 911 Turbo (930) received vacuum-assisted power brakes that used a 7-inch booster acting directly on the master cylinder. The servo effect of the vacuum booster was 2.2 for the 911S and 1.8 for the 911 Turbo.

The Group 4 934s and Group 5 935s used the 917-style brakes in 1976, and the IMSA version of the 934 and the 935s used them again in 1977. In 1978, with the introduction of the 3.3 Turbo, a production version of the

917-style brakes were installed on the 911 Turbo. In 1978, the brake booster for the Turbo was increased in size from 7 inches to 8 inches, and the internal servo factor was increased from 1.8 to a 2.25 ratio. These brakes continued to be used on the 3.3 Turbo over the ensuing 10 model years until the model was discontinued in 1989. They were also used on the newer Turbo-look cars from 1984 to 1989. The servo factor was increased again in the 1984 model year from the 2.25 to a 3.0 ratio.

When Porsche built its *Moby Dick* 935/78 it designed a new set of big brakes to haul down this faster version of the 935. These new big brakes were made available on the customers' version of the 935 in 1979.

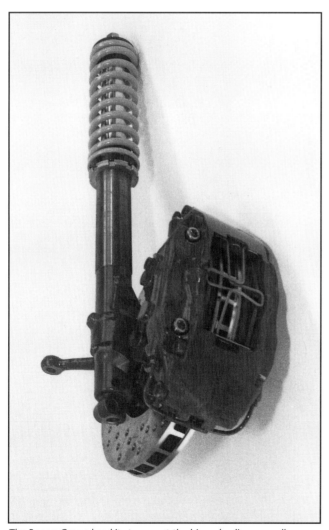

The Racers Group has kits to mount the big red calipers on all cars from the 911SC forward. This one shows the front strut for the 1969-1989 911 with 13-inch-rotor big red calipers with Pagid pads, Bilstein struts, and the Racers Group springs.

This is the Racers Group's modified caliper adapted for the rear of cars with 911 aluminum rear banana arms.

This is the Racers Group's modified caliper adapted for the rear of cars with 930 rear banana arms. These modified calipers mount in the standard location and require no modification of the trailing arm.

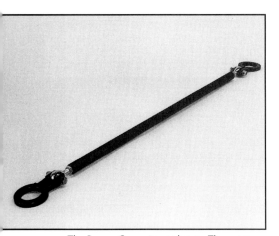

The Racers Group tower brace. These are useful for coil-spring cars, but they do little good with the earlier torsion-bar cars.

In 1978, some of the first 911SCs continued to use the aluminum S front calipers and the M rear calipers, but by 1979 all SCs used the A caliper and the S caliper was gone forever.

The brakes were revised again for the introduction of the 3.2 Carrera in 1984 as follows:

• A vacuum amplifier increased the vacuum for the brake booster.
• The brake booster increased in size from 7 to 8 inches.
• Brake disc thickness front and rear increased from 20.0 mm (0.78 inches) to 24 mm (0.94 inches). The thicker rotors provide better heat sink capabilities.
• Brake calipers were adapted to a thicker disc with spacers.
• The A and M caliper designs were still used for the 1984 models. The brake caliper piston diameter for the rear brakes was increased from 38 mm to 42 mm. The M caliper design was still retained for the rear but with larger pistons. The front caliper pistons remained at 48 mm, unchanged since 1969 and the aluminum S calipers.
• The brake pressure regulator in the rear axle brake circuit was set for 33 bar.
• Brake pads, rear axle: Textar changed from Textar TP 22 to T269.

Porsche said that better rear-wheel braking with low brake pressure was accomplished by using larger pistons in the rear calipers. However, because the rear brakes were more effective, a brake-pressure regulator was needed to prevent excessive braking and lock up. Porsche explains that with the regulator there is equal pressure in the front and rear brake circuits until a brake pressure of 33 bar. When brake pressure is above

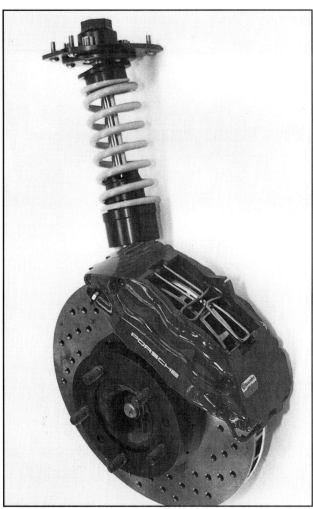

This is the Racers Group's 964 strut with big red caliper adapted, 13-inch disc and hardware, Bilstein short racing shocks, and the Racers Group uniball mounting hardware and springs.

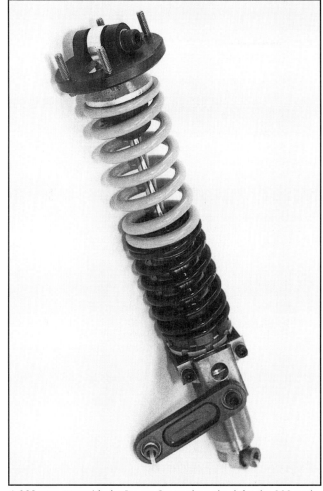

A 993 rear strut with the Racers Group short shock for the 993 and with different mounts for the 964 and the earlier 911s. The Racers Group even has hardware that will allow mounting upside down in early 911s.

A special Porsche device that allows stiffening of the springs on coil-spring race cars. If you wind more of the solid piece into the coil you make the spring stiffer by reducing the length of the coil.

Rear multilink suspension on a factory Supercup car with the spring stiffness adjusters. This car has special uniball links in the suspension and adjustable sway bars front and rear.

33 bar, for example under full-stop braking, only 46 percent of the additional brake pressure goes to the rear axle compared with 54 percent to the front. For the Turbo-look car, the switching pressure of the brake regulator was increased from 33 bar to 55 bar to better match the braking characteristics to the car's larger brakes. Porsche made this change in an effort to improve the overall braking. Still, for safety reasons it has to be sure that the rear wheels do not lock up.

Brake Pads

I have experimented with different brake pad makes over the years, and I have found pads that I feel work better than others in some specific applications. A compromise pad is a hard thing to come up with, however, and the pads that the various Porsche models come with are probably the best compromise for most applications. The real problem is that Porsche owners are unwilling to compromise their driving to make compromise solutions really work.

Modern brake pads have had the asbestos removed and as a result no longer function like brake pads of a few years ago. For a street car you are probably best off using the Porsche-recommended pads; however, for competition there is a broad selection of pads available: Cool Carbon, Performance Friction, and Pagid, to name a few of the more popular pads. What these pads

have in common is that they are all carbon-based combined with Kevlar or metal. They stop the car very well, hot or cold, but they are noisy, and as a result, may not make a reasonable compromise for street use.

Brake Cooling

Beyond changing brake pads, there are several other things that can be done to improve the braking of your 911 for competition or track use. The first thing you should do is work on ducting more air into the brakes, particularly the fronts. It is important for a race car to duct forced air into the brakes for cooling because, for example, if you have changed to Ferodo DS 11 brake pads they will only work up to 1,050 deg F.

The first phase of cooling vented rotors is to duct forced cooling air into the eye of the rotor so that the cool air is forced out through the internal ventilating core. Start with the front brakes, because that's where most of your braking power is. You can either fabricate your own brake scoop and ducting or purchase one as a kit. One such kit that looks like a good approach to the problem and doesn't require cutting holes in front air dams is the "COOL-brake." The fiberglass scoop mounts on the bottom of the front A arm where there is always plenty of cool air. From the scoop, the cool air is ducted via hose and funnel to the eye of the rotor.

Ralph T. Boothe wheel adapters that allow the use of late-style offset wheels on the early 1969–89 911s.

The next step in brake cooling would probably be the addition of wheel fans.

Brake Fluid

All brake fluid comes in DOT 3, DOT 4, or DOT 5 ratings. The DOT standards for brake fluids were established in 1972. When the National Highway Traffic Safety Administration(NHTSA) Department of Transportation devised the requirements for brake fluids it determined that there was a need for two fluid grades until an all-weather fluid was developed with viscosity and boiling point characteristics suitable for all braking systems. In order to provide added protection against vapor locking and fade in severe braking service, DOT 4 fluid is recommended. But in such applications it is important to note that the same higher viscosity that helps eliminate vapor lock and fade may result in poorer system performance in very cold weather. Also, it should be noted that high boiling-points are sacrificed in the DOT 3 fluid for low viscosities for use at low temperatures. These differences between the viscosities of the DOT 3 and DOT 4 fluids are necessary to cover the specified operating temperature ranges and as such make it necessary to maintain both DOT 3 and DOT 4 brake fluids.

DOT 5 fluid is supposed to be the all-weather fluid that is mentioned in the preceding paragraph. All three fluids are tested for a variety of characteristics, the most interesting of which are the equilibrium reflux boiling point (dry boiling point), the wet equilibrium reflux boiling point (wet boiling point), and the kinematic viscosities (viscosity at cold temperatures).

Dry boiling point: These are the minimum boiling temperatures allowed for the various grades of fluid (this test simulates the boiling point when the fluid is new).

DOT 3: 401 deg F
DOT 4: 446 deg F
DOT 5: 500 deg F

Wet boiling point: These are the minimum boiling temperatures allowed for the various grades of fluid when wet (this test is a simulation of the boiling point after the absorption of moisture from air).

DOT 3: 284 deg F
DOT 4: 311 deg F
DOT 5: 356 deg F

Note: These are the minimum requirements, and there are brake fluids available that will exceed these specs.

Kinematic viscosities: All brake fluids (DOT 3, DOT 4, and DOT 5) must meet a minimum viscosity test of not less than 1.5 centestokes at 100 deg C (212 deg F) and must not be more than the following to meet their various classifications (the larger numbers indicate higher kinematic viscosities just like with motor oils).

DOT 3: 1,500 centestokes at -40 deg F
DOT 4: 1,800 centestokes at -40 deg F
DOT 5: 900 centestokes at -40 deg F

For the Porsche 911, I break down the brake fluids that should be used into three applications:

Street: New Porsches now come with a new ATE brake fluid called DOT 4-200. Porsche's new DOT 4-200 brake fluid clearly outperforms the existing DOT 3, DOT 4, and DOT 5 fluids in both dry and wet boiling points. While it may not be as good as the really high-temperature, specialized racing fluids, this stuff is excellent brake fluid and is marketed by the manufacturer as a racing brake fluid under the label "ATE Blue."

This new DOT 4-200 fluid will also last much longer than conventional DOT 3 and DOT 4 fluids because of its excellent wet boiling point and improved moisture activity. Because of this longer life Porsche has extended the change interval to three years. This DOT 4-200 fluid should be used in all street-driven Porsches and changed at least every three years.

Racing: High-temperature DOT 3 or DOT 4 fluids such as Motul, Castrol, Pentosin, and so on. Silicone brake fluid, which meets the DOT 5 specification, is unsuitable for high-temperature applications because of its compressibility. Silicone brake fluid should not being used in disc brakes for racing.

Storage: DOT 5 silicone brake fluid. Silicone fluid works well for storage because it prevents corrosion and deterioration of the brake components. I think this is the only legitimate application for DOT 5 fluid. Because of its ability to ab-

A Rightwood Racing brake kit to put big brakes and rotors on the 964. Warren Gardner

Vehicle Craft Incorporated (VCI) has rotors and caliper kits to mount all of the different brakes on all of the different 911 models. Here is a wide selection of floating and nonfloating rotors and hats for the 911 (early and late), the 964, and the 993. VCI

A VCI 928 S4 caliper mounted on a 930. VCI

Above and above right
Cool Carbon brake pads for all occasions and all sizes of Porsche brakes.

Brake System Problems

Frequent brake fluid changes help extend the life of the brake system's rubber components. One of the problems that will surface because of rubber deterioration is brake line or hose deterioration. This problem seems to take about 10 years and can sometimes be deceptive and hard to diagnose because the brakes will appear to operate normally, except that they will not retract when the pedal is released. The problem is caused by the fact that the brake lines have swollen up internally. The hydraulic system has enough of a mechanical/hydraulic advantage to overcome the restriction when you are braking, but the seals that retract the pistons do not have enough force to push the fluid back so that the pistons can't retract. The swelling of the brake lines is probably caused by petroleum contamination of either the brake fluid or some other portion of the brake system.

After corrosion and rubber deterioration, the next most common problem caused by not changing the brake fluid and bleeding the system will be the gumming up of the pistons in the calipers. When the pistons gum up, they stick in the seals when they try to retract and cause the pads to drag on the rotors, similar to the swollen brake line problem. Usually the only cure is to disassemble and rebuild the calipers. However, it is always worth trying to exercise the calipers by extending and retracting each piston several times. This proce-

sorb air, it is unsuitable for any high-performance application because of the spongy, compressible pedal it creates.

dure requires two people; one to pump the brake pedal to extend the pistons and the other to force them back with a hard wood or aluminum bar. The brake fluid should be renewed and the brakes bled at the same time.

If you ever have a master cylinder fail on your 911—and it is one of the pre-booster-brake 911s—you should remove your pedal assembly and replace the pedal bushings. What usually happens to the pedal bushings is that the master cylinder fails and leaks brake fluid past the seal and into the pedal box area. The stock pedal bushings are hygroscopic, so the brake fluid causes them to swell and bind, keeping them from returning when you remove your foot from the brake pedal. If you ever have a sticking pedal, check the brake fluid level and the floor boards down around the pedals for moisture. If the fluid level is low and you find fluid around the pedals, then you probably have a bad master cylinder. I recommend that you use the original-style nylon type bushings and not the bronze type being offered as a replacement. The new set of plastic bushings will last until the next master cylinder goes bad, which will probably be another 5 to 10 years and nearly 100,000 miles.

If you use your 911 in speed events plan to flush your brake system more

Front-wheel clearance in front on a 911SC with 8x16-inch wheels with 225/50x16-inch tires. The fender lip was rolled and 1 1/2 degree of negative camber helped to provide clearance. Joel Reiser

221

The heim-jointed rear suspension pickup point on a club track car.

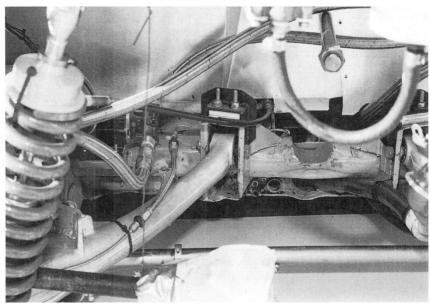

The inner suspension pickup point on a club track car. This also copies the rear suspension used on the 935s. This modified rear suspension pickup allows the camber to be adjusted at the inner end of the trailing arms.

Rear-wheel clearance in back on a 911SC with 9x16-inch wheels with 245/45x16-inch tires. Joel Reiser

frequently than the once every two or three years recommended in the owner's manual. Racers flush their brake systems and bleed their brakes at each racing weekend. If you get your brakes too hot you will boil the brake fluid. When the fluid boils it forms air bubbles; since air bubbles are compressible, the pedal will move closer to the floor. The solutions for this problem are brake fluid with a higher boiling point and the ducting of cooling air to the rotors and calipers. Simply maintaining fresh fluid in the system will reduce the boiling problem because the fluid will not have picked up moisture.

Improving the Brake System

For competition or track use the next step to improve your 911's braking is to install larger brakes or brake calipers. Over the years, a number of people have installed the larger 917-style brakes that have been used on the 911 Turbo since 1978. Owners making this modification usually choose to use a twin master cylinder assembly with a built-in balance bar for adjusting the bias between the front and rear brakes. Some owners have fabricated their own pedal assembly and incorporated a balance bar, while others have adapted a Neal Pedal assembly, which has built-in twin master cylinders with a balance bar. The easiest way to solve this problem is to purchase the latest version of the pedal assembly that Porsche uses with these types of brakes. The latest version is part number 954.423.003.00, which was used in the 911SC RS. The factory pedal assembly will require some slight modification to the floorboards and firewall where it mounts. As an al-ternative to the double master cylinder pedal assembly some owners have installed the Turbo brakes using the vacuum booster assembly and master cylinder from the 911 Turbo. There are also several dual master-cylinder pedal assemblies available from the Porsche aftermarket, such as BRD and Auto Associates.

Over the past decade, Porsche has switched all of its cars to the high-tech, Brembo fixed calipers with four pistons per wheel all the way up to the big red Brembo calipers that Porsche uses on the twin turbo and Carrera 4S. The big red brakes are the ones that Porsche says offer "almost 2,000 hp at the command of the brake pedal." These as well as the other Brembos are great brakes, and they are reasonably priced, so I recommend looking at one of the conversions available for your car from the various aftermarket suppliers. Most of these new Brembo calipers are radial-mount calipers, so it is relatively easy make a side-mount adapter for the earlier cars (1965–1989). Most of the rear calipers remain side-mount calipers but with different spacing than what has been used on the earlier cars. The suppliers machine the side mounts off and bolt radial mount adapters to these rear calipers as well, making them much easier to fit on all of the Porsche 911 models. There are good brake kits available from Vehicle Craft, Inc., Ruf GmbH, Wrightwood Racing, and the Racers Group, just to name a few. These companies supply all necessary mounting brackets and the correct rotors and hats. Wrightwood Racing also has some larger racing brakes available that use the Alcon calipers.

If you are converting your 911 into a race car or if it is primarily going to be a track car you should probably switch the rubber brake lines for Teflon braided-steel, carbon-Kevlar, or Kevlar brake hoses. Rubber hoses are fine for a street car—in fact, I prefer them. They are a low-maintenance item, and the only problem I have ever seen with them is swelling from old age and contaminated brake fluid. If you do switch to special racing brake lines be sure that they are "dash three" or smaller size hoses; the "dash four" that were common a few years ago on the aftermarket actually cause a spongy brake pedal. All of the successful race cars in the world use special brake hoses. However, if you get an inferior product, or if they are improperly installed, you may actually create a worse problem for yourself than the one that you think you are solving.

Even though it might seem like a good idea, I discourage drilling your brake rotors unless you have special rotors from either Porsche or Automotive Products (AP) that were made to be drilled. The problem is excessive cracking. The alternative is the slotted rotors where slots are cut into the rotors' surface. The purpose of these slots is to wipe the hot brake dust from the operating surface of both the pad and the disc. The slots should be cut into the surface of the rotor so that they are parallel with the leading edge of the pad as they are rotated under the pads.

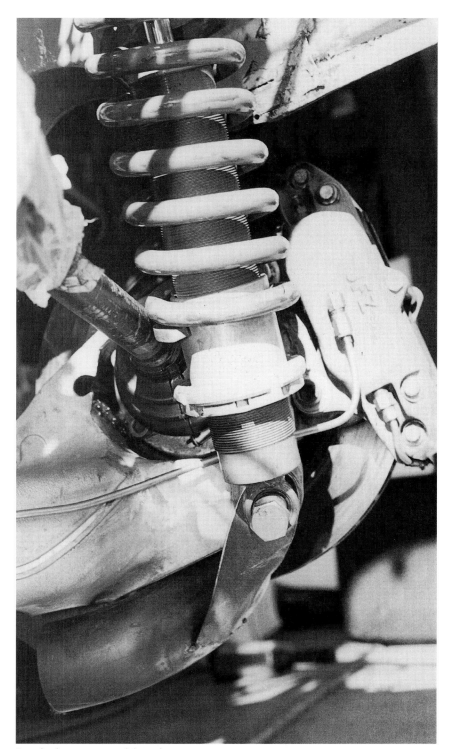

Rear-brake scoop on a club track car.

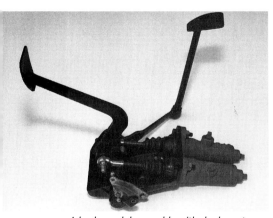

A brake-pedal assembly with dual master cylinders and a balance bar to adjust the brake balance between the front and rear brakes. Pedal assemblies are available from Greg Brown, BRD, Mark Stevens, and Jim Newton Auto Associates.

A Carrera RSR pedal assembly with dual master cylinders and a balance bar to adjust the brake balance between the front and rear brakes. This is the best setup for adjusting front-to-rear brake balance.

A 935 pedal assembly with a dual master cylinder and a balance bar for adjusting the brake balance between front and rear brakes. Note that the clutch pedal is kept separate from the brake and throttle, and that the clutch cable goes back directly under the driver's seat.

A 954 pedal assembly from a 911SC RS. This pedal assembly is easily adapted to a production 911 and only requires some minor modifications to the car's floorboards. Porsche AG

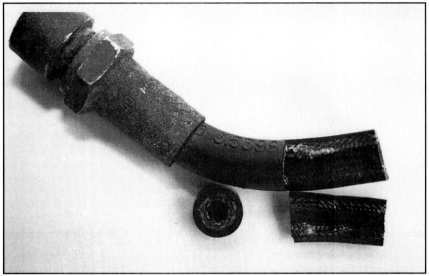

With age, the rubber brake lines can deteriorate and cause the brakes to malfunction. The malfunction is kind of sneaky in that the brakes seem to stop and work fine. The problem is a dragging caliper, where the pads never fully retract and drag on the rotor. One of the first symptoms will be one black wheel from the brake dust. The problem is caused by the brake lines swelling up internally. The hydraulic system has enough of a mechanical/hydraulic advantage to overcome the restriction when you are braking, but the seals that retract the pistons do not have enough force to push the fluid back, so the pistons can't fully retract. The swelling of the brake lines is probably caused by petroleum contamination of either the brake fluid or some other portion of the brake system.

Chapter 7

Transmission

The original transmission used in the 911 was the five-speed 901 transmission which used Porsche's own synchronizing system. The transmission was originally housed in a sand-cast aluminum housing, but this was changed to a magnesium casting in 1969. Later, there were both four- and five-speed versions of the 901 transmission available.

The 904, 906, and 909 competition cars all used special versions of the 901 gearbox consisting of 901 internal components and unique transmission housings. This was done to take advantage of the wide selection of gears available for the 901 transmission. The 914 and 914/6 also used modified versions of the 901 transmission with a unique case. There were three different versions of the shifting mechanism for these 914 transmissions, two with side-angled tail shifters—one each for the four and the six—and the side shifter for the 914/4.

915 and 916 Transmissions

The Type 916 transmission became the replacement for the racing transmissions in 1969 because of the added demands placed on the transmission by the 3.0-liter 908 engines. The 915 transmission used in the production cars was a derivative based on this 916 racing transmission and was introduced in 1972 along with the 2.4-liter engine. The 915 transmissions were available in both four- and five-speed versions and used Porsche's synchronizing system. A magnesium housing was employed until 1978 when the larger, more powerful 3.0-liter SC engines were introduced for the world market.

The 901 transmission had what was considered at the time a conventional shift pattern—the common H-pattern—with low and reverse placed out to the left and both with a spring-loaded lockout. Reverse was to the left and forward and low gear was to the left and back; the remaining four gears were on the regular H-pattern. When the 915 transmission was introduced the pattern was revised, and reverse and fifth were spring loaded and placed out to the right of the H-pattern.

930 Transmission

When the 930 was introduced for 1975 it had a new Type 930 transmission. This was a much larger transmission, designed to cope with the power outputs of a generation of turbocharged race cars. The 930 transmission is a four speed with a conventional H shift pattern and reverse out to the left and forward. It, too, used Porsche's synchronizing system.

A large rubber-centered clutch was incorporated in 1978 so the bell housing was made 30 mm longer to accommodate it. The production 911 Turbo (930) has an aluminum transmission housing. There have been different versions of this transmission made for both the 934 and the 935. In fact, there were two versions for the 935, a conventional right-side-up version and the "upside down" gearbox which was incorporated to permit a reduction of the axle angles in the 935s.

For 1987 an all-new, stronger G50 five-speed transmission was introduced for the normally aspirated Carrera 3.2 911 which used a cone-type (Borg-Warner design) synchronizing system in all forward gears and reverse. The shift pattern had been changed again with reverse moved to the left front of the H-pattern and fifth moved to the right front. The pinion was a hypoid-drive design to gain extra strength without increasing the size over that used in the 915 transmission. The transmission had a new, larger clutch activated by a hydraulic master and slave cylinder. The rear torsion bar tube had a bent center section to provide additional clearance for the transmission.

G50, G50/50, and G64/00 Transmissions

In 1989, there was also a version of the G50 transmission for the 911 Turbo. Porsche called this the G50/50 and it had different gear ratios than the version of the G50 transmission used in the normally aspirated cars. The G50/50 was longer and stronger to cope with the Turbo's added power.

A 901 transmission. An aluminum housing was used from 1965 to 1968. There was also a mainshaft available for the 904 version of the transmission that had no fixed second gear on the mainshaft (as with the 911) so that all five speeds could have different ratios selected. One of the weaknesses of the 901 transmission was the mainshaft. First gear was cantilevered outside of the intermediate plate so that when excessive torque is applied to first gear, the tendency is to pull the gear right off the end of the shaft.

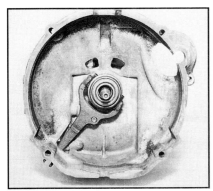

A 901 transmission with the original pivot for the push-type clutch with guided throw-out bearing.

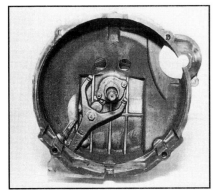

A 901 transmission with the revised pivot point for the pull-type clutch used in 1970 and 1971.

A 901 transmission. A magnesium housing was used from 1969 through 1971.

A 915 transmission with a magnesium housing.

A version of this new G50-style transmission called the G64/00 was used in the C4 when it was introduced in 1989. This transmission had a front power take-off for front-wheel drive. There had been a similar transmission built for the Type 953 Paris-Dakar car. Porsche called that transmission a Type 964, and it was based on the same design as the G-50 transmission and was a forerunner of the C4 transmission.

In 1990, with the addition of the C2 to the product line, a new version of the G50 transmission was designed that would mount in the new 964 platform. This was essentially the same transmission as the G50 used in the 1987–89 911 but with a new nosepiece and different mounts.

When the 993 was introduced in 1994, the transmission was changed to a six-speed version of the G50 type. The most significant change was making it a six-speed for improved performance and fuel consumption. Porsche improved the shifting by installing a dou-

ble-cone synchromesh on both first and second gears and reduced gear noise by using ground gears. Great effort was made to hold the weight of the six-speed to that of the previous five-speed used in the 964.

European versus North American Gearing

The RS America and all of the C2, C4, and 993 non-turbo cars for North America have taller gearing than their European street and sport counterparts because of the gas guzzler laws. By raising the gearing, most of these cars came in exempt from the extra tax. Un-

less you need to run 175 mph—with the time needed to achieve that speed no object—you would be better off with any of the shorter European gearsets. More top speed is great, depending on whether your straightaways and your power level permit you to actually reach those speeds. By lowering the gearing, you can get there faster. The paradox is that since you get better acceleration, you increase the odds of needing the extra top speed gearing you traded away to get there.

The European RS 964, and the Carrera Cup car, had a shorter ring and pinion (like all of the European 964's) and

A 915 transmission with an oil pump. When these oil pumps were used in the production cars, they were used just to recirculate the transmission lubricant around to be sure that it would provide proper lubrication to all of the gears.

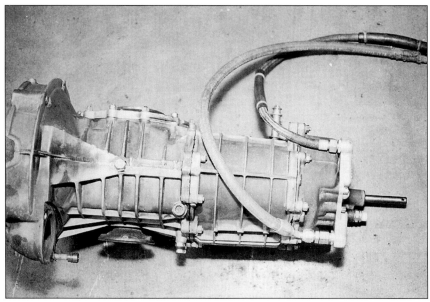

A 915 transmission with an oil pump, as used in the RSR competition cars. In the RSR, the oil was circulated to an oil cooler and then returned to lubricate the transmission, thus ensuring that the transmission was properly lubricated with cooled oil.

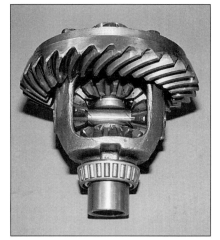

An open differential of the type used in Porsche transmissions.

taller first and second gears. This closed the gap between second and third, which causes a car on the track to "fall off the cam." Because the rev drop is more than 2,000 rpm when you shift from second to third at 6,000 to 6,500 rpm, and because the power does not come on much below 4,500 rpm, it feels like you have a "flat spot" in your engine's responsiveness. At certain race-tracks this problem is worse, because those are the speeds and gears you will carry through certain corners.

For the 993 models, the problem should not have been as severe because of the new six-speed gearbox, and the more favorable ring and pinion ratios. Unfortunately, the second to third problem persisted. Changing to the European gearset again solves the problem,

but this time you have to change second through sixth gears, not first and second as in the 964. If you have an early 993, perhaps the best solution to this problem is through the powerband improvements included with the Vario-Ram engines for 1996.

For the RSR and other 964- and 993-based racing vehicles, the factory has made other gear sets and ratios available for a wide variety of applications.

Sportomatic

Porsche made Sportomatic transmissions for the 911s for a number of years, starting in 1968 and phasing them out in the 1980s. The Sportomatic transmissions combined a torque converter and a vacuum-operated clutch with a manual transmission to create a "semi-automatic" transmission. The original version was the four-speed Type 905.

In 1972, a four-speed version of the 925 transmission replaced the 905 for most models, while the 905 was continued for the 1972 and 1973 Euro 911T. The 925 transmission was equivalent to the 915, as the 905 transmission had been the Sportomatic equivalent to the 901 transmission. Porsche limited the 925 Sportomatic to a three speed in the United States for 1975 because it felt that with the broad torque curve of the 2.7-liter engines the four-speed was no longer necessary. For the European market, the three-speed version was held off another year until the introduction of the 1976 3.0-liter Carrera.

Tiptronic Transmission

In 1990, Porsche offered its Tiptronic Transmission as an option for the 964 C2. The Tiptronic was a load-shiftable four-speed automatic transmission with a torque converter that would appeal to sporting drivers. The big advantage was that both upshifts and downshifts could be made without changing the position of the accelerator pedal.

The gear selection lever had two selected gates. Upshifts and downshifts are automatic in the left gate, depending upon the gear selector's position (P-R-N-D-3-2-1), just like a fully automatic transmission. The torque converter has a lockup clutch that remains closed from the second drive range on up.

Automatic shifts can be controlled by five different shift programs. The control learns the driver's style and adjusts accordingly. The various automatic shifting tricks must be learned to be appreciated. The one that I like best is the ability to downshift by dabbing the accelerator pedal.

If the manual gate on the right side of the shift selector is used, the driver has control of the shifting by pushing forward for upshifts and back for downshifts.

During the 1994 model year, a Tiptronic S version was added to the model line. The Tiptronic S offered two rocker switches for shifting, one on each side of the top spokes on the steering wheel. To shift up you pushed upward on either of the switches (la-

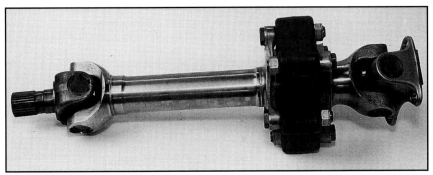

The titanium rear axle used on the 935.

A limited-slip differential, the late style introduced in 1969. A multidisc limited-slip differential was available from the beginning because it was used in the 904 version of the transmission. The later style limited-slip differentials were both more reliable and more effective.

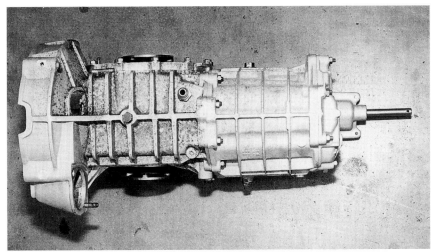

The 930 transmission, early style with the small bell housing.

beled "+"), and to shift down you pushed downward on the button (labeled "–"). All of this was aimed at adding to the enjoyment of driving a Porsche. The steering wheel controls were supplemental to the Tiptronic's standard dual-range console. The steering wheel-mounted toggle switches only worked with the shifter in the right-hand, manual gate.

There is no kickdown feature in the manual mode, and shifting had to be done manually. In the manual gate the driver could at any time shift up or down depending on the road speed and engine rpm. Tapping the selector twice in rapid succession caused the transmission to shift down two gears in one motion. As soon as the engine speed limit was reached the transmission would automatically shift up without any required action on the part of the driver. The Tiptronic transmission has proven to be a popular option.

In the automatic gate the following are the maximum permissible shifting speeds:

From D to 3 at 4,400 rpm or 111 mph
From 3 to 2 at 3,800 rpm or 72 mph
From 2 to 1 at 2,800 rpm or 35 mph

In the manual gate you can shift to the next higher or lower gear at anytime, as long as you do not exceed the same downshift speeds as in the automatic mode.

From 4 to 3 at 4,400 rpm or 111 mph
From 3 to 2 at 3,800 rpm or 72 mph
From 2 to 1 at 2,800 rpm or 35 mph

Ruf Semi-Automatic Shifting System

One of my favorite Porsche shifting systems is the Ruf semi-automatic shift. This is the *Electronische Kupplung* System (EKS, or in English "Electronic Clutch System"), which provides the convenience of clutchless driving without the loss of power normally associated with any of the other clutchless systems that use a torque converter.

The Ruf cars with EKS have no clutch pedal and are similar in operation

The titanium spool used in the 935 instead of any differential providing a locked rear end.

to the transmissions used in modern Formula 1 cars. Clutch operation is controlled by electronic signals from a computer controlling hydraulic circuits. The system responds to several different sensors: a gas pedal sensor for throttle position, a torque sensor in the gearshift lever so that it knows when you want to shift, and engine and car speed sensors. Monitoring the signals from these various sensors, the EKS computer decides when and how to engage or disengage the rather conventional single-plate clutch through a hydraulic actuator that moves the clutch throw-out bearing. The EKS system is manufactured by the Sachs Company. Ruf was Sachs' first customer, and it helped Sachs develop the system. Sachs wanted a small manufacturer to work with so that it could gain practical experience with the system before it went after a mass market. Saab was the first large-volume manufacturer to use the EKS system in a production car. Saab used the system in the 1995 Saab 900SE turbo and called its version of the clutchless EKS "Sensonic."

I had not really expected to be impressed with the EKS or the Porsche using the system because I have already had some clutchless Porsche experience with both the Sportomatic and the Tiptronic. My wife had a 911 Sportomatic for about 10 years in the 1970s and early 1980s, and I really expected this to be more of the same. I have always felt that clutchless transmissions like the Sportomatic and the Tiptronic serve a purpose and are nice to drive, but are usually difficult to defend in a macho conversation.

After I drove the Ruf 993 prototype with the EKS I was so impressed with the operation of this combination of automatic clutch and manual six-speed transmission that I am now willing to defend it in one of those "manly" conversations. You lose absolutely no performance, yet you don't have to bother with a clutch. Its operation is computer controlled and it is definitely more consistent than most drivers, and I would guess a lot smarter than some, including me. I honestly didn't miss the clutch pedal at all and only poked at the clutchless floor once, and that was when I pulled to a stop to photograph the car.

The Ruf EKS clutch has been available since spring 1992. More than 120 Ruf EKS cars have been built and sold and most of the cars that Ruf is building now are delivered with this option.

Porsche has also built some 3.6 Turbos with EKS but uses its own five-speed transmissions. Porsche says that this is a special-order option that, unfortunately, will not be available for U.S. cars because it has not been approved for this market and Porsche is concerned about product liability.

Unlike the Sportomatic or the more contemporary Tiptronic, the EKS has no losses through a torque converter because the system uses a clutch. Performance is improved because there is no clutch lag time. With the EKS you have both the performance and the fuel economy of the manual transmission with the advantage of being able to shift as fast as you can move your hand. And you don't have to worry about coordinating that with the movement of your left foot.

The EKS system is sophisticated and there are a number of potential advantages over a conventional clutch. Clutch engagement is more precise, so there is less clutch wear. You cannot abuse the clutch as a lazy driver might with a normal foot-activated clutch. If you miss a shift the computer will protect the engine by not engaging the clutch. The EKS system provides the pleasure of shifting gears without the inconvenience of a clutch pedal in stop-and-go traffic or high-speed conditions. It is sporty yet comfortable, with flawless clutch engagement.

You can start out in first or second gear, but the computer won't let you start out in third. If you miss a shift on a downshift, the clutch will not engage—the EKS will save you and your engine from yourself.

Gear Selection

The Porsche transmissions have always had a wide selection of gear ratios to choose from. How do you know what gear ratios your car has? If your car is stock and no one has modified the transmission, then check the type number stamped in the transmission case

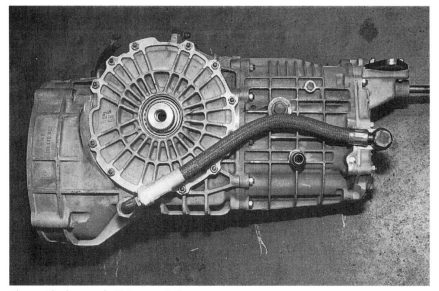

The upside-down-style 935 transmission.

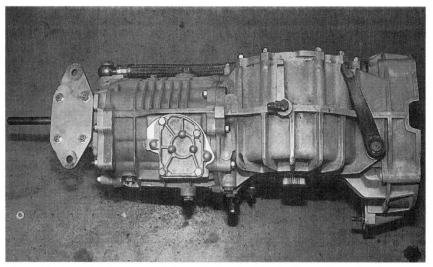

The upside-down-style 935 transmission; note the plumbing for the auxiliary oil cooler.

and look up the ratios up in your *Technical Specifications* booklet.

The first step in choosing a set of gears is to assume a differential ratio and tire diameter and pick first gear. First gear should be a compromise between being too long (meaning too many mph/rpm), which would cause too much clutch wear from the slippage required to get started, and too short, (not enough mph/rpm) that is, a "stump puller" gear. A good first gear ratio for a street 911 would be around 4–6 mph/1,000 rpm. The range of a first gear for a race car could be from 4–10 mph/1,000 rpm depending on what first gear will be used for. In a race car, first gear might just be used as a starting gear for some tracks and as both a starting gear and the gear you could use for one or more corners on other tracks.

Next, select top gear; let's call it fifth gear. This gear is determined by one of

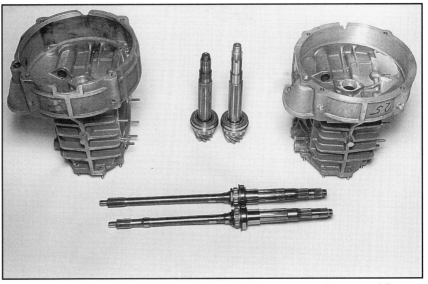

A Ruf five-speed (right) compared to a Porsche four-speed (left). Some of the major differences between the Porsche four-speed and the Ruf five-speed. Exclusive Motorcars, Inc.

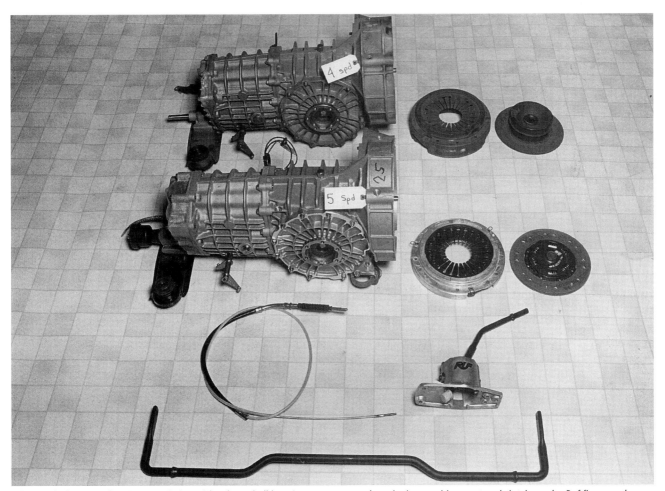

A late-style four-speed 930 transmission with a large bell housing to accommodate the large rubber-centered clutch, and a Ruf five-speed transmission. The Ruf five-speed has all different castings from those used by the Porsche four-speed. The differential housing is a special casting with a shorter bell housing like that of the 935. The center section is a special casting that provides support for the reverse gear. Exclusive Motorcars, Inc.

three things: (1) absolute top speed of the car, (2) highest speed the car will be driven (such as a long straightaway), and (3) an economical cruising gear for the highway.

If you were gearing your 911 for top speed you would need to know, or extrapolate from other data, what the car's top speed would be. If you were going to gear the car for the highest speed that it will reach, this will be dictated by the length of the longest section on the race track. You would either know the maximum speed reached on a straight section of a race track from experience or you could calculate it.

The maximum speed and maximum engine rpm desired at that speed are then entered into the following equation (or a gear chart) to calculate the fifth gear ratio:

$$T.R. = \frac{(RPM)\ (TIRE\ DIA)\ (o.002975)}{(MPH)\ (D.R.)}$$

Where:
  T.R = transmission ratio
  RPM = engine speed
  Tire Dia. = rear tire diameter
  MPH = desired speed in mph
  D.R. = the final drive ratio-ring and pinion

Next divide the range between first gear and fifth gear into even increments. For this example let's say that first is a ratio of 11:35, or 3.18, and fifth is 28:23, or 0.82. To divide this into even steps, a step-up ratio is calculated as follows:

$$STEP\text{-}UP\ RATIO = \sqrt{\frac{(1st\ RATIO)}{(5th\ RATIO)}}$$

$$= \sqrt{\frac{(3.18)}{(0.82)}}$$

STEP-UP RATIO = 1.4 (for this example)

Where n = number of intervals between gears; i.e., one less than the number of gears. (eg. n = 4 for a five speed).

In this case the step-up ratio calculates out to 1.4.

This step-up ratio is the ratio between gear ratios. If fifth gear is 0.82, then fourth gear ratio is 0.82 times 1.4, or 1.15, which is approximately a 24:28 gear set. Third then is 1.15 times the step-up ratio or 1.15 times 1.4, which equals 1.60, approximately a 20.32 gear set. Second would be 1.60 times the step-up ratio of 1.4 or 2.25; which is approximately a 14:31 gear set.

You can see by looking at the ratio that we selected on the gear chart that in each gear the car will run in the same rpm band, from about 5,700 to 8,000 rpm. Though this may sound reasonable, you probably won't find many 911s geared like this. Let's analyze why.

Ruf accommodated the fifth forward gear inside of the front cover with the reverse gear, much like the original 901 transmission.
Exclusive Motorcars, Inc.

A Porsche four-speed with only reverse out in the front cover.
Exclusive Motorcars, Inc.

A Porsche center section (left) and an Ruf center section (right). Exclusive Motorcars, Inc.

A Porsche end cover (left) and Ruf's end cover (right). Exclusive Motorcars, Inc.

Consider the speeds at which you would be shifting with shifts required at 8,000 rpm. The first to second shift would be at 49 mph, the second to third shift would be at 69 mph, the third to fourth would be at 96, and fourth to fifth at 132 mph. As the speed goes up, the range of speed in which each gear is used would increase. Shifting is frantic in the lower gears, but finally the car is expected to pull all the way from 132 to 180 mph. So this system I have just described that uses even, geometric steps to select your gear ratios is not necessarily the best selection process.

Generally, the best way to select gears is with a method that is quite simple. Divide the speed range between maximum rpm in first and fifth by the number of intervals between gears, four in this example of a five speed, for a constant speed range in each gear. Each gear is used for approximately a 35-mph range and each upshift starts the next higher gear a successively higher rpm. Usually this is best because "long pulls," from 4,700 rpm to 8,000 rpm in second gear for example, are at low speeds where the time involved is very short. This allows the "short pulls," from 6,500 rpm to 8,000 rpm in fifth for example, to occur at high speed where the time in gear is much longer because of aerodynamic drag. In other words, the time lost at lower speeds is more than made up at the higher speeds. This is a fairly standard method of gear selection for street cars from 356s through 959s, including most racing applications.

The gear selection process just discussed is great for straight-line acceleration from standing start to the 911's top speed. If we are gearing our 911 for a race track or autocross, which has corners that must be taken at awkward

A 915 transmission adapted for use in the 911 Turbo. Extra oiling was added in an effort to extend the life of the 915 transmission. Oil is sprayed at the point where each gear set meshes. Tom Hanna

speeds, our gear selection process will require some modification. Intermediate gear must be juggled up or down, if possible, to allow the car to exit corners at as high an rpm as possible while minimizing the number of shifts required per lap. This juggling is done based on past experience at a particular track, or a very good course diagram which allows cornering speeds to be calculated.

If you are an autocrosser and the courses on which you compete are similar, you will want to try to gear your transmission to minimize shifting—a great deal of time is wasted by shifting. Take advantage of your engine's strong

A 915 transmission adapted for use in a 911 Turbo. A special reinforced side cover has been made for the transmission. One of the late-model 915 oil pumps has been incorporated in the reinforced side cover to recirculate the transmission lubricant. Tom Hanna

A Tilton self-priming transmission cooler pump and integral cooling fan—which weighs just 3.5 lb and may be mounted remotely from the transmission—can be used for other things. Temperature 265 deg F (130 deg C) constant and 300 deg F (149 deg C) intermittent. Tilton

For a race car mechanic, one of life's pleasures is choosing all the gears for a new race track and having the driver come back in after the first practice and say, "the gears are just right!" Doesn't happen too often.

Gear chart equations

The gear charts are all based on the equation

MPH = ((RPM) x (tire diameter) x 0.002975) ÷ ((T.R.)x(D.R.))
Where:
RPM is engine speed
Tire diameter is in inches
D.R. is differential ratio
T.R. is transmission ratio

The tire diameter is best determined with a tire on the car at the rated pressure. Measure the distance in inches that the car moves for a few revolutions of the tire and then calculate the diameter from:

$$\text{Diameter in inches} = \frac{\text{Distance}}{(\pi)(\text{revolutions})}$$

The tire diameter increases with speed because of centrifugal force, until at about 180 mph the diameter has increased roughly 3 percent (for a bias ply race tire).

Differential ratio and transmission ratio are always calculated as driven gear divided by driving gear. For example, a 7:31 ring and pinion has a ratio of 31 (number of teeth on the driven gear) divided by 7 (number of teeth on the driving gear) or 4.428. When a gear set is given on a chart, or parts book, the first number is always the driving gear and the second is always the driven gear. So, just divide the second gear by the first and you have the correct ratio.

In order to calculate a speed for a different differential ratio than is shown on the chart use the following:

$$\text{MPH for new ratio} =$$
$$\text{MPH for old ratio} \times \frac{\text{old ratio}}{\text{new ratio}}$$

To calculate speed for a different tire diameter use the following:

$$\text{MPH for new tire diameter} =$$
$$\text{MPH for old tire diameter} \times \frac{\text{old tire diameter}}{\text{new tire diameter}}$$

characteristics. If it pulls well at low rpms, choose a gear that will take advantage of that. If it pulls well at higher rpms, choose a gear that will take advantage of that.

The most important corner on a track to consider when selecting gears is the one leading onto the longest straight. The correct gearing on this corner is vital to minimizing lap times. The gear for this corner should allow exiting the corner at a high rpm, but one which still allows the car to be well away from the corner before the next shift is required. At a given speed, acceleration out of a corner is increased by running the engine nearer its maximum horsepower, as opposed to running it at its maximum torque rpm. A compromise must be made so that an upshift is not required too close to the corner exit or to require too much shifting.

A bilge pump mounted in a special track car for recirculating transmission lubricant to the oil cooler and back to the transmission. When making such a modification, be sure that large lines are used so that the lines do not restrict the flow.

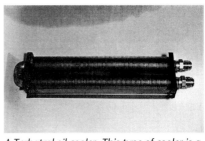

A Terbatrol oil cooler. This type of cooler is a good idea for cooling a transmission. Lemke Design

The RS 3.6 version of the G-50 transmission. Porsche AG

The G-50 transmission, an all-new transmission used in the 1987 911 Carrera. This new transmission extends so far forward that it necessitated a new torsion-bar carrier and motor mount.

A Porsche short shifter. This short shifter was part of the 911SC RS Type 954, part number 954.424.010.00. Porsche AG

The GT2 six-speed racing transmission with an external oil cooler. Porsche AG

A Porsche PDK transmission. The PDK transmission uses two separate clutches. The driver does not have to use the clutch to shift. The power flows from one clutch to the other, and the actual gear change occurs with this clutch change. Two gears are engaged at one time, and the engine output is transferred from one gear to the other with the two clutches. The shift itself resembles a motorcycle shift. Pushing the gear lever forward shifts down, and pulling the lever back shifts up. Porsche AG

A Tiptronic shifter. Porsche AG

A Ruf six-speed transmission.

A Tiptronic S shifter with toggles on the steering wheel and gear selection indicator in the speedometer. Porsche AG

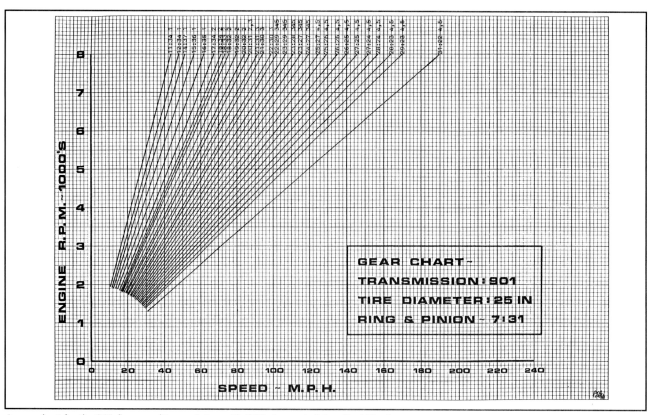

A gear chart for the 901 five-speed transmission with 7:31 ring and pinion. Paul Bingham

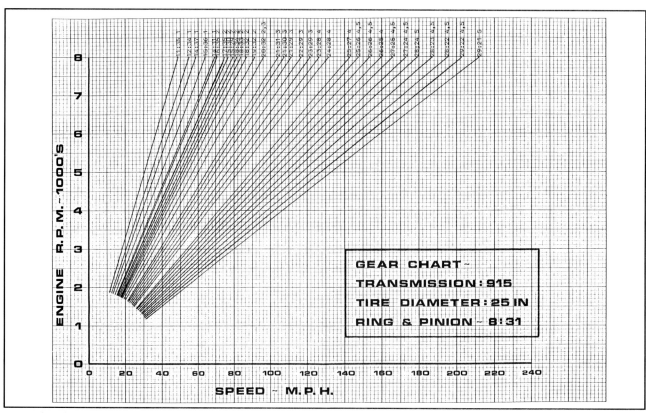

A gear chart for the 915 five-speed transmission with 8:31 ring and pinion. Paul Bingham

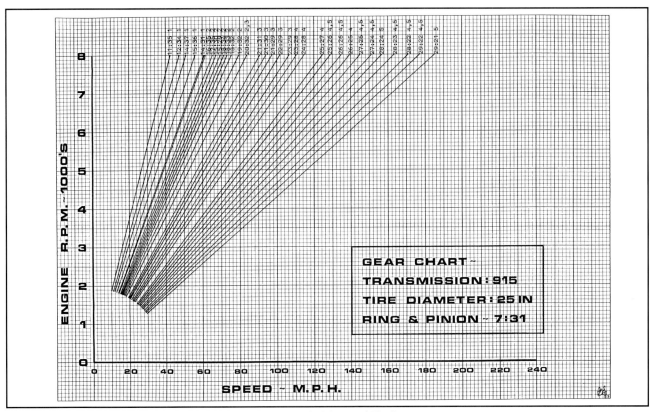

A gear chart for the 915 five-speed transmission with 7:31 ring and pinion. Paul Bingham

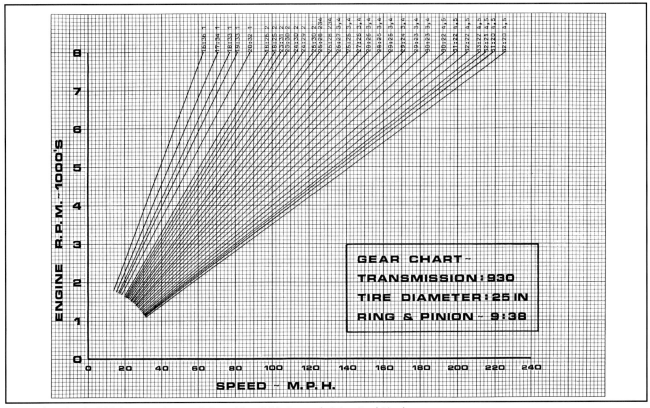

A gear chart for the 930 four-speed transmission with a 9:38 ring and pinion. Paul Bingham

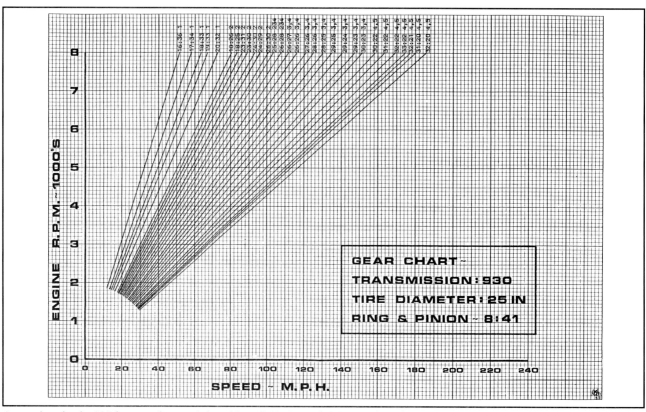

A gear chart for the 930 four-speed transmission with an 8:41 ring and pinion. Paul Bingham

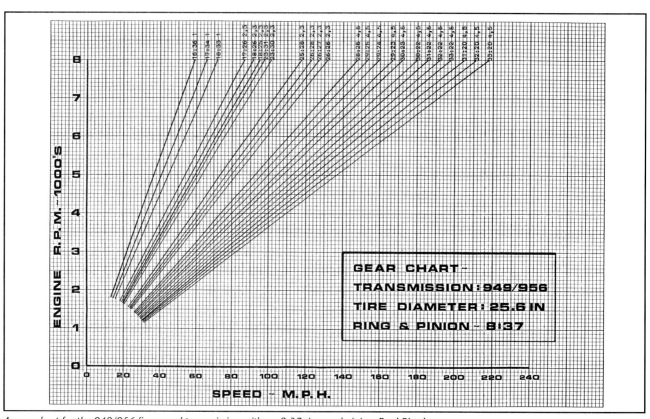

A gear chart for the 949/956 five-speed transmission with an 8:37 ring and pinion. Paul Bingham

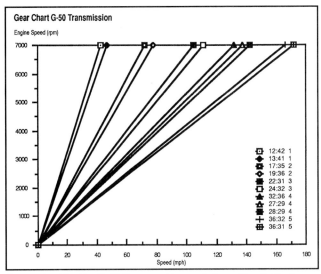

A gear chart for the G-50 five-speed transmission with a 9:31 ring and pinion.

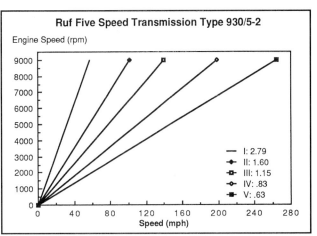

A gear chart for the Ruf five-speed transmission with a 9:36 ring and pinion. The advantage of the Ruf five-speed over the Porsche four-speed is that low gear is lower for faster acceleration and the remaining four gears have closer ratios, allowing the engine to remain on the boost. The 930 gears are interchangeable for gears two through five.

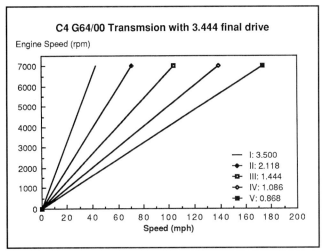

A gear chart for the C4 G-64/50.

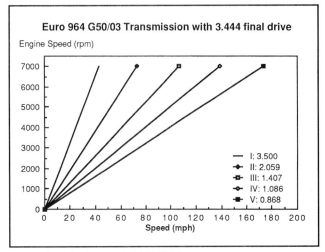

A gear chart for the Euro 964 G-50/03.

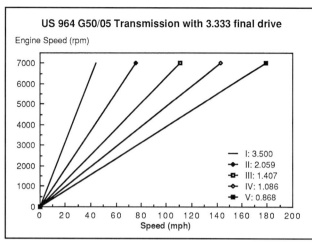

A gear chart for the U.S. 964 G-50/05.

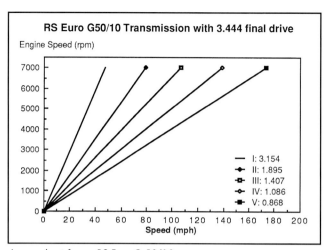

A gear chart for an RS Euro G-50/10.

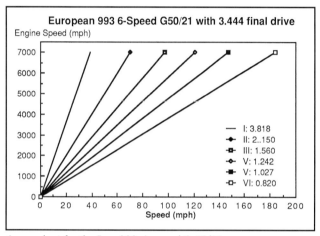

A gear chart for the Euro 993 six-speed G-50/21.

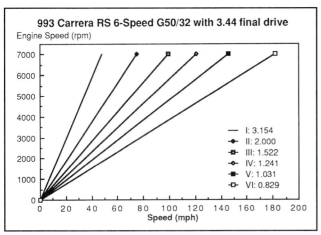

A gear chart for the RS G-50/32.

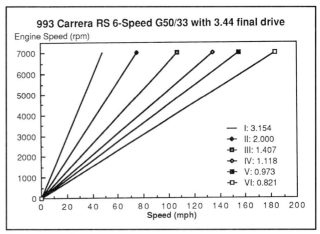

A gear chart for the RS G-50/33.

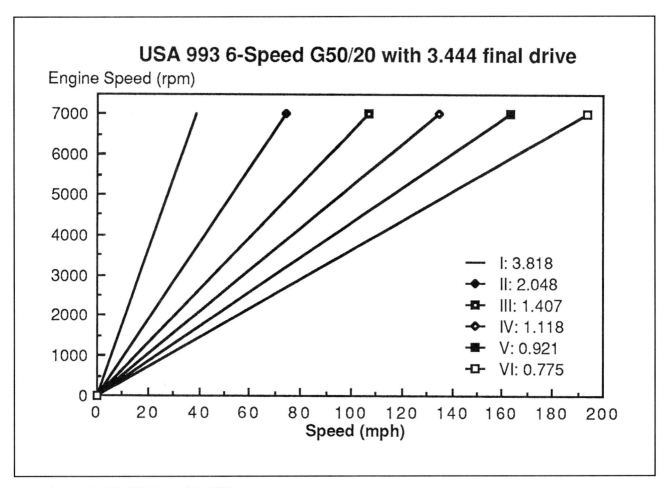

A gear chart for the U.S. 993 six-speed G-50/20.

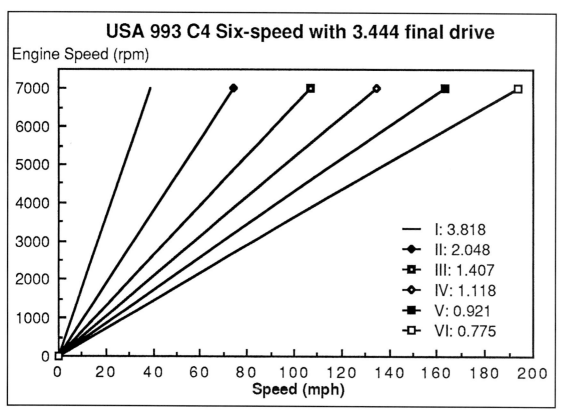

A gear chart for the U.S. 993 C4.

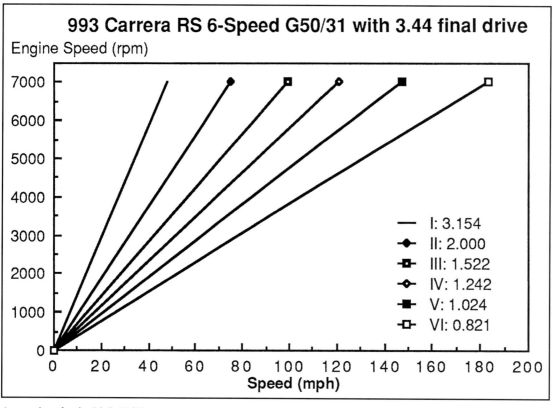

A gear chart for the RS G-50/31.

Chapter 8

Custom Treatment Photo Gallery

The 911 has always been a popular car to modify. When the 911 R was introduced in 1967 it had fender flares in the rear to fit what were then very large, 7-inch rear wheels (it had 6-inch wheels in the front). It was not long before owners started flaring their rear fenders to fit larger wheels and tires. This was a pretty small styling statement, but it marked the beginning of a custom craze that is still going on 30 years later.

The pace quickened when in 1970 Porsche offered the mechanicals to convert the Grand Touring 911 into a street racer. Usually the styling changes followed something that Porsche had done to make the 911s more competitive on the track, but not always. In the late 1960s, a fellow named Stan Townes cut the top off of a 911 coupe and made a Speedster. Others have followed suit, including Peter Schutz, president of Porsche from 1981 to 1987, who had a Speedster made at Werks I in 1985, rumored then to be the prototype of a future production 911 Speedster.

For the most part custom 911s have emulated Porsche's racing cars of one form or another. Back in 1979, Kremer's and Design Plastic were the first to capitalize on what became the slope-nose fad when they offered their 935 Street Turbo. In 1981, Porsche introduced a slope-nose (or slant-nose) version of its own as part of its *Sonderwunsch programm* (Special Wishes Program). Now it seems every population center in the world has someone doing slope-nose conversion work.

The photos that follow offer just a small sampling of the possibilities that exist for customizing and personalizing your 911. After all, who wants to drive a 911 just like everybody else's?

Stan Townes built this 1967 Porsche Speedster, shown at the 1971 Oakland Roadster Show, in the late 1960s from a wrecked 911 coupe. The fenders were flared to fit the larger American mag wheels and tires. Photo courtesy of the *Nugget*, PCA GGR's newsletter

It's a Coupe, it's a Cabriolet, and it's a Speedster. Richard and Lori Riley

The Speedster as a coupe. Only the black seam of the gasket between the top and the red paint is visible. The Porsche hardtop is right from the Special Wishes program catalog from Werk I. Richard and Lori Riley

Peter Schutz, former president of Porsche, took advantage of the flexibility and skills of Porsche's Werk I to try out some of his pet ideas for the 911. Working with Rolf Sprenger at Werk I, they converted one of the 911s into a coupe with the aid of a hardtop from the Sounderwunschprogramm ("Special Wishes program") and then, with a little magic, into a "Speedster." The project was a great success; the transformation was started June 1985 with a U.S.-legal Cabriolet chassis, including DOT, EPA, and June 1985 ID plate in the driver's door. The conversion took 650 hours and was finished June 30, 1986. Peter Schutz drove his Speedster to work in the fall of 1986, putting 4,226 miles on it. The Speedster was purchased by Bob Snodgrass of Brumos Porsche and imported to Jacksonville, Florida, in December 1986. Richard and Lori Riley

The windshield removes much like the one on the original Porsche Speedster. Richard and Lori Riley

The side-view mirrors and their fairings are built onto the wind-wing assembly so that when the wind-wing assembly is removed, the mirrors go with them. Richard and Lori Riley

In 1979, the Kremers, in collaboration with Design Plastics (DP), introduced the slope-nose look for street cars. Their slope-nose was a copy of the simplest of the slope-nosed 935s. Porsche Kremer Racing

This is a special car that was built for Mansour Ojjeh, the owner of TAG, with special air-dam running boards, 935 rear fenders, and a 935 rear wing. Mansour Ojjeh's car also has a roll bar and a special high-output engine. Porsche AG

Left
The Kremer slope-nose conversions were done in fiberglass, and the fiberglass components were made by DP. The quality of the fiberglass work is impeccable. Jerry Woods

Porsche introduced its own slope-nose in the fall of 1981 as part of its new Special Wishes program. Porsche's slope-nose was done in metal; only the air dam was made of fiberglass. Most of the conversions in the 1960s to the big-fender look had been done in fiberglass. There were conversion kits for any wide-fendered version of a Porsche imaginable, available from AIR, Hoesman, and Mitcom. But now that the slope-nose look was in, the trend was toward having the conversions done all in metal, and only the originators in Europe still do the conversions in fiberglass. Porsche's original slope-nose cars were pretty simple, with their cutoff fenders, running boards, and the air dam/bumper. The air dam/bumpers had the headlights mounted in them and there was nothing in the fenders. Porsche AG

The Special Wishes program at Werk I was expanded, and more options were available. The options included the slope-nose kit, the running boards, and the rear brake vents. Porsche AG

John Paul Racing also made a slope-nose conversion for sale using fiberglass bodywork styled like the Kremer K3 bodywork. Leonard Turner, Porsche Panorama

The Special Wishes program at Werk I offered the slope-nose with built-in headlights. This car also has the running boards and the rear brake vents. Porsche AG

Special Wishes don't just end with what can be done at Werk I; there are tuners and custom body builders in Europe and in the U.S. that will convert your 911 or 911 Turbo into almost anything that you can imagine. This is the Kremer line-up. The car in the center is a very special wish; it is a Kremer K3 935 that has been converted for the street. Porsche Kremer Racing

A DP Motorsport 935 II Cabriolet U.S. version. Ekkehard Zimmerman has built all of the bodywork for the Kremer racing cars. In 1979 they collaborated to make a road-going 935 based on the 911 Turbo. Originally, the cars were sold only as Kremer Street 935s with DP bodywork. They now both offer their own versions of the slope-nose 911 Turbo. DP

The Special Wishes program at Werk I offered the slope-nose treatment with louvers. Porsche AG

Walter Wolf's Porsche Kremer K3 street car, the ultimate weapon. Porsche Kremer Racing

A Strosek Auto Design Program 911 Turbo coupe. Strosek Auto Design GmbH offers these body conversions for the Turbo and Carrera. Strosek Auto Design

A Strosek Auto Design Cabriolet. Strosek Auto Design

Two interesting cars by Sport Performance in California. In the foreground is the owner's 935-bodied 911 Turbo, and in the background is a slope-nose 911SC without Turbo look. Van Tune, provided by Sport Performance

A slope-nose Cabriolet by Sport Performance. Bill F. Martin

A Ruf 911 Turbo slope-nose with running boards, rear brake vents, and 17-inch wheels. Exclusive Motorcars, Inc.

A 935 dashboard in a 1976 factory team car. Porsche AG

A rear brake vent made of metal.

A custom dashboard in a Sport Performance 911 Turbo Cabriolet. Note the center console and the LED-enunciated boost gauge.

A slope-nose fender in bare metal ready for primer.

Bob Akin's "The Last 935" dashboard.

In addition to being able to purchase special gauges, you can have your gauges modified, refinished, and restored by any number of people in the Porsche custom business. These gauges were done by North Hollywood Speedometer. North Hollywood Speedometer

An LED boost gauge.

A 934/935 boost gauge. This style of boost gauge is the most accurate. When the LED boost gauges were standard equipment in the 935s, all of the teams that raced them added one of these more-accurate boost gauges.

These Davtron Digital charge air temperature gauges can be hooked up with a switch and two senders, so you can monitor the charge air temperature before and after the intercooler to see how effective your intercooler is.

Performance Air makes this AC vent that doubles the size of the underdash vent and more than doubles the cooling capacity.

A lasting fad in the United States has been tinted windows—not just stock tinted windows, but dark tinted windows. This is a brand-new 1987 911 Turbo Targa in the process of having its windows tinted. Removing the rear window from a Targa is a major chore, but it must be done to ensure a quality job applying the tint film. With its complex curves, the Targa window is one of the more difficult windows to have tinted. To ensure that the film conforms to the complex shape of the Targa rear window, it is cut into eight narrow strips. The rear window is marked with masking tape to guide the cutting of these strips. The window is wetted, and the narrow strips are laid on and burnished to the glass one at a time. Each strip is then overlapped by the next strip. After a few strips of film are laid down and burnished, the overlap is cut along the edge of one of the window-heater wires with a surgeon's scalpel. The cuts are made along the edge of the heater wires so that the seams will not be visible. After the film is cut along the heater wires, the overlapping strips are removed and the film is reburnished.

In 1986, Porsche built the 961, which was to have been a Group B car based on the 959. The 961 did use the complete monocoque because the rules required it.

Bob Akin had Dave Klym build what they called "The Last 935" for the IMSA GTX rules. The rules required that it use steel tubing instead of aluminum tubing, but they were allowed to completely discard the monocoque chassis and make a tube-frame car. Dave Klym, FABCAR Engineering

The resulting car is a TopTime of Day club car. Moto Foto

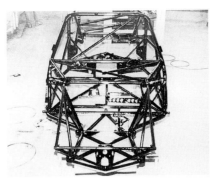

A steel-tube-framed 935. Dave Klym, FABCAR Engineering

The original body for "The Last 935" was made from aluminum. It was then used as a mold for the Kevlar and carbon-fiber body. Dave Klym, FABCAR Engineering

The local club rules require that cars be built from the original monocoque chassis. What you see is a monocoque chassis with a steel roll cage attached. John Hammill

A C4 Lightweight built by Jürgen Barth's Customer Racing Group.

A 1992 lightweight Turbo. These cars were built to celebrate victory in the IMSA Supercar series. They were built as a series by Rolf Sprenger's Customer Service group. Porsche AG

A custom 1989 Speedster, made to look like a 934 Speedster with an IMSA 962 600-hp engine.

A C2 Turbo 3.6 S2 slope-nose. A series of these cars was built by Rolf Sprenger's Customer Service group. Porsche AG

A Strosek Auto Design Program Speedster. Strosek Auto Design

A rear view of the Strosek Auto Design Program Speedster. Strosek Auto Design

A Strosek Auto Design Program Targa. Strosek Auto Design

Detail of a Techart CT3 supercharged car. Techart

Rear-end detail of a Techart CT3 supercharged car. Techart

Tom Hessert's FABCAR mid-engined GTS-2 car.

Kevin Jeannette's latest creation, the "G-93," a mid-engined 911, with a 962 engine, transmission, and suspension. This is a full unibody car that was built to fit the rules that were in effect in 1994; by the time the car was completed, it was deemed no longer eligible by IMSA. Gunnar Racing

Kevin Jeannette's "G-93." The engine will come out without removing the intercooler, and the intercooler will come out without removing the engine. There is enough room in there that he could change the rods with the engine in the car. The cam towers and the heads will come right off with the engine in the car. There is even room to time the cams. The whole rear end comes out in one piece; the wheels, gearbox, and motor all drop right out of the car. The rear suspension is from the 962, too, but the lower control arms had to be changed because of the geometry of moving everything forward. The suspension pickup points had to be in a different location because of the changed location in the car. But the suspension rockers and all of that are right from the 962, and all of the roll centers are standard off of the late-model 962. The front suspension is a strut with 962 front hubs. Gunnar Racing

The FABCAR mid-engined GTS-2 car front end, showing the fuel cell and front suspension. Bruce Anderson

Right
A view from the rear of the FABCAR mid-engined GTS-2 car engine.
Bruce Anderson

Frank & Partner's modified 993 Turbo. Frank & Partner

A rear quarter-view of Frank & Partner's modified 993 Turbo. Frank & Partner

ProtoTech, working with Protomotive Engineering in California, has spent a great deal of effort in improving the efficiencies of all the various systems on the turbocharged engines. ProtoTech also has the capability to do custom bodywork, upholstery, and sound systems.

ANDIAL installed a fully water-cooled 962 engine in the back of a C4.

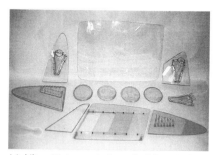

Mukilteo Motorsports has all of the windows and headlight covers for everything 911 in lightweight, tough plastic (shown here). Mukilteo claims that its lenses have never been cracked while in use in an endurance race. Mukilteo Motorsports also makes windshields.

Mukilteo Motorsports headlight lenses.

A Mukilteo Motorsports rear quarter window.

911 Options

The following is a table of optional equipment numbers used by the 911. Since 1982, Porsche has included these numbers on the vehicle identification labels. Some M numbers are considered standard in the country that they are built for, so they are not shown as optional equipment in the vehicle records or identification labels. Some numbers have been used to represent more than one option depending on model and year; in some instances several options are grouped together and sold as a package. For instance, here in the United States such things as air bags, sun roof, impact bumpers, tinted windows, seats with electric height adjustment, central locking, alarm system, and hi-fi sound systems were all standard equipment on some of our 911s.

Option #	Description	World	USA	Not USA
M 9	Three-speed Sportomatic transmission	✓		
M 18	Sport steering wheel with elevated hub	✓		
M 20	Speedometer with two scales, KPH/MPH	✓		
M 24	Version for Greece			✓
M 26	Activated charcoal canister		✓	
M 27	Version for California		✓	
M 34	Version for Italy			✓
M 58	Bumpers with impact absorbers		✓	
M 61	Version for Great Britain			✓
M 62	Version for Sweden			✓
M 70	Tonneau cover, Cabriolet	✓		
M 97	Anniversary Model 1989			✓
M 98	Anniversary Model 1989		✓	
M 99	Anniversary Model 1989	✓		
M 103	Adjustment of shock absorber strut	✓		
M 111	Version for Austria			✓
M 113	Version for Canada			✓
M 119	Version for Spain			✓
M 124	Version for France			✓
M 126	Digital Radio 1982	✓		
M 126	Stickers in French			✓
M 127	Stickers in Swedish			✓
M 130	Labeling in English	✓		
M 139	Seat self-heating, left	✓		
M 148	Modified engine 930/66			✓
M 151	Engine with differing parts			✓
M 152	Engine noise reduction			✓
M 154	Control unit for improved emissions		✓	
M 155	Motronic control unit for cars with catalytic converter	✓		
M 156	Quieter muffler			✓
M 157	Oxygen sensor and catalyst		✓	
M 158	Radio "Monterey" 1986, "Reno" 1987		✓	
M 160	Radio "Charleston"		✓	

Option #	Description	World	USA	Not USA
M 167	Tires made by Bridgestone	✓		
M 176	Oil cooler with fan		✓	
M 185	Automatic two-point rear seat belts	✓		
M 186	Manual two-point rear seat belts			✓
M 187	Asymmetric headlamps			✓
M 190	Increased side door strength		✓	
M 193	Version for Japan			✓
M 195	Prepared for cellular-telephone system			✓
M 197	Higher amperage battery	✓		
M 215	Version for Saudi Arabia			✓
M 218	License brackets, front and rear		✓	
M 220	Locking differential	✓		
M 221	Porsche-locking differential	✓		
M 240	Version for countries with inferior fuel			✓
M 241	Shorter shifting travel	✓		
M 241	Tires (Bridgestone, Continental, Dunlop, or Michelin) 1994 911			
M 243	Shorter gearshift lever	✓		
M 261	Passenger side mirror; electric, plain	✓		
M 277	Version for Switzerland			✓
M 286	High-intensity windshield washer	✓		
M 288	Headlight washer	✓		
M 298	Prepared for unleaded fuel, manual transmission			✓
M 323	Sticker: without ECE-Regulations		✓	
M 325	Version for South Africa			✓
M 326	Radio, Blaupunkt, Berlin IQR 87 with ARI			✓
M 327	Radio, Blaupunkt, Koln SQR 22 with ARI			✓
M 328	Radio, Blaupunkt, Bremen SQR 46 with ARI, −1990			✓
M 329	Radio, Blaupunkt, Toronto SQR 32			✓
M 330	Radio, Blaupunkt, Toronto SQR 46			✓
M 335	Automatic three-point rear seat belts	✓		
M 340	Seat heating, right	✓		
M 341	Central locking system	✓		
M 347	Platinum anodized wheels	✓		
M 348	Forged wheels, grand prix white	✓		
M 375	Clutch lining without asbestos	✓		
M 377	Combination seat, left adjustable	✓		
M 378	Combination seat, right adjustable	✓		
M 379	Series seat, left electric vertical adjustable	✓		
M 380	Series seat, right electric vertical adjustable	✓		
M 381	Series seat, left manual	✓		
M 382	Series seat, right manual	✓		
M 383	Sport seat, left electric vertical adjustable	✓		
M 384	Bucket seat, left			✓
M 385	Bucket seat, right			✓
M 387	Sport seat, right electric vertical adjustable	✓		
M 389	Porsche CR stereo/manual antenna	✓		

Option #	Description	World	USA	Not USA
M 391	Stone guard foil, added separately	✓		
M 392	Interior Tartan cloth	✓		
M 395	Light metal wheels, forged	✓		
M 397	Forged wheel, black, 7J x 16, rear, Turbo	✓		
M 399	A/C without front condenser	✓		
M 400	Light metal wheel, 6Jx15, 1973–1976	✓		
M 401	Light metal wheels	✓		
M 402	Stabilizer bars & Koni shocks, 1973–1976	✓		
M 402	Cast wheel "Cup" design, 16 inch	✓		
M 403	50 year anniversary car, 1982	✓		
M 403	Cast wheel "Cup" design, 17 inch	✓		
M 405	Level control system	✓		
M 407	Rear seats, with static seat belts			✓
M 409	Sport seats, left and right leather	✓		
M 410	Seats, left and right leatherette/cloth	✓		
M 411	License bracket, front			✓
M 418	Automatic seat belts			
M 419	Rear luggage compartment instead of rear seats			✓
M 424	Automatic heating control	✓		
M 425	Rear wiper	✓		
M 436	Targa folding top	✓		
M 437	Comfort seat, left	✓		
M 438	Comfort seat, right	✓		
M 439	Electric Cabriolet top	✓		
M 439	Special model "Weissach," 1980		✓	
M 439	Special model, 1980		✓	
M 441	Radio speakers and antenna amplifier	✓		
M 443	Tinted front and side glass, heated windshield			✓
M 444	Cabriolet	✓		
M 446	Parts for type "Targa" belonging to stipulated assembly	✓		
M 451	Prepared for radio for sport group, two speakers in door			
M 454	Automatic Speed Control	✓		
M 455	Wheel locks	✓		
M 462	Sekuriflex windshield	✓		
M 463	Clear windshield	✓		
M 464	Without compressor and tire pressure gauge		✓	
M 467	Driver's side mirror, convex			✓
M 468	Graduated tint windshield, green side glass	✓		
M 469	Black headliner	✓		
M 470	Without spoilers in conjunction with Turbo look	✓		
M 473	With spoilers	✓		
M 474	Sport shock absorbers	✓		
M 475	Brake pads without asbestos	✓		
M 476	Brake pad with abrasive pad	✓		
M 479	Version for Australia			✓
M 481	Manual transmission	✓		

Option #	Description	World	USA	Not USA
M 482	Engine compartment light	✓		
M 483	Right-hand drive			✓
M 484	Symbols for controls		✓	
M 484	Version for USA, 1989–		✓	
M 487	Connection for fog headlamp with parking light	✓		
M 488	Stickers in German			✓
M 489	Symbols and insignias in German			✓
M 490	Hi-fi sound system	✓		
M 491	Turbo look	✓		
M 492	H4 headlights for left-hand traffic			✓
M 494	Two speakers on back shelf	✓		
M 494	Amplifier system 1986–on	✓		
M 496	Black trim, painted headlight rims	✓		
M 496	Prepared for telephone, Philips "C-Network"			✓
M 498	Without rear model designation	✓		
M 499	Version for West Germany			✓
M 503	Cabrio-variant (Speedster)	✓		
M 504	RS America		✓	
M 505	Slant-nose	✓		
M 506	Slant-nose variant			✓
M 513	Lumbar support, right seat	✓		
M 525	Alarm with continuous sound			✓
M 526	Cloth door panels	✓		
M 528	Passenger side mirror, convex			✓
M 529	Outside mirror-passenger side, convex, manual	✓		
M 533	Alarm system	✓		
M 545	92-liter gas tank			✓
M 553	Version for USA		✓	
M 559	Air conditioner	✓		
M 562	Airbag driver and passenger side, 1990–on		✓	
M 565	Safety steering wheel, leather	✓		
M 566	Rectangular front fog lights	✓		
M 567	Windshield, green graduated tint	✓		
M 568	Tinted windshield and side glass	✓		
M 572	Heating	✓		
M 573	Air conditioner	✓		
M 577	Heated and tinted windshield	✓		
M 579	Version for Hong Kong			✓
M 580	Antidive-off feature (Immobilizer),1995–			
M 586	Lumbar support, left seat	✓		
M 590	Center console	✓		
M 592	Antilock brake system (Bosch-Teves)	✓		
M 592	Brake fluid warning system			✓
M 593	Antilock brake system (Bosch)	✓		
M 594	Antilock brake system (Wabaco)	✓		
M 602	Third brake light "High mount"		✓	
M 605	Vertical headlight adjustment			✓
M 612	Prepared for telephone, Phillips "C2-network"			✓

Option #	Description	World	USA	Not USA
M 630	Equipment for police			✓
M 637	Sport Group	✓		
M 650	Sunroof	✓		
M 651	Electric windows	✓		
M 652	Intermittent wiper	✓		
M 656	Manual steering	✓		
M 657	Power steering	✓		
M 659	On board computer, 1989 911C2/4	✓		
M 666	Without lacquer preservation and chrome preservation	✓		
M 673	Prepared for lead-sealed odometer	✓		
M 684	One piece rear seat	✓		
M 686	Radio, "Ludwigsburg" SQM, ARI			✓
M 688	Radio, Blaupunkt, Boston, SQM 26, ARI			✓
M 690	CD-Player "CD-10" Radio, ARI			✓
M 691	CD-Player "CD-01" with Radio –1988, "CD-2" with radio 1989–		✓	
M 692	CD changer, "Porsche CDC-1"	✓		
M 694	1996 911 Turbo			
M 701	Car-version, slant-nose	✓		
M 702	Tuned engine 930/66			✓
M 718	Next year VIN			
M 780	Remove safety certificate		✓	
M 900	Tourist delivery		✓	
M 912	Without vehicle identification plate		✓	
M 930	Seat cover, rear LLL	✓		
M 931	Seat cover, rear KKK	✓		
M 933	Seat cover, rear SKK	✓		
M 934	Seat cover, rear SSK	✓		
M 935	Seat cover, rear RLL	✓		
M 947	Seat cover front, cloth/leatherette/leatherette	✓		
	Seat cover rear, cloth/leatherette/leatherette	✓		
M 948	Seat cover, front SLL	✓		
M 970	Floor mats, front			✓
M 975	Velour carpet in luggage compartment	✓		
M 980	Seat cover, Raff-Leather	✓		
M 981	All-leather lining	✓		
M 986	Partial leather lining	✓		
M 975	Velour carpet in luggage compartment	✓		
M 981	All-leather lining	✓		
M 986	Partial leather lining	✓		

Preventive Maintenance

To ensure that your 911 is always in good operating condition it is essential that it is well maintained. My experience with 911s indicates that the 2.0, 2.2, and 2.4-liter cars should have routine maintenance performed every 6,000 miles, and all of the newer 911s should have routine maintenance performed every 10,000 miles. In addition to this routine preventive maintenance, it is always a good idea to keep an eye out for anything that may show up between the scheduled maintenance. Check the belts often and keep an eye out for fuel and oil leaks.

Recommended Preventive Maintenance Checklist

Engine oil and filter	____	Change
V-belts	____	Adjust or replace as necessary
Valve clearance	____	Check and adjust
Rocker shaft tightness	____	Check and correct
Spark plugs	____	Replace and compression test
Dwell and timing	____	Adjust with electronic equipment
Fuel filter	____	Replace
Engine idle speed and CO%	____	Check with machine and adjust
Brake pads	____	Visual check and % reading
Hand brake	____	Adjust if past 5 clicks
Exhaust system	____	Check for leaks or damage
Door hinges	____	Lubricate
Door latch	____	Lubstick
Accelerator linkage	____	Lubricate
Transmission oil	____	Check level every 10,000 miles
	____	Change every 30,000 miles
Ball joints and tie rod ends	____	Check
Front wheel bearing play	____	Check
Operation of lights, horn	____	Check
Operation of lights, wipers	____	Check
Headlight adjustment	____	Check
Battery level	____	Check and correct
Tires wear and condition	____	Check, correct pressure and note wear
Windshield washer operation	____	Check and correct
Filter element for air pump	____	Replace
Air pump, control valves	____	Check
Air injection hoses	____	Check
E.G.R., OXY counter	____	Reset
Evaporative control system	____	Check visually
Crankcase ventilation filter	____	Clean
Crankcase hoses	____	Check visually
Clutch free-play	____	Check and adjust

Road Test
Check braking, clutch, steering, heating, ventilation, cruise control, and air conditioning system (a/c should be recharged and serviced every two years). Check all instruments, controls, and warning lights.

Appendix 3

Tune-up Specifications

Model Year / Type	1968	1969 911T	1969 911E	1969 911S
Fuel system	Weber 40IDTP3C	Weber 40IDTP3C	Bosch mech. inj.	Bosch mech. inj.
Secondary air pump	Yes	No	No	No
Throttle compensat.	Yes	Yes	No	No
Ign. desrib. vacuum	Yes	Yes	No	No
Diverter valve	Yes	No	No	No
Spark plugs	W250C /W4DC	W225T30/W5D	W265C /W3DC	W265C /W3DC
Spark plug gap	0.35mm	0.6mm	0.55mm	0.55mm
Ignition distributor	Bosch	Marelli	Bosch	Bosch
Part number	0.231.159.001	S112AX	0.231.159.006	0.231.159.007
Dwell angle	38° ±3°	40° ±3°	38° ±3°	38° ±3°
Ignition timing	30° BTDC/6000	35° BTDC/6000	30° BTDC/6000	30° BTDC/6000
Idle RPM	900±50	900±50	900±50	900±50
CO%	4.5 sec pmp disc	3.5% +0.5 at idle	3.5% +0.5 at idle	3.5% +0.5 at idle
Exhaust system	Regular 3 into 1	Regular 3 into 1	Regular 3 into 1	Regular 3 into 1
Engine code No.	901/14 901/17	901/17 901/198	901/09 901/11	901/10

Model Year / Type	1970/71 911T	1970/71 911E	1970/71 911S	1972 911T
Fuel system	Zenith 40 TIN	Bosch mech. inj.	Bosch mech. inj.	Bosch mech. inj.
Secondary air pump	No	No	No	No
Throttle compensat.	No	No	No	No
Ign. desrib. vacuum	No	No	No	Yes
Diverter valve	No	No	No	No
Spark plugs	W225T30/W5DC	W265C /W4DC	W265C /W4DC	W265C /W4DC
Spark plug gap	0.6mm	0.55mm	0.55mm	0.6mm
Ignition distributor	Bosch	Bosch	Bosch	Bosch
Part number	0.231.159.008	0.231.159.006	0.231.159.007	0.231.169.003
Dwell angle	40° ±3°	38° ±3°	38° ±3°	38° ±3°
Ignition timing	35° BTDC/6000	30° BTDC/6000	30° BTDC/6000	5° ATDC idle
Idle RPM	900±50	900±50	900±50	900±50
CO%	3.5±.05 at idle	3.0±0.5 at idle	3.0±0.5 at idle	1.5-2.0 at idle
Exhaust system	Regular 3 into 1	Regular 3 into 1	Regular 3 into 1	Regular 3 into 1
Engine code No.	911/07 911/08	911/01 911/04	911/02	911/51 911/61

Model Year / Type	1972 911E	1972 911S	1973 911T	1973 911E
Fuel system	Bosch mech. inj.	Bosch mech. inj.	Bosch mech & CIS inj.	Bosch mech. inj.
Secondary air pump	No	No	No	No
Throttle compensator	No	No	Decel valve for CIS	No
Ign. distributor vacuum	Yes	Yes	Yes	Yes
Diverter valve	No	No	No	No
Spark plugs	W265C /W3DC	W265C /W3DC	W235P2/W5DC	W265C/W3DC
Spark plug gap	0.55mm	1.55mm	0.6mm	0.55mm
Ignition distributor	Bosch	Bosch	Bosch	
Part number	0.231.169.004	.0231.169.005		
Dwell angle	38° ±3°	38° ±3°	38° ±3°	38° ±3°
Ignition timing	5° ATDC	5° ATDC	5° ATDC	5° ATDC
Idle RPM	900±50	900±50	900±50	900±50
CO%	2.0-2.5 at idle	2.0-2.5 at idle	1.5-2.0 at idle	2.0-2.5 at idle
Exhaust system	Regular 3 into 1	Regular 3 into 1	Regular 3 into 1	Regular 3 into 1
Engine code No.	911/52 911/62	911/53	911/51/91/92	911/52/62

Model Year / Type	1973 911S	1974 911	1974 911S	1975 911
Fuel system	Bosch mech. inj.	Bosch CIS	Bosch CIS	Bosch CIS
Secondary air pump	No	Yes	Yes	Yes
Throttle compensator	No	Decel valve	Decel valve	Decel valve
Ign. distributor vacuum	Yes	Yes	Yes	Yes
Diverter valve	No	No	No	No
Spark plugs	W265C/W3DC	W215C/W6DC	W235C/W5DC	W235C/W5DC
Spark plug gap	0.55mm	0.55mm	0.55mm	0.55mm
Ignition distributor	Bosch	Bosch	Bosch	Bosch
Part number				
Dwell angle	38° ±3°	38° ±3°	38° ±3°	38° ±3°
Ignition timing	5° ATDC	5° ATDC	5° ATDC	5° ATDC
Idle RPM	900±50	900±50	900±50	900±50
CO%	2.5±0.5	1.5±0.5	1.5±0.5	1.5-2.0 sec air dis
Exhaust system	Regular 3 into 1	Regular 3 into 1	Regular 3 into 1	49 state reg/Cal therm reactors EGR
Engine code No.	911/53	911/92/97	911/93/97	49 state 911/43/48 Cal 911/44/49

Model Year / Type	1976 911	1977 911	1978/79 911SC	1980 911SC
Fuel system	CIS fuel injection	CIS fuel injection	CIS fuel injection	CIS fuel injection
Secondary air pump	Yes	Yes	Yes	No
Throttle compensator	Decel valve	Decel valve	Decel valve	No
Ign disributor vacuum	Yes	Yes	Yes	Yes
Diverter valve	No	No	No	No
Spark Plugs	W235C /W5DC	W235C/W5DC	W145T30/W8DC	W225T30/W5DC
Spark Plug Gap	0.55mm	0.55mm	0.8mm	0.8mm
Ignition Distributor	Bosch	Bosch	Bosch	Bosch
Part number			0.237.306.001	0.237.304.016
Dwell Angle	38°±3°	38°±3°	Pointless	Pointless
Ignition Timing	5° ATDC	49 state OT±2° Calif. 15°±2° ATDC	5°±2°BTDC	5°±2°BTDC
Idle RPM	900±50	49 state 950±50 Calif. 1000±50	900±50	900±50
CO%	2.0-3.5 sec. air disc	1.5-3.0 sec. air disc	2.5±1.0 sec. air disc	0.4-0.8 oxygen sensor disc
Exhaust system	49 state reg/Cal. therm. reactors EGR	EGR therm. reactors	CAT EGR	3-way Cat. Oxy. Sens.
Engine code No.	49 state 911/82/89	911/85/90	930/04 Cal 930/06	930/07

Model Year / Type	1981/82/83 911SC	1984/85 Carrera	1986/89 Carrera
Fuel system	CIS fuel inj.	L-Jetronic DME	L-Jetronic DME
Secondary air pump	No	No	No
Throttle compensator	No	Idle stabilizer	Idle stabilizer
Ign. disributor vacuum	Yes	No	No
Diverter valve	No	No	No
Spark plugs	225T30/W5DC	W7DC, WR7DC, WR7DC	WR7DC,WR7DC
Spark plug gap	0.8mm	0.7±0.1mm	0.7±0.1mm
Ignition distributor	Bosch	Bosch	Bosch
Part number	0.237.304.016	0.237.505.001	0.237.505.001
Dwell angle	Pointless	DME 0.261.200.050	DME
Ignition timing	5°±2° BTDC	3°±3° ATDC	3°±3° ATDC
Idle rpm	900±50	800±20	800±20
CO%	0.4-0.8 oxy. disc	0.8±0.2 oxy. disc	0.8±0.2 oxy. disc
Exhaust system	3 way Cat oxy. sens	3-way Cat oxy. sens	3 way Cat oxy. sens
Engine code No.	930/16	930/21	1986 930/21; 1987 930/25

Model Year / Type	1989-94 C2/4 964	1984-96 Carrera 993	
Fuel system	L-Jetronic DME	L-Jetronic DME	
Secondary air pump	No	Yes U.S. cars	
Throttle compensator	Idle stabilizer	Idle stabilizer	
Spark plugs	Bosch FR5DTC	Bosch FR6LDC/FR5DTC	
	Beru 14FR-5DTU	Beru 14FR5DTU	
Spark plug gap	0.7mm	0.7 mm	
Ignition distributor	DME double ignition	DME double ignition	
Idle rpm	880±40	800±40 manual; 750 ±40 tiptronic	
CO% at idle	0.4 without converter	0.8±0.2 oxy. disc	
Exhaust system	3-way cat with heated oxygen sensor	3-way cat with heated oxygen sensor	
Engine code No.	M64/01 manual trans.	M64/05/07manual trans.	
	M64/02 tiptronic trans.	M64/06/08 Tiptronic	

Model Year / Type	1976 911 Turbo	1977 911 Turbo	1978/79 911 Turbo
Fuel system	CIS fuel inj.	CIS fuel inj.	CIS fuel inj.
Secondary air pump	Yes	Yes	Yes
Throttle compensator	decel. valve	decel. valve	decel. valve
Ign. distributor vacuum	Yes	Yes	Yes
Diverter valve	Yes	Yes	Yes
Spark plugs	W3CS/W4CS*	W3CS/W4CS*	W3CS/W4CS*
Spark plug Gap	0.6 mm	0.6 mm	0.6 mm
Ignition distributor	Bosch	Bosch	Bosch
Dwell angle	Pointless	Pointless	Pointless
Ignition timing	5° ±2° ATDC	7° ±2° ATDC	10° ±2° ATDC; 5° ±2° ATDC, Calif.
Idle rpm	950±50	1000±50	1000±50
CO%	1.0-3.0 sec. air disc.	2.0-4.0 sec. air disc.	2.5±0.5 sec. air disc.
Exhaust system	Thermo reactors	Thermo reactors, EGR	Thermo reactors, EGR
Engine code No.	930/51	930/53	930/61/63

Model Year / Type	1981/82 911 Turbo	1983/84/85 Turbo	1986/89 911 Turbo
Fuel system	CIS fuel inj.	CIS fuel inj.	CIS fuel inj.
Secondary air pump	Yes	Yes	Yes
Throttle compensator	decel. valve	decel. valve	decel. valve
Ign. distributor vacuum	Yes	Yes	Yes
Diverter valve	Yes	Yes	Yes
Spark plugs	W3CS/W4CS*	W3CS/W4CS*	W3CS/W4CS*
Spark plug gap	0.7 mm	0.7 mm	0.7 mm
Ignition distributor	Bosch	Bosch	Bosch
Dwell angle	Pointless	Pointless	Pointless
Ignition timing	29° BTDC/4000	29° BTDC/4000	26°±1°BTDC at 4000; RPM vac. hosed disc.
Idle rpm	1000±50	900±50	900±50
CO%	2.5±0.5 sec air disc.	2.0±0.5 sec air disc.	0.4-0.8 measured before CAT, oxy., sen. discon.
Exhaust system	Regular	Regular	3-way CAT
Engine code No.	930/60	930/66	930/68

Model Year / Type	1991/92 C2 Turbo	1993 C2 3.6 Turbo	1996 993 Twin Turbo
Fuel system	CIS fuel inj.	CIS fuel inj.	DME engine management .
Secondary air pump	Yes	Yes	No
Ign distributor vacuum	Digital spark control (pressure controlled)	Digital spark control (pressure controlled)	DME dual plug kNock control
Spark plugs	W3CS/W4CS*	W3CS/W4CS*	FR6LDC/FR6LCS
Spark plug gap	0.7 mm	0.7 mm	0.7 mm
Ignition distributor	Bosch	Bosch	Bosch
Ignition timing	0 deg BTDC at idle	0 deg BTDC at idle	via DME
Idle rpm	900±50	900±50	900±50
CO%	1.0 ±0.2% measured before CAT oxy., sen. disconnected	1.0 ±0.2% measured. before CAT oxy, sen. disconnected	0.4-0.8 measured before CAT
Exhaust system	3-way CAT	3-way CAT	3-way CAT
Engine code No.	M30/69	M64/50	M64/60

* W4CS for stock cars and W3CS for cars running more boost or with some other engine modifications.

Units of Measure and Conversions

Metric Conversions

Length

Metric	U.S.
1 millimeter	0.039 inch
1 centimeter	0.393 inch
1 centimeter	0.032 feet
1 meter	39.370 inch
1 meter	3.280 feet
1 meter	1.093 yard
1 kilometer	0.621 mile
1 kph	0.621 mph

U.S.	Metric
1 inch	25.4 millimeter
1 foot	0.304 meter
1 mile	1.609 kilometers
1 mph	1.609 kph

Area

Metric	U.S.
1 square centimeter	0.155 square inch
1 square meter	10.763 square feet

U.S.	Metric
1 square inch	6.451 square centimeters
1 square foot	0.092 square meter

Volume

Metric	U.S.
1 cubic centimeter	0.061 cubic inch
1 cubic meter	35.314 cubic feet
1 cubic meter	1.307 cubic yard
1 liter	1.056 quarts
1 liter	33.8 fluid ounces
1 liter	0.264 gallons
1 liter	61.032 cubic inches

U.S.	Metric
1 cubic inch	16.387 cubic centimeters
1 cubic foot	0.028 cubic meter
1 quart	0.946 liter

Mass (weight)

Metric	U.S.
1 gram	0.035 ounce
1 kilogram	2.204 pounds
1 kilogram	35.273 ounces

U.S.	Metric
1 ounce	28.349 grams
1 pound	0.453 kilogram

Force

Metric	U.S.
1 Newton (N)	0.224 foot-pound (ft-lb)
1 kilogram/meter (kgm)	0.224 foot-pound (ft-lb)

Torque

Metric	U.S.
1 newtonmeter (Nm)	0.737 foot-pound (ft-lb)
1 newtonmeter (Nm)	8.850 inch-pound (in-lb)
1 kilogram meter	7.15 foot-pound (ft-lb)

U.S.	Metric
1 inch pound (in/lb)	0.113
1 foot pound (lb/ft)	1.356

Power

Metric	U.S.
1 watt (1 Nm/sec.)	0.001 horsepower
1 kilowatt (kW)	1.340 horsepower
1 PS (European hp)	0.986 hp

U.S.	Metric
1 horsepower	0.746 kilowatt

Pressure

1 newton per square meter (N/m^2)	1 pascal
1 pascal	0.00014 psi
1 kilopascal (kPa)	0.145 psi
1 bar	100,000 pascals
1 bar	14.5 pounds per square inch
1 atmosphere	14.7 pounds per square inch
1 atmosphere	29.921 inches of mercury

Temperature Conversions

Celsius to Fahrenheit	Fahrenheit to Celsius
• °C = (1 ÷ 1.8) x (°F-32)	• °F = 1.8 x °C+32
• 1°C= 1.8 or 9/5 ° F	• l°F= 5/9 of 1°C

Other Cases

Converting fractions to decimals
• Divide the numerator by the denominator
Example: 3/4 to a decimal 3 ÷ 4 = 0.75

Converting inches to millimeters
• Multiply by 25.4
Example: use the results from converting the fraction 3/4 to a decimal, which was 0.75. Multiply 0.75 x 25.4 = 19.050 mm. From this example you can see that 3/4 inch is almost exactly 19 mm, which means that you can use your 3/4-inch lug wrench on your Porsche 911's 19-mm wheel nuts.

Converting millimeters to inches
• Multiply by 0.0393701
Example: 19 x 0.039 = 0.748. From this example you can see that your 19 mm lug wrench would be a little tight on 3/4-inch lug bolts.

Compression Ratio
- Compression = (V1+V2+V3-V4) ÷ (V2+V3-V4)
  Where:
  - V1 = swept volume
  - V2 = deck height volume
  - V3 = cylinder head volume
  - V4 = piston dome volume

Swept Volume
- $(V1) = Bore^2$ x Stroke x 0.7854 *
  *Simplified formula

Engine Displacement
- Displacement = π x R^2 x S x N
  Where:
  - π = 3.141
  - R = radius of the bore in centimeters
  - S = stroke of the cylinder in centimeters
  - N = number of cylinders

or

- Displacement = $((\pi D^2) \div 4)$ x S x N = displacement
  Where:
  - D = diameter of bore in centimeters
  - π = 3.141
  - S = stroke of the cylinder in centimeters
  - N = number of cylinders

These same formulas will work for inches as well as centimeters, and the resulting answers can be converted from cubic inches to cubic centimeters by dividing cubic inches by 0.061 or from cubic centimeters to cubic inches by multiplying cubic centimeters by 0.061.

Piston speed
- Piston speed in feet per minute (FPM) =
  (RPM x S) ÷ 152.4
  Where: S = stroke in millimeters

Horsepower calculation
- Horsepower (HP) = (Torque (ft-lb)) x (RPM ÷ 5250)

- Metric horsepower (PS) = HP (U.S.) x 1.015

Horsepower is a unit of work, an effort to relate the work of an engine to the work of a horse. One horsepower is the amount of work a horse could do in one minute and is equal to 33,000 ft-lb of torque per minute. When related to an engine the torque is measured as a rotational force on a dynamometer with some form of absorption unit. With this torque figure and the engine rpm we can calculate horsepower using the above formula

Calculation for speed in mph
- MPH = (RPM x tire diameter x 0.002975) ÷ (T.R. x D.R.)
  Where:
  - RPM = engine speed
  - Tire diameter is in inches
  - D.R. = differential ratio
  - T.R. = transmission ratio

Tire diameter is best determined with a tire on the car at the rated pressure. Measure the distance in inches that the car moves for a few revolutions of the tire and then calculate the diameter from:

- Tire diameter = distance traveled ÷ (π x revolutions)

To calculate speed for a different tire diameter; use the following:

- MPH for new tire diameter = MPH for old tire diameter x (old tire dia. ÷ new tire dia.)

In order to calculate a speed for a different differential ratio use the following:

- MPH for new ratio = MPH for old ratio x (old ratio ÷ new ratio)

Appendix 5

Resources

The following recommendations are offered as an aid to finding parts and services for your 911 or 911 Turbo. The recommendations are for the most part either based on my own personal experience or the experiences of friends. When I make recommendations I realize that someone else may offer a similar service and/or parts, but the ones that I am recommending are the ones that I am familiar with, and you may get just as good or better service and/or parts from someone else.

Air Conditioning
Scott Hendry
Dianna Eaton
Performance Aire
1885 Santa Cruz St.
Anaheim, CA 92805
714-634-9184
FAX: 714-634-9251

Bodywork
New England Metal Crafters
Joe Stafford
508-388-2692
Makes Spyders

American Designers, Inc.
100W Morgan Bldg. 4 , Box 8
Knightstown, IN 46148
800-628-5442   FAX: 317-345-2258
Factory direct Porsche sheet metal 356 and 911 pans

Dan McLoughlin
American International Racing
11237 Vinedale
Sun Valley, CA 91352
818-504-2500
FAX: 818-504-9348

Blackburn-Daly LTD
33 N Dearborn Suite 730
Chicago, IL 60602
313-346-7661
Slope nose conversions

Bodystyle
408-295-0535
A quality Porsche body shop
Bruce Canepa Motorsports

Canepa Design
1191 Water Street
Santa Cruz, CA 95062
408-423-5704
FAX: 408-423-2239
Custom Porsches, restorations, and specialty components

GT Racing
Hank Godfredson
8854 Birchwood Lane
Bloomington, MN 55438
612-943-2911
FAX: 612-943-2781
Fiberglass body parts

Hoesman Fiberglas
3072 Rubidoux Blvd.
Suite J
Riverside, CA 92509
714-788-0970
Custom fiberglass body parts

Mitcom
12621 Sherman Way
North Hollywood, CA 91605
800-423-3224

Brakes and Brake Parts
White Post Restorations
White Post, VA 22663
703-837-1140
Recondition corroded calipers

The Racers Group
Kevin Buckler
29187 Arnold Dr.
Sanoma, CA 95476
707-935-3999 Phone
FAX: 707-935-5889
Brembo brake kits and Pagid pads

Tilton Engineering Inc.
McMurry Road & Easy Street
Buellton, CA 93427
805-688-2353
FAX: 805-688-2745
Clutch, brake, and suspension components

Pete Bartelli
53 Hillside Ave
Berkeley Heights NJ 07922
201-665-6889
Stainless steel brake pistons

Porterfield Enterprises
1767 Placentia
Costa Mesa, CA
714-548-4470.
Brake pads

Vehicle Craft Inc. VCI
Doug Arnao, Jim Foster.
288 Route 46
Dover, NJ 07801
800-845-5948
201-366-6577
FAX: 201-366-6344.
Brake kits and brake parts
Brembo
1579 Sunland Lane
Costa Mesa, CA 92626
714-641-5831

Cool Carbon
David Waits
PO Box 9240
Huntsville, AL 35812
205-882-1756
FAX: 205-882-9301
Brake pads
Mr. Steve Holroyd
Alcon Components Ltd.
Northside
Reddicap Trading Estate
Sutton Coldfield
West Midlands,
B75 7BU
England

JFZ Engineering
Simi Valley, CA
805-581-3674
Racing brake components

Jim Newton
Auto Associates
5 Albany Turnpike
PO Box 213
West Simsbury, CT 06092.
203-693-0278 or 203-651-8117
FAX: 203-693-6798.
Dual master-cylinder pedal assembly

Wilwood Engineering
4580 Calle Alto
Camarillo, CA 93010
805-388-1188
Racing brake components

Cams
Dema Elgin
Elgin Racing Cams
53 Perry Street
Redwood City, CA 94063
415-364-2187

Web-Cam
1815 Massachusetts Ave.
Riverside, CA 92507
909-369-5144
FAX: 909-369-7266
Performance camshafts

Carburetors and Fuel Injectors
Eurometrix
Norbert Eberhardt
PO box 1361
Campbell, CA 95009
408-296-1533
Rebuilds fuel injection throttle bodies
and carburetor throttle bodies

H &R Fuel Injection LTD.
1648C Locust Avenue
Bohemia, NY 11716
516-589-1600
Mechanical injection pump rebuilding

Gus Pfister
Pacific Fuel Injection
153 Utah Ave.
San Francisco, CA 94080
415-588-8880
FAX: 415-588-2031
Mechanical injection pump rebuilding
Motec Systems USA
5355 Industrial Drive
Huntington Beach, CA 92649
714-897-6804
FAX: 714-897-8782
Mobile Phone: 714-812-2974

PMO
Richard Par
135 17th Street
Santa Monica, Ca 90402
310-393-5423
FAX: 310-394-6313
Weber carburetors

KRT Electronics
Ken House
2432 Crestwood Dr.
Huntsville, AL 35805
205-430-3041
Motronics repair and custom chips

Automotion
3535 Kifer Road, Unit 5
Santa Clara, CA 95051
408-736-9020
FAX: 408-736-9013
Performance chips

AutoThority
3763 Pickett RD.
FairFAX, VA 22031
sales: 703-323-0919
service: 703-323-7830
FAX: 703-323-7325
Performance chip makers

Robert Bosch Corporation
2800 S. 25th Ave.
Broadview, IL 60153
708-865-5200 or 312-681-5000
Electric and fuel systems

ESI Technology, Inc.
Grahm Western
386 Beech Ave #4
Torrance, CA 90501
213-320-5238

The Carburetor Refactory
815 Harbor Way South #5
Richmond, CA 94804
415-237-1277
Carburetor remanufacturing

Clutch Parts and Cables
Sachs
909 Crocker Road
Westlake, OH 44145
216-871-4890
FAX: 216-871-6904
Original equipment clutches

Kennedy Engineered Products KEP
38830 17th Street East
Palmdale, CA 93550
805-272-1147
Adapter kits and clutches

Tilton Engineering Inc.
McMurry Road & Easy Street
Buellton, CA 93427
805-688-2353
FAX: 805-688-2745
Clutch components

Terry Cable
17376 Eucalyptus
Hesparia, CA 92345
919-244-9353

Cablecraft
PO Box 28164
Oakland, CA 94604
101-A Filbert St.
Oakland, CA 94607
415-444-3730
Custom-built cables

Connecting Rods
Carrillo Industries
33041 Calle Perfecto
San Juan Capistrano, CA 92675
714-493-1230

Crankshafts
Moldex Crankshaft Company
Mr. Bob Gillen
25249 W. Warren Ave.
Dearborn Heights, MI 48127
313-561-7676
Repair damaged crankshafts or make
all new billet crankshafts

Sammy Hale Crankshafts, Ltd.
20 D Pamaron Way
Novato, CA 94949
415-883-3141
Home: 415-883-8279

Elgin's Custom Crankshaft Repair
53 Perry Street
Redwood City, CA 94063
800-994-2726 or 415-364-1747

Cylinder Heads
Michael Stimson
Pacific Performance
51 Perry
Redwood City, CA 94063
415-361-8636

C. R. Axtell
10949 Tuxford Unit # 17
Sun Valley, CA 91352
818-768-5595

Extrude Hone
8800 Somerset Blvd.
Paramount, CA 90723
310-531-2976
FAX: 310-531-8403.

K & N Hi-Performance Air Filters
POBox 1329
Riverside, CA 92502
714-682-8813

Exhaust System
European Racing Headers
George Narbel
27601 Forbes Road, Suite 20
Laguna Niguel, CA 92677
714-582-1061
Racing headers

Pete Weber Performance Products
37350-A Cedar Blvd.
Newark, CA 94560
Phone/FAX: 510-794-7748
Phase 9 Silencers and complete exhaust systems

B & B Fabrication, Inc.
5642 N. 51st Avenue
Glendale, AZ 85301
602-842-1234
FAX: 602-842-2285

Monty Manufacturing
PO Box 375
Emerald, Victoria 3782
Australia
059-68 5532
FAX: 059-68 5432

SSI
John Daniels
24 Pamaron Way
Navato, Ca 94949
415-883-2000
800-227-1486
Stainles steel exhaust systems

Stahl Headers
1515 Mt. Rose Ave.
York, PA 17403
717-846-1632
Racing headers

Flowmaster Mufflers
2975 Dutton Ave., Unit 3
Santa Rosa, CA 95407
707-544-4761
FAX: 707-544-4784

Pressler Parts
Kurt Pressler
PO Box 644
Bethel Island, CA 94511
510-684-9437 or 510-684-3820
Maker of "bull horn sport muffler"

Flywheels
Pat Williams
177 Magnolia
Memphis, TN 38122
901-382-1727
Flywheel for 964 installation into 915 gear box

Patrick Motorsports
4750 North 16th Street
Phoenix, AZ 85016
602-266-4040
FAX: 602-266-4888
Flywheel for 964 into 915 transmission, cable shifters, shortened G 50 transmission, transmission gear sets

Renntech Performance Systems
313-856-2245
915 Gear sets

Gaskets and Seals
Charlie Spira
Wrightwood Racing
1401 Vanguard Drive
Oxnard, CA 93033
805-385-7191
FAX: 805-385-7194
Source for quality aftermarket gaskets and seals for the 911 engine

Ignition Systems
Per-Lux
1242 E. Edna PLace
Covina, CA 91724
Per-Lux Ignitor, inductively triggered ignition

Bill Evans
458 Wildbriar
Garland, TX 75043
214-270-1146
Rebuilds Bosch CD units

IAE International Auto Electric
Barry Hershon
14379 Rockdale Street
Detroit, MI 48223
313-532-5350 or 313-532-3169.
Distributor rebuilding and recurving

Jerry Woods Enterprises
491 McGlincey Lane #1
Campbell, CA 95008
Phone-FAX: 408-369-9607
Programmable crank fire ignition

Instruments
Davtron
427 Hillcrest
Redwood City, CA
415-369-1188
Digital charge air temperature gauge for turbocharged cars

Palo Alto Speedometer
Claus H. Mees
718 Emerson St.
Palo Alto, CA 94301
415-323-0243
FAX: 415-323-4632
VDO repair, conversion, and restoration

VDO Instruments
980 Brooke RD.
Winchester, VA 22601
703-665-0100

North Hollywood Speedometer
6111 Lankershim Blvd
North Hollywood, CA 91606
818-756-5136
VDO repair, conversion, and restoration. Offers a wide selection of custom instrument services.

Lubricants and Chemicals
Dow Corning
Midland, MI 48640
517-636-8000

HRL Lubricants, Inc.
7340 Florence Ave.
Downey, CA 90240
213-927-4781
Moly lubes for assembly

Red Line Synthetic Oil Corporation
3450 Pacheco Boulevard
Martinez, CA 94553
415-228-7576
Full line of synthetic engine and gear oil

Pat Dewitt
916-488-1076
SWEPCO and Ate Super Blue

SWEPCO
Southwestern Petroleum Corporation
POBox 789
Fort Worth, TX 76101
817-332-2336
817-877-4047
Telex: 758300 or 6829053
Quality engine and gear oils and fuel additives

SWEPCO
John Svabenik
117 "H" ST
San Rafael, CA 94901
415-454-1698

Oil Coolers
Lemke Engineering Company
Eugene Lemke
9226 Gleann Loch
Indianapolis, IN 46256
317-849-2821
Oil cooler, heat exchanger, and spoiler design

Terbatrol
POBox 20410
2501 East 56th Street
Indianapolis, IN 46220
317-257-6050
FAX: 800-900-8654
Terbatrol oil heat exchangers

B & B Fabrication, Inc.
Oil cooler and intercooler
5642 N. 51st Avenue
Glendale, AZ 85301
602-842-1234
FAX: 602-842-2285

Southwest Cooler Service
3939 Platinum Way
Dallas, TX 75237
Phone: 214-330-7214
Cleaning oil coolers

FG Enterprises
Fred Garretson
PO Box 3446
609-15th Street
Manhattan Beach, CA 90266
213-545-4997
Oil coolers and intercoolers

Pistons and Cylinders
ANDIAL
3207-P South Shannon Street
Santa Ana, CA 92704
714-957-3900
Mahle pistons and cylinders

Cosworth Engine Components
23205 Early Ave.
Torrance, CA 90505
213-534-1390
Custom racing pistons

Frank Terarousky
Applied Porsche Engineering
41960 Keith Wilson Road
Chilliwak, BC V2R 4B2
Office Phone/FAX: 604-823-4536
Machine Shop Phone/FAX: 604-850-7997
Wiseco pistons

Shasta Design Engineering Co.
22403 Ladeene Avenue
Torrance, CA 90505
Days: 310-813-8753
Evenings: 310-378-3032
FAX: 310-813-9171
Pistons and cylinders

JE Pistons
15681 Cumper Lane
Huntington Beach, CA 92649
714-898-9763

Cosworth Engineering
St. James Mill Road
Northampton, England
TelePhone 51214
Custom racing pistons

David Weber
Malvern Racing
Rt. 3, Box 162
Charlottesville, VA 22901
804-971-9668
FAX: 804-971-5652
Cosworth pistons

Jerry Woods Enterprises
491 McGlincey Lane #1
Campbell, CA 95008
Phone/FAX: 408-369-9607
Special piston designs

Plumbing and Metric Hardware
Aeroquip Corporation
300 South East Avenue
Jackson, MI 49203
517-783-2585
Lines and fittings
Earl's Supply Co.
14611 Hawthorne Blvd.
Lawndale, CA 90260
213-679-1438
Lines and fittings

Global Metrics, Inc.
519-J Marine View Ave
Belmont, CA 94002
800-227-9981 or 415-592-2722
FAX: 415-591-5396

Metric & Multistandard Components Corp.
120 Old Saw Mill River Road
Hawthorne, NY 10532
914-769-5020 or 800-431-2792
FAX: 914-769-5049

Metric & Multistandard Components Corp.
Midwest
261 Shore Court
Burr Ridge, IL 60521
708-655-9009 or 800-221-4469
FAX: 708-655-9062

Metric & Multistandard Components Corp.
Southwest
9840 Monroe Drive
Dallas, TX 75220
214-358-4106 or 800-527-5177
FAX: 214-358-4729

Metric & Multistandard Components Corp.
Southeast
1725 Corporate Drive Suite 360
Norcross, GA 30093
770-935-9520 or 800-444-9560
FAX: 770-935-9511

Rod Bolts and Specialty Hardware
RaceWare
Race-Tech Engineering
11320 Brydan Dr. #222
Taylor, MI 48180
Phone: 313-946-4477 or 800-486-1977
FAX: 313-946-9913

Carrillo Rods
990 Calle Amanecer
San Clamente, CA
714-498-1800

Time Fasteners
5103G Longley Lane
Reno, NV 81511
702-829-1026
800-423-4070
"Time-Certs" threaded inserts

Suspension Components
Bilstein of America
11760 Sorrento Valley Road
San Diego, CA 92121
619-453-7723
800-537-1085
Racing and street shock absorbers

Cary Eisenlohr
Eisenlohr Racing Products ERP
565 21st Street
Hermosa Beach, CA 90254
310-798-9335
Trick suspension parts

Wrightwood Racing
1401 Vanguard Drive
Oxnard, CA 93033
805-385-7191
FAX: 805-385-7194
In my opinion the best sway bars for the 911

Tilton Engineering Inc.
McMurry Road & Easy Street
Buellton, CA 93427
805-688-2353
FAX: 805-688-2745
Suspension components

Pressler Parts
Kurt Pressler
PO Box 644
Bethel Island, CA 94511
510-684-9437 or 510-684-3820
Repairs worn out Bilsteins

Longacre Racing Products
14959 NE 95th
Redmond, WA 98052
206-885-3823
Scales for weight checking cars.

Bob Love
800-388 8783
Coil over strut conversions for 911
struts

Glen Sander Engineering
3155 Kashuwa Street
Torrance, CA 95050
310-534-1210
Quality torsion bars both solid and
hollow

Carrera Industries, Inc.
5412 New Peachtree Rd.
Atlanta, GA 30341
404-451-8811
Source of coil springs, shock absorbers
and coil over conversions

Eibach Springs
15311 Barranca
Irvine, CA 92718
714-727-3700

Hyperco Hypercoils
7606 Freedom Way
Fort Wayne, IN 46818
219-489-8959 or 800 365 COIL.
FAX: 219-489-8286

Koni ITT Parts Supply Division Koni
8085 Production Ave.
Florence, KY 41042
606-727-5000
tech: 606-727-5035
sales: 800-994-KONI

Boge of America, Inc.
3658-E Atlanta Industrial Drive, N.W.
Atlanta, GA 30331
404-699-1131
FAX: 404-699-1130

Penske
150 Franklin Street
PO Box 301
Reading, PA 19603
215-375-6180
FAX: 215-375-6190
Racing shocks

Sachs
909 Crocker Road
Westlake, OH 44145
216-871-4890
FAX: 216-871-6904
Shock absorbers, clutches, and gas
hood struts

Springs and Torsion Bars
Sway-A-Way Co.
7840 Burnet Ave.
Van Nuys, CA 91405
818-700-9712
Torsion bars, adjustable spring plates,
other suspension components

Weltmeister
Automotion
3535 Kifer Road, Unit 5
Santa Clara, CA 95051
408-736-9020
FAX: 408-736-9013

Kelly-Moss Motorsports
3017 Perry Street
Madison, WI 53713
Phone 608-274-5054
FAX: 608-274-6252
Porsche racing specialty parts

H&H Specialties
20 Reid Road
Chelmsford, MA 01824
508-256-9465

Vision Motorsports, Inc
15801 Rockfield, Unit L
Irvine, CA 92718
714-770-2888
Swaybars

Super Boots
Richard and Laura Lyly
702-372-5335
CV joints and axles for race cars.

CV Express
30369 Beck Road
Wixom, MI 48393
1 800-458-4418
Special CV joints

Synthetic Oil
Mobil 1: 800-662-4525; for Technical
information and sources: 703-840-
3000
Mobil 1 is now available in 5W-30,
10W-30, and 15W-50 grades in the
U.S.

Tools
Cylinder Head Abrasives
3250 Monier Circle
Rancho Cordova, CA 95742
916-638-1212

Aircraft Spruce and Specialty Company
201 W. Truslow Avenue
PO Box 424
Fullerton, CA 92632

Mr. Assenmacher
Assenmacher Specialty Tools
6440 Odell Place
Boulder, CO 80301

Baum Tools Unlimited
PO Box 5867
Sarasota, FL 34277
800-848-6657
Source for special metric tools

Sir Tools
Paradise CA
800-845-4542

Stahlwille Tools Inc.
3451 I-35 N. , Suite 103
San Antonio, TX 79219
210-222-1997
FAX: 210-222-0261

Go-Power Systems
37050 Industrial Road
Livonia, MI 48150
313-591-2110
Dynos

Graduated Burrets
Tri-Ess Science
622 West Colorado Street
Glendale, CA 91204
213-245-7685

Mac Tools, Inc.
Washington Court House
Washington, OH 43160
614-355-4112

Snap-on Tools Corporation
Kenosha, WI
414-654-8681

Superflow
Neal Williams
3512 North Tejon
Colorado Springs, CO 80907
303-471-1746
Dynos and flow benches

Zelenda
Machine and Tools Corp.
66-02 Austin Street
Forest Hills, NY 11374
718-896-2288
Special metric tools

Transmission
Jabsco Products
A Unit of ITT Corporation
1485 Dale Way
PO Box 2158
Costa Mesa, CA 92628-2158
714-545-8251
Telex 67-8357 or 472-2035
Electric pumps for circulating gear lu-
bricant to transmission cooler

Turbo Equipment
HKS USA INC.
20312 Gramercy Place
Torrance, CA 90501
310-328-8100
FAX: 310-618-6911
Electronic Valve Controller (EVC)

Upholstery and Interior
Auto's International
148 N. Cedros
Solana Beach, CA 92075
619-481-1603

ONCALL and Associates
209 Bulen Street
Rosville, CA 95678
916-783-6082 or 916-973-2020
FAX: 916-786-7328

Paterek Preferred
Care Care Products
Post Office Box 1014
Chatham, NJ 07928
Phone/FAX: 201-635-0689

Alan Gun Leather Accessories
8840 N. Lake Dasha Dr.
Plantation, FL 33324
800-780-4500
FAX: 305-472-9836

CBE Interiors
1960 Airport Industrial Park Drive
Marietta, GA 30062
404-952-0928

Color-Plus
Leather reconditioning treatment
dies and reconditions leather
PO Box 404
Kearny, NJ 07032

Valve Guides
Tom Manning
L&S Machining
209-836-5827
Phosphorus bronze valve guides

Vintage Racing Porsches and Parts
Kerry Morse
GTS Motorsport
714-259-0844
FAX: 714-259-9577

The Parts Shop
Bill Perrone
15725 Chemical Lane
Huntington Beach, CA 92649
714-894-3112
FAX: 714-894-8694

International Mercantile
PO Box 2818
Del Mar, CA 92014-5818
619-438-2205
FAX: 619-438-1428
Restoration and rubber parts

Porsche Parts Obsolete
Gary Emory
13851 Eola Village Road
McMinnville, OR 97128
503-835-2300
800-354-9307
FAX: 503-835-4000

Kevin Jeannette
Gunnar Racing
4110 West Roads Dr.
West Palm Beach, FL 33407
407-844-8482 or 407-844-8547
Vintage race car restoration and parts

Wheels
Revolution Wheels
215-945-3834.

Robert W. Wood, Inc.
Greg Wood
1537 Pontius Avenue
Los Angles, CA 90025
310-473-6649
FAX: 310-473-9672

Wheel Enhancement
Mr. Robert Wood
10129 W. Jefferson Blvd.
Culver City, CA 90232
310-836-8908 or 310-276-2654
FAX: 310-836-8924

General Parts Sources
Stuttgart Connection
Mark King
P.O Box 911
Leigh-on-Sea
Essex SS9 @RS
UK
44 702 559911
FAX: 44 702 555 944

Jean Buser
44, rue Voltaire
92300 Levallois
France
Phone 1-47 47 58 59 54
FAX: 1-47 58 74 76

Auto Mechanika
2100 West Dartmouth Ave.
Englewood, CO 80110
800-582-2886
303-781-1140
FAX: 303-762-9881

Engine Builders Supply Co.
John Freismidl
155 Glendale Ave. #24
Reno-Sparks, NV 89431
800-462-3774 or 702-331-2334
FAX: 702-331-8268

AJ-USA, Inc. Alan Johnson Racing Inc.
6620 Mira Mesa Boulevard
San Diego, CA 92121-4300
619-452-8900 or 1-800-877-1911
FAX: 619-452-8999

Holbert Motor Cars
1607 Easton Rd.
Warrington, PA 18976
215-343-4810
FAX: 215-343-4269

Automotion
3535 Kifer Road
Santa Clara, CA 95051
800-777-8881 or 408-736-9020
FAX: 408-736-9013

PAR
206 South Broadway
Yonkers, NY 10705
914-476-6700
800-367-7270

The Racers Group
Kevin Buckler
29187 Arnold Dr.
Sanoma, CA 95476
707-935-3999
FAX: 707-935-5889

Pine Ridge Enterprises
13165 Center Road
Bath, MI 48808
1-800-5 CARBAG
FAX: 517-641-6444
Omnibag car storage systems

Mr. Willi Brombacher
F.V.D. Brombacher
Waldmatten-2
Umkirch/Freiburg
Freiburg in Umkirch
Germany
011-49-7665-9899-0
FAX: 011-4907665-9899-20

Windward
930 Performance Products.
Sawmill Racing Comples Bay #1
Route 5, Box 241
Putney, VT 05346
802-387-4500
FAX: 802-387-5579

Europroducts
PO Box 20944
St. Petersburg, FL 33742
orders: 800-962-0911
information: 813-527-2583

Griffiths Technical Inc
195-19 N. Beverwyck RD
Lake Hiawatha, NJ 07034
800-451-7225
Power steering racks

RSR/Reichenberg Schwalm Racing
4118 W. Valley Blvd
Walnut, CA 91789
714-594-2921 or 800-237-4318
FAX: 714-594-9559

Recaro
905 W. Maple Road, Suite 100
Clawson, MI 48017
800-873-2276

Imparts
9330 Manchester RD
St. Louis, MO 63119
314-962-0810
800-325-9043

Electrodyne
4750 Eisenhower Ave.
POBox 9670
Alixandria, VA 22304-9670
703-823-0202
800-658-8850
FAX: 703-823-0842
Porsche aftermarket parts source

Manfred Freisinger Motorsport
Südliche Uferstrasse 5
76189 Karlsruhe - Germany
011-49 0721-554926
FAX: 011-49 0721-554925

Zims Al/Autotechnik
Restoration Parts
1804 Reliance Parkway
Bedford, TX 76021
817-267-4451
FAX: 817-545-2002

NLA Limited
Restoration Parts.
POBox 41030
Reno, NV 89504
702-829-8187
order: 800-438-8119
FAX: 702-827-2666

Performance Products
16129 Leadwell Street
Box #B-4
Van Nuys CA 91406-3488
800-423-3173 USA
800-787-7500 CA
818-787-7500
FAX: 818-787-2396

Stoddard Imported Cars, Inc.
38845 Mentor Avenue
Willoughby, OH 44094-0908
216-951-1040
800-342-1414
FAX: 216-946-9410

MY Porsche
Mike Hayworth
One Geary Plaza
Monterey Peninsula Auto Center
Seaside, CA 93955
408-899-5555
FAX: 408-899-5606
Good source for manuals

Tweeks
8148 Woodland Drive
Indianapolis, IN 46278
317-875-0076
800-428-2200
FAX: 317-875-0181

Tweeks
3301 E. Hill Street, Unit 408
Long Beach, CA 90804
213-494-4777
FAX: 213-494-9084

Otto's
John Williamson
707 South Hampton Drive
Venice, CA 90291
213-399-3221
FAX: 213-399-9399

Troutman LTD, Inc.
3198-L Airport Loop Dr.
Coata Mesa, CA 92626
714-979-3295
800-356-9307
Telex 181-579

Vasek Polack
199 Pacific Coast Highway
Hermosa Beach, CA 90254
213-376-7434
FAX: 213-374-0169
Telex 9103447393

Bill Yates Racing Service
32852 Valle Road
San Juan Capistrano, CA 92675
714-493-4511
FAX: 714-493-3473

Brumos Motor Car, Inc.
10231 Atlantic Boulevard
Jacksonville, FL 32225
904-724-1080
904-725-9155
904-725-5006
FAX: 904-725-4193

Champion Porsche
500 West Copans Road
Pompano Beach, FL 33064
305-946-4020
800-940-4020
FAX: 305-942-8871

New and Used Parts
Aase Brothers Inc.
701 Cypress
Anaheim, CA 92805
714-956-2419 or 800-444-7444
FAX: 714-956-2635

Parts Heaven
Alan Uejo
23694 Bemhardt Street
Hayward, CA 94545
510-782-0354 or 800-767-7250
FAX: 510-782-0358

Active Foreign Auto Parts
Hays Patrick
6803 Ward Road
Millington, TN 38053
800 321-9732
CompuServe: 76752,1127

EASY
European Auto Salvage Yard
Jim Brazil
4060 Harlan Street
Emeryville, CA 94608
510-653-EASY
FAX: 510-653-3178

Mr. Robert Hills
H.S.A. plc
9 The Square
Foodford Green, Essex
Great Britain
Phone 0277 812221 or 0860 300190
FAX: 0277 812221

P.A.P Inc.
Joe and Ginger Cogbil
6394 Buford Hwy
PO Box 910
Norcross, GA 30091
Phone 404-449-3146
Parts: 800-944-2964
FAX: 404-449-3146

Machine Shop Service
Jerry Woods Enterprises
491 McGlincey Lane #1
Campbell, CA 95008
Phone/FAX: 408-369-9607

Jay Robison
408-980-0743
1744 Grant St.
Santa Clara, CA 95050

Ted Robinson
German Precision
1270 Lawrence Station Road #H
Sunnyvale, CA 94089
408-747-0728
FAX: 408-747-0782

Ollie's Automotive Machining
510 Terminal St.
Santa Ana, CA 92701
714-558-7334

Red Line Service Inc.
Peter Zimmerman
720 Colorado Avenue
Santa Monica, CA 90401
213-450-7414
213-452-0378
FAX: 213-396-3042

Competition Engineering
Ray Litz & Walt Watson
3409 Seclusion Road
PO Box 1967
Lake Isabella, CA 93240
619-379-3879
FAX: 619-379-6305

Metal Finishing
Metal Improvement Company, Inc.
Subsidiary of Curtiss Wright Coprporation
3239 East 46th Street
Vernon, CA 90058
213-585-2168
Telex 62911792
Shot peening

Mr. Roger F. Reynolds
5139 W. 13th Street
Speedway, IN 46224
317-241-5544
Dow Corning Process for refinishing magnesium

Paragon Productions
11352 Trask Ave. Suite 103
Garden Grove, CA 92643
714-534-8489
OEM "Bright Dip" aluminum anodizing

Porsche Development Work
Jerry Woods Enterprises
491 McGlincey Lane #1
Campbell, CA 95008
Phone/FAX: 408-369-9607

Autosport Engineering, Inc.
Lenny Cummings
370 Hudson Road
Stow, MA 01775
508-562-7300
FAX: 508-584-8172

Alex Job Racing
1495 Seminola Blvd. Suite 9
Casselberry, FL 32707
407-695-5526

Protomotive Engineering
Cynthia & Tod Knight
Phone/FAX: 909-926-2694
Engine building

Proto Tech
David Hart
954-771-2654
FAX: 954-492-4062
Engine, body, upholstery, and sound
system

Supercharging of Knoxville
123 Perimeter Park Road
Knoxville, TN 37922
423-579-1534
FAX: 423-579-9001
Supercharger installations

Motorsport Design
Bob Holcombe
7905E Greenway Suite 102
Scottsdale, AZ 85260
602-483-9514
FAX: 602-483-6134

Exclusive Motor Cars
256 Park Street
Upper Montclair, NJ 07043
201-744-1932
Telex: 706617
FAX: 201-744-7885

Perfect Power
Saul and Beth Snyderman
844 Liberty Drive
Libertyville, IL 60048
708-367-8837
FAX: 708-816-6876

Mr. Peter Dawe
Promotion Motorsports
4 John Street
Building C
Morristown, NJ 07960
201-984-95555

AASCO Performance
2017 West Commonwealth Ave.
Fullerton, CA 92633

714-992-2283
Engine and chassis development, performance valve springs

Norwood Autocraft Inc.
Bob Norwood
5020 Tracy
Dallas, TX 75205
214-526-0260
FAX: 214-526-0949
Engine and car development

BRD/Precision Performance
Greg Brown
930 E. Orangethorpe, Suite F
Anaheim, CA 92801
714-879-9072 or 714-879-1576
FAX: 714-526-6002.

Fabricators, Designers, and Builders
Blakely Engineering, Inc.
Glenn Blakely
23052 Alcalde
Unit C.
Laguna Hills, CA 92653
Design and fabrication of race cars

GAACO
Charles W. Gaa
2801 Cole Court
Norcross, GA 30071
404-448-4766
Design and fabrication of race cars

FABCAR
Dave Klym
4385 West 96th Street
Indianapolis, IN 46268
317-872-3664
FAX: 317-872-3835

Car Creations
Paul Newman
271 La Cuesta Drive
Scotts Valley, CA 95066
408-438-4328

Fabrications
Roger Hamlin
Sears Point International Raceway
29255 Arnold Drive
707-935-6825

**German Tuners and Specialty Car
Builders and Their Agents in the U.S.**
DP Motorsport
Ekkehard Zimmermann Gmbh + Co.
KG
Zum Alten Wasserwerk
5063 Overath 6
Germany
TelePhone 02204-71068

E & M Kremer
Achim Stroth
011-49-221-171025
FAX: 011-49-221-174841

Alois Ruf
Ruf Automobile, GMBH
Mindelheimer Strasse 21
D 8949 Pfaffenhausen
Germany
0 8265 1012
Telex 531446ruf d
FAX: 08265 1213

Ruf Automobile
Mr. Alois Ruf
Mindelheimer Strasse 21
D-8949
Pfaffenhausen
Germany
0 82 65-10 12 or 0 82 65-12 13
Telex 531 146 ruf d

Louis Fubare
POBox 249
Jupiter, FL 33468
407-743-3201
FAX: 407-743-3260
Ruf U.S. importer

Gulf Performance Center
Felix Amore
450A NE 27th St.
Pomoano Beach, FL 33064
Phone 305-783-7345
FAX: 305-783-7453
U.S. Ruf dealer

Bodymotion
Michael Bavaro
21 Cindy Land
Ocean, NJ 07712
908-493-2700
FAX: 908-493-0157

Koenig Specials GmbH
Flossergasse 7
D-8000 Munchen 70
Germany
089-724970
Telex 528145 koevmd

Strosek Autodesign
Eduard-thony Strasse 40
D-8919 Utting/Ammersee
Germany
TelePhone 08806-1428
Telex 59921
One of Europes best know customizers

Fred Opert Racing
138 North Central Avenue
Ramsey NJ 07446
FAX: number 201-327-8222
Phone number 201-327-1111
Strosek kits

Porsche
Porsche Sports Department
Mr. Jürgen Barth
Dr. Ing.h.c.F. Porsche
Entwicklung
Abteilung Kundensport
Postfach 1140
Porschestrasse
7251 Weissach
Germany
011497044352687
FAX: 011497044352022

Porsche Motorsport North America,
Inc.
Alwin Springer
3203 South Shannon Street
Santa Ana, CA 92704
714-546-6939
FAX: 714-957-1386

Factory Cardex Information
Certificate of Authenticity
Porsche Cars North America
POBox 30911
Reno, NV 89501
Send request with $30.00 and a copy
of your registration to Howard Adams

Porsche Cars North America
Importer for Porsche automobiles and
parts
100 West Liberty Street
PO Box 30911
Reno, NV 89520-3911
702-348-3000

Porsche Cars North America 800
Phone numbers
800-443-0340 Porsche Cars North
America
800-545-8039 Owner Relations Department
800-438-1409 24hrs Roadside Assis-
tance
800-767-7243 Location Information
for nearest Authorized Porsche Dealer

Appendix 6
Recommended Reading

Books

Bob Bondurant on High Performance Driving. Bondurant, Bob and John Blakemore. A good book with lots of illustrations and descriptions of how to drive faster.

Bosch Automotive Handbook, 3rd Edition. This book is chock full of more information that you will ever need to know.

Excellence Was Expected. Karl Ludvigsen is one of the classic books about Porsche cars. Unfortunately this book was written in 1978, and it is starting to show its age a bit. Still, I feel that it is one of the best. Hopefully Karl Ludvigsen will update this book in the not too distant future.

Guide to Purchase & D.I.Y. Restoration of the Porsche 911. Lindsay Porter and Peter Morgan. A good guide for what to look for when buying an older used 911 and what to do to fix it up once you have bought it.

How to Make Your Car Handle. Fred Puhn. Detailed descriptions of how the suspension is engineered and of how to set up your car yourself.

Original Porsche 911. Peter Morgan. The restorer's guide to all of the production models 1963–93 including the Turbo. This is a good book on the details of the production Porches with photos of cars in Germany, England, and the United States.

Porsche 911 Story. Paul Frère is one of my favorite books. The book has a lot of photos, but is a well-written technical look at the design and evolution of the 911.

The Porsche Book. Jürgen Barth and Lothar Boschen. This is a detailed history of all of the Porsche models. Dean Batchelor. A good book with lots of photos and tables.

Porsche Forever Young. Tobias Aichele. Covers the 911's history from the original concept through the 993.

Porsche Racing Cars of the 70s. Paul Frère. This is a very detailed technical description of the development of the Porsche racing car built in the 1970s, including the Carreras, Turbo Carrera, and the 934, 935, and 936 racing cars.

Porsche Specials. Lothar Boschen and Jürgen Barth. An interesting book generously illustrated with pictures of all of the Porsche specials the authors could find. A description accompanies each car.

Porsche Story. Julius Weitmann. This book is in its fourth edition and was revised and edited by Michael Cotton. A photo history of Porsche from 1951 through 1991.

The Used 911 Story. Peter Zimmerman. This is a good guide to checking out a used 911 for purchase. Covers 911s from 1965 through the 993.

Factory Workshop Manuals. Though not faultless, these are the best manuals covering 911 repair. They are written to support Porsche's own trained technicians. The 911 workshop manuals are written in such a manner that each new manual is dependent on it predecessors. Consequently, if you are working on a 993 it is possible that you will need the 964 manuals, the Carrera 3.2 manuals, the manual covering the 1972–1973 911s, and the original manual which covered the 1965–1971 911s to understand all of the details. The Turbo manuals were similar with manuals to cover the 1967–1989 Turbos, the 1991–92 Turbos, the 1993–94 Turbos, and the current manuals covering the 993 Twin Turbo.

Owners Manuals for the various 911 models. Owners manuals are available for most of the 911s built. The amount of information available in these books is amazing. No 911 owner should be without one.

Porsche Specifications Books. These amazing little books are full of all of the details of all of the different Porsche models, including everything from the chassis numbers to all of the 911's specifications. Anyone planning to work on their own 911 shouldn't be without one.

Periodicals

The 911 & Porsche Magazine
Nagoya Magazine Company.
2-52-1, Yada-cho
Higashi-ku
Nagoya City
461 Japan
052-711-0002

911 and Porsche World
CHPublications Ltd.
PO Box 75
Tadworth Surrey KT20 7XF
UK
01737 814311
Fax: 01737 81459

911 and Porsche World
USA, Canada, Mexico
369 Sprinfield Ave.
Box 188
Berkeley Heights, NJ 07922
908/665-7811
Fax: 908/665-7814

Christophorus
Postfach 400640
D-7000 Stuttgart
Germany
Telephone 0711/827-5278
Porsche factory magazine

Excellence
42 Digital Drive, Number 5
Navato, CA 94949
415/382-0580

Flat 6 Magazine
B. P. 137
80103 Abbeville Cadex
R.C.SB 334 078 052
France
22 31 28 28
Fax: 22 24 90 27

Panorama
PCA National Executive Office
P. O. Box 10402
Alexandria, VA 22310
703/922-9300
Monthly magazine of the Porsche Club of America

Porsche Owners Club Newsletter
P. O. Box 7293
Van Nuys, CA 91409-7293

Porsche Market Letter
Phil Van Buskirk
4705 Morning Canyon Road
Oceanside, CA 92056
888-928-9111 or 619/727-4856
Fax: 619/940-9170

Index